Preventing a Biological Arms Race

Preventing a Biological Arms Race

edited by Susan Wright

The MIT Press
Cambridge, Massachusetts
London, England

This book was set by Asco Trade Typesetting Ltd. in Hong Kong, and was printed and bound in the United States of America.

Library of Congress Cataloging-in-Publication Data

Preventing a biological arms race / edited by Susan P. Wright.

   p. cm.
  ISBN 0-262-23148-4
  1. Biological warfare (International law)   2. Biological weapons.
I. Wright, Susan Presswood
JX5133. C5P74   1990
327.1′74—dc20   89-39284
                                     CIP

Contents

IV
CHARGES OF VIOLATION OF THE BIOLOGICAL WARFARE LEGAL REGIME *197*

V
THE INTERNATIONAL LEGAL REGIME ON BIOLOGICAL WARFARE *239*

VI
STRENGTHENING THE BARRIERS TO BIOLOGICAL WARFARE *289*

Foreword

The Council for Responsible Genetics (CRG) is a public-interest organization that monitors military and commercial applications of applied genetics and provides a forum for public education and discussion on the directions of biotechnology.

Since its formation in 1982 as the Committee for Responsible Genetics, CRG has been concerned about the possible militarization of biological knowledge. The inaugural issue of the Council's publication *GeneWatch* (1973) contained an essay by the editor of this volume, Susan Wright, that expressed the sentiment and hope of the organization as well as countless people throughout the world: "Before nations begin to build major military dependencies on the new biological technologies, we need to intervene to ensure that these technologies are directed exclusively toward peaceful applications."

At a time when there is a seed of hope that the threat of nuclear confrontation and the buildup of nuclear weapons may be reduced, we should not neglect the possibility of a biological arms race. The Biological Weapons Convention is a hopeful sign, but no single treaty and no lofty promises of governments can substitute for the active vigilance of the world's citizenry. The challenge to international, civil, and model law is to ensure that the life sciences are used only to enhance and not to destroy life.

The CRG is pleased to have supported this volume and to be associated with the distinguished efforts of its contributors. This book will succeed if it educates, informs, and advises the global community about strengthening the goals of the Biological Weapons Convention.

Sheldon Krimsky
Chairman, Board of Directors
Council for Responsible Genetics

Acknowledgments

Addressing the many dimensions of the issues currently associated with biological warfare and disarmament could not have been accomplished without the support of the authors, whose varied perspectives and experiences were essential for producing a comprehensive treatment of the subject. I thank them not only for providing their own chapters but also for responding to those of others and for doing so in the spirit of commitment to public education that has informed this project throughout.

For specific guidance on various aspects of this book, I am especially indebted to the reviewers for MIT Press, for detailed and perceptive responses to the manuscript, and to Paul Grams, whose fine editorial assistance often went beyond style to substance, strengthening arguments in the process. I also thank my fellow members of the Committee on Military Use of Biological Research of the Council for Responsible Genetics, whose ideas and actions related to the question of biological warfare have provided stimulation and encouragement.

Several people influenced the book's development in a more general way. I thank especially Richard Falk and Robert Sinsheimer, whose visions of the respective roles of law and of science in a just and peaceful world have been important sources of guidance and inspiration, and Matthew Meselson and Julian Perry Robinson, whose writing about chemical and biological warfare and disarmament has contributed greatly to public understanding and awareness of these issues.

The production of the book depended crucially on the contributions of several people. Sue Meyer skillfully negotiated the tricky terrain of manuscript preparation with efficiency, humor, and reassurance. Jo Ann Berg played an essential role in her scrupulous reading of page proofs. My research assistants, Christine Skwiot,

Framji Minwalla, Liz Joffe, Anne-Marie Phillips, and Tara Tuomaala, helped with the details of manuscript production, not least through their curiosity and enthusiasm. The staff of the MIT Press provided excellent guidance and editorial support.

This project also owes a great debt to Claire Nader, who first proposed a book about biological warfare and encouraged its progress at every stage, to Sheldon Krimsky, Chairman of the Board of Directors of the Council for Responsible Genetics for wise counsel on practical issues as well as for helpful comments on several chapters, to Nachama Wilker, Executive Director and the Board of Directors of the Council for Responsible Genetics for support throughout, and to the Safety Systems Foundation and the New England Biolabs Foundation for generous grants that allowed the project to be brought to fruition.

Finally, I thank my son Jonathan Wright and all the friends and colleagues at the University of Michigan and elsewhere who gave their encouragement when it was most needed in their belief in the goal of disarmament and in their commitment to a more peaceful world.

List of Abbreviations

AEC	Atomic Energy Commission
AMIIA	U.S. Army Medical Intelligence and Information Agency
AMRDC	U.S. Army Medical Research and Development Command
AMRIID	U.S. Army Medical Research Institute of Infectious Diseases
BDRP	Biological Defense Research Program
BL	Biosafety Level
BW	Biological Warfare
BWC	Biological Weapons Convention
CBW	Chemical and Biological Warfare
CCD	Conference on the Committee on Disarmament
CERN	Conseil Européen pour la Recherche Nucléaire
CRDEC	Chemical Research, Development, and Engineering Center
CW	Chemical Warfare
DOD	Department of Defense
DPG	Dugway Proving Ground
DTIC	Defense Technical Information Center
FOIA	U.S. Freedom of Information Act
HEW	U.S. Department of Health, Education, and Welfare
IAEA	International Atomic Energy Agency
NAS	National Academy of Sciences
NIH	National Institute of Health
ONR	Office of Naval Research
rDNA	Recombinant DNA
SIPRI	Stockholm International Peace Research Institute
WRS	War Research Service

Preventing a Biological Arms Race

Introduction

Susan Wright

In theory, the menace of biological warfare should no longer be with us. Developing, producing and stockpiling biological and toxin weapons—which deploy living organisms and natural poisons to spread disease and debilitation in humans, animals, or plants—are unconditionally banned by international treaty: the United States, the Soviet Union, and most other nations have signed, ratified, and apparently complied with the 1972 Biological Weapons Convention. Given its support and many years of operation, the Convention provides some grounds for believing that governments and military establishments will not unleash biological agents under the compulsion of warfare, or consider developing such weaponry as a means of intimidation.

Developments in the 1980s, however, have drawn the adequacy of the Biological Weapons Convention as an instrument of reassurance into question. East-West military rivalry and confrontations in the Middle East have eroded confidence, at least temporarily, in the treaty regime. The advent of genetic engineering and other new biotechnologies has stimulated renewed military interest in the biological sciences, generating in turn concern about the potential weapons applications of certain lines of research. Despite international efforts to strengthen the treaty, the situation remains precarious, with ominous signs of increasing military development of the biological sciences, a trend which if continued could provoke a biological arms race.

The problem of biological warfare is closely related to that of chemical warfare (the use of toxic agents to cause disease in humans, animals or plants). Both types of weapons are biospecific, harming living things rather than inflicting physical damage. Both are effective over large areas and have indiscriminate impact. Both are likely to be devastating against the unprotected and less effective when used against a protected adversary. Both are relatively cheap to produce, thus providing tempting alternatives to conventional or nuclear weaponry (particularly for beleaguered states threatened by superior military force) and, once accepted, raising the possibility of rapid global proliferation.

To date, use of chemical and biological weapons has been comparatively rare, but when it has occurred, it has generally been highly destructive. The first large-scale use of chemical weapons in World War I caused over one million casualties, ten percent of which were fatal. Use of herbicides (defined by the majority of the world's nations as a chemical weapon) by the United States destroyed thousands of acres of forest and cultivated land in Vietnam. Iraq's use of chemical weapons against Iranian soldiers and its own Kurdish people is estimated to have caused 10,000 casualties. Biological weapons, though intensively researched, developed, produced, and stockpiled during and after World War II, have never been used openly in armed conflict, although their possible strategic, tactical, and covert uses have been explored by military planners. Charges of use abound, and at least one case of covert use —by Japan against China in 1940–44—has been well documented.

Particularly because of their association with disease and poison, as well as in view of their destructive power and indiscriminate impact, biological and chemical weapons have evoked deep psychological aversion and moral repugnance within the military as well as the general public. Prolonged efforts have been made internationally to prohibit not only their use but also their possession. The 1925 Geneva Protocol bans use of both biological and chemical weapons. The 1972 Biological Weapons Convention, in committing parties to the treaty to pursue chemical disarmament, established an international legal regime of prohibition of both types of weaponry that aims to preclude recourse to these weapons by removing the means for their development and production. The Chemical Weapons Convention currently under negotiation will, if widely signed and ratified, complete this regime. Although this book focuses on the present issues associated with biological warfare and disarmament, connections with the problem of chemical warfare and with the larger goal of comprehensive chemical and biological disarmament are also emphasized.

In the 1970s, the sense that the problem of biological warfare was successfully contained was reinforced by a virtual lack of serious military interest in biological weapons. They were seen as unreliable, slow in action, and unpredictable in effect, and consequently as having dubious battlefield utility. Furthermore, all known stockpiles of biological weapons were destroyed. In the United States, the Biological Weapons Program was cut back and reoriented toward defense. Support for the program, which was renamed the Biological Defense Program (and, in 1987, the Biological Defense Research Program) remained at a low level throughout the 1970s.

In the 1980s, however, the intensification of superpower tensions and growing military interest in the biological sciences in the United States and elsewhere reactivated fears, and possibly ambitions, relating to the possible future development of biological weapons. Advances in genetic engineering and other biogenetic technologies produced speculation in certain military circles that these techniques could be used to produce new kinds of biological weapons superior to those using naturally occurring organisms. Although such possibilities were and remain controversial, they were influential in justifying plans for expanding military research and development in biotechnology, as were suspicions that these activities elsewhere could create new security vulnerabilities unless matched by countervailing efforts.

The legal prohibition of chemical and biological warfare seems today considerably less solid than it did in the 1970s. Repeated charges by the United States of Soviet treaty violations in the early 1980s cast doubt on the effectiveness of the regime and undermined confidence in it, despite the fact that the most important charges were eventually discredited or have remained inconclusive. U.S. military spending on the Biological Defense Research Program, which was increased in response to these accusations, has not subsequently declined. Furthermore, as superpower relations improved and U.S. anxieties about Soviet intentions with respect to chemical and biological weaponry receded in the late 1980s, new concerns emerged. Claims of the proliferation of chemical and biological weaponry in the Middle East have been aired regularly in the last few years. Intense and often sensationalist media coverage of these matters, based largely on undisclosed intelligence reports with limited attention to verifiability, has reinforced doubts in public and governmental circles about the effectiveness of the chemical and biological warfare legal regime.

A further issue has developed recently in connection with the capacity of biotechnology to produce novel biochemical substances whose classification as "toxins" (potent natural poisons) is unclear, either because these substances are less potent than conventional toxins or because their chemical composition is novel. This problem has generated debate about how or even whether such substances should be covered by either the Biological Weapons Convention or the new Chemical Weapons Convention. Such issues open up possible new grey areas in relation to these treaties.

In this climate of suspicion and rapid innovation, the United States, as well as some European countries, has reactivated and expanded biological defense research, including projects in which offensive and defensive aspects can be distinguished only by claimed motive. Military research in new forms of biotechnology was initiated in the United States in 1980 and continues unabated. This work, while not formally excluded by the Biological Weapons Convention, risks undermining the treaty's primary purpose. Particularly because genetic engineering provides the means to construct novel organisms and to make novel substances, the military exploration of biotechnology could trigger a spiral of suspicion and exploratory development among rival nations, eventually producing weapons innovations that could prove tempting to military establishments. Indeed, this book documents how in the United States, Department of Defense officials, impressed by the dazzling advances in biotechnology, painted a frightening picture of the military attractions of weapons applications of this new field to potential adversaries and urged initiation of just such exploration in the name of protecting national security. (In this case, it is research and development—as opposed to application, production, and stockpiling—that could stimulate such a qualitative arms race, challenging in the most concrete manner traditional conceptions of the moral and political neutrality of science.)

At the same time, some developments in the 1980s are encouraging. Despite the noise about treaty violations and concern about military applications of the biological sciences, all major states have reaffirmed their willingness to respect the Biological Weapons Convention and work toward its greater effectiveness. At the Second Review Conference on the Convention held in September 1986, the participating governments addressed two areas of treaty weakness: first, by establishing informal mechanisms for the exchange of information and second, by agreeing to consult about suspicious events that could be perceived as being caused by a treaty violation. A positive sign at the conference was an indication of Soviet willingness to provide additional, reassuring evidence about the 1979 epidemic of anthrax at Sverdlovsk—the event which became the central element in the U.S. government's campaign to allege an illicit Soviet biological warfare program. Since the review conference, a regular exchange of information has been initiated about high-containment facilities that handle hazardous biological agents, including facilities used by the military.

In the United States, legislators, scientists, and public interest organizations have achieved some success in challenging the direction taken by the Biological Defense Research Program in the 1980s and in halting, at least temporarily, some of the most ambiguous and provocative military-sponsored research. In addition, the introduction in 1987 of congressional legislation to implement, on a domestic level, the 1972 Biological Weapons Convention, its endorsement by the Bush administration in 1989 and approval in the Senate represented a first step towards reinforcing the treaty at home, especially by making its obligations directly binding on individuals and corporations.

Thus in the 1980s the restraints on biological warfare encoded in the Convention and the 1925 Geneva Protocol were subject to contradictory trends—threatened by an incipient spiral of suspicion, secrecy and military development but strengthened by continuing efforts to make the renunciation of biological weapons endure.

The course of biological disarmament in the 1990s is likely to be determined by which of these trends comes to dominate. The existing regime banning biological weapons could well be undermined if nations persist in irresponsible charges of violations, or if military establishments are allowed to apply advances in the biological sciences in the course of research into new weaponry. On the other hand, barriers against military assimilation of the biological sciences could be fortified through steps at the Third Review Conference on the Biological Weapons Convention in 1991 to reinforce the treaty and close remaining loopholes, through governmental behavior that avoids jeopardizing the treaty, and through active acceptance and more diligent dissemination of cultural norms that repudiate biological weaponry and abjure research likely to produce results relevant to weapons applications. The relaxation of superpower tensions since 1985 provides a favorable climate for international collaboration in these areas not only among nations, but also among scientists and citizens throughout the world.

In the United States, President George Bush has regularly voiced his commitment to biological as well as chemical disarmament.

However, whether his commitment translates into strengthening the ban on biological and chemical warfare depends crucially on reversing the expansionary impulse of the Chemical Warfare and Biological Defense Research programs and ensuring that the "new biology" is not introduced into the military realm. If Bush succumbs to arguments advocating the extension of deterrence to biological weaponry and supports ambiguous and provocative research programs in the biological sciences that pave the way for the military assimilation of these fields, the chemical and biological warfare legal regime is an almost certain casualty.

Preventing a Biological Arms Race examines the interests and interactions behind the present expansion of military involvement in the life sciences, develops the case for strengthening national and international commitments to biological disarmament in the 1990s, and proposes policies and action to achieve those goals. While the underlying assumption of this book is that biological warfare is an international problem that requires international cooperation for its solution, particular attention is given to the role of the United States. As a leading nation in the development of biotechnology and in its military application, the United States sets crucial precedents, whether for biological armament or disarmament, that deserve special scrutiny.

This book comprises fifteen chapters written by experts who, while they may differ in their assumptions and approaches to the problem of biological warfare, are united by their conviction that a comprehensive international prohibition on biological weaponry is desirable and necessary. Designed for a general audience—scientists, legislators, policymakers, students, and others interested in preserving biological disarmament—the book seeks to present the essential historical, political, ethical, legal, and technical background necessary to arrive at informed judgments about biological warfare issues. It also seeks to stimulate public concern, and thereby to encourage creative and instructive action.

I

A History of U.S. Biological Warfare Policy

1

Origins of the U.S. Biological Warfare Program

Barton J. Bernstein

> *The wise assumption is that any method which appears to offer advantages to a nation at war will be vigorously employed by that nation. There is but one logical course to pursue—namely, to study the possibilities of biological warfare from every angle.*
> —National Academy of Sciences Committee Report, February 17, 1942

> *We had a crop destroyer, which we could use in September or October 1945 against Japan and destroy the food sources . . . nail them down until they sued for peace. A very logical enterprise . . . we recommended it.*
> —Assistant Secretary of War for Air Robert Lovett, 1960

> *The atomic bomb . . . is far worse than gas and biological warfare because it affects the civilian population and murders them wholesale.*
> —President Harry S. Truman, January 19, 1953

Until World War II, no modern state had employed or even developed a significant capacity for offensive biological warfare. Although legal barriers to the development and use of biological weaponry were weak—the United States had signed but never ratified the 1925 Geneva Protocol banning the use of biological as well as chemical weapons—the idea of deliberately spreading pestilence and creating disability then, as now, evoked widespread revulsion. Yet, in a manner that roughly parallels the development of the atomic bomb, the United States government's fear of Axis development of biological weapons encouraged American work on such weaponry and lowered barriers to its use.

America's World War II work on biological warfare, which like the A-bomb project was kept top secret, cost under $60 million and involved about 4,000 workers, including scientists. Unlike the $2 billion A-bomb project, little is generally known about America's wartime biological warfare activity. Publications on the subject are sparse, and even the archival sources are skimpy.[1]

Nevertheless, some important questions can be usefully addressed, often by teasing out the answers from archival materials. How and why did the program arise? Why was it administered through a "cover" agency, the War Research Service (WRS)? Did Presidents Franklin D. Roosevelt and Harry S. Truman or their top advisers ever explicitly define policy for deterrence or combat use of biological weaponry, as Roosevelt did for gas? How great was presidential knowledge, and oversight, of the biological warfare program? What role did morality play for scientists and high-level officials in considering the program? Was there any wartime effort at establishing international control of biological warfare? How close did the United States come to using biological weaponry in the war?

Initiation of the U.S. Biological Warfare Program

The U.S. Army started conducting biological-warfare research in 1941 through its Chemical Warfare Service, but American efforts did not become substantial until 1942. In February of that year, a special committee appointed by the National Academy of Sciences submitted a report to Secretary of War Henry L. Stimson containing recommendations for the future of the biological-warfare program. Stimson had requested the report a few months before the bombing of Pearl Harbor.[2]

The committee, composed of eminent biologists such as Edwin B. Fred of the University of Wisconsin and Stanhope Bayne-Jones of Yale University, concluded that an enemy attacking with biological weapons could gravely harm human beings, crops, and livestock. Although the report stressed defense and called for work on vaccines and protection of the water supply, the committee also recommended that the U.S. develop bacterial weapons.[3]

Spurred by the scientists' warnings, Stimson sought presidential approval for a formal biological warfare program that would include a small group of advisers to coordinate and direct all government research. "We must be prepared," Stimson wrote to Roosevelt in an April 1942 memorandum. "And the matter must be handled with great secrecy as well as great vigor."[4]

Stimson never mentioned that the Chemical Warfare Service had already begun research into biological weaponry; and the president probably did not know of the program. Still, the chemical service later received millions of dollars in appropriations through the Army's budget and became more instrumental in the biological warfare program than the small advisory group that directed it. Why did Stimson press for the group?

Perhaps it was because, as he told Roosevelt, "biological warfare is dirty business." Stimson hoped to legitimize the research at the Chemical Warfare Service by naming civilians as monitors. Whereas some members of the National Academy of Sciences committee thought the program should be administered by the War Department, top Army officials preferred the establishment of a civilian agency with ties to the armed services. Stimson explained their reasoning to Roosevelt: "Entrusting the matter to a civilian agency would help in preventing the public from being unduly exercised over any ideas that the War Department might be contemplating the use of this weaponry offensively." He implied that the United States would not initiate biological warfare but added, significantly, that "reprisals by us are perhaps not beyond the bounds of possibility any more than they are in the field of gas attack, for which the Chemical Warfare Service . . . is prepared."[5]

Stimson suggested hiding the "germ warfare" advisory group in a New Deal welfare agency, called the Federal Security Agency, that oversaw the Public Health Service and Social Security.[6] He wanted an academic luminary to direct the program, someone familiar with the university research system and skilled in administration. After a cabinet meeting on May 15, Roosevelt admitted he had not yet read the secretary's plan but told him to go ahead with it anyway.[7] A week later, Stimson discussed his ideas with Secretary of Agriculture Claude R. Wickard, whose agency would later take part in the research coordinated by the advisory group, and with Paul V. McNutt, who directed the Federal Security Agency.[8]

By midsummer, three candidates had rejected an offer to head the new group: economist Walter W. Stewart, who chaired the Rockefeller Foundation, geographer Isaiah Bowman, president of Johns Hopkins University, and economist Edmund Ezra Day, president of Cornell University. Finally, in August, chemist George W. Merck, president of the pharmaceutical firm Merck & Co., Inc., accepted the position.[9]

Organizing Biology and Medicine for Biological Warfare

The innocuously named War Research Service (WRS) started out in mid-1942 with an initial allocation of $200,000. Wide contacts with major biologists and physicians enabled the eight-member directorate to initiate secret work in about 28 American universities, including Harvard University, Columbia University, the University of Chicago, Northwestern University, Ohio State University, the University of Notre Dame, the University of Wisconsin, Stanford University, and the University of California. By January 1943, the WRS had contracted with William A. Hagan of Cornell to explore offensive uses of botulism and with J. Howard Mueller of the Harvard Medical School to study anthrax.[10]

Anthrax and botulism remained the foci of biological warfare research during the war. Both deadly diseases are of bacterial origin, and the bacteria are hardy and prolific. Both have very short incubation periods, lasting for only a few days or even hours. The tough but virulent anthrax spores can be inhaled or absorbed through breaks in the skin; botulism results from ingestion of the bacterial poison botulin.

At the same time, the WRS empowered the Army's Chemical Warfare Service to expand greatly its own work on biological warfare. In 1942 and 1943, the chemical service received millions of dollars to build research facilities. The most notable one was Camp Detrick in Frederick, Maryland (now Fort Detrick), which cost nearly $13 million. The service also hired many scientists to work there and elsewhere in the newly enlarged system.[11]

The scientists, drawn largely from university faculties, put aside their repugnance at developing agents of death because the work seemed necessary in the exceptional situation of World War II. Theodor Rosebury, a Columbia University microbiologist, argued in early 1942 that "the likelihood that bacterial warfare will be used against us will surely be increased if an enemy suspects that we are unprepared to meet it and return blow for blow."[12] Soon afterward Rosebury entered the Chemical Warfare Service's laboratory and became a leader at Camp Detrick. "We were fighting a fire [the Axis]," he later wrote, "and it seemed necessary to risk getting dirty as well as burnt."[13]

Stimson and McNutt might well have applauded these sentiments, but they would have been astonished at Rosebury's view of who held the reins. Rosebury believed the ethical concerns of the scientists in his laboratory governed the use of the weapons they were creating. He wrote years later: "Civilians, in or out of uniform, made all the important decisions; the professional military kept out of the way. We resolved the ethical question just as other equally good men resolved the same question at Oak Ridge and Hanford and Chicago and Los Alamos."[14]

History tells a different story. Even though the president himself did not set the course of the War Research Service, it seems clear that the key decisions were made by civilian leaders and military chieftains in Washington. The scientists provided the necessary expertise to conceive and develop the weapons, and even to suggest how to deploy them, but they had no controlling authority, and even little influence, over when and under what political conditions the weapons would be used.

Expanding the Program

In spite of Paul McNutt's primary concern with welfare and social services, he kept an eye on the secret biological-warfare program hidden in his agency. In February 1943, McNutt informed President Roosevelt that the last of the WRS' $200,000 was being spent. The president, McNutt said, would have to decide whether to "go more deeply into two or three . . . projects now under way."[15] By April, with Stimson's approval, McNutt requested another $25,000 for the WRS FY1943 budget and a total of $350,000 for FY1944. Two days later, Roosevelt endorsed McNutt's request with a laconic notation: "O.K. F.D.R." The WRS 1944 budget grew again several months later, when Roosevelt expanded it to $460,000.[16]

In keeping with the tight security of the program, McNutt did not commit particular projects or details to writing, even in his correspondence with the president. Roosevelt's own files contain fewer than a dozen letters and memoranda on biological warfare. Of the handful pertaining to 1942 and 1943, most deal with the small appropriations and administrative arrangements for the War Research Service. Perhaps in discussions with McNutt and Stimson or in meetings with General George C. Marshall, the trusted Army chief of staff, Roosevelt was kept informed of the additional millions of dollars in appropriations going to the biological warfare work of the Chemical Warfare Service. Not one of the available records, however, shows that Roosevelt was receiving such reports.[17]

Meanwhile the chemical service was enlarging its facilities for development, testing, and production. In addition to the 500-acre Camp Detrick site, a 2,000-acre installation for field trials was established on Horn Island in Pascagoula, Mississippi. A 250-square-mile site near the Dugway Proving Ground in Utah was designated for bombing tests, and 6,100 acres were secured for a manufacturing plant to be built near Terre Haute, Indiana.[18]

The technology of delivery and dissemination was also advancing. With British technical assistance, the chemical service made considerable progress in devising biological bombs and in late 1943 began work on 500-pound anthrax bombs. These bombs held 106 four-pound "bomblets" that would disperse and break on impact.[19] The bombs were untested, but it was known that pulmonary anthrax, which causes lesions on the lungs, was almost invariably fatal.[20]

The chemical service also succeeded in producing botulism toxin, one of the most potent of all gastrointestinal poisons. Merely tasting food infected with the toxin is usually sufficient to cause severe illness or death. In natural outbreaks the death rate ranges from 16 to 82 percent,[21] but by varying the toxin and the delivery mechanism, the scientists at Camp Detrick aimed at producing a reliably lethal weapon.

Bolstered by these developments, in 1944 the Chemical Warfare Service pressed for and received an additional $2.5 million to finance the manufacture of anthrax and botulism toxin bombs. The service could produce either 275,000 botulinum toxin bombs or one million anthrax bombs every month with that allocation. It was anticipated that by 1945, these weapons might be needed in the war with Japan.[22] The most immediate threat, however, was that of possible German use of biological weapons.

Early in 1944, Allied intelligence experts were beginning to fear that Germany's powerful new V-1 "buzz bombs" might soon be directed against Britain or allied troops in Normandy, and that the missiles' warheads might be loaded with germ-warfare agents. The German high command, the experts warned, was facing a strategic crisis; it was assembling all its resources and might resort to biological warfare to gain a permanent advantage.[23] The analyses were based on so-called worst-case assumptions. They were not comforting.

By June 1944, the U.S. had probably prepared only a few anthrax bombs for testing, if any. Certainly no bombs were available for use against an enemy.[24] To deter Germany from launching a biological strike, military leaders arranged to inoculate about 100,000 soldiers against botulin, hoping to convince the Germans that Allied troops were preparing for biological retaliation.[25] If Germany have actually staged a biological attack, Anglo-American forces would probably have retaliated with gas.[26]

Germany never called the bluff. Hitler used only conventional explosives in the V-1. As a matter of fact, for reasons that are still not known, he had barred all research on offensive biological warfare.[27] The American program—developed substantially to deal with a German threat that never existed—remained untried.

America's biological warfare effort moved at a brisk pace. In May 1944, Stimson and McNutt presented Roosevelt with a brief research summary that allotted only five lines to scientific developments.[28] Much more could have been said about developments. An anthrax plant soon received authorization through the Chemical Warfare Service to manufacture a million bombs, and the service was making headway with short-range dispersal techniques for botulin in paste form.

In November 1944, Merck sent a report to Stimson and Marshall—but not to Roosevelt—that cryptically referred to research on four additional "agents against men."[29] Judging from other sources, these were probably brucellosis (undulant fever), psittacosis (parrot fever), tularemia (rabbit fever), and the respiratory disease glanders.[30]

Merck said the Chemical Warfare Service was also developing "at least five agents for use against plants." (These agents are actually chemicals, but at the time they were defined as part of the biological program because they could kill crops.) A sixth compound, ammonium thiocyanate, was recommended for the destruction of "Japanese gardens."[31]

These developments constituted 12 lines in Merck's short November report on biological warfare. The document is tucked away in Stimson's declassified Secretary of War records in Washington. There is no evidence that the secretary or the president devoted any attention to the details of the program.

U.S. Biological Warfare Policy: Roosevelt's Legacy

In spite of the considerable progress at Camp Detrick and fears of a German biological offensive, Roosevelt seems to have given little thought to the matter of biological warfare and the question of the policy that should guide development of biological weapons. In 1942 and again in 1943, Roosevelt had promised publicly not to initiate gas warfare, but he threatened retaliation in kind if the Axis used gas. Apparently he never considered issuing a similar statement on germ warfare. Nor did any adviser propose such a warning to deter action by Germany or Japan.[32]

In May 1944, Roosevelt's ties to the biological-warfare program became even more tenuous when Stimson and McNutt urged him to abolish the War Research Service and make Merck a consultant to Stimson. The president readily acceded to this reorganization, which may have further distanced him from the secret enterprise.[33] Roosevelt himself never indicated whether he would launch a biological-warfare attack in retaliation for Axis first-use, or whether he might even countenance first-use against Japan. (During the war, there were some then-unsubstantiated claims that Japan had used biological warfare against China.[34]) American use of biological warfare was never a central issue, and Roosevelt had a penchant for delaying decisions and keeping his options open.

The issue of America's first-use against Japan did come up, briefly, in July 1944, when Admiral William Leahy, military chief of staff to the president, and some other presidential advisers conducted in Roosevelt's presence what Leahy later called "a spirited discussion of bacteriological warfare," apparently focusing mostly on an effort to destroy Japan's rice crop.[35] Leahy, perhaps alone among the participants, "recoiled from the idea." A crusty old admiral who had gone on active duty in the 1890s, he was wedded to older moral principles about how America should conduct war even amid the horror of World War II. He recalled saying to Roosevelt, "Mr. President, this [using germs and poison] would violate every Christian ethic I have ever heard of and all of the known laws of war. It would be an attack on the noncombatant population of the enemy. The reaction can be foretold—if we use it, the enemy will use it." Leahy stated that the president "remained noncommittal through this discussion."[36]

Thus, in stark contrast to President Roosevelt's public pledges that America would not initiate gas war, he bequeathed to Harry S. Truman an ambiguous legacy regarding biological warfare. It fell into a penumbra of new, unused, fearsome weapons where neither policies of deterrence nor of use had even been defined.

Attempts to Achieve International Control of Biological Weapons: The Proposals of Bush and Conant

Somewhat like a monopoly in nuclear weaponry, a near-monopoly in biological weaponry could bestow great military and political power on a nation. Such superiority might also produce a feverish arms race in future years. Foreseeing such developments in October 1944, Vannevar Bush and James Conant, Roosevelt's two scientist-administrators who directed the Office of Scientific Research and Development and had recently warned against the president's policy of atomic-energy secrecy toward the Soviet Union, feared the international-political effects of the administration's similar secrecy policy toward the Soviets on biological warfare.[37]

These two top advisers knew that the American biological-warfare program, like the top-secret A-bomb program, had established close links to the British program but had maintained a policy of secrecy toward the Soviets.[38] Bush and Conant probably even knew the details—unavailable from the skimpy records now available—of precisely who had devised this American policy of secrecy on biological warfare. The two scientist-administrators implied that the policy had been conceived to help assure that the United States, and presumably Britain, would have greater military power than the Soviets in the postwar period.

Bush and Conant hoped to avoid a postwar biological arms race. They believed that some international arrangement on biological warfare, possibly with a sharing of information under the future United Nations organization, might also serve as a rough model for handling the more disruptive problem of atomic energy in international relations. On October 27, 1944, they wrote to Stimson to plead their case on biological warfare and to request permission to take their proposal directly to President Roosevelt.[39]

"If this war ends without the use of biological warfare by any country and without it being clear whether or not any country has solved the extremely difficult technical problems involved," they warned, "the United States will be confronted with a serious problem as to the future. Shall research and development along this line be pushed? . . . [F]ear and distrust of other countries might be intensified if the rumors spread [of work] on the perfection of this new weapon of destruction."[40]

They argued that the United States, by gaining information of other nations' research and having the work placed under an international organization, would actually be safer. They admitted that their hope for international control and inspections, with a rollback of national secrecy, might pose problems for the Soviet Union. "Granted that evasion on the part of Russia might take place," they wrote, but "is not the scheme proposed less dangerous to [American] security . . . than to assume that Russia would proceed with this development without any reference to the activities of the other nations." If Russia were allowed to develop its work without any participation in such an international arrangement, Bush and Conant warned, the results would be corrosive fear, a souring of the postwar peace, and great difficulty in planning for America's defense establishment. Bush and Conant emphasized that their primary concern was American security and that their proposed international arrangements would enhance, not impair, their own nation's security.[41]

In mid-February 1945, Bush again pushed on the issue of international control of biological weapons. This time, in a draft letter to Roosevelt (which was never sent), Bush argued for a U.N. agency "recommend[ing] means for policing aggression. . . . It should provide for full interchange between peace-loving nations [so] that no nation shall be caused to fear the scientific activities of another. . . ."[42]

The proposals of Bush and Conant failed, as did their related efforts to move America toward international control on atomic energy. There is no evidence in the relevant archives—Stimson's papers, his Secretary of War records, Roosevelt's files, or in the Bush-Conant materials—that their bold October and February recommendations went any further than Stimson in late 1944 or early 1945. In May 1945, however, when their October proposal was circulated to the recently created Interim Committee on atomic energy, the paper was read primarily, as Bush and Conant intended, as a suggestion about atomic energy and not as a proposal to be dealt with on the seemingly less threatening matter of biological warfare. It failed then, too.[43]

Contemplation of Biological Warfare Against Japan

Two weeks after Truman entered the White House in April of 1945, and a day after the president had received a lengthy briefing on the atomic bomb, Secretary Stimson got a memo from his special assistant Harvey H. Bundy. Bundy wrote that Merck and several other members of the biological warfare program were proposing the use of chemicals against Japanese food crops. "It is a pretty serious step," the assistant cautioned, and you may want to speak to the President." Stimson sent a note to General Marshall asking to confer with him at his convenience.[44]

From that point until the war's conclusion, emphasis on biological warfare shifted from bacteriological agents to crop defoliants.[45] American scientists certified that the chemicals were not poisonous to humans; the Judge Advocate's office concluded that their use would be legal because they were nontoxic to people and because the United States, as a warring nation, "is entitled to deprive the enemy of food and water, and to destroy the sources of supply in his fields."[46]

Stimson, although deeply troubled by the mass killing of non-combatants that American bombing had already caused, seemed prepared to accept the poisoning of Japanese crops.[47] Given that General Marshall wanted to use gas against Japanese troops, he too was probably not unnerved by the tactic of crop poisoning.[48] In May and June an air force general drew up an elaborate plan for destroying Japan's rice crops by dropping ammonium thiocyanate on rice-producing areas near six major cities: Tokyo, Yokohama, Osaka, Nagoya, Kyoto, and Kobe.[49] General Henry H. Arnold, the commander of the air force, rejected the plan on tactical rather than moral grounds. Bombing Japan's industry and cities, he judged, would have "earlier and more certain impact."[50]

At least one sector of the military did raise moral questions about biological warfare, including the poisoning of crops. "It is likely that this form of warfare will become more and more militarily practicable," the Chemical Warfare Service stated in July 1945. "This presents us with an important moral and political problem. These are all weapons of great hazard to the civilian population of an enemy, and the U.S. must . . . face the issue of determining whether in defeating an enemy we are willing to destroy not alone his property, as we have been doing from the air . . . but life on a large scale."[51]

Assistant Secretary of War For Air Robert Lovett approved a plan for destroying Japan's rice crop.[52] But some questioned whether the supply of chemicals was sufficient; some thought the destruction of the 1945 rice crop would not have any effect until 1946. By then, they believed, the war would have been won and American occupation forces would have the added burden of feeding a hungry civilian population.[53] On August 3, a few days before the bombing of Hiroshima, Arnold's deputy, Lieutenant General Ira C. Eaker, asked for a comprehensive report on crop destruction by air, including the capabilities of the air force, the best chemicals available, and the best techniques for their application.[54] He received the report on August 10, shortly after the Nagasaki bombing.[55] Four days after that report, the war in the Pacific ended.

The nation's secretly developed germ-warfare arsenal was not forgotten in the final months of the war. One high-ranking Army general had commented earlier in the program's history that the Administration might consider a policy of first use against Japan.[56] Later, strategists discussing retaliation concluded that if Japan broke the Geneva Protocol and resorted to gas agents, the U.S. should be prepared to respond with both gas and germ weapons. Admiral Donald B. Duncan, a staff member of the Joint Chiefs of Staff, pointed out that in some situations bacteriological attacks might be more effective than gas.[57]

American beliefs about the morality of biological warfare, however, were never put to the test in World War II. The ultimate decision to use biological weapons would have fallen to Truman; he probably would have relied on the counsel of General Marshall, whom he greatly admired, and Secretary Stimson, whom he regarded as a moral man. Having sanctioned the use of atomic bombs on Japanese cities, these key advisers probably would not have taken exception to poisoning rice fields to compel Japan's surrender. They would have probably endorsed Assistant Secretary Lovett's plan to "nail down" the Japanese by killing their crops.

But germ warfare, with its specters of epidemic and invisible poison, would have been harder to endorse. Years later, however, Truman implied in a letter to an associate that if the war in the Pacific had dragged on past mid-August, he would have employed both bacteriological and chemical agents—that, in effect, the atomic bombing he had approved was so much worse.[58]

The Legacy of World War II

In World War II, the governments of all the major nations except Germany worked to develop biological weapons. No major nation other than Japan used these weapons during the war. But the establishment of America's scientific-technological capacity for biological warfare left a powerful legacy for the early postwar years: the continuation of general secrecy surrounding research and development, the creation of military institutions for biological warfare work, and a desire by some military and civilian advisers to pursue such work for possible deterrence and use in the emerging Cold War. In articulating the rationale for such efforts, George Merck advised President Truman soon after V-J Day, "Work in this field, born of the necessity of war, cannot be ignored in time of peace."[59] Others agreed.

Acknowledgments

This essay is drawn substantially from my brief article, "The Birth of the U.S. Biological-Warfare Program," *Scientific American* 256 (June 1987), 116–121; and also from my larger study, "America's Biological Warfare Program in the Second World War," *Journal of Strategic Studies* 11 (September 1988), 292–317.

I am indebted to Larry Bland of the George Marshall Papers, Lynn Eden of Carnegie-Mellon University, Julian Perry Robinson and Rod McElroy of Sussex University, Lt. Col. Charles F. Brower IV of West Point, Bruce Russett of Yale University, and Dale Birdsell for assistance with sources, and to Stanford's Center for International Security and Arms Control (ISAC), to the Japan Fund, and the Values, Technology, Science and Society (VTSS) Program for assistance. Members of the VTSS Forum and the Peace Studies seminar provided valuable comments on my analysis.

Notes

1. Leo Brophy, Wydham Miles, and Rexmond Cochrane, *The Chemical Warfare Service: From Laboratory to Field* (Washington, D.C.: Government Printing Office, 1959), 101–122; Stockholm International Peace Research Institute, *The Problem of Chemical and Biological Warfare* (New York: Humanities Press, 1971), I, 119–123, mostly a summary of the official history; Seymour Hersh, *Chemical and Biological Warfare: America's Hidden Arsenal* (Garden City: Doubleday, 1968), 6–17; Stephen McFarland, "Preparing For What Never Came: Chemical and Biological Warfare in World War II," *Defense Analysis* 2 (June 1986), 108–09; 114; and Robert Harris and Jeremy Paxman, *A Higher Form of Killing* (New York: Hill and Wang, 1982), 94–97.
2. National Academy of Science Committee Report (WBC Committee), February 17, 1942, Surgeon General (Army) Records, Record Group (RG) 112, Washington National Records Center; and "History of the Relation of the SGO to BW Activities," n.d. (1945–46), 37–41, Surgeon General (Army) Records.

3. NAS Committee Report (WBC Committee), February 17, 1942.

4. Henry L. Stimson to President, April 29, 1942, President's Secretary's File (PSF) 104, Franklin D. Roosevelt Library.

5. Stimson to President, April 29, 1942.

6. Stimson to President, April 29, 1942.

7. Henry L. Stimson Diary, May 16, 1942, Yale University Library; and Stimson, "Notes After Cabinet Meeting," May 15, 1942, Stimson Papers, Yale.

8. Stimson Diary, May 22, 1942.

9. Stimson Diary, August 27, 1942.

10. Contracts in War Research Services files, now in HEW Records, RG 235, National Archives (N.A.). For a partial summary and names, see "Appedix: Biological Warfare," n.d. (about February 1944), attached to Florence Newsome, Assistant Secretary, General Staff, to Joint Chiefs of Staff, "Biological Warfare," March 3, 1944, CCS 385.2 (12–17–43), Records of the Joint Chiefs of Staff, RG 218, National Archives

11. Brophy et al., *Chemical Warfare Service: From Laboratory*, 108–110.

12. Theodor Rosebury and Elvin Kabat, with assistance of Martin Boldt, "Bacterial Warfare," *Journal of Immunology* 56 (May 1947), 11 (from a 1942 paper).

13. Rosebury, "Medical Ethics and Biological Warfare," *Perspectives in Biology and Medicine* 6 (Summer 1963), 514–515.

14. Rosebury, "Medical Ethics," 514. Also see Albert Krueger, "History of a Medical Reasearch Program," *Military Surgeon* 110 (June 1952), 410–412.

15. McNutt to President, February 9, 1943, summarized in Official File (OF) 5381, Roosevelt Library.

16. To Secretary of the Treasury, April 5, 1943, summarized in OF 581, Roosevelt Library.

17. See PSF 104 and 10, and OF 5381 and 3700, at Roosevelt Library (a total of 19 pages).

18. George Merck, "Summary Status of Biological Warfare," November 24, 1944, Records of the Secretary of War, RG 107, National Archives.

19. "Appendix: Biological Warfare," n.d. (about February 1944); Ernest Brown to Prime Minister (Churchill), both in Premier (Prem) 3/65, Public Record Office (PRO), Kew, Great Britain.

20. Rosebury and Kabat, with Boldt, "Bacterial Warfare," 42–43.

21. Rosebury and Kabat, with Boldt, "Bacterial Warfare," 34.

22. Maj. Gen. William Porter, Chief, Chemical Warfare Service, to Commanding General, (Somervell), Army Service Forces, "Plant, production, BW," February 2, 1944, CCS 385.2 (12–17–43), Records of the Joint Chiefs of Staff. Attached to this document is an undated note by Florence Newsome about General Joseph McNarney's "off the record" comment that Japan was a likely target.

23. Col. John Weckerling, Deputy for Intelligence, G-2, "Bacteriological Warfare Summary Report, Germany's Intentions and Capabilities," January 26, 1944, Joint Intelligence Staff 21, CCS (12–17–43), Records of the Joint Chiefs of Staff.

24. Report By the Joint Committee on New Weapons and Equipment, JCS, "Biological Warfare," February 20, 1944, JCS 625/6, CCS (12–17–43), Records of the Joint Chiefs of Staff.

25. Philip Noel-Baker, *The Arms Race* (New York: Oceana, 1958), 351–354. For partial confirmation, see n.a. to Commanding General, Army Service Forces,

"Protection Against Bacteriological Warfare," January 13, 1944, Marshall Library. Unfortunately, the only strong statement about this application of the strategy of deterrence is from a source, a Canadian general, whose other recollections are flawed.

26. See Annex 2 ("Other Forms of Warfare"), attached to "Military Considerations Affecting the Initiation of Chemical and Other Forms of Warfare," n.d. (probably July 26 or 27, 1944), Prem 3/89, PRO; and Merck, "Summary Status of Biological Warfare," November 24, 1944.

27. See various Alsos reports in the Surgeon General (Army) Records: "Translation, Resume of England-America BW Intelligence Gathered by German Intelligence Organizations" (May 24, 1945); "Official German Documents and Reports on BW, H-H 168, dated 24 May 45"; "A Review of German Activities in the Field of Biological Warfare," n.d. (1945); and "Bacteriological Warfare," n.d. (1947). Information on Hitler appears in all of these reports, but see especially "A Review of German Activities," 6.

28. Stimson and McNutt to President, May 12, 1944, PSF 104, Roosevelt Library.

29. Merck, "Summary Status of Biological Warfare," November 24, 1944. Earlier, the plant had been scheduled to produced 625,000 anthrax bombs monthly. (Ernest Brown to Prime Minister, May 9, 1944, Prem 3/65, PRO).

30. Theodor Rosebury, *Peace or Pestilence* (New York: Whittlesey House, 1949), p. 49; Calderon Howe et al., "Acute Brucellosis Among Laboratory Workers," *New England Journal of Medicine* 236 (May 15, 1947), 741–747; Howe et al., "Streptomycin Treatment in Tularemia," *Journal of the American Medical Association* 132 (September 28, 1946), 195–200; and Howe et al., Human Glanders: Report of Six Cases," *Annals of Internal Medicine* 26 (January 1947), 93–115.

31. Merck, "Summary Status of Biological Warfare," November 24, 1944.

32. Roosevelt in Samuel Rosenman, ed., *The Public Papers and Addresses of Franklin D. Roosevelt* (New York: Harper, 1950), 1942, 258 (June 5, 1942 warning to Japan), and *ibid.*, 1943, 243 (June 8, 1943 general warning to Axis). For evidence that FDR's 1943 statement was intended to refer *only* to gas warfare, see Cordell Hull to President, May 11, 1943, with "Statement by The President on Gas Warfare," Speech File 1469, Roosevelt Library; and Roosevelt to Secretary of State, May 21, 1943, and Roosevelt to Leahy, June 5, 1943, PSF 93, Roosevelt Library. For a different but mistaken view (that FDR's 1943 statement included BW), see Gen. Brehon Somervell to Chief of Staff (Marshall), on "Biological Warfare," February 21, 1944, CCS 385.2 (12–27–43), Records of the Joint Chiefs of Staff.

33. Stimson and McNutt to President, May 12, 1944, and Roosevelt to Dr. (Ross) McIntire, June 1, 1944, PSF 104, Roosevelt Library; and Roosevelt to Stimson, June 8, 1944, Records of the Secretary of War. For background on the May 12 letter, see Harvey Bundy to Secretary (Stimson), February 13, 1944, Marshall Library.

34. H.L. Ismay to Churchill, July 9, 1942, Prem 3/85, PRO (on China's claims); and John Powell, "Japan's Germ Warfare: The U.S. Cover-up of a War Crime," *Bulletin of Concerned Asian Scholars* 12 (October-December 1980), 2–17. Also see Sheldon Harris, "Japanese Biological Warfare Experiments and Other Atrocities in Manchuria, 1932–1945: A Preliminary Statement" (1988 ms.), courtesy of Harris, California State University, Northridge.

35. Leahy, *I Was There* (New York: Whittlesey, 1950), 439.

36. Leahy, *I Was There*, 440.

37. Bush and Conant to Stimson, October 27, 1944, with attached "Memorandum on the Future of Biological Warfare As An International Problem in the Postwar World," n.d., AEC Doc. 283, in Department of Energy Historical Office (Germantown, MD) Records and also in Bush-Conant Files, Office of Scientific Research and Development (OSRD) Records, RG 227, National Archives. For background, see Bush to Conant, October 24, 1944, AEC Doc. 188.

38. On American-British relations on the A-bomb project, see Bernstein, "The Uneasy Alliance," *Western Political Quarterly* (June 1976), 220–230.

39. Bush and Conant to Stimson, October 27, 1944, AEC Doc. 283; and John Anderson to Bush, April 19, 1944, and reply, May 15, 1944, Prem 3/89, PRO. On British secrecy and Russia, Chairman, BWIC, "The Capabilities of Our Defeated and Possible Future Enemies in the Field of B.W. During The Next Ten Years," January 18, 1946, BW (46) 3, Surgeon General (Army) Records. On U.S.-Soviet WW II relations on BW, see Joint Intelligence and Chemical Weapons," January 27, 1949, JIG 297/3, Records of the Joint Chiefs of Staff.

40. Bush and Conant to Stimson, October 27, 1944.

41. Bush and Conant to Stimson, October 27, 1944.

42. Bush, "Draft of Letter," February 15, 1945, Secretary of War Records.

43. James Conant to George Harrison, May 22, 1945, Harrison-Bundy files (H-B), Manhattan Engineer District Records, RG 77, N.A.

44. Bundy to the Secretary (Stimson), April 26, 1945, and handwritten Stimson note to Marchall, n.d. (April 1945), both in box 84, folder 27, George C. Marshall Papers, Marshall Library, called to my attention by Lt. Col. Charles F. Brower, IV.

45. For the official definition of BW as including chemical compounds against crops, see Brophy et al., *Chemical Warfare Service: From Laboratory*, 102.

46. Frank Jewett, President, National Academy of Sciences to Gen. William Porter, April 20, 1945, with attachments, and Maj. Gen. Myron Cramer, Judge Advocate General to Secretary of War, "Destruction of Crops by Chemicals," March 5, 1945, box 84, folder 27, Marchall Papers.

47. Bundy to Secretary (Stimson), April 26, 1945; and Gen. Barney Giles to Gen. Arnold (Stimson's concern about Dresden), March 7, 1945, box 223, Henry H. Arnold Papers, Library of Congress; and Stimson Diary, May 16, 1945.

48. John J. McCloy, "Memorandum of Conversation with General Marshall," May 29, 1945, Records of the Secretary of War.

49. Maj. Gen. V. E. Bertrandias to Gen. H. H. Arnold, May 29, 1945, box 115, Arnold Papers.

50. Brig. Gen. John Samford, Director, Joint Target Group, to Bertrandias, June 4, 1945, box 115, Arnold Papers.

51. "Conference General Policy Board Notes," July 19–21, 1945, File 337, Records of the Chemical Warfare Service, RG 175, N.A.

52. Robert Lovett oral history (1960), Columbia University.

53. Report by the Joint Staff Planners and the Joint Logistics Committee, "Policy on the Use of Chemical Agents For The Destruction of Japanese Food Crops." n.d. (June 1945), enclosure A to JCS 1371/1, ABC 475.92 (2–25–44), Records of

the Army Services Forces, RG 319, N.A. This report may have been considering a poison other than ammonium thiocynate.

54. Lt. Gen. Ira Eaker, Deputy Commander, AAF, to Deputy Chief of Staff, August 3, 1945, "Experiment in Destruction of Crops By Air," box 115, Arnold Papers.

55. Lt. Gen. Hoyt Vandenberg, Assistant Chief of Air Staff, to Chief of Air Staff, "Experiment in Destruction of Crops By Air," August 10, 1945, which mentioned a June 1945 report (not found), "Developments of Tactics and Techniques for Dissemination of Chemicals from Aircraft for Crop Destruction," box 115, Arnold Papers.

56. Florence Newsome note, n.d. (about February 1944), attached to Maj. Gen. William Porter, Chief, Chemical Warfare Service, to Commanding General, (Somervell), Army Service Forces, "Plant, production, BW," February 2, 1944, CCS 385.2 (12–17–43), Records of the Joint Chiefs of Staff.

57. Minutes of the JPS 206th Meeting, June 13, 1945, CCS 441.5 (8–27–42), Records of the Joint Chiefs of Staff.

58. Harry S. Truman to AEC Commissioner Thomas Murray, January 19, 1953, PSF, Harry S. Truman Library.

59. George Merck, "Biological Warfare: Report to the Secretary of War by Mr. George Merck, Special Consultant For Biological Warfare," n.d. (about November 1945), PSF, Truman Library. This document is also in CCS 385.2 (12–17–43), Records of the Joint Chiefs of Staff.

2

Evolution of Biological Warfare Policy: 1945–1990

Susan Wright

World War II left a major legacy for the future development of chemical and biological weapons. Fear of the use of these weapons by the other side resulted in the production of large arsenals of lethal chemicals by both the Allies and the Axis powers; the development in Germany of new chemical agents (nerve agents, many times more potent than their predecessors); the development in Britain and the United States of defoliants as anti-plant chemical weapons; and finally, as shown in the previous chapter, the intensive development, especially in the United States and Britain, of biological weapons, transforming them from crude instruments of sabotage into weapons of mass destruction.

This chapter surveys the post-war evolution of the U.S. CBW institutions and their policies, focusing on biological warfare policy and use of the biological sciences for military purposes. A full analysis of developments in biological warfare requires discussion of chemical warfare policy as well. For institutional as well as technical reasons, policies in both fields were linked. The similar technical properties and complex operational and logistical requirements of chemical and biological weapons, as well as the overlap of their research bases in the biological and chemical sciences, encouraged their sponsorship within the same military institutions. Conversely, this institutional linkage encouraged the formation of similar policies for both types of weaponry.

In broad terms, U.S. CBW policy since World War II evolved through three main phases: first, the period following the war until the late 1960s, in which an active CBW program was pursued; second, the period from the late 1960s until the late 1970s, a period characterized by efforts towards chemical and biological disarmament, in which military influence in this area declined; finally, the period from the late 1970s until the present, in which military interest in CBW has revived, alongside and partially in conflict with U.S. efforts to achieve chemical disarmament.

At no time in the period under consideration were chemical and biological weapons central elements of military theory and practice. Technological limitations, cultural factors, domestic political pressures and legal restraints all played roles in restricting the introduction of these weapons into military arsenals. However, these restraints prevented neither the pursuit of major research and development efforts nor the assimilation and use of chemical and biological weaponry in particular instances. My concern in this account is to draw attention to the social and political forces that promoted military assimilation of these weapons (and with them, the relevant areas of science) as well as the social and cultural pressures that have restrained that process.

This chapter is based largely on sources on biological and chemical warfare available in the open literature, supplemented by declassified documents. In particular, for the period 1945 to 1973, the account makes use of the six-volume series on the history of chemical and biological warfare, *The Problem of Chemical and Biological Warfare*, published by the Stockholm International Peace Research Institute in 1971–1973 and the materials relating to biological warfare activities in the 1950s and 1960s that came to light as a result of Congressional investigations in the 1970s. For developments in recent years, the account makes use of materials on the U.S. Biological Defense Research Program generated by Congressional inquiries and lawsuits that have probed the compliance of this program with the National Environmental Policy Act, as well as of materials obtained through requests under the Freedom of Information Act.[1]

Expansion of Chemical and Biological Warfare Programs, 1945–1969

Shortly after the end of the war, George Merck, director of the War Research Service during the war, presented the case for continuation of biological warfare operations. In a report to the Secretary of War written in January 1946, Merck argued that biological warfare could not be "discounted by those of this nation who are concerned with the national security," and that continuation of BW operations was imperative:

Our endeavors during the war provided means of defending the nation against biological warfare in terms of its presently known potentialities, and explored means of retaliation which might have been used, had such a course been necessary. Although remarkable achievements can be recorded, the metes and bounds of this type of warfare have by no means been completely measured. Work in this field, born of the necessity of war, cannot be ignored in time of peace; it must be continued on a sufficient scale to provide an adequate defense.[2]

While it was recognized that continuing to develop the offensive potential of biological weaponry risked making war with the new weapons inevitable,[3] Merck's rationale for in-kind BW deterrence was broadly accepted in the post-war years. With their increased effectiveness biological—as well as chemical—weapons acquired regular sponsorship in military establishments. Although some reduction of expenditures on chemical and biological warfare occurred immediately after World War II, chemical and biological weapons operations in the United States (and elsewhere) were not phased out, and the institutions responsible for these operations remained in place.

The lead agency for chemical and biological warfare was the Army Chemical Corps (the former Chemical Warfare Service) which was responsible for the principal biological warfare facility at Fort Detrick as well as for the chemical warfare facilities. Overall technical direction for chemical and biological warfare research and development was provided initially by the Research and Development Board of the Office of the Secretary of Defense, which established a Committee on Chemical and Biological Warfare, and later, by the Office of the Director of Defense Research and Engineering.[4]

Immediately following the war, official policy apparently continued President Roosevelt's pledge in 1943 of no first use of chemical weapons and extended it to biological weapons. Until 1956 the U.S. Army Field Manual 27-10, "The Rules of Land Warfare," stated that "gas warfare and bacteriological warfare are employed by the United States against enemy personnel only in retaliation for their use by the enemy." (There was, however, no public affirmation of this policy.)[5] For several years, production and field testing of biological weapons was discontinued. The United States supported the United Nations General Assembly Resolution of 14 December 1946 committing nations to eliminate all "major weapons adaptable now or in the future to mass destruction."[6] It is questionable, however, whether U.S. support for these and other General Assembly proposals for the elimination of weapons of mass destruction had any significant impact on the U.S. CBW program. In any case, the intensification of cold-war tensions towards the end of the 1940s eroded American support for disarmament proposals and legitimated military pressures for expansion of the program.

The history of the BW program in this period displays repeated policy reviews. An Army report written in 1958 describes the years 1947 to 1952 as "an era of boards, committees, Ad Hoc groups, panels, contractors, etc. investigating, evaluating, and advising on various phases of the BW program." At one point there were some 23 groups committed to such studies and surveys.[7] Generally, these reports appear to have reached very similar conclusions: that the United States was unprepared to meet a BW threat (assumed to be posed primarily by the Soviet Union) and therefore needed to expand its BW capabilities. Subsequent expansion naturally furthered the military assimilation of biological weaponry. The reports described below are used to illustrate these tendencies.

An early review, conducted by a panel on biological warfare of the Research and Development Board, was designed to assess subversive use of biological warfare. In a report in October 1948, the Committee concluded that the United States was especially susceptible to subversive BW operations—a position also expressed in a report issued in February 1950 by the Chief of the Research and Engineering Division of the Chemical Corps. The principal recommendation of the 1948 biological warfare panel was that the vulnerability of ventilation, subway and water supply systems should be assessed—recommendations that were approved and eventually implemented in the 1950s and 1960s in an extensive series of secret open-air tests (see below).[8]

A further review not only reinforced those conclusions but went considerably further. The review was conducted by an Ad Hoc Committee on Biological Warfare appointed by the Secretary of Defense and chaired by Caryl Haskins of Haskins Laboratories, New York, and resulted in a report issued on July 11, 1949. In this report, the committee depicted biological and chemical weapons, as well as a third category of weaponry based on radioactive materials and known as "radiological weapons," as having great potential for strategic use as well as for subversion. In the case of biological weaponry, advances in the life sciences were seen as enhancing that potential, possibly making them comparable in

military utility to nuclear weapons: "Medical and biological sciences are on the threshold of great new advances comparable to
those in the atomic field. New biological weapons more potent than
any now known may be expected—for example, weapons causing
epidemics, glandular or hereditary changes, or other biological
'chain-reactions'."[9]

Furthermore, the report shows that a primary concern was the
possibility that the Soviet Union could disrupt the prevailing balance of power through achieving a major advance in biological,
chemical, or radiological warfare. As the report stated,

The committee wishes to call attention to a consideration of particular
importance having a major bearing on the international balance of power.
Accurate appraisal of this matter will require much wider information,
particularly of an intelligence nature, than has been available to the Committee. This is the bearing which the Soviet estimate of its own military
capabilities vis-a-vis those of the rest of the world has on its courses of
action. Such Soviet self-appraisal will affect both the emphasis given to the
development of weapons of biological warfare within the U.S.S.R., and
Soviet policy with respect to the international armaments agreements.
Thus the Soviets might well feel that a major technical advance in biological warfare in their own country could put them in a position of weapons
parity in this field. On this basis, they might expect to press for the elimination of atomic weapons in return for the prohibition of biological
weapons. Further, the development of effective CEBAR [chemical, biological and radiological] weapons, particularly if accompanied by success in
the atomic field might lead the Soviets to believe that they possessed overall weapons superiority and that the time had come to precipitate openly
'the inevitable conflict between capitalists and communist societies.'[10]

The implication of these speculations about the possible emergence
of Soviet superiority in chemical, biological, and radiological
weaponry was that the United States should initiate a build-up in
biological weaponry in order to maintain the United States' superior position at the bargaining table. The report urged the Secretary
of Defense not only to strengthen defenses against biological warfare but also to stimulate strategic planning for biological (as well
as chemical and radiological) weapons and to expand weapons
research programs. Significantly for the future, it noted close connections between defensive and offensive activities: "The offensive
employment of BW is predicated upon the ability to immunize our
troops, those of our allies, or other personnel likely to come within
range of infection by our own BW weapons." Defense, therefore,
was an integral part of offense. Furthermore, "information

obtained from research on the defensive aspects of BW is, in the greater part, applicable to offensive problems as well."[11]

Perhaps the most influential of these post-war reports on chemical and biological warfare policy was issued in June 1950 by a further ad hoc committee convened by the Secretary of Defense and chaired by Earl P. Stevenson, president of Arthur D. Little. Reflecting cold-war fears about Soviet intentions, the Stevenson report recommended that the "necessary steps be taken to make the United States capable of effectively employing toxic chemical agents at the onset of war." According to the report, such a readiness demanded expanding all aspects of CBW research and development, field tests of CBW agents and munitions, and establishment of CBW production facilities. Most significantly, the report also proposed abandoning the policy of no-first-use.[12] The onset of the Korean War in June 1950 triggered the adoption in October 1950 of all these recommendations, except that of revoking the no-first-use policy. However, from that point on, Roosevelt's policy was frequently depicted as obstructing development of the CBW programs. In the late 1950s, this proved sufficient to overturn the policy.[13]

In 1955, a further report issued by a civilian advisory committee chaired by Otto N. Miller, vice-president of the Standard Oil Company of California, advised that the "proper place of chemical and biological warfare" be given "more candid recognition." The report also proposed that the advice of the Chemical Corps be "weighed early and frequently at critical points within the military, in order that maximum consideration be given in overall Department of Defense thinking to meshing chemical, biological and radiological warfare into plans of warfare and plans of defense as they are being developed."[14] In short, what was being proposed was a closer integration of CB weaponry into war planning. This advice was given reinforcement in 1956 by the Defense Department's interpretation of Soviet Defense Minister Marshal Zhukov's speech to the twentieth Communist Party Congress. Zhukov's statement that "future war, if they [the United States] unleash it, will be characterized by . . . various means of mass destruction such as atomic, thermonuclear, chemical, and bacteriological weapons" was taken as further evidence of a Soviet CBW threat.[15]

In 1956, the no-first-use policy was finally revoked and replaced by a policy of preparedness for use at the discretion of the President.[16] In retrospect, it is significant that the passage in the

Army Field Manual 27-10 stating the no-first-use policy disappeared in 1956, and elsewhere in the manual, a passage was inserted to the effect that the United States was not bound by any treaty prohibiting or restricting the use of chemical or biological weapons. At the time, however, the precise change of policy was kept secret and efforts on the part of certain members of Congress to clarify it in the late 1950s failed. The only official reference to U.S. policy during the Eisenhower administration was vague and misleading: questioned about a change in the policy of no-first-use at a press conference in January 1960, President Eisenhower responded: "No such official suggestion has been made to me, and so far as my own instinct is concerned, [it] is not to start such a thing as that first." The real policy change was not officially acknowledged until the Army's release of a report on the history of its biological warfare activities at Congressional hearings in 1977.[17]

Still more reports urging expansion of the CBW effort followed. A symposium on CBW at the Rand Corporation convened by the Defense Science Board in December 1958 produced recommendations to develop new chemical and biological weapons, formulate strategies for use, expand CBW research, and initiate a public relations champaign aimed at gaining public acceptance of chemical and biological weaponry. These recommendations were accepted by the Director of Defense Research and Engineering, Herbert York, who proposed to the Secretary of Defense a fivefold expansion of the CBW research and development over the following five years. York's recommendation was reinforced by the Joint Chiefs of Staff in September 1959. Among other things, the Joint Chiefs advised the Secretary that the Army's chemical and biological warfare capabilities were out of date and needed to be modernized if it was to be "operational," that an "increasingly active research and development program" was required, and that "nonlethal incapacitating chemical agent-munitions" might be "highly desirable in a variety of limited war situations." Both retaliatory use and first use were contemplated. As the report stated: "In order to place the United States in a position to initiate CW or BW in war, at the decision of the President, U.S. forces must possess the ability to live and fight in a toxic environment. Thus protected, the U.S. forces would survive enemy use of similar munitions or be able to exploit any advantage resulting from United States use." In October 1959, the Chief Chemical Officer was directed to prepare an expanded five-year program that included revival of anti-crop efforts phased out two years earlier. Significantly, the policy of preparedness for use at the discretion of the President was secretly revalidated in the summer of 1960, despite efforts on the part of some members of Congress to reaffirm the policy of no first use.[18]

Further examination of the CBW program at the beginning of the Kennedy administration again produced recommendations for even greater expansion, with the cost of achieving a full range of chemical and biological weaponry estimated at four billion dollars. A DOD task force, established by the Director of Defense Research and Engineering, was assigned the task of preparing a comprehensive plan for this expansion, designated "Project 112." At this point, both the increase in hostilities between the United States and the Soviet Union as well as the shift in strategic doctrine from "massive retaliation" to "flexible response" endorsed by the Kennedy administration reinforced commitments to the integration of chemical and biological weaponry into war planning proposed in 1955 by the Miller committee.[19]

At the same time, Kennedy's Secretary of Defense, Robert McNamara, ordered a reorganization of the functions of the Chemical Corps. A Joint Technical Coordinating Group was set up to coordinate research between the three armed services. Effectively, this arrangement gave members of the military committed to the expansion of chemical and biological functions high-level representation within the Pentagon. The CBW research, development, production, and stockpiling functions of the Chemical Corps were absorbed into the Army Matériel Command, while testing and evaluation became the responsibility of a new Test and Evaluation Command.[20]

This succession of high-level recommendations to expand the CBW programs and assimilate them into military planning was influential. The role and status of CBW programs rose. Total support for the CBW programs increased from approximately $10 million in the early 1950s to $352 million in 1969—an increase of over 2,000 percent, allowing for inflation. Support for CBW research and development trebled in real terms between 1958 and 1964 to $129 million (figure 2.1). The Chemical Corps launched a public relations campaign known as "Operation Blue Skies" that used briefings with journalists, Congressional hearings, and a steady flow of news articles to try to persuade the public that chemical and biological weapons were humane and to overcome traditional aversion to their use. Barriers to the assimilation and use of CB weaponry were lowered.[21]

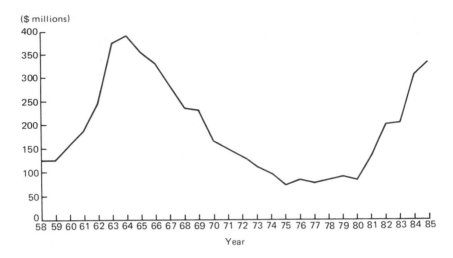

($ millions)

Figure 2.1
U.S. Department of Defense support for chemical and biological warfare research
and development (constant 1982 dollars).
Sources: 1963–73, SIPRI, *The Problem of Chemical and Biological Warfare*, II, 204–5
(expenditures); 1974–86, Department of Defense, Annual Reports to Congress on
Chemical Warfare and Biological Defense Program Obligations (obligations).

The chemical warfare program focused on development and production of nerve agents, irritant and incapacitating agents, and
herbicides. Nerve agents, knowledge of which was acquired from
the Germans at the end of World War II, were further developed,
tested and produced in the United States, Britain and elsewhere in
the 1950s and 1960s. VX, the most lethal nerve agent known, was
selected for development in the U.S. and its production began in
1961. By 1969, the U.S. chemical weapons stockpile included
roughly 42,000 tons of poison gas. In addition, secret research and
development of a binary nerve gas weapon—a munition consisting
of two comparatively nontoxic components that mix and produce a
nerve agent when the weapon is on its way to a target—was initiated in 1949. (The results were made public in 1969). Irritant
agents (tear gas) developed and produced in the 1950s and 1960s
were used extensively in Vietnam. (Roughly 7000 tons of the tear
gas CS were shipped to Southeast Asia.)[22] Also explored for the
CW arsenal were incapacitating agents, such as BZ, a psychotropic
substance capable of blocking nerve pathways to the heart and
brain; psychochemicals such as LSD; and toxins, poisons made by
bacteria and other organisms, which are hundreds of times more
lethal than nerve agents.[23] Finally, herbicides, developed in Britain

and the United States in the 1940s, became a major military focus. First used by the British in Malaya to destroy vegetation and crops in the 1940s, herbicides were further developed and field tested in the U.S. in the 1950s and shown to be capable of destroying Indochinese crops and vegetation. Following operational trials in 1961, they were authorized for use by President Kennedy and deployed in Vietnam.[24]

Biological weapons were similarly integrated into the military arsenal. In the 1950s and 1960s, an extensive biological weapons program, much of it carried out in secret and involving all stages from research and development to production of pathogenic organisms as weapons, came into existence. The expanding program was bolstered by its exclusive possession of data transferred to Fort Detrick from the brutal Japanese BW program, obtained from Japanese officials in the late 1940s in exchange for immunity from war crimes prosecution. A research and development network extending far beyond the boundaries of Fort Detrick, the principal Army research and development facility for biological warfare, to contractors in approximately 300 universities, research institutes and corporations, was formed. Biological agents were developed and standardized as weapons against humans, animals and plants: in all, eight anti-personnel agents and five anti-crop agents were adopted. Many methods of dissemination were explored and developed, including use of insects as carriers of disease. Extensive field testing with simulants as well as pathogens was carried out at the Army's chemical and biological warfare test facility at Dugway Proving Ground, Utah and many other locations. After research on human subjects was authorized in 1955, a large program that used hundreds of human subjects was pursued. Anti-personnel agents were produced from 1954 onwards at Pine Bluff, Arkansas. Anti-crop agents were also produced and stockpiled. By the end of the 1960s, the U.S. government had available at least ten different biological and toxin weapons.[25]

In the 1950s and 1960s, chemical and biological weaponry was also broadly developed and assimilated by the Central Intelligence Agency for clandestine operations. (As in the case of military development the climate of the cold war, supporting fears of use of CB weaponry by adversary nations, was influential in justifying development.) Hearings conducted by the Senate Select Committee to Study Governmental Operations with Respect to Intelligence (the Church Committee) in 1975 and by the Senate Subcommittee on Health and Scientific Research in 1977 revealed several highly sensitive CIA programs aimed at covert use of chemical and biological agents.[26]

The principal CIA operation, code-named MKULTRA, began in 1953, focusing on techniques for controlling human behavior. Over the next ten years, investigations were pursued secretly in some 86 universities and research institutions, often with ruthless insensitivity to ethical considerations. Hundreds of human subjects were involved in tests of hallucinogenic and other drugs, sometimes without their knowledge or consent. Another CIA operation, code-named MKNAOMI, was pursued in collaboration with the Army's Special Operations Division (SOD), based at Fort Detrick, Maryland, in developing, testing, and maintaining biological agents and delivery systems. The collaboration was motivated by interests in developing both defensive and offensive applications. According to the final report of the Church hearings, the primary interest of the SOD was "to assess the vulnerability of sensitive installations, such as the Pentagon, air bases, and subway systems, to biological sabotage by an enemy." In addition, however, a 1951 study conducted by the Joint Chiefs of Staff reveals that the Army also viewed these studies as a source of useful information for offensive purposes. The primary interest of the CIA was to develop offensive systems.[27] Between 1952 and 1970, the CIA and SOD pursued their goals through an extensive series of secret measurements of the diffusion of biological agents through the Pentagon, the White House, the Manhattan subway system, Washington National Airport, and other major national systems and institutions. Biological simulants (normally harmless organisms whose molecular properties were similar to those of certain biological warfare agents) were sprayed from canisters and other easily concealed devices and their spread monitored. The test results were used both defensively, for assessing vulnerability to covert BW attack, as well as offensively, for matching delivery systems with lethal or incapacitating agents. The Army-CIA collaboration underscores the possibility of an easy passage from defensive to offensive application: the same project produced results relevant to both goals (chapter 8).

In addition, the army directly advised the CIA on using biological weapons in covert operations: SOD scientists prepared briefing papers for the CIA listing pathogens native to various parts of the world. (Covert uses of indigenous pathogens in these areas would probably go undetected.) The CIA also explored the use of biological warfare against plants; a memo in 1962 noted that the agency had developed "three methods and systems for carrying out a covert operation attack against crops and causing severe crop loss" in anticipation of actual use.[28]

In summary, the end result of the expansion of CBW activity in the 1950s and 1960s was an unprecedented assimilation of CB weaponry by the military and the CIA. The period saw the formation of a huge chemical and biological warfare infrastructure of laboratories, test facilities, and production plants, and a network of institutional ties with the civilian sector. This system produced biological and chemical weapons systems capable of dispersing lethal CB agents over vast areas. Plans for use both in military and covert operations were formed. The United States used herbicides and irritant agents on a massive scale in Vietnam, thereby undermining the clarity of the 1925 Geneva Protocol's ban on "the use in war of asphyxiating, poisonous and other gases and of all analogous liquids, materials or devices." Possibly in response to growing public and international criticism of such use, a no-first-use policy for lethal chemical and biological agents began to be articulated by U.S. spokesmen in the mid-1960s. Other aspects of the United States CBW policy remained obscure to the public and by no means unambiguously restrained by international law.[29]

CBW Disarmament Efforts, 1969–1975

The second phase of U.S. policy began in the 1960s when international and domestic pressures for CBW disarmament mounted, stimulated partly by dissemination of information about the nature of these weapons, partly by strong opposition to the continued use of herbicides and irritant agents in Vietnam, and partly by several well-publicized events within the United States, including a major accident resulting from the testing of nerve gas at Dugway Proving Ground.[30]

In various international arenas, the question of chemical and biological disarmament achieved prominence. The United Nations heard repeated complaints against American use of chemicals in Vietnam.[31] U.N. Resolution 2603A introduced by Sweden in November 1969 affirmed the position of the majority of nations that the Geneva Protocol prohibited "any chemical agents of warfare . . . which might be employed because of their direct toxic effects on humans, animals or plants" and implicitly censured American use of defoliants and irritant agents. (Only the United States, Australia, and Portugal voted against the Resolution.) In addition, various initiatives were taken to place the question of chemical and biological disarmament on the international agenda. In August 1968, the United Kingdom submitted a working paper to the Eighteen-Nation Disarmament Committee proposing a Convention banning biological weapons. A report issued by U.N. Secretary-General U Thant in July 1969 warned of the growing destructive capacity of CB weaponry. In a strongly worded foreword, he appealed to all nations to accept the Geneva Protocol's prohibition on the use of chemical and biological agents, including irritant agents, and to eliminate them from military arsenals.[32] Amidst considerable international debate about how best to achieve chemical and biological disarmament, two draft conventions, the first aimed at biological disarmament and the second aimed at comprehensive chemical and biological disarmament, were proposed by the United Kingdom and the countries of the eastern bloc respectively in the summer of 1969.[33]

Within the United States, the CBW programs drew the fire of those appalled at the complicity of modern science in warfare. Critics attacked the use of herbicides and anti-personnel weapons in Vietnam, the open-air testing of chemical and biological weapons, and generally, the use of science for the creation of weapons of mass destruction. Scientists contributed to the growing protests by publicizing these issues and focusing attention on the moral contradictions entailed by weapons research. In 1967, thousands of scientists signed a petition to President Lyndon Johnson urging an end to the use of anti-personnel and anti-crop weapons in Vietnam and a review of U.S. CBW programs and policies. A number of scientific societies took action to express concern over or opposition to chemical and biological warfare.[34]

Members of Congress were also influential in raising the visibility of the CBW issue and pressing for a change of policy. Congressional interest in the largely secret CBW program was activated in part by growing media coverage of the issue that focused public attention on the hazards associated with the storage, transportation, disposal and open-air testing of chemical weapons. Congressional hearings on these matters in the spring of 1969 further fanned public and congressional opposition.[35]

By the summer of 1969, congressional committees were flexing their muscles. By July, a House resolution urging the President to submit the Geneva Protocol to the Senate for ratification had gained 95 cosponsors. In addition, members of Congress were threatening major cuts in the authorization for the CBW program. In the same month, the Senate Armed Services Committee voted to eliminate the entire $16 million authorization for offensive CBW research and development. In August, amendments to the defense procurement authorization bill placed a series of restrictive conditions on the CBW program including prohibitions on open-air tests of lethal CBW agents and procurement of delivery systems for such agents and a requirement that the Secretary of Defense submit semiannual reports to Congress accounting for expenditures on the CBW program. By the middle of 1969, the U.S. CBW programs had become the focus of a major public controversy.[36]

In this climate of strong criticism of the CBW program at home and abroad, the Nixon administration initiated a review of CBW policy by the National Security Council (NSC) in May 1969. Information and policy proposals flowed to the NSC from a variety of sources including the Joint Chiefs of Staff, the President's Science Advisory Committee, the DOD Office of Systems Analysis, and the State Department's Bureau of Politico-Military Affairs. Following a lengthy process of discussion and negotiation, Richard Nixon announced in November 1969 several major changes in CBW policy: an unconditional renunciation of the development, production, and stockpiling of biological weapons; the renunciation of first use of lethal chemicals and incapacitating agents; and finally, his historic renunciation of biological weapons. Henceforth, Nixon affirmed, U.S. interests in biological warfare would be confined to research for defensive purposes, and stockpiles of biological weapons would be destroyed.[37] Toxin weapons were not mentioned in the president's statement, but following substantial congressional comment on the omission, the U.S. renunciation was extended in February 1970 to include these weapons.[38]

The precise reasons for Nixon's decision to alter U.S. CBW policy remain obscure. In a general way, the policy change responded to growing public and international criticism of the U.S. CBW policy. In some respects, the decision may be seen as a compromise, going part way to satisfy the demands of critics of U.S. policy by renouncing those weapons which had the least military utility yet preserving the U.S. option to use herbicides and tear gas in Vietnam. As critics of the U.S. CBW policy noted immediately after Nixon's announcement, the United States did not consider those chemicals to be covered either by the Geneva Protocol or by Nixon's renunciation of "lethal chemical weapons." In addition, the only chemical agent in the U.S. arsenal defined as an incapacitant—BZ—was both expensive and unreliable. Its elimination had no impact on the conduct of the Vietnam War.[39]

Nixon's renunciation of biological and toxin weapons was, on the other hand, comprehensive. It is likely that several factors entered into the Nixon administration's calculations. First, the military utility of biological weapons was seen as dubious; thus renunciation did not deny the U.S. an advantage over chemical or conventional weaponry. It is possible also that the decision was in part a response to concerns within the scientific community about the future military use of advances in biology.[40] Evidence for this interpretation comes from the reasons for supporting biological disarmament given by the director of the Arms Control and Disarmament Agency during the Nixon Administration, Fred Iklé, in testimony before the Senate Foreign Relations Committee in 1974. Among other things, Ikle stated that "without such a prohibition, new developments in the biological sciences might give rise to concern because they could be abused for weapons purposes. Such anxieties could foster secretive military competition in a field of science that would otherwise remain open to international competition and be used solely for the benefit of mankind."[41] A third and possibly decisive reason for the change of policy was that advances in biological weaponry were unlikely to serve U.S. interests. As one observer of U.S. CBW policy had argued in 1964: "The introduction of radically cheap weapons of mass destruction into the arsenals of the world would not act as much to strengthen the big powers as it would to endow dozens of relatively weak countries with great destructive capability. . . . It is obviously to the advantage of great powers to keep war very expensive."[42] This argument was also stressed by former Defense Department adviser Han Swyter at a symposium on chemical and biological warfare at the National Academy of Sciences in October 1969: "The proliferation of chemical and biological capability would tend to change the world's balance of power, reducing ours. We would lose some of the relative advantages of nuclear and conventional capability which wealth gives to us and to the Soviets. Consequently, we have a strong incentive to discourage other nations from acquiring chemical and biological capabilities."[43]

The details of Nixon's new biological warfare policy were articulated in National Security Decision Memorandum 35, signed by Nixon's National Security Adviser, Henry Kissinger, and issued on the same day as Nixon's renunciation of biological weapons. The memorandum defined the permissible areas of biological research: The United States... biological program will be confined to research and development for defensive purposes. . . . This does not preclude research into those offensive aspects of. . . biological agents necessary to determine what defensive measures are required." According to this guideline, the operative criterion for permissible biological defense research was not the *product* of research but the *motive* guiding it. This criterion thus allowed research in a gray area where defensive and offensive activities could not be easily distinguished.[44]

Meanwhile, at the international level, the question of whether the problem of chemical and biological disarmament should be addressed by a single comprehensive convention or by separate conventions remained controversial, with the socialist and non-aligned nations favoring the former and the United Kingdom, the United States, and some other western nations the latter. However, the virtual deadlock on this issue at the Geneva Conference on the Committee on Disarmament (CCD) was broken in the spring of 1971 when the Soviet Union reversed its position and tabled a draft convention for biological disarmament only. Nixon's renunciation may have played an important role in this reversal, signalling to the Soviet Union a new willingness to negotiate on BW disarmament.[45] Rapid progress on a Biological Weapons Convention prohibiting biological and toxin weapons followed. The Convention was completed in September 1971 and opened for signature in London, Moscow and Washington on April 10, 1972.[46]

The treaty was (and is) a major achievement in the history of disarmament. Until the 1988 INF treaty, it was the only treaty in modern times to prohibit possession as well as use of weapons. However, the formal language of the treaty is in some respects weak and does not entirely preclude the possibility of activities aimed at the development of biological weapons. (For a discussion of the Convention's provisions, see chapter 11.) In addition, the treaty does not contain provisions for verification of compliance. To a great extent, the Biological Weapons Convention depended on the good faith, self-interest, and commitment of the parties to it.[47]

In 1975, when the treaty entered into force, the United States also ratified the Geneva Protocol and committed itself once again to a policy of no-first-use of chemical weapons. A period of relative restraint with respect to chemical and biological weapons followed.

Stockpiles of biological and toxin weapons were ordered to be dismantled.[48] The Biological Warfare Program (now renamed the Biological Defense Program) was cut back, confined to research, and reoriented toward defense, as defined by National Security Decision Memorandum 35. The program also underwent some important institutional changes at this point. Research and development activities related to biological agents and toxins were transferred from the Army Matériel Command to the Health Services Command under the Army Surgeon General. Research related to crop diseases was transferred to the U.S. Department of Agriculture. Physical defense—that is, activities related to detection devices and protective clothing—continued under the Army Materiel Command at Edgewood Arsenal. Testing and evaluation remained under the Testing and Evaluation Command and continued to be carried out, with reduced staffing, at Dugway Proving Ground.[49] In effect, research and development activities focusing on the properties of biological warfare agents appear to have been separated from the Chemical Warfare Program and reoriented toward defense. At the same time, an unofficial moratorium on the manufacture of chemical weapons occurred. (No chemical weapons were produced from 1969 until December 1987.) Support for research and development for the Chemical Warfare and Biological Defense Programs continued to decline, reaching its lowest point in the post-war period in 1975 (figure 2.1). The CBW programs were essentially mothballed.

Also in the 1970s, negotiations on the development of a treaty prohibiting chemical weapons were initiated between the two superpowers. (These bilateral talks supplemented the multilateral efforts being pursued under joint U.S.-Soviet leadership by the Conference of the Committee on Disarmament.) President Nixon and Secretary Brezhnev's intention to begin such negotiations, announced at the Moscow summit meeting in 1974, was reaffirmed by President Ford and Secretary Brezhnev at Vladivostok, and bilateral negotiations began in Geneva in August 1976. Progress was slow, but it was not insignificant. By August 1979, broad agreement had been reached on the scope of the treaty (the quantities and types of chemicals to be covered) and on the national and international measures for verifying compliance, including the use of on-site inspection. In the joint communiqué issued by President Carter and Secretary Brezhnev in Vienna in June 1979, the superpowers agreed to intensify their efforts to produce a joint draft convention for presentation to the Committee on Disarmament, which succeeded the CCD. Although pressure from the U.S. Army to initiate production of binary chemical weapons had begun to mount, the Ford and Carter administrations and Congress seemed generally committed to seeking to disarm, rather than rearm, chemically, and the prospects for an eventual Chemical Weapons Convention appeared quite promising.[50]

Resurgence of Military Interest in CB Warfare, 1975–1987

The third phase of U.S. CBW policy was characterized by a renewed reliance on deterrence as the basis of chemical warfare policy and by growing skepticism toward chemical and biological disarmament in official circles. Military spending on chemical and biological warfare was no longer inhibited by public perceptions that chemical and biological weapons should be internationally ostracized, or, significantly, by military perceptions that these weapons were likely to be battlefield liabilities.

A principal cause of this change was the general deterioration of international relations, particularly East-West relations, that developed from the late 1970s onward. As cold-war hostilities were renewed and the arms race accelerated, the U.S. commitment to arms control and to international law generally weakened—a trend that intensified following the election of Ronald Reagan and a republican Senate. Although the United States remained formally committed to its obligations under the Geneva Protocol and the Biological Weapons Convention, its accusatory posture toward the Soviet Union transformed official behavior on matters related to chemical and biological warfare. Beginning in 1981, Reagan administration officials promulgated accusations that the Soviet Union had produced toxin weapons ("yellow rain") for use by the Vietnamese in Southeast Asia, deployed chemical and toxin weapons in Afghanistan, and maintained an offensive biological warfare program—all violations or circumventions of the Geneva Protocol and the Biological Weapons Convention.

These charges climaxed in the early 1980s, providing much ammunition for conservative political analysts to use to attack the viability of the chemical and biological warfare regime. In 1983, *Wall Street Journal* editor Robert Bartley and journalist William Kucewicz averred that "there is no great argument about the facts of what is happening in Southeast Asia. The reality is that we have here arms control violations that are unambiguous, militarily important and totally cynical." Mark Storella of the Institute for Foreign Policy Analysis at Tufts University found the evidence for Soviet use of lethal chemicals in Southeast Asia and Afghanistan "substantial and compelling." Joseph Douglass and H. Richard Lukens worried about U.S. vulnerability in the face of a Soviet CBW "threat," because the Sverdlovsk outbreak "offered strong evidence that the Soviets have not been complying with the 1972 Convention, and have been actively engaged in the manufacture and storage of biological weapons." Further, Kucewicz penned an eight-part feature in the *Wall Street Journal* claiming that the Soviet Union was using genetic engineering to construct a first-strike biological weapon and concluding that "[i]t's clear that the Soviet interest in chemical and biological warfare calls into question all arms control."[51]

As documented in chapters 9 and 10, all of these imputations were either discredited or remained inconclusive. The yellow rain charges collapsed under the weight of contrary evidence, much of it generated by the United States government itself (chapter 10). Defense Department officials, pressed to substantiate the existence of a Soviet biological weapons program, admitted that their contention was little more than a "working hypothesis."[52] However tenuous, the Reagan administration's charges did damage the chemical and biological warfare legal regime. The difficulty of producing a definitive resolution of these charges raised doubts as often about the effectiveness of the chemical and biological warfare legal regime as about the commitment of the Soviet Union to disarmament. Some conservative analysts even advocated withdrawal from the Biological Weapons Convention.[53]

In this changed political climate, the Chemical Warfare and Biological Defense programs, after their decline in the 1970s, experienced a resurgence of military interest and support. This renewed interest in chemical warfare was probably spurred by technical progress in the development of a new generation of chemical weapons known as "binary" weapons, whose activation at the moment of deployment was claimed to eliminate the most severe hazards of chemical weaponry to the user. Beginning in 1975, the military services, the Defense Science Board, and other government units undertook reviews of U.S. chemical warfare capabilities in relation to the Soviets', concluding, generally, that the Soviet Union presented a major chemical warfare "threat" which the United

States was ill-prepared to counter. This position was supported by a secret report issued in 1980 by a panel of the Defense Science Board chaired by MIT chemistry professor John Deutch, which urged production of binary weapons. In the increasingly tense context of superpower relations in the early 1980s, it was also argued that the United States had to be prepared to fight in an "integrated battlefield"—a combat zone in which nuclear, chemical, and conventional weapons might be combined.[54]

These pressures resulted in renewed growth of the chemical warfare program from the late 1970s onwards. In 1976–1980, Congress and the Carter administration generally resisted military pressures for renewal of production of chemical weapons on the grounds that this would be destabilizing. (No production funds for chemical weapons were requested for FY 1977 to FY 1980).[55] Other Defense Department goals for the chemical warfare program were pursued, however: improvement of protective equipment, upgrading of training programs, stockpile renovation, and research and development on both defensive and offensive aspects of chemical warfare proceeded. (Spending on the program doubled between 1976 and 1980.) The Reagan administration went much further, repeatedly pushing Congress to appropriate funds for production of binary weapons. The charges of Soviet violations of the CBW legal regime were influential in supporting the administration's position.

The issue of the use of chemical and toxin warfare in Southeast Asia and Afghanistan was first raised in Congress in 1979 when Congressman James Leach (R-Iowa) aired his belief that use of lethal chemicals in Laos was "well established" and his suspicion that the chemicals came from the Soviet Union.[56] No direct charges against the Soviet Union were made, however, until Secretary of State Haig's accusation of Soviet complicity in Vietnamese use of chemical warfare in Laos and Cambodia in September 1981 (Chapter 9). Following Richard Burt's dramatic announcement of the discovery of the "smoking gun" providing definitive confirmation of Haig's charge at a Congressional hearing in November 1981, the truth status of the so-called yellow rain charges changed abruptly from "suspicions" to "demonstrated facts." By 1982, administration officials were referring regularly to "Soviet use of chemicals in Southeast Asia," and qualifiers concerning the evidence for the claims were quickly dropped. The claims crescendoed in Congress in 1982 and 1983 (they were made on at least 12 separate occasions during these years). Thereafter, the frequency of the claims decreased. Ironically, by the time that a rival theory of yellow rain emerged in 1983, it appears that members of Congress had generally come to accept the claims. At least, no member of Congress publicly expressed skepticism. Senate Resolution 201, introduced by Larry Pressler, (R-South Dakota) in February 1984, which aired the yellow rain charges and called for further investigation of them was approved unanimously by a voice vote; no dissent was formally expressed by members of Congress. The "facticity" of yellow rain (that is, the status of yellow rain as received fact, for which earlier processes of inquiry and debate were forgotten) apparently had moved beyond dispute in this setting.[57]

As the charges against the Soviet Union were progressively reified, they were instrumental in changing political attitudes toward renewed production of chemical weapons. After resisting the pressure from the Reagan administration for several years Congress finally succumbed in 1985, appropriating $130 million to produce these weapons, albeit with several important conditions attached. Overall, support for the Chemical Warfare and Biological Defense Programs rose by 555 percent (allowing for inflation) to $1.44 billion.[58]

Signs of a parallel change of emphasis for the Biological Defense Program also emerged at this time. A series of reports in the mid-1980s not only urged the Defense Department to address the Soviet "threat" (as demonstrated by the Sverdlovsk incident and yellow rain) but also conceptualized this threat in terms of future military use of biotechnology. The successful industrial application of biotechnology demonstrated in the preceding decade, proof of its ability to construct new life forms, had given the field a luster sufficient to make it irresistible to military advisers. In June 1985 Reagan's Chemical Warfare Review Commission, in addition to urging the production of binary weapons, turned its attention to biological warfare (appendix N). The Commission warned that "the rapid advances of genetic technology—in which the United States for now is fortunately the leader—offer the predictable likelihood of new agents being developed for which no vaccines or counteragents are known or available." Pointing an accusing finger at the Soviet Union (it was claimed in the report that the Soviets were "believed to be pursuing development of both lethal and incapacitating toxins that could produce, for example, sudden panic or sleepiness" in troops), the Commission concluded that "the only sensible response . . . is again for the United States not to ignore the problem, but rather to conduct comprehensive defensive research on biological agents and toxins under conditions of extreme care. The need is to be able to assess the likely threat, to develop detection measures and defenses, and to create sufficient uncertainty in the minds of Soviet leaders as well as those of other governments that they would hesitate to trust in such a method of warfare. . . . The Department should be devoting much more resources and talent to addressing the chemical and biological threats of the future as well as those of the present. A moderate but intensive course of research, which does not include actual development of biological weapons, appears the only prudent one to follow."[59]

The Chemical Warfare Review Commission's report was followed in September 1985 by a secret report from the Defense Science Board to the Department of Defense which again pointed to the use of biotechnology, particularly by the Soviet Union and Third World countries as a major threat to national security. Furthermore, the report claimed that biotechnology was dissolving the once clear distinctions between chemical and biological agents: "toxins can be produced by chemical synthesis, and genetic engineering can be employed to manufacture chemicals in a manner previously unimagined." In the view of the members of the Board, "technology has made obsolete much of the distinctions and language of the BW treaty."[60]

In March 1986, a secret report from the Pentagon's own scientific, technical, and national security experts contended that the lack of verification and compliance mechanisms in the Biological Weapons Convention meant that the United States had to develop defenses against biological warfare.[61] Finally, a report issued by the Army Science Board in July 1987 recommended steps which, if adopted, would inevitably lead to the production of novel BW agents. The report urged the appointment of a "red team" under the Army Training and Doctrine Command. The team, which would include biologists, would be responsible for developing realistic BW "threat scenarios," including the use of BW in warfare and terrorism. Also proposed was an assessment of the use of molecular genetics and biotechnology "by potential adversaries to modify, enhance or greatly alter the pathogenicity, survival capacity, dissemination potential, susceptibility to detection, and identification of viable BW agents." The report claimed that this assessment could be performed without the actual creation of new genomes but did not, however, explain the feasibility of such a proposal. And last, in a move reminiscent of the efforts to induce public acceptance of the growing CBW program in the 1950s, the Army Science Board recommended a public relations effort aimed at improving "public understanding" of its activities.[62]

A Pentagon report to Congress in May 1986 reflected the reorientation of military thinking about the relevance of biotechnology to biological warfare that had occurred in the 1980s. Iterating the views of the Chemical Warfare Commission, the Defense Science Board, and Defense Department's own experts, the report argued that military use of biotechnology (particularly in the hands of the Soviet Union) now presented an immediate threat, having succeeded in making biological warfare easier, cheaper, and far more effective. The Pentagon's vision recalled the exuberant speculation in the 1970s about civilian application of biotechnology except that now, the emphasis was on the dark side of the field. The possibility of using genetic engineering to construct microorganisms with novel properties and to invent biological "factories" for the production of novel substances, previously portrayed in glowing terms, was now projected as a biological warfare threat of menacing proportion. "Biological warfare is not new, but it has a new face," the report concluded. The strong message to members of Congress was that increased funding was needed to maintain national security in the face of a biological warfare threat based on the use of biotechnology by hostile nations.[63]

It is important to note that the report's claims were dismissed as ill-informed hype by many scientists (chapter 5). What is significant in this report is not so much its content as its reflection of a new military attention to biogenetics and interest in exploring its weapons implications. The Pentagon's new view of biological warfare had followed the heyday of industrial expansion into bioengineering by less than a decade.

The Reagan administration's new CBW policies resulted in substantial increases in support for research and development for the chemical and biological warfare programs. Allowing for inflation, the funds available for chemical warfare and biological defense research, development, evaluation and testing rose steadily until 1985, peaking that year at $372 million—a real increase (adjusting for inflation) of 310 percent over the 1980 level. In real terms, funding for CBW research and development was close to the highest levels of the Cold War (figure 2.1). Support for the Biological De-

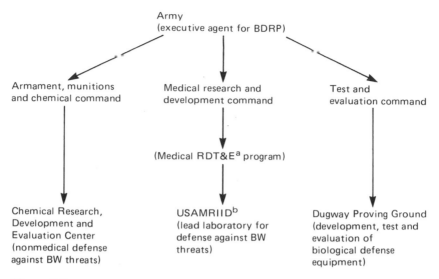

Figure 2.2
U.S. Department of Defense coordination of Biological Defense Research
Program. a. Research, Development, Testing, and Evaluation. b. U.S. Army
Medical Research Institute of Infectious Diseases.

fense Research Program alone rose in a similar manner—by 262
percent, to $86.5 million, between FY 1980 and FY 1985.[64]

Within the Department of Defense, primary responsibility for the
BDRP remained with the Army, under which three institutions
oversaw activities within the program: (1) the U.S. Army Medical
Research and Development Command (AMRDC) (responsible for
medical research and development); (2) the Chemical Research,
Development and Engineering Center (CRDEC) (responsible for
developing nonmedical defenses against biological warfare, e.g.
detection systems and protective clothing); (3) the U.S. Army
Dugway Proving Ground (DPG) (responsible for developing, testing and evaluating biological defense matériel).[65] The U.S. Army
Medical Research Institute of Infectious Diseases (AMRIID), a
subordinate unit of the AMRDC, is designated as the lead laboratory for defense against BW threats, with responsibility for coordinating medical defense activity in all other military, government,
and civilian institutions (figure 2.2).[66]

Priorities for expansion of the BDRP were defined in an
AMRIID report issued in 1985 in terms of three possible lines of
development. First, a "base" program addressed vaccines, therapy,

and early diagnosis for conventional BW agents and toxins. Stepping up the development of vaccines for natural pathogens and toxins had been urged in a U.S. Army report issued in 1983. In fact, reports on the BDRP to Congress and summaries of specific projects shows that this "base" program expanded substantially in the 1980s, encompassing a wide range of natural pathogens and toxins as well as large-scale production of tularemia, anthrax, and botulinum vaccines (appendix A, table 2). Second, an "expanded and realigned" program included new research aimed at responding to areas defined by AMRIID as "new biothreats." These new "threats" included further toxins, such as saxitoxin, "altered organisms" (presumably modified through genetic engineering, microencapsulation, or other means), and "endogenous bioregulators," (substances that are normally present in the body in minute quantities and appear to have essential physiological and psychological functions). Finally, an even larger program (described as "required") included further activities aimed at addressing "additional threats" assumed to be posed by use by an adversary of still further toxins (e.g., post-synaptic toxins, membrane active compounds, protein inhibitors) and hybrid compounds (e.g., immunotoxins designed to destroy a specific type of cell.) This document appears to indicate that in 1985, only the first two programs were fully funded.[67]

Beyond research and development in the life sciences and medicine, the two other main organizational components of the BDRP, the CRDEC and Dugway Proving Ground, pursued development of new, fast-acting detection devices and protective equipment on the one hand, and tests of equipment on the other. The latter program included open-air tests using "simulants" of biological warfare agents (organisms such as *Bacillus subtilis* claimed to be harmless by the Army). Also supported under the BDRP were theoretical "threat assessments," aimed at evaluating the effectiveness of modern biological weapons and the vulnerability of targets, conducted by the Army Forces Intelligence Center and a new organizational unit known as the "Biological Threat Analysis Center."[68] For example, studies of target vulnerability and the possibility of delivery of biological agents by intercontinental ballistic missiles were conducted in the early 1980s.[69]

The use of genetic engineering, hybridoma technology, and other new biogenetic technologies within these programs was increasingly emphasized in the 1980s. Up to April 1980, the Department of Defense had consistently stated that it was not supporting and did not plan to support recombinant DNA research, although the possibility was not ruled out for the future. The only reference to genetic engineering in the Defense Department's reports to Congress on the Chemical Warfare and Biological Defense programs in the late 1970s was to a theoretical analysis of its biological warfare potential.[70]

In the early 1980s, however, the Defense Department began to encourage the development of biogenetic technology for military purposes. Beginning in September 1980, the Defense Department began to award contracts for research and development using genetic engineering under the Chemical Warfare and Biological Defense programs. In 1981, the Advanced Research Projects Agency, whose mission is to facilitate transfer of technology from academic and industrial laboratories to the military, specifically targeted new biotechnology.[71] Military support on research and development involving new biotechnology expanded rapidly. While precise figures are elusive, support for research in the life sciences and medical defense under the Chemical Warfare and Biological Defense programs rose by about 400 percent in real terms to $180 million from 1980 to 1987. Total Defense Department support for biotechnology rose in the same period from virtually nothing to $119 million. A measure of the pressure exerted on biologists in the civilian sector to seek military support is reflected in the fact that Defense Department support for the life sciences increased in real terms by 35 percent from 1980 to 1987 (to $273 million), 9 percent over the federal average (22 percent) for this period.[72]

By 1988, the number of military projects using genetic engineering for the Chemical Warfare Program Biological Defense Research Program stood at 99 (appendix L). Some of these projects were located abroad in countries such as Britain, Israel, and Sweden. Thus one important side effect of the Defense Department's sponsorship of new biotechnology was the transfer of the use of this technology for CBW purposes to other nations. (Whether this was intended or not is unclear.)[73]

Interpreting this surge of military activity in biotechnology is difficult (see chapter 8). All of this work was justified by Defense Department officials as fully complying with the requirements of the Biological Weapons Convention. But the ambiguities both in the treaty and in the character of biological research left open the possibility of grey areas where defensive and offensive interests could overlap. Even research and development aimed at a product as seemingly "peaceful" as a vaccine could have an ominous dimension since developing a vaccine generally entails the isolation, identification, modification, and growth of the biological agent for which it is designed to give protection—all steps that would also be part of an offensive program (chapter 6). Furthermore, the Convention did not bar the exploration ("for defensive purposes") of even the weapons potential of biotechnology. National Security Decision Memorandum 35 noted above provided scope for just such exploration. And the United States accusations that the Soviet Union was engaged in suspicious BW activity rationalized Pentagon interest in moving in this direction.

In fact, in the 1980s, there were many indications of Pentagon interest in such exploratory activity. By 1980, the Department of Defense was reporting the possibility that recombinant DNA technology might enable "a potential enemy to implant virulence factors or toxin-producing genetic information into common, easily transmitted bacteria such as *E. coli*," calling for new lines of research aimed at "providing an essential base of information to counteract these possibilities and to provide a better understanding of the disease mechanisms of bacterial and rickettsial organisms that pose a potential BW threat, with or without genetic manipulation," and requesting the National Academy of Sciences to undertake partially classified studies on defenses against genetically engineered weapons." (The Academy turned down the request.)[74]

As the accusations against the Soviet Union intensified in the 1980s, the Biological Defense Program moved further in the direction of weapons exploration. Particularly indicative of this interest in operating in grey areas of the BWC was the revelation late in 1984 that the Pentagon planned to construct a high-containment facility for testing and evaluating large aerosols of lethal chemical and biological agents at the Army's chemical and biological warfare test site at Dugway Proving Ground, Utah. Although these plans were stalled by a lawsuit brought by the Foundation on Economic Trends and remained in abeyance in 1988, they provide an important indication of the future direction of the Biological Defense Program envisaged by the Department of Defense.

According to the Army's plans, the aerosol chamber at the facility would have a total area of 483 square feet—large enough to hold several people—and would be used to handle what the Army called "substantial volumes of toxic biological aerosol agents" under conditions of extremely high containment in order to test protective equipment such as detectors, filters, and clothing. The scheme represented a new initiative since, as an Army document noted, "the DoD does not have any other laboratory capable of studying aerosols of biological pathogens for nonmedical purposes."

The Defense Department justified the expanded facility as necessary to meet the Soviet biological warfare "threat," references to which had lost much of their earlier tentativeness by this point. In 1984, Secretary of Defense Caspar Weinberger defended the need for the facility in the following terms:

We continue to obtain new evidence that the Soviet Union has maintained its offensive biological warfare program and that it is exploring genetic engineering to expand their program's scope. Consequently, it is essential and urgent that we develop and field adequate biological and toxin protection.

Our development efforts in this area are driven by the Soviet threat. To ensure that our protective systems work, we must challenge them with known or suspected Soviet agents.[75]

Responding to the Foundation on Economic Trends lawsuit, the Army insisted that it planned to use the Dugway aerosol chamber to test only "conventional" biological warfare agents (naturally occuring pathogens) and that the testing of genetically engineered pathogens, while contemplated, was not specifically proposed. If the logic of Weinberger's rationale was any guide to the future, however, such tests would eventually be initiated. Defense Department reports from this period, cited earlier, indicated similar interest. Thus by the mid-1980s there were serious signs that the Department of Defense would proceed by incremental steps into the use of new genetic technologies for inquiry and development with significant offensive implications.

The changing expectations surrounding genetic engineering are illustrated by the two conferences reviewing progress under the Biological Weapons Convention that have been held since the treaty came into force. At the first (March 1980), new scientific and technological developments, such as genetic engineering, were not deemed significant problems. A briefing paper submitted by the three depository nations, the Soviet Union, the United Kingdom and the United States, called the development of fundamentally new, dangerous microorganisms or toxins a task of "insurmountable complexity." (This opinion was in harmony with the general "no hazard" stance adopted by scientists with respect to genetic engineering during this period, when strenuous efforts to deregulate biogenetic research were underway in the United States and elsewhere.) The report argued further that there would be little motivation for inventing novel organisms for weapons purposes since "naturally occurring disease-producing microorganisms and toxins already span an exceedingly broad range, from some which are extraordinarily deadly to others usually producing only temporary illness." Only Sweden in a separate paper dissented somewhat from that view. Generally, however, the conference maintained that new developments in biotechnology did not appear to threaten the Convention in any significant way.[76]

In contrast, by the time the Second Review Conference was held in September 1986, the military potential of biotechnology had become a significant concern. Briefing papers by Sweden, the United Kingdom, the Soviet Union, and the United States noted that biogenetic technologies could alter the virulence, stability, or immune characteristics of living things, and could maximize production of potent toxins, previously available only in minute quantities; also cited were new techniques of dissemination (developed in agriculture for the control of pests) and novel fermentation techniques that greatly enhanced the efficiency of production. Every paper claimed or implied that these would tempt military establishments, and that the small scale and ease of production would make verification of treaty compliance—always assumed to be difficult in the case of biological warfare—even more problematic. The United States report concluded that

In many ways, recent progress in biological technology affects the ease of concealment of manufacturing plants and the availability of new delivery systems, particularly for biological chemicals such as toxins and peptides. Verification of the Convention, always a difficult task, has been significantly complicated by the new technology. The confidence derived from the belief that certain technical problems would make biological weapons unattractive for the foreseeable future has eroded. The ease and rapidity of genetic manipulation, the ready availability of a variety of production equipment, the proliferation of safety and environmental equipment and health procedures to numerous laboratories and production facilities throughout the world, are signs of the growing role of biotechnology in the world's economy. But these very same signs also give concern for the possibility of misuse of this technology to subvert the Convention.[77]

It is important to note that in fact, fundamental scientific advances had not appreciably fueled renewed military exploration of biotechnology. As the briefing papers for the United Kingdom and the United States noted, there had been no further fundamental scientific advances in the 1980s comparable in their scope to that of recombinant DNA in the 1970s. What *had* changed was first, the political context in which weapons policy was set and second, prospects for the successful application of biotechnology in industry and agriculture, proof of its power to manipulate life forms. Perceptions of the military implications of biotechnology, always complex, shifted in the 1980s for both reasons.

Prospects for Restraining the Biological Defense Research Program

The communiqué issued by Ronald Reagan and Mikhail Gorbachev after the November 1985 summit, in which the two leaders expressed their commitment to prevent the proliferation of chemical weapons, heralded not only a thaw in the cold war but also a marked change in the emphasis of the U.S. and Soviet chemical and biological warfare policies. Gorbachev's subsequent willingness to accept previously unnegotiable American proposals for the chemical weapons convention, to open the Soviet chemical weapons plant at Shikhany to an international group of experts, and to provide details of the anthrax epidemic at Sverdlovsk also skillfully seized the moral initiative and disarmed American charges of Soviet intentions to undermine the CBW legal regime.[78] In response, Reagan in his second term of office cultivated an image of commitment to the global elimination of chemical and biological weapons and of willingness to work with the Soviet Union to achieve that end—an image also adopted by George Bush in the presidential campaign.[79]

But the details of the new American CBW policy were far more complex. Beginning in the mid-1980s, new charges of "proliferation" of chemical and biological weapons began to replace "Evil Empire" rhetoric. This new claim portrayed chemical and biological weapons as spreading rapidly, particularly to nations in the Middle East and possibly also to terrorist groups. Claims of the proliferation of chemical weapons were made as early as 1985 by the Chemical Warfare Review Commission. In addition to its emphasis on the Soviet "threat," the report also described the spread of chemical weapons as "an extremely serious danger which requires more vigorous action than heretofore" and noted further that biological weapons lent themselves to terrorist uses.[80] A secret Defense Science Board Task Force report which appeared in the same year was reported to have concluded similarly that "[t]he chemical and biotechnology threats are increasing, Third World proliferation is getting worse, and the possible consequences are extremely serious."[81] In the late 1980s, these claims, broadcast regularly in the American press (generally without qualification) emphasized the role of Middle Eastern countries such as Libya, Iraq, Iran, and Syria. While reports focused on the spread of chemical weapons, biological weapons were often implicated as well.[82] At hearings on "the global spread of chemical and biological weapons" before the U.S. Senate Committee on Governmental Affairs, William Webster, Director of the CIA, charged that "as many as 20 [Third World] countries may be developing chemical weapons" and "we expect this trend to continue, despite ongoing multilateral efforts to stop their proliferation." Furthermore, he claimed that "[a]t least 10 countries are working to produce both previously known and futuristic biological weapons."[83]

As in the case of yellow rain, solid evidence for the rapid spread of chemical and biological weapons was scant. Iraq's violation of the Geneva Protocol was confirmed by a United Nations team in March 1986, but evidence of possession of chemical weapons by nations other than Iraq, France, the United States and the Soviet Union remained uncertain. Evidence for possession of biological weapons was even weaker. A detailed and cautiously worded assessment of the charges was given in a report of the Stockholm International Peace Research Institute published in 1988:

To be skeptical about proliferation reports is not to deny that they may be true. The use of chemical weapons by Iraq in the Gulf War is unquestionable evidence of proliferation; and the now-accepted fact that chemical weapons of Iraqi manufacture were employed indicates that motors of proliferation are at work other than those of the international arms trade or of state-to-state arms transfer such as the trade in precursor chemicals, those which react to form chemical warfare agents and applicable technology. But the now rather widely disseminated picture of advanced and still accelerating proliferation, though not demonstrably untrue, cannot be accepted on the evidence as unquestionable fact.[84]

Despite the uncertainties, the claim of "rapid proliferation" of chemical and biological weapons began to be reified through frequent repetition. With this new rationale, the U.S. government justified continued production of binary weapons and continued to emphasize the need for exploration of the offensive potential of biotechnology.[85] Although funding for the BDRP dropped somewhat after FY 1986, the program continued at a substantial level.[86]

Thus, the U.S. biological (as well as chemical) warfare policy ended the decade of the 1980s in contradiction: on the one hand, both Ronald Reagan and George Bush claimed to be committed to the goal of biological disarmament; on the other hand, they also supported an expanding military research and development program in the biological sciences and an ominous and provocative militarization of biotechnology.

The tendencies within the United States towards increasing military assimilation of biotechnology and of the biological sciences generally have been countered somewhat by a variety of moves at home and abroad to restrain military development and to strengthen the CBW legal regime. The sixty nations represented at the Second Review Conference on the Biological Weapons Convention held in 1986 succeeded in establishing several substantial confidence-building measures as well as a procedure for consultation on suspected treaty violations (chapter 12).[87] Moreover, reflecting the new policies of the U.S.S.R. under Gorbachev, important progress occurred during the 1986–1987 negotiations for a parallel Chemical Weapons Convention prohibiting development, production and stockpiling of chemical weapons. In particular, the Soviet Union agreed to several highly intrusive verification measures including the declaration of the location and inventories of all chemical weapons stockpiles, verification of the destruction of these stockpiles, and "challenge" inspections at short notice and without the right of refusal. Barring the emergence of further contentious issues, the Chemical Weapons Convention appeared to be near completion. Since toxin weapons would be covered by both the biological and the chemical treaties, the progress achieved in the chemical area seemed likely to yield useful precedents for future approaches to developing verification and enforcement provisions in the biological area.[88]

Within the United States, the expanding Chemical Warfare and Biological Defense programs have encountered increasing public scrutiny and criticism. Plans for the chemical and biological warfare test facilities at Dugway Proving Ground, particularly the aerosol facility, have been a special target. In 1985, the lawsuit brought by the Foundation on Economic Trends forced the Defense Department to prepare an environmental impact statement for the program. The resulting proceedings provided scope for intensive examination of the future use of and rationale for the aerosol facility. In Utah, these evoked skepticism toward official reassurances about safety and strong resistance among citizens sensitized to the dangers of weapons tests. As a Salt Lake City television station stated in an editorial, "There are too many unknowns with nuclear testing. There are too many unknowns with nerve gas testing. And there are too many unknowns with the proposed biological weapons testing. Utah has seen enough of testing of lethal weapons."[89]

The broad political and technical rationales for the CBW programs were also challenged. Dugway's critics argued that the virtually infinite array of BW agents deployed by an adversary brooked no defense; at the same time, the ambiguity of defensive research made its political impact dangerous and destabilizing, undermining the Biological Weapons Convention. These arguments were well articulated at a joint hearing in May 1988 of three Congressional subcommittees with oversight responsibilities for biological warfare in May 1988. According to Representative Wayne Owens of Utah,

[T]here appear to be serious treaty implications involved in constructing the Dugway facility, implications that did not surround research projects of the past. According to a number of experts, the line between defensive and offensive research would be so hopelessly blurred by the construction of a level-four aerosol facility, that the Dugway lab may be perceived by other nations as a provocative violation of the 1972 Bio-weapons Treaty. Given the advances in biotechnology over the past decade, which are potentially very dangerous, it seems appropriate to ask ourselves: why not work towards building a stronger treaty, rather than risk the world's judgment that we are breaching the line between defensive and offensive biological testing.

At the same hearing, the past president of the American Public Health Association, Anthony Robbins, insisted: "Even if defense were possible, which it is not, it would be impossible to convince other nations that our testing activities are not intended for an attack rather than for protection of our population."[90]

A second lawsuit brought by the Foundation on Economic Trends in September 1986 sought to halt the Pentagon's entire Biological Defense Program until the Department submitted a satisfactory environmental impact statement for it. In a court settlement in February 1987, the Department agreed to write the statement while work under the program continued. The volume, scope, safety and rationale of the program were publicly questioned, particularly the use of aerosol testing, open-air testing and genetically modified pathogens, and the implications, for the proliferation of biological warfare expertise, of contracts with other countries.[91]

Several further actions bearing on biological warfare were taken in Congress. Representatives Peter Rodino and Hamilton Fish introduced legislation implementing the provisions of the Biological Weapons Convention in July 1986 and again, in January 1987 (chapter 13). Similar legislation, introduced in 1989 in the House and Senate by Representative Robert Kastenmeier (H.R. 237) and by Senators Herbert Kohl and David Pryor, along with Senators Leahy, Hatfield and Glenn (S. 993), was approved by unanimous consent by the Senate in November 1989, and the prospects for passage in 1990 appeared promising (appendix I). Second, Senator Carl Levin, chair of the Senate Subcommittee on Oversight of Government Management, initiated a review of the safety of the biological as well as the chemical warfare programs that revealed major flaws in precautions taken with respect to both programs: for example, violations of state and federal hazardous waste management regulations in 89 different areas of Aberdeen Proving Ground, one of the Army's principal chemical and biological warfare test sites; the lack of formal risk assessment and safeguards management procedures for the Biological Defense Program; and major safety problems at the U.S. Army Medical Research Institute of Infectious Diseases, including the loss of approximately 2500 milliliters of Chikungunya virus, a highly infectious virus for which no specific therapy is available.[92] Third, Representative Wayne Owens (Utah) introduced a bill (H.R. 806) requiring public disclosure of all biological agents used in military research programs (appendix J). This bill was adopted by the House in 1990 as an amendment to the FY 1990 Defense Authorization Bill but was opposed by the Department of Defense on the grounds that its provisions would compromise national security. Its future in July 1989 was uncertain.

Finally, scientists began to organize to reinforce the broad cultural norm that renounced use of the life sciences for military purposes. By July 1989, over 800 scientists had signed a statement circulated by the Council for Responsible Genetics and the Coalition of Universities in the Public Interest opposing the use of science for the development of chemical and biological weapons (appendix K).

Whether the biological sciences can be walled off from military use remains an open question. In the absence of public opposition, the inertia of current programs and the military's tendency to be ever uncovering new threats to meet may yet keep the Biological Defense Research Program quite alive. But it may be that the chief benefit to the Pentagon in funding this program in the 1980s lay in its propaganda value; total spending for it would not have launched half a submarine at today's prices, after all. And the Pentagon's own assessment acknowledges that present biological weapons are ineffective from a military standpoint. But at least to *appear* prepared to counter supposed Soviet biological weapons became a necessity in the context of worst-case analyses, deterrence-style thinking, and distrust of arms control agreements that became the hallmark of the strategic and diplomatic orientation of the Reagan administration. Whether the relaxation of super-power tensions of the late 1980s and the emergence of international and national resistance to the military assimilation of the biological sciences can restrict the direction and scope of the biological defense program remains to be seen.

Acknowledgments

This chapter draws on several articles previously published in the *Bulletin of the Atomic Scientists* from 1984 to 1989. This expanded treatment of the history of biological warfare policy has greatly benefited from my discussions with Richard Falk, Paul Grams, and Robert Sinsheimer and from detailed responses to drafts from Barton Bernstein, Matthew Meselson, Rodney McElroy, and Julian Perry Robinson. Research for the chapter was supported in part by the National Science Foundation (Grant No. SES-8511131).

Notes

1. Stockholm International Peace Research Institute, *The Problem of Chemical and Biological Warfare* (Stockholm: Almqvist and Wiksell, 1971–1973), 6 Vols.; U.S. Senate, Select Committee to Study Governmental Operations with Respect to Intelligence Activities, *Hearings: Intelligence Activities*, I: *Unauthorized Storage of Toxic Agents*, 94th Cong., 1st Sess., September 16–18, 1975, and *Final Report: Foreign and Military Intelligence*, 26 April 1976; U.S. Senate, Committee on Human Resources, Subcommittee on Health and Scientific Research, *Hearings: Biological Testing Involving Human Subjects by the Department of Defense*, 95th Cong., 1st Sess., 8 March and 23 May 1977 and *Hearings: Human Drug Testing by the CIA*, 20–21 September 1977; U.S. Senate, Select Committee on Intelligence and the Subcommittee on Health and Scientific Research of the Committee on Human Resources, *Joint Hearings: Project MKULTRA, the CIA's Program of Research in Behavioral Modification*, 95th Cong., 1st Sess., August 3, 1977.
2. George Merck, "Biological Warfare" (Report to the Secretary of War by Mr. George Merck, Special Consultant for Biological Warfare), 3 January 1946, reprinted in U.S. Army *U.S. Army Activity in the U.S. Biological Warfare Programs* (24 February 1977) in the U.S. Senate, Committee on Human Resources *Hearings: Biological Testing Involving Human Subjects by the Department of Defense*, 23–234 (hereafter cited as *U.S. Biological Warfare Programs*), Annex A, 71.
3. Theodor Rosebury, "An Opinion on BW as a Weapon," (memorandum to Technical Director, Research and Development Department, Camp Detrick, Maryland), 8 August 1946, cited in SIPRI, *The Problem of Chemical and Biological Warfare*, I 156–157.
4. *U.S. Biological Warfare Programs*, 30, 42.
5. U.S. Department of the Army, Rules of Land Warfare, in *Field Manual* 27–10, 1954.
6. U.N. General Assembly Resolution 41 (I).
7. Department of the Army, Office of the Chief Chemical Officer for Scientific Activities, H.I. Stubblefield, "A Resume of the Biological Warfare Effort," 21 March 1958. I thank Rodney McElroy for providing a copy of this document as well as of JCS 1837/26, cited in note 28.
8. *U.S. Biological Warfare Program*, 31–32; Colonel William M. Creasy, "Presentation to the Secretary of Defense's Ad Hoc Committee on CEBAR," 24 February, 1950 (kindly provided by Barton Bernstein); Leonard Cole, *Clouds of Secrecy*, (New Jersey: Rowman, Littlefield Publishers, 1987), ch. 2.
9. U.S. Office of the Secretary of Defense, "Report of the Secretary of Defense's Ad Hoc Committee on Biological Warfare," 11 July 1949, Lamont Library, Harvard University, p. 2. I thank Christine Skwiot for drawing my attention to this report, as well as to the Twining memorandum cited in note 19.
10. U.S. Office of the Secretary of Defense, "Report," 10.
11. U.S. Office of the Secretary of Defense, "Report," 12.
12. *U. S. Biological Warfare Programs*, 35–36, Julian Perry Robinson, "Chemical Arms Control and the Assimilation of Chemical Weapons," *International Journal* (Summer 1981), 523–524.
13. Julian Perry Robinson, "Chemical Arms Control and the Assimilation of Chemical Weapons," 523–524.

14. O.N. Miller et al., "Report of the Ad Hoc Advisory Committee on Chemical Corps Mission and Structure," August 1955, cited in SIPRI, *The Problem of Chemical and Biological Warfare*, II, 195.

15. *U.S. Biological Warfare Program*, 41. Marshal Zhukov's statement is cited in SIPRI, *The Problem of Chemical and Biological Warfare*, II. 162.

16. *U.S. Biological Warfare Programs*, 40–41, This source does not elaborate on how the no-first-use policy was changed, and by whom.

17. *U.S. Biologicla Warfare Programs*, 41–44; SIPRI, *The Problem of Chemical and Biological Warfare*, II, 195–196.

18. *U.S. Biological Warfare Programs*, 41–46; N.F. Twining, Chairman, Joint Chiefs of Staff, Memorandum for the Secretary of Defense, Subject: Chemical and Biological Warfare, 14 September 1959, Lamont Library, Harvard University; Forrest Frank, "U.S. Arms Control Policymaking: The 1972 Biological Weapons Convention Case," Ph.D. Diss., Stanford University, 1974, 30–31.

19. *U. S. Biological Warfare Programs*, 41–46; SIPRI, *The Problem of Chemical and Biological Warfare*, II, 195; Frank, "U.S. Army Control Policymaking," 31–33.

20. *U. S. Biological Warfare Programs*, 46–47; Hersh, *Chemical and Biological Warfare*, 34–35.

21. Statement of Han Swyter in Proceedings of the Conference on Chemical and Biological Warfare, sponsored by the American Academy of Arts and Sciences and the Salk Institute, July 25, 1969 in the U.S. House, Committee on Foreign Affairs, *Hearings, Chemical-Biological Warfare: U.S. Policies and International Effects*, 91st. Cong., 1st Sess., 1969, 465; *Congressional Record* (8 August 1969), 23072; SIPRI, *The Problem of Chemical and Biological Warfare*, II, 204–205. Walter Schneir, "The Campaign to Make Chemical Warfare Respectable," *The Reporter* (1 October 1959), 24–28. Here and elsewhere in this chapter, GNP implicit price deflators are used to convert current dollars to constant 1982 dollars to adjust for inflation.

22. SIPRI, *The Problem of Chemical and Biological Warfare*, I 75, 190; Julian Perry Robinson, "The Changing Status of Chemical and Biological Warfare: Recent Technical, Military and Political Developments," in *Stockholm International Peace Research Institute Yearbook 1982* (London: Taylor and Francis, 1982), 324; "Old Fears, New Weapons: Brewing a Chemical Arms Race," *The Defense Monitor* IX (10) (1980): 6. The size of the U.S. chemical weapons stockpile is based on U.S. official statements about its size in 1979 and the fact that no new chemical weapons were produced after 1969 until 1987.

23. SIPRI, *The Problem of Chemical and Biological Warfare*, I, 75–78; II, 35–36.

24. Julian Perry Robinson, "Environmental Effects of Chemicla and Biological Warfare," in Royal Swedish Ministry of Agriculture, Environmental Advisory Council, *War and Environment* (Stockholm: Liber Förlag, 1981), 73–117; SIPRI, *The Problem of Chemical and Biological Warfare*, I, 162–185; E.W. Pfeiffer and Gordon Orians, "The Military Uses of Herbicides in Vietnam," in J. Neilands (ed.), *Harvest of Death* (New York: The Free Press, 1972), 117–175.

25. *U.S. Biological Warfare Programs*, 40–51, 101–140, 177–209, 225–226; SIPRI, *The Problem of Chemical and Biological Warfare*, II, 202–211; John W. Powell, "Japan's Germ Warfare: The U.S. Cover-up of a War Crime," *Bulletin of Concerned Asian Scholars* 12, No. 4 (1980), 2–17; Peter Williams and David Wallace, *Unit 731: The Japanese Army's Secret of Secrets* (London: Hodder and Stoughton, 1989).

26. U.S. Senate Committee to Study Governmental Operations With Respect to Intelligence Activities, Final Report: Foreign and Military Intelligence (April 26, 1976); U.S. Senate Subcommittee on Health and Scientific Research of the Committee on Human Resources, *Hearings, Human Drug Testing by the CIA*, 95th Cong., 1st Sess., September 20 and 21, 1977; U.S. Senate, Select Committee on Intelligence and the Subcommittee on Health and Scientific Research of the Committee on Human Resources, *Joint Hearing, Project MKULRA, The CIA's Program of Research in Behavioral Modification*, 95th Cong., 1st Sess., August 3, 1977.

27. U.S. Senate, Select Committee to Study Governmental Operations with respect to Intelligence Activities, *Final Report* (26 April 1976), 360–362; Joint Advanced Study Committee, "Biological Warfare," JCS 1837/26, 25 February 1952. See also Department of the Army, Office of the Chief Chemical Officer for Scientific Activities, H.I. Stubblefield, "A Résumé of the Biological Warfare Effort," 21 March 1958.

28. U.S. Senate, Select Committee to Study Governmental Operations With Respect to Intelligence Activities, *Final Report*, 360–362.

29. SIPRI, *The Problem of Chemical and Biological Warfare*, II, 195–197.

30. *1969 Congressional Quarterly Almanac*, 797. Other incidents which stirred public concern about the CBW programs included the disclosure of an Army plan to dump 27,000 tons of obsolete chemical warfare agents into the Atlantic Ocean and the news that CBW agents were being transported and stored outside the United States.

31. These developments are described in SIPRI, *The Problem of Chemical and Biological Warfare IV*, Part I, ch. 9 and Part II.

32. U.N. Secretary-General, *Chemical and Bacteriological (Biological) Weapons and the Effects of Their Possible Use* (New York: United Nations, 1969). The conclusions of the U.N. report were reinforced by a report of the World Health Organization which emphasized the destructive power of CB weapons and the special threat they posed to civilians: *Health Aspects of Chemical and Biological Weapons* (Geneva: World Health Organization, 1970).

33. SIPRI, *The Problem of Chemical and Biological Warfare*, IV, 295–297.

34. Eleanor Langer, "CBW, Vietnam Evoke Scientist's [sic] Concern," *Science* 155 (20 January 1967), 302; J.V. Reistrup, "500 Scientists Ask Ban on Gas in Vietnam," *Washington Post* (15 February 1967).

35. House Committee on Foreign Affairs, *Hearings: International Implications of Dumping Poisonous Gas and Waste Into Oceans*, May 8–15, 1969; House Committee on Government Operations, Subcommittee on Conservation and Natural Resources, *Hearings: Environmental Dangers of Open Air Testing of Lethal Chemicals*, May 20–21, 1969; Senate Committee on Foreign Relations, *Hearings: Chemical and Biological Warfare*, April 23 and June 23, 1969.

36. "Chemical-Biological Weapons Stir Controversy," *Congressional Quarterly* (1 August 1969), 1398–1403; *1969 Congressional Quarterly Almanac* 83–84, 89, 258–259, 797–801; *Congressional Record-Senate* (5 August 1969), 22282–22292; *Congressional Record-Senate* (11 August 1969), 23188–23225; Richard D. McCarthy, *The Ultimate Folly* (New York: Knopf, 1969); P.L. 91–121, section 409.

37. "Statment on Chemical and Biological Defense Policies and Programs, November 25, 1969," in *Public Papers of the President of the United States: Richard Nixon, 1969* (Washington, D.C.: U.S. Government Printing Office, 1970), 968.

38. For a detailed account of the policy process that led up to this major change in chemical and biological warfare policy, see Forrest Frank, "U.S. Arms Control Policymaking," 98–126.

39. Anon. "President Nixon Renounces Chemical and Biological Warfare (Or Does He?): An Examination of the United States CBW Program in the Light of the President's Recent Announcement of Profound Changes Therein," (unpublished ms., ca. December 1969).

40. For discussion of biologists' apprehensions in the 1960s about the future military use of the biological sciences, see Susan Wright, "Biotechnology and the Military," in Michael Warren (ed.), *Agricultural Bioethics* (Ames; Iowa State University Press, 1990).

41. U.S. Senate, Committee on Foreign Relations, *Hearing: Prohibition of Chemical and Biological Weapons*, 93rd Cong., 2nd Sess. (10 December 1974), 15–16.

42. Matthew Meselson, Review of *Tomorrow's Weapons, Chemical and Biological* by Jacques Hirshon Rothschild, *Bulletin of the Atomic Scientists* 20 (October 1964), 35–36.

43. Han Swyter, "Political Considerations and Analysis of Military Requirements for Chemical and Biological Weapons," *Procedures of the National Academy of Sciences* 65 (1970), 266.

44. National Security Council, National Security Decision Memorandum 35 (25 November 1969) (appendix H). For further analysis, see Susan Wright and Robert Sinsheimer, "Recombinant DNA and Biological Warfare," *Bulletin of the Atomic Scientists* 39 (November 1983), 24.

45. Julian Perry Robinson, personal communication, 12 June 1989.

46. For the history of negotiation of the Biological Weapons Convention, see SIPRI, *The Problem of Chemical and Biological Warfare* IV, 253–279, 290–321; Frank, "U.S. Arms Control Policymaking," chapter 5.

47. Arthur Westing, "The Threat of Biological Warfare," *Bioscience* 35 No. 10 (November 1985), 627–633.

48. It appears that Nixon's order was largely carried out. However, in 1975, it was revealed that the CIA had retained quantities of toxins in violation of the order: U.S. Senate, Select Committee to Study Governmental Operations with Respect to Intelligence Activities, *Final Report*, 362–363. The disposition of this illegally retained stockpile remains unclear.

49. *U.S. Biological Warfare Program*, 57–58.

50. James McCullough, "Chemical and Biological Warfare: Selected Issues and Developments During 1978 and January 1–June 30, 1979," Report No. 79–156 SPR, Congressional Research Service (1 July 1979); Matthew Meselson and Julian Perry Robinson, "Chemical Warfare and Chemical Disarmament," *Scientific American* 242 (April 1980), 38–47.

51. Robert Bartley and William Kucewicz, "'Yellow Rain' and the Future of Arms Agreements," *Foreign Affairs* 61 (Spring 1983), 821; Mark Storella, *Poisoning Arms Control: The Soviet Union and Chemical and Biological Weapons* (Cambridge, Mass: Institude for Foreign Policy Analysis, 1984), 31; Joseph Douglass and H. Richard Lukens, "The Expanding Arena of Chemical-Biological Warfare," *Strategic Review* (Fall 1984), 76; William Kucewicz, "Beyond Yellow Rain: The Threat of Soviet Genetic Engineering," *Wall Street Journal*, (April 23, 25, 27; May 1, 3, 8, 10, 18, 1984); Jack Anderson, "Biological Warfare Update," *Seattle Post*

Intelligencer (5 December 1984); "Soviets Maintain Biological Weapons," *Seattle Post Intelligencer* (1 March 1985).

52. John Birkner, Scientific and Technical Intelligence Manager, Defense Intelligence Agency, response to question at Symposium on Biotechnology: International Trade Considerations, annual meeting of the American Association for the Advancement of Science, 27 May 1984.

53. Bartley and Kucewicz, "'Yellow Rain' and the Future of Arms Agreements," 817–820.

54. Steven Bowman, "U.S. Chemical Warfare Preparedness Program," Congressional Research Service Issue Brief No. IB822125, March 7, 1983, 5.

55. However, with pressure from certain members, Congress approved $3.15 million in 1980 for construction of a binary nerve gas plant. Wayne Biddle, "Restocking the Chemical Arsenal," *New York Times Magazine* (24 March 1981), 32–49.

56. U.S. House, Committee on Foreign Affairs, Subcommittee on Asian and Pacific Affairs, *Hearings, Use of Chemical Agents in Southeast Asia Since the Vietnam War*, 96th Cong., 1st Sess. (12 Dec 1979), 8.

57. I thank Christine Skwiot for her assistance in gathering data on the hearings in which the claims were aired. For text of Senate Resolution 201, see *Congressional Record* (22 Feb 1984), S1459–60.

58. Wayne Biddle, "Restocking the Chemical Arsenal," *New York Times Magazine* (24 May 1981); U.S. Senate, Committee on Armed Services, *Hearings on Department of Defense Authorization for Appropriations for Fiscal Year 1983*, 97th Congress, 2nd Session, March 22, 1982, 5065–68; Julian P. Robinson, "Chemical and Biological Warfare: Developments in 1983," *Stockholm International Peace Research Institute Yearbook 1984*, 322–329; Rodney McElroy, "Green Light for U.S. Chemcial Rearmament," *Unmask*, No. 4 (November 1986), 3–7. Data on support for Chemical Warfare and Biological Defense programs: Office of Atomic Energy, Office of the Secretary of Defense.

59. Walter Stoessel et al., *Report of the Chemical Warfare Review Commission* (Washington, D.C.: U.S. Government Printing Office, June 1985), 69–71. The members of the Commission were Walter J. Stoessel, Jr. (former ambassador and Under Secretary of State), Philip J. Bakes, Jr. (President, Continental Airlines), Zbigniew Brzezinski (National Security Adviser to President Carter), Richard E. Cavazos (General, U.S. Army, retired), Barbar B. Conable, Jr. (Senior Fellow, American Enterprise Institute), John N. Erlenborn (attorney, former U.S. Representative from Illinois), Alexander Haig, Jr. (former Secretary of State), and John Kester (attorney). The administrative staff of the Commission was drawn from the Pentagon, the Army, and the Navy.

60. Charles A. Fowler, Final Report of the Defense Science Board on Chemical Warfare and Biological Defense, 11 September 1985 (secret), quoted in Department of Defense, "Biological Defense Program," Report to the Committee on Appropriations, House of Representatives, May 1986.

61. U.S. Army Chemical Research and Development Center, Aberdeen Proving Ground, MD, "Technologic Changes Since 1972: Implications for a Biological Warfare Convention," (Secret) March 1986; cited in Department of Defense, "Biological Defense Program," 1.6.

62. Department of the Army, Army Science Board, "Final Report of the Ad Hoc Subgroup on Army Biological Defense Research Program," July 1987.

63. U.S. Department of Defense, "Biological Defense Program," part I, 13.

64. Department of Defense, *Annual Report on Chemical Warfare and Biological Defense Research Programs, FY 1980,* and *Annual Report on Chemical Warfare and Biological Defense Research Programs, FY 1985.*

65. Department of the Army, *Final Programmatic Environmental Impact Statement: Biological Defense Research Program* (April 1989), 2.3–2.9.

66. U.S. Army Medical Research Institute of Infectious Diseases, *Biological Defense: Functional Area Assessment: Overview,* C.3.

67. *Ibid.,* C.6–C.28a; W.C. Anderson and J.M. King, "Vaccine and Antitoxin Availability for Defense Against Biological Warfare Threat Agents," Final Report, September 1983 (U.S. Army Health Care Studies Division Report, #83–002).

68. Army Science Board, *Final Report of the Ad Hoc Subgroup on Army Biological Defene Resaerch Program* (July 1987), 2.

69. Foundation on Economic Trends v. Caspar W. Weinberger et al., Civil Action No. 86–2456, Defendants' Answers to Plaintiffs' First Set of Interrogatories and Request for Production of Documents, 3–5.

70. Minutes, Federal Interagency Committee of Recombinant DNA Research, 23 November 1976, in U.S. Department of Health, Education and Welfare, *Recombinant DNA Research* 2 (March 1978), 241; Nicholas Wade, "BW and Recombinant DNA," *Science* 208 (19 April 1980), 271; Department of Defense, "Annual Report on Chemical Warfare and Biological Research Programs," *Congressional Record* (5 August 1980), S10865.

71. U.S. Army Medical Research and Development Command, *Request for Proposals,* advertisment in *Science* 209 (12 September 1980), 1282; Anon., "DoD Offers Dollars for Far-Out Research Ideas in Molecular Detection," *McGraw-Hill's Biotechnology Newswatch* (21 September 1981), 1–2.

72. Department of Defense, Annual Reports on Chemical Warfare and Biological Research Programs, FY 1980, FY 1987; Office of Technology Assessment, *New Development in Biotechnology, No. 4: U.S. Investment in Biotechnology* (Washington, D.C.: U.S. Government Printing Office, July, 1988); National Science Foundation, *Federal Funds for Research and Development: Federal Obligations for Research by Agency and Detailed Field 1967–1988* (n.d.).

73. U.S. Department of Defense, *Draft Environmental Impact Statement for the Biological Defense Research Program,* May 1988, Appendix 3; Office of the Under Secretary of Defense, Acquisition (R&AT), "Recombinant DNA Research Projects Currently Conducted in DoD Biomedical Laboratories," 3 August 1987; "IBC-Approved Recombinant DNA Research Projects Funded by the Department of Defense," 8 September 1983; Work Unit Summaries of Defense Department-sponsored projects obtained in response to requests filed under the Freedom of Information Act, 1987–1988.

74. Department of Defense, *Annual Report on Chemical Warfare and Biological Defense Programs, FY 1980* (15 December 1980), sec. 2, p. 4; *Annual Report on Chemical Warfare and Biological Defense Programs, FY 1981* (30 December 1981), 16; Stephen Budiansky, "U.S. Looks to Biological Weapons: Military Takes Interest in DNA Devices," *Nature* 297 (24 June 1982). 615; Alvin Lazen, interview with author, February 7, 1983. For further discussion of these Pentagon initiatives, see Susan Wright and Robert L. Sinsheimer, "Recombinant DNA and Biological Warfare," *Bulletin of the Atomic Scientists* 29 (November 1983), 20–26.

75. Caspar Weinberger to James Sasser, November 20, 1984. A similar justification was made two years later in a Defense Department report to Congress on the Biological Defense Program: see Department of Defense, "Biological Defense Program," Report to the Committee on Appropriations, House of Representatives, May 1986, Chapter 1.

76. Report of the Preparatory Committee for the Review Conference of the Parties to the Convention on the Prohibition of the Development, Production and Stockpiling of Bacteriological (Biological) and Toxin Weapons and on their Destruction (8 February 1980), U.N. Document BWC/CONF. I/5; Views of States Parties on New Scientific and Technological Development Relevant to the Convention (29 February 1980), U.N. Document BWC/CONF. I/6.

77. Background Document on New Scientific and Technological Developments Relevant to the Convention on the Prohibition of the Development, Production and Stockpiling of Bacteriological (Biological) and Toxin Weapons and on Their Destruction, U.N. Documents BWC/CONF. II/4 (18 August 1986), BWC/CONF. II/4/Add.1 (29 August 1986) and BWC/CONF. II/Add.2 (8 September 1986).

78. Jozef Goldblat, "Multilateral Arms Control Efforts," *SIPRI Yearbook 1986* and *SIPRI Yearbook 1987*; Gordon Burck, "Recent Progress Toward Chemical Disarmament," *Federation of American Scientists Public Interest Report* 40 No.10 (December 1987); Jesse James, "Glasnost Spreads to Chemical Weapons," *Arms Control Today* (1 November 1987), 22; S.J. Lundin, J.P. Perry Robinson, and Ralf Trapp, "Chemical and Biological Warfare: Developments in 1987," *SIPRI Yearbook 1988*; Matthew Meselson, "The Biological Weapons Convention and the Sverdlovsk Anthrax Outbreak of 1979," *Federation of American Scientists Public Interest Report* 41 No.7 (September 1988).

79. Julie Johnson, "U.S. Asks Stiff Ban on Chemical Arms," *New York Times* (27 September 1988), 1, 6; Transcript of the First TV Debate Between Bush and Dukakis, *New York Times* (26 September 1988), 12.

80. Walter J. Stoessel et al., *Report of the Chemical Warfare Review Commission*, June 1985, 30–31.

81. U.S. Army Science Board, *Final Report of the Ad Hoc Subgroup on Army Biological Defense Research Program* (July 1987), 6.

82. See, e.g., Gary Thatcher, "Poison on the Wind," *The Christian Science Monitor* (four-part series, December 13–16, 1988). A purported chemical weapons plant in Libya was the subject of intense coverage in January 1989: see, e.g., "Chemical Warfare: The Fight Against 'The Wings of Death;' A Showdown With Kaddafi," *Newsweek* (16 January 1989); Stephen Engelberg, "American Officials Say Iraq Is Developing Biological Arms," *New York Times* (18 January 1989).

83. Testimony of William H. Webster, U.S. Senate, Committee on Governmental Affairs, *Hearings: Global Spread of Chemical and Biological Weapons: Assessing Challenges and Responses* (9 February 1989).

84. S.J. Lundin, J.P. Perry Robinson and Ralf Trapp, "Chemical and Biological Warfare: Developments in 1987," 103.

85. Lundin, Perry, and Trapp, "Chemical and Biological Warfare," 101–102.

86. According to the Department of Defense Annual Report on Chemical Warfare — Biological Defense Program to Congress, support for the BDRP for FY 1987 was $62.5 million.

87. Barbara Rosenberg, "Updating the Biological Weapons Ban," *Bulletin of the Atomic Scientists* 43 (January/February 1987), 40–43; Nicholas Sims, "Biological and Toxin Weapons: The 1986 Outcome," *The Council for Arms Control Bulletin* No. 29 (November 1986), 6–7; Judy Foreman and Allison Bass, "A New Look at Anthrax Outbreak," *Boston Globe* (25 April 1988), 33–34; Ad Hoc Meeting of Scientific and Technical Experts from States Parties to the Biological Weapons Convention, 15 April 1987, U.N. Document BWC/CONF.II/EX/.

88. Report of the Ad Hoc Committee on Chemical Weapons to the Conference on Disarmament, 26 August 1987, U.N. Document CD/782; Gordon Burck, "Recent Progress Toward Chemical Disarmament," *F.A.S. Public Interest Report* 40 (December 1987), 22–31.

89. KSL.AM.TV Salt Lake City, Utah, "Reject Germ Test Facility," (Editorial comment broadcast 8 March 1988).

90. Testimony of Anthony Robbins and Wayne Owens, House of Representatives, Subcommittees on Armed Services, Foreign Affairs, and Interior and Insular Affairs, *Joint Hearing: Biological Warfare Testing*, 3 May 1988.

91. U.S. Department of the Army, *Draft Environmental Impact Statement: Biological Defense Research Program*, May 1988; Francis Boyle to Philip K. Russell, Major General, Medical Corps Commander, U.S. Army Medical Research and Development Command, 5 August 1988; Committee for Responsible Genetics to Philip K. Russell, 8 August 1988.

92. "Preliminary Report of the Majority Staff of the Senate Subcommittee on Oversight of Government Management on DoD's Safety Programs for Chemical and Biological Warfare Research, 11 May 1988; United States General Accounting Office, "DoD's Risk Assessment and Safeguards Management of Chemical and Biological Warfare Research and Development Facilities," 27 July 1988; Harold Lloyd Dye, Jr., Maryland Department of the Environment, Hazardous and Solid Waste Management Administration, Hazardous Waste Enforcement Division, Testimony before the Senate Subcommittee on Oversight of Government Management, 27 July 1988; Neil Levitt, Testimony before the Senate Subcommittee on Oversight of Government Management, 27 July 1988.

II

Ethical Issues Posed by Biological Warfare

3

Scientists and Research

Robert L. Sinsheimer

And thus the native hue of resolution is sicklied o'er with the pale cast of thought.
—William Shakespeare

The Question

Should scientists be concerned with the likely uses of their research findings and should such concern influence the directions of their research endeavors? If a scientist is to be a morally aware, self-responsible human being, the answer to both questions must be. yes.

However, "yes" is but the prelude to another series of other difficult and vexing questions that limn the human condition. For the world is complex and allegiances conflict; human knowledge is always finite and time waits not and logic falters, adrift in a sea of uncertainty.

Most scientists in the United States worked gladly on military projects during World War II. They were convinced their cause was right and their foe was evil. A few scientists to be sure had deep-lying concerns about the atomic bomb, which they foresaw to be a weapon of such fateful power that no cause could justify its use. Some hoped to prove it could not be built. Later, some opposed its deployment.

And, of course, many scientists devoted their talents to the cause of our foe, which they conceived to be righteous. Indeed, on both sides there was a foreboding sense of awful scientific competition.

Contrarily, many, but surely not all, scientists in this country eschewed military research during the Vietnam War—a war that they perceived to be unjust, even unfair. One element of that "unfairness" perhaps derived from the use of advanced military technology (e.g., the electronic battlefield, defoliants, napalm, and antipersonnel gases)—the military product of sophisticated scientific research and development—against a scientifically less advanced culture.

⌜Currently, biologists are concerned with the propriety of research that might—or would—be applied for purposes of biological warfare. Nature already provides a variety of viruses and microorganisms pathogenic to humans, animals, or crops. Now the newer developments in molecular genetics offer the potential either to enhance the utility of these agents for military use or to develop wholly new disease-producing organisms—to increase their survivability, their resistance to dessication or sunlight, to augment their virulence, to vary their means of dissemination, to alter their antigenicity in myriad ways so as to circumvent attempts at immunological protection.

It is argued that since this potential exists, the military forces must be prepared to defend against it and must therefore engage in the relevant research. And since an effective defense must be based upon a realistic understanding of the offensive military potential of such agents, the research must encompass offensive as well as defensive techniques, even though we have no offensive intentions.⌟

The Scientist's Quandary

⌜The scientist engaged in basic research, seeking only to enlarge the store of human knowledge, may often claim with justice to be unable to predict the uses to which scientific discoveries may be put. When Einstein deduced the equivalence of matter and energy he could not plausibly have anticipated that his equations would find expression in the atomic bomb. Nor could Scheele, the discoverer of chlorine gas, have conceived of its military application.

But in an increasingly technological age, scientists have become increasingly aware of the potential applications for commercial or other uses, of the most basic discoveries of their laboratories. So also has the government which largely funds their research.

At some point in the transition from elemental scientific fact to commercial product, medical technique, or military weapon, the intent becomes clear and the effort focuses on design and development—as in the Manhattan project or the attack on AIDS—and here the ethical issue cannot be shirked.⌟

Scientists are citizens of three communities: their national society with its history, goals, and ideals; the international fellowship of scientists with its history, goals, and ideals; and the human race, past, present, and future. To each of these they owe allegiance in greater or lesser degree and it is the conflicts of these allegiances, the divergence of values, and the temporal disjunctions among these communities that give rise to the moral dilemmas.

Only the second of these is strictly unique to the scientist, but just as scientists play a special role in society, so do their allegiances to the first and third have a special character.

The allegiance of scientists to their national society rests initially upon the basic obligations of every citizen—obligations accepted in return for the provision of protection, of education, of our economic "safety net" and agencies to maintain public health, of constitutional freedoms—all the more binding in a democracy where the governmental functions are chosen by the citizenry. But scientists receive from the national society additional benefits without which they surely could not function: direct support in institutional and social arrangements such as universities, federal grants, tax incentives for the support of research and the distribution and application of its results that are essential to the conduct of their research, as well as the indirect but powerful motivations inherent in the society that (mostly) believes in the virtues of rationality and the value of scientific progress.

The perspective the scientist acquires through allegiance to the world-wide community of scientists is unique: the history of science, the practice of science is an international endeavor. Each scientist in any country adds to the cathedral of knowledge. Every scientist engaged in research is the intellectual heir of Galileo and Newton and Einstein, of Lavoisier and Mendeleev and Fisher, of Linnaeus, Darwin and Mendel, to cite but a few. Every scientist is also dependent today upon advances made in a global network as much as upon the advances made in his own society. National boundaries are meaningless to the quest for knowledge. To pit the scientists of one country against those of another is inherently a violation of the scientific ethos.

All human beings owe allegiance to the human race, but the scientist is perhaps peculiarly able to view the trajectory of our species with both detachment and compassion. The scientist knows of the long history of life on our planet prior to the recent emergence of

Homo sapiens. Scientists are aware of the enormous effort humanity has expended to wrest from nature our present treasure of human knowledge. They understand how this treasure has enabled us to triumph over animal foes, climatic vagaries, and deadly diseases—to multiply our numbers and prosper on our planet—to expand our intellectual horizons again and again as we gain a truer vision of our origins and our place in the cosmos, in an unending task.

And they have a more sound realization of our future prospects for greatness or alternatively, for catastrophe.

The obligations that bind scientists to the national societies are manifest and strong; historically that allegiance has, with rare exception, been dominant. When called upon to serve the needs of society as expressed by a democratically elected government, the scientist, conscious of his social obligation to that society, needs a powerful reason to refuse.

Allegiance to the world scientific community has seldom provided such a motivation. The international structure of science is a voluntary confederation. Without strong international organization and large internationally based resources, the obligations of such an allegiance are tenuous, and the short-term penalties for its rupture, weak. To date, nationalism has repeatedly transcended internationalism, even in science.

The third allegiance, however—seemingly the most abstract—may well entail the most acute moral imperative. Can a scientist rightfully apply the triumphs of human knowledge to the arts of human destruction—especially the arts of human destruction on a super-human scale. Some modalities of warfare—nuclear and biological weapons—would seem to have the potential for unprecedented catastrophe and for the destruction of the very cathedral of knowledge which scientists have striven to create. They represent a perversion of the greatest accomplishments of cumulative generations of scientific endeavor and insight. Their use—and their development certainly makes possible their use—would make meaningless the lives of every scientist of every time.

Biological Warfare Research, No

The proper balance of this set of three allegiances must be a personal one. Only dedicated pacifists would exclude all military research. In the twentieth century it is naive to believe we live in a harmonious world order. We cannot expect to be unarmed and live in peace.

All weapons aim at military defeat of an adversary but some weapons (e.g., radar) are primarily defensive, aiming to thwart the opposition. Others, such as smart bombs, are of limited scale and higher specificity. In research on biological weapons, however, the distinction between "defensive" and "offensive" becomes hopelessly blurred.

Lacking any such distinction, development of biological warfare seems especially repugnant. Having conquered through centuries of effort most of the microbial diseases of humanity, to now use our insights to create new diseases, new and indiscriminate plagues on behalf of any cause, cannot be considered a sane act. We may presume that scientists promoting or pursuing biological warfare research justify their activity either as morally neutral or as a route to national security. In either case, their justification is short-sighted; it does not confront the perilous consequences of the militarization of advanced fields of science and technology and the arms acceleration that inevitably follows.

It must be recognized that some weapons are simply unfit for any human use at any time in any cause. Too powerful and indiscriminant, they make hideous mockery of the entire scientific adventure. Biological weapons and nuclear weapons are such.

Some of the physicists who under very different circumstances developed the atomic bomb recognized this peril and were placed in a fearful quandary.

V.F. Weisskopf has written, "Many physicists...worked hard to understand more about fission. Many of us hoped that the number of neutrons per fission would be low enough to prevent the making of a bomb. But it wasn't."[1]

I.I. Rabi declined a formal association with the Los Alamos Laboratory; he was too distressed by the concept that a nuclear bomb would be "the culmination of three centuries of physics."[2]

In opposing the proposal to develop the hydrogen bomb, Enrico Fermi and I.I. Rabi wrote:

Necessarily such a weapon goes far beyond any military objective and enters the range of very great natural catastrophes. By its very nature it cannot be confined to a military objective but becomes a weapon which in practical effect is almost one of genocide.

It is clear that the use of such a weapon cannot be justified on any ethical ground which gives a human being a certain individuality and dignity even if he happens to be a resident of an enemy country . . . Any postwar situation resulting from such a weapon would leave unresolvable enmities for generations. A desirable peace cannot come from such an inhuman application of force.[3]

Weisskopf has more recently written, "In today's world, loaded with nuclear explosives, any use of nuclear bombs would be a crime against humanity. There are ways to avoid the holocaust and we must never cease to search for them. If we do not succeed, our century will be remembered by the unfortunate survivors as the time of preparation for the great catastrophe and science will be seen as the main culprit."[4]

These physicists in World War II were confronted with a most cruel dilemma. Intelligent and well-meaning, they could foresee the horror of nuclear weapons. But their countries were clearly engaged in a dreadful war with an advanced, ruthless foe, a foe who might well already be designing such weapons. There was no chance for anticipatory agreement, to achieve a reasoned understanding of the mutual peril.

Fortunately, we are not yet enmeshed in such a dire situation. There is yet time to avert the development of another threat of planet-wide destruction. But the militarization of physics and chemistry should serve as a grievous warning. Biologists need to take steps now to avoid the militarization of their achievements. If history is any guide to the future, waiting to protest the use of novel weapons in a future conflict will be of no avail.

The advances of science will doubtless continue to create new opportunities to develop other weapons of gross, indiscriminate, uncontrollable destruction. Scientists especially must be "eternally vigilant" to resist all such threats to the human future on this planet. Rather than develop new dimensions of warfare, scientists should work to outlaw all such weapons and to reinforce such proscriptions with adequate means for international verification.

Notes

1. Weisskopf, V.F., "A Peril and a Hope," *Bull. Atom. Sci.* 35 (January, 1979), 10–13.
2. Quoted in a letter from Robert Oppenheimer to I.I. Rabi, February 26, 1943.

Text of letter in A.K. Smith and C. Weiner, eds., *Robert Oppenheimer, Letters and Recollections*, Cambridge, Mass: Harvard University Press, 1980, 250–251.

3. Addendum by I.I. Rabi and E. Fermi to the report by the General Advisory Committee of the Atomic Energy Commission concerning development of the hydrogen bomb, October 31, 1949. The complete text of the addendum is presented in John S. Rigden, *Rabi, Scientist and Citizen*, New York: Basic Books, Inc., 1987, 206–207.

4. Weisskopf, V.F., "Looking Back on Los Alamos," *Bull. Atom. Sci.* 41 (August, 1985), 206–207.

4

Ethics in Biological Warfare Research

Marc Lappé

1 Introduction

To be morally acceptable, an activity must comport with the value structure of society and be consistent with the laws, mores and ethical behavioral norms of its participants. Biological warfare (BW)—that is, warfare conducted with organisms or products of living systems—deserves special moral scrutiny both because its participants often include health professionals who have special moral duties and also because its military objectives often include civilian or other nonmilitary targets.

There is a long history of efforts in international law to implement moral norms condemning the use of weapons deemed to cause unnecessary and indiscriminate suffering. Biological and chemical weapons have been a particular focus of these efforts.[1] The preamble to the first major international measure prohibiting the use of chemical and biological weapons, the 1925 Geneva Protocol, stated that the use in war of "asphyxiating, poisonous or other gases, and of analogous liquids, materials or devices, has been justly condemned by the general opinion of the civilized world" and expressed the view that the Protocol would "[bind] alike the conscience and the practice of nations." That of the 1972 Biological Weapons Convention, which bans possession of biological and toxin weapons, expressed the conviction that signatory States that use such weapons would be "repugnant to the conscience of mankind" and stated their determination to "exclude completely the possibility" of such use (see appendixes B and C).

The preamble of the Biological Weapons Convention appears to be an unequivocal disavowal of any research directed towards developing—or making feasible the development of—biological weapons. However, the scope of Article I, which formulates the basic treaty requirement, is significantly less comprehensive. Article I prohibits "development, production and stockpiling" of biological weapons, but it is silent on the question of research. It also permits retention of biological agents "of types and in quantities" that can be justified for "prophylactic, protective or other peaceful purposes" (chapter 9). Significantly, under the terms of a guideline that originated in a memorandum to the National Security Council written by Henry Kissinger in 1969, the United States interprets its responsibilities under the Biological Weapons Convention as permitting "research into those offensive aspects of bacteriological/biological agents necessary to determine what defensive measures are required" (chapter 2 and appendix H).

The ambiguity in the operational part of the Biological Weapons Convention thus leaves a legal loophole through which much research that anticipates or defends against biological weapons may pass. It is for this reason that the moral analysis of the acceptability of biological warfare research is important and of significantly broader scope than the prohibitions currently encoded in international law. My purpose in this chapter is to show that moral analysis raises serious ethical issues about any activities that contribute to the development of biological weapons.

2 The Morality of Biological Warfare Research

Participants in BW programs bear varying degrees of moral responsibility for the consequences of their activities in perfecting these systems. Those who directly prepare biological agents for use in warfare are more morally culpable than are those whose participation contributes only indirectly to the ultimate machinery of biological warfare. The major weapons systems that constitute the core of a biological weapons system, namely toxin delivery systems, pathogen aerosol generators, etc., must by their nature be developed with the complicity of scientists and medical practitioners. But the moral responsibility of the public health or bacteriological scientist in BW activities can only be determined with some difficulty because of the ambiguity between medical and military uses of scientific knowledge and the often vague distinction between offensive and defensive BW operations.

From one viewpoint, research aimed at developing agents that overcome natural defenses and resistance, whether found in the medical or military sector, is intrinsically immoral. While medical practitioners can justify occasional needs to impair human resistance (such as performing grafts of allogenic tissue), those who have done so in the context of warfare (doctors who collaborated with the Nazi regime, for instance), are considered grossly immoral. Military researchers who intentionally develop weapons that override natural resistance to disease incur a similar moral onus, since their activities are likely to lead to unnecessary suffering and injury for combatants and noncombatants alike; they thereby pervert the ethics of medicine and medical research to benefit, not harm, humans (see sections 4 and 5, below).

To be effective, biological weapons must be designed and perfected by those who understand the physiological and immunological prerequisites of health. Those researchers who convert medical knowledge to potentially harmful ends warrant particular moral sanction because of the opportunity principle: had their efforts and special skills been turned to aiding humanity rather than creating weapons, the likelihood of human suffering would be reduced and future generations would not be jeopardized.

To investigate this blameworthiness of participants in BW programs, it is necessary to distinguish those who participate in projects clearly designed to perfect offensive weapons from those who contribute only to defensive preparations. Since in practice these distinctions are often blurred, the first task is to clarify defensive and offensive BW activities.

3 The Moral Ambiguity of Military Research

A fundamental ambiguity exists in the moral and legal standing of BW research, even that aimed solely at perfecting detection systems or at developing effective defenses against specific weapons systems. These categories embrace numerous grey areas: even purely "defensive" research (such as the development of vaccines to protect civilian populations) can be an integral part of a broader offensive effort, such as preparing troops to engage in biological warfare by prior vaccination against offensive weapons (chapter 6). It should be noted that the Department of Defense has argued that we are entitled under our treaty obligations to engage in activities that constitute reasonable measures of self-defense.[2]

It is in the context of ostensibly defensive research that the lines between acceptable and unacceptable become blurred. At one extreme, it might be argued that *any* participation in a system of research activities that supports military operations acquiesces to the immorality of warfare. At the other, it can be argued that self-defense is a morally justified, if not mandated, activity. It is therefore helpful to distinguish three kinds of BW research:

1. research that directly aids an offensive BW delivery system;

2. research of a defensive nature that simultaneously creates an offensive *and* defensive capability; and

3. research whose ends are "purely" defensive in nature. ⌋ 80-81

As distinct from the legality of these forms of research (an analysis of which is beyond the scope of this chapter), their moral acceptability ranges along a continuum from possible acceptability to censure, depending on two factors: the likelihood of conversion of the project to blatantly nefarious ends; and the system of moral analysis used. From a purely deontological perspective in which both the intention and the end of avoiding any contribution to the conduct of war are seen as morally necessary, all three forms of research are unacceptable. From a consequentialist viewpoint, research in any category could be considered morally blameworthy (or supportable) to the extent that it generates more (or less) harm than benefit. I shall examine the three different research categories separately from both perspectives.

Category 1. Offensive Research

It is clear that any products of biological research that by scale or form have immediate offensive military utility are proscribed by the Biological Weapons Convention. Signatories have foresworn activities that produce materials for biological weapons. However, as we have seen, the United States has expressly identified research into offensive aspects of biological agents as acceptable as long as it is conducted for defensive purposes. That does not preclude a moral test of such research. All research directed towards *assisting* a biological weapons program is morally suspect for all the reasons that biological warfare is itself immoral. ⌋ 81

Category 2. Simultaneous Utility

A consequentialist test of the moral acceptability of research with joint applicability is the following: research that has both offensive and defensive applications is morally questionable to the extent that the incorporation of its results, whether into a weapons system or a vaccination program, is more likely to harm than protect humanity. Where military BW research *diminishes* the likelihood of harm, its morality is ambiguous, and it may possibly be acceptable. One difficulty with such an analysis is that it weighs future harms of indeterminate extent against the likelihood of safeguarding the public from the unquantifiable danger of biological war.

Another instance of ambiguous research is that which *could* lead to health-related applications, but is designed primarily for military objectives. This problem is particularly troublesome when the military research centers on an extremely dangerous agent or process that could have great public health benefit (research into the attachment and entry into cells by RNA viruses analogous to the AIDS virus, for example). By consequentialist analysis, the net potential benefit of such research might be so great as to outweigh the consequences of using such an agent in warfare.

Nevertheless, such arguments do not adequately justify BW research program with simultaneous utility. First, research directed solely to beneficial ends is more likely to achieve such ends than is research split between offensive and defensive objectives. Second, risk should only be balanced against benefits when both accrue to the same parties—and when those parties are given a freely informed opportunity to consent to their acceptance. Any harm to innocent persons is considered to be morally unacceptable by virtually all codes of medical ethics (see below). Thus, benefits accruing to soldiers on some potential battlefield cannot be weighed against risk to society as a whole. Third, because any program which increases the likelihood of offensive weapons development is morally proscribed by signatories of the Biological Weapons Convention, the "proportional-good" test is legally as well as morally questionable.

Category 3. Defensive Research
There are at least six general areas of proposed defensive biological warfare research that warrant moral scrutiny:

(i) isolation of preparation of toxins and pathogenic organism:

(ii) prophylactic measures (vaccines, toxoids);

(iii) therapeutic measures (antibiotics, antiviral drugs, antidotes);

(iv) protective clothing and equipment;

(v) monitoring and detection devices;

(vi) methods of decontamination.

The Department of Defense claims that research of type (i) is necessary to test the measures developed under (ii)–(vi). However, since biological agents and molecular analogs of toxins can effectively simulate true pathogens and biotoxins, it is difficult to justify research of type (i) except for the development of prophylactic and therapeutic measures against specific agents that pose a current health risk. The pursuit of research in these areas raises further questions.

The military justification for expanding the most morally ambiguous research—types (ii) and (iii)—is both that it is necessary for defending troops and that it has "high civilian potential."[3] However, it is unlikely that vaccination programs designed to increase the resistance of military personnel to future biological warfare encounters could be effective since it will be extremely difficult to anticipate the nature of the specific biological weapon that might be used by an aggressor. Furthermore, such research may be seen by adversary nations as provocative since they may assume that its most likely function is to increase the capacity of protected troops to use their own weapons systems, or to permit biological weapons system to be applied more aggressively (chapter 6).

Nor can developing immunological defenses be justified as providing civilian protection to BW agents, since human civilian populations under attack by biological agents are not likely to be adequately defended by any of the systems under development. For civilian populations, the overall level of effective immunological protection is dependent on the delivered dose of a toxin or the number of pathogenic organisms. At low levels of immunity, high concentrations of toxin or large numbers of organisms can overwhelm host defenses. If an adversary knew that a civilian population were vaccinated, it could design its attack strategies accordingly.

Vaccine use is also highly time-dependent, and unsuitable for defending civilian populations from surprise attack. By the United States' own admission, the development and apparent use by the Russians of an effective vaccine did not prevent the occurrence of deaths in the civilian population after the alleged release of anthrax spores in the Sverdlovsk incident in 1979.[4] In that event, the vaccination of the civilian population came much too late to protect against bacterial anthrax infection.

The work at the U.S. Army Medical Research Institute of Infectious Diseases, which has the formal mission of developing effective protections against exotic diseases with biological warfare potential, is principally suspect in this context; nonetheless, exploiting the ambiguity inherent in "defensive research" rationales, it continues to justify its work on biological warfare pathogens by citing its civilian applications.[5]

The development of protective clothing or other materials, monitoring devices and detection devices, and decontamination procedures is also double-edged in that all types of such activities, while ostensibly "purely" defensive in nature, are in fact required to assure that any offensive attack take place under controlled conditions. To the extent that these activities are thus tightly linked to waging biological warfare, they are also appropriately criticized.

4 The Nature of Physicians' Duties

Physician-researchers are in a special category in terms of the morality of their participation in biological warfare-related research. Physicians' actions are delimited by both their Code of Ethics, including the Hippocratic Oath, and by several specific covenants which govern their behavior in both war and peacetime. Under the Geneva Rules governing the establishment and protection of the Red Cross, it is clear that physicians are to be considered noncombatants, because it is assumed that they will render care to combatants and noncombatants without regard to their military roles.[6] The key proviso is that the Red Cross personnel are unarmed and not directly involved in offensive actions. Clearly, any active participation of physicians in a biological warfare program such as the one conducted by the Japanese at Harbin, Manchuria, toward the end of World War II would violate the norms of this agreement.

The Hippocratic Oath and its accompanying maxims are the major repository of moral guidance for physicians. The specific section of the Oath which most closely relates to the participation of physicians in activities analogous to biological warfare is that which says; "I will neither give a deadly drug to anybody if asked for it, nor will I make a suggestion to this effect."[7]

While the historical context of these stipulations indicates that the Pythagoreans intended to avoid the social opprobrium associated with suicide, it is also possible to read the Oath more broadly. The Greeks may well have wished to disassociate the healing profession from the taint of participation in internecine feuds or battles in which political assassination and other activities frequently involved the clandestine administration of poisons *per os*. If so, the Oath can be seen as a forerunner of modern injunctions against physicians' participation in biological warfare.

Elsewhere in the Oath and in other oaths generated in other versions and jurisdictions, the injunction to use knowledge to benefit (and not harm) mankind is evident. For instance, the first Section of the Principles of Medical Ethics of the American Medical Association (1957) states: "The principal objective of the medical profession is to render service to humanity with full respect for the dignity of man."[8] This too is an incomplete basis for deriving a specific ethic against medical participation in the often ambiguous research that undergirds biological warfare defenses, but strongly endorses the principle of nonparticipation with biological warfare research generally.

The intentional infliction of harm on another person, or the creation of means or circumstances that condone or support such infliction, is contrary to international codes of medical ethics, such as those of the World Medical Association.[9] In a proposed variation of the Hippocratic Oath, it would be unethical for a physician to assist in torturing another person—or even to offer passive assistance by performing physical examinations whose ultimate purpose is to determine the tolerance of a prisoner for additional torture.[10] By analogy, even those physician-researchers who simply *participated* in developing the foundations for a biological weapon (such as diagnostic, detection or dispersal systems) could be morally culpable in assisting in the development of an immoral device to the extent that their efforts made its use more feasible. Physician-researchers thus have a strong moral obligation to abstain from participation in work that can contribute directly or indirectly to biological warfare.

5 The Nature of Scientists' Duties

Unlike physicians, scientists are under no formal covenant to assure that their work is used for the betterment of mankind. A recently proposed declaration, the Buenos Aires Oath, seems to imply a balancing test when it states (in part) that scientists examine the consequences of their work to assure that it is "truly in the best interests of society and peace."[11]

In a simple sense, biological weapons research can be seen as violating a universal moral maxim against using knowledge to cause suffering. But no codes of ethics exist that forbid the use of biological or medical knowledge to inflict human pain or harm if that harm is an *indirect consequence* of scientific study. Those codes that exist are presently limited to animal or human subjects of experimentation, and do not pertain to conditions of war or to the second order (social) consequences of research. Moreover, work at Department of Defense installations, not directly funded by the Department of Health and Human Services, was until recently outside the purview of the 1981 regulations that protect subjects of research.[12]

Where lines linking research directly to offensive weapons development are clear, it may be relatively straightforward to define the moral duty of scientists to foreswear participation in research programs. Scientific personnel who engage in perfecting biological weapons can be said to have corrupted their duty as practitioners of the life sciences to understand and apply knowledge about living systems for the ultimate improvement of life. For physicians and scientists alike, the duty of beneficence proscribes providing, no matter how unintentionally, a maleficent power with the capacity to produce harm.

The moral status of biological research which *could* be used to study or develop weapons systems is rarely so straightforward. Much unclassified, military-directed research is described as being directed towards public health ends, and is centered at institutions such as the Walter Reed Army Institute for Research, which has a long history of public health support. The challenge to any critic is thus to document those instances where public health research directly lends itself to, or has been used for, weapons systems development.

Many researchers believe strongly that the duties of scientific researchers should be limited to assuring that they take due care in protecting subjects of research from immediate harm in the pursuit of knowledge. Under this notion research, especially "basic" research, is considered in itself morally neutral. I have previously argued that even at the stage of formulation of a hypothesis, moral arguments demand that the consequences of embarking on a course of inquiry be considered.[13]

The line where scientific responsibility begins for unforeseen (but not unforeseeable) consequences of the use of the fruits of research remains highly controversial. Where immediate applications of work that can harm or injure are clear, the responsibility for exercising care to control possible harmful consequences is self-evident: we require all pesticides to be tested for their putative harmfulness before registration. But where only distant applications create the likelihood of harm, for example where spinoffs of the original project lead to weapons of mass destruction, responsibility is diffuse and less morally weighty. An instance would be the responsibility of laser researchers for the application of their invention to construct "smart" bombs used in Vietnam against civilian and military targets. At some point, scientific responsibility for adverse consequences is thus rendered moot by the distance that separates the initial invention from its final (unintended) applications.

6 Ethical Criteria for Assessing Biological Warfare Research

The most difficult question about the ethics of scientific research thus hinges not on the moral acceptability of engaging in perfidious forms of research, but on the culpability of scientists who carry out *collateral* research that ultimately permits weapons to be produced. An example would be a biological weapons system made functional by the development of a special aerosol generator that *by itself* was not a weapon. The more *direct* the applicability of collateral research is to the weapons system, the more morally suspect it is (table 4.1).

Context

Most collateral research can be rationalized by its practitioners as having some benign application, and thus it is essential to examine carefully the context of the research project before judging it. A classic instance of an ostensibly bidirectional form of research in which good applications cannot be separated from evil ones is the development of immunotoxins at Army facilities, in which toxic agents are linked to specific antibodies. This work does not violate medical ethical norms when conducted in a cancer research laboratory, but might do so when done under military aegis in the context of biological warfare preparedness. The two types of immunotoxins are almost certainly going to be qualitatively different in construction, purity, specificity and host range. Cancer immunotoxins are linked to specific monoclonal antibodies for action at a strictly cellular level in the cancerous lesion. Military immunotoxins will likely select toxins with specific neurotoxicity linked to antibodies

Table 4.1
Criteria for judging the likelihood of misuse of potential biological warfare research

| | Likelihood | |
	High	Low
Applicability: linkage of research to functional needs of an extant or proposed biological warfare system	Immediate or direct	Tangential or indirect
Setting: locale and context of proposed research	DOD facility or DOD aegis	University or public sponsorship
Offensive Capability: role of research in offensive applications (weapons component)	Essential	Nonessential
Facilitation Scale: degree to which research increases probability of first/offensive use	Great	Small
Security Status: degree of security attached to work	Secret	Nonsecret
Proximity Standard: congruence of endpoint of research to needed element in a weapons system	Close	Distant
Overall Probability of Nefarious Use: likelihood that research aids or abets the eventuality of use of biological weapons systems	High	Low

directed at acetylcholine receptors or similar molecular targets. Conceivably, immunotoxins also may be made with broad-spectrum antibodies. Even if the distinctions between therapeutic and military immunotoxins are blurred for some toxins, they are not for their delivery systems. Clearly a syringe would suffice for clinical use, while some form of broad-range applicator would be needed for large-scale military use.

Applications
Some research applications to biological warfare needs appear genuinely *coincidental* to non-military applications. An example would be the development of vaccines or neutralizing antibodies to extremely virulent organisms. The morality of such work is at least questionable if the organism is a rare one. Research which

is directly part of military work but is designed solely to *assist* in passive defense against BW (such as research designed to improve protective equipment and closing or efforts to design monitoring and detection equipment intended simply to alert a populace or troop concentration of the imminence of a warfare attack) seems less problematic.

Content

These observations suggest that the most ethically difficult issue to be resolved is the one facing scientists whose work *may lend itself* to warfare applications. This is particularly problematic where the researchers claim to be ignorant of the warfare utility of their studies. Such circumstances should be rare since such a claim is hardly in keeping with the acumen and foresight required of any competent scientific researcher. Admittedly, subversion of innocent research to military ends can occur—chromatographic techniques have abetted chemical weapons preparation. But to argue in such instances that scientists were morally irresponsible is untenable because of the remoteness of the connection between the research or technique and its final application.

It is thus unclear from an investigation of the content of research whether all research that might possibly abet a biological warfare program is necessarily morally egregious. Many of the techniques presently used to protect the population from epidemic disease (vaccination, immunization, etc.) are often indistinguishable from those used to augment the capacity to wage war (i.e., by pre-vaccinating invading troops against an intended weapon), or to defend a nation-state against putative attack. Such a moral grey area may be clarified by the use of further criteria.

Locus

First, does the social context of the research, particularly the mission of the agency supporting the research, further define the goals being pursued? If research on vaccines, pathogens or toxins is genuinely in the public health interest, it seems reasonable to require that it be conducted by a civilian agency. The counterargument, that military troops frequently encounter novel or foreign pathogens not commonly occurring within civilian populations, is only partially valid. Pursuing research in those areas potentially serves an ulterior purpose—that of guaranteeing a minimum capacity to engage in or defend against overt biological warfare, or acts that encourage the spread of endemic disease.

The overall acceptability of so-called defensive research may be partially evaluated by the locus of the activity. While the locale neither ensures beneficence nor the likelihood of morally acceptable outcomes, there is a greater likelihood of acceptability when the work is conducted in public and private civilian institutions than in military installations. This is so, in part because of the higher degree of public accountability in the former institutions, as well as the requirement of many public universities (like the University of California) that only unclassified work be permitted on its campuses.

Beneficence

Second, is there really an overall likelihood of beneficial application? A basic moral maxim of ethical science is that scientists by virtue of their training and the potential power of their instruments have great capacity to "disturb the universe."[14] According to philosopher and ethicist Daniel Callahan, the nature of this power imputes a special obligation of scientists to use moral imagination to anticipate the immediate and foreseeable consequences of their work.[15] A corollary to this principle is that the extent to which moral imagination is required is directly proportional to the likely adverse impact of the chosen field of inquiry. Thus, less moral imagination is needed to foresee the consequences of isolating and separating the so-called "kappa" or killer particles in *Paramecium* species (no matter how aggressive-sounding the name) than in perfecting the laser. In the first instance, it is unlikely because of species specificity and scale that serious deleterious consequences could accrue to humans from the internecine warfare conducted by paramecia. In the second instance, the ability to harness and focus vast amounts of energy into a sharply defined beam creates almost an instantaneous weapons potential, as well as the ability to cauterize or otherwise destroy diseased or cancerous tissue.

The latter case is the most difficult, since maleficent and beneficent ends, *both* extremely valuable, can be derived from the same device. Anticipating the worst possible uses of a technological innovation—and being able to somehow rein in or otherwise control it—is an extremely taxing proposition. While some would say that such an exercise is either futile or would effectively paralyze all research, a middle ground is to argue for the scientist's responsibil-

ity to anticipate the *maximum negative impact* of foreseeable consequences of the work. Such a view is consistent with virtually all
theories of moral behavior. What is at stake in evaluating the moral
legitimacy of any piece of research then is anticipating the most
likely outcomes to its application within a set of societal values.
While many (and perhaps most) outcomes of basic research cannot
be so anticipated, many of the short-term applications can.

Secrecy

Third, is the research open and unclassified and will the results of
the research be made freely available? Classified or secret research
violates traditional norms of scientific inquiry, which call for the
open and free sharing of ideas and data in a community of scholars.
A further problem of secret research is that of deception and nondisclosure, where scientists and potential human subjects alike are
ignorant of the intended or actual uses of research data. Although
violations of these norms may be accepted in periods of national
emergency, the exceptions confirm the rule. (These norms have
also been eroded by the recent increase in the volume of proprietary
research conducted at universities.)

Safety

Fourth, is the research being conducted safely? The safety of research for human subjects is not in itself a sufficient criterion for
assessing moral acceptability. The issue of *public* right to know and
be protected from risk-generating activities has become legitimized
in the last two years with the spate of legislation requiring public
disclosure of hazards posed by chemical or toxic substances
general.[16] The question of the safety of biological warfare research
is morally distinct from, and in a sense easier to resolve, than is the
issue of choosing what form of research to pursue in the first place.
The duty of protecting the public—and more specifically human
subjects—from nefarious and morally problematic research is well
developed in the form of required impact statements or appropriate
institutional reviews. These reviews are often limited to first-order
effects of the intended project.[17] This means that even extremely
nefarious and morally problematic research projects (like that
directed toward perfecting Zyklon B, an asphyxiating nerve gas
developed by German researchers to be used in the gas chambers)
could be favorably reviewed—in terms of physical risk to the public
or laboratory personnel—although it is morally repugnant because

of its intended applications. Additional review criteria are therefore desirable.

7 Case Studies

An instructive example of the application of these criteria is the case of the scientists who first isolated ricin toxin, a powerful, two-component cytological poison that has lent itself to medical studies involving selective killing of cells. It may be argued that these scientists could have been expected to foresee that it might also be used as a surreptitious agent for conducting political assassinations. Indeed, it was apparently the agent used in the infamous "umbrella murder" in Great Britain in which a Bulgarian agent was killed by being stabbed with an umbrella equipped with a syringe containing ricin.

But this same agent has been used (in modified form) as the second half of a "magic bullet" immunotoxin targeted against thyroid tissue[18] and is being tested for its effectiveness against ovarian cancer.[19] Knowing that both military and medical eventualities were plausible outcomes of their research, would the scientists who developed the immunotoxin technique be morally culpable for not alerting their colleagues about the potential misuses of their work? The answer depends on the application of the criteria developed above. In the first place, the nature of the sponsoring agency and its goals for such research would play a crucial role in this assessment. Research conducted by a public health agency and clearly aimed at achieving a cancer cure may be judged to be morally desirable, whereas similar work sponsored by a military agency may be judged to be morally suspect. In the second place, the magnitude of beneficent uses of a toxin for large numbers of cancer victims may be seen morally to outweigh the rather remote and exotic clandestine use of the same agent in covert operations directed against selected individuals.

A second example is the case of a graduate student in marine biology who was approached by the Army Command at Fort Detrick, Maryland in 1966 for a post-doctoral scholarship. Fort Detrick was then a major installation conducting both defensive and offensive biological warfare research. This biologist was a young authority on the toxic properties of a particular toxin known as saxitoxin produced by the Gonylaux organism. This toxin is responsible for the phenomenon known as "red tide," causing large economic losses for fisheries and shellfish beds. Gonylaux toxin has caused human fatalities in those who have ingested contaminated shellfish.

In his conversations with me, this scientist (who wished to remain anonymous) argued that the Detrick laboratories offered the best facilities for conducting his research, since by the nature of their ongoing projects, they housed the most sophisticated instruments for isolation and toxicity testing.[20] This researcher was also aware of the possibility that some of his work might be applied to the ongoing warfare programs at the Detrick facilities, but assured me and presumably himself, that his *own* research was going to be directed at studying the health consequences of ingestion of the red tide organism's toxin. He subsequently went to Fort Detrick and isolated the red tide toxin, some of which was allegedly used in CIA-mediated assassination schemes. Could he be held morally blameworthy for this decision?

From the perspective developed in this chapter, the answer would be yes. He knew in advance both the extreme toxicity of the chemical he was isolating and the context of his work (a military installation conducting classified research). That context virtually assured that others would study, use or otherwise subvert his own efforts to maintain ideological purity by amalgamating the research to the ends of the institution. Fort Detrick was a known biological warfare facility during this period, and its staff would be likely to bring his toxin studies to bear on warfare-related issues.

The counterargument is that as long as the research was legal (in 1966–1969—the period of this research—the 1925 Biological Weapons Treaty had not yet been ratified by the United States) and his own research was designed and directed toward resolving and perhaps reversing a major human health problem, he was blameless for the uses to which others eventually put his work. This view is based on the premise that scientific knowledge is morally neutral, and that the eventual uses to which it may be put are outside the ken of even the most percipient researcher. Such a position belies a duty (argued here) to assess the likelihood that certain knowledge or data will be misused. It would be disingenuous for the scientist who is isolating a potent biotoxin to claim that his research is morally equivalent to work on the size of stamens or petals on a flowering plant.

In the saxitoxin instance, the scientist may be held to the moral requirement to assess the likelihood of misuse of his toxin. Moral imagination is the lifeblood of the scientist. It is in the very nature of science to anticipate the causal links and uses of knowledge, and to generate those chains of association and linkage into the future that have the most likely prospect for success. Researchers who design studies of the toxicity of particular biological agents in the setting of a biological warfare institution must be seen as lending themselves to, if not actually participating in, evil.

8 Implementing the Ethical Assessment of Biological Warfare Research

It is one of the contentions of this chapter that moral criteria independent of treaty compatibility or public health questions can suffice to condemn biowarfare research. On the basis of the preceding analysis, a series of questions concerning biological warfare research may be developed, the answers to which help determine the moral culpability of scientists engaging in this research:

1. How direct is the applicability of research results to weapons development or production?

2. What is the mission of the agency sponsoring the research?

3. What potential has the work for achieving beneficial and nonmilitary application?

4. May the results be freely published?

The criteria these questions invoke take cognizance of both deontological and consequentialist perspectives; they embrace the more restricted criteria used in table 4.1; and they summarize the essential moral questions uncovered in examining the test cases considered. The legality of the research or its safety is omitted as tangential to strictly ethical evaluation.

Below, I discuss several mechanisms for screening research and for discouraging morally proscribed research that could be implemented by research institutions, the scientific community, and legislatures.

Human Subject and Animal Experimentation Committees in Research Institutions

At present there is no formal mechanism for assessing the goals and societal implications of research. Peer review panels established by funding agencies evaluate only the scientific validity of research design and purpose. Human subject and animal experimentation committees in research institutions would provide a reasonable mechanism for reviewing biological research for its social and ethical impact. Presently, these committees are governed by federal regulations that limit their purview to certain identifiable classes of subjects.[21] These committees are also limited to assessing the impact of research on human subjects or on animals. Although scientists are often asked (although they are not required) in federal grant forms to provide an assessment of possible societal *benefits* from their research, there is no parallel request for assessment of *risks* or *harms*.[22]

The responsibilities of human subject and animal research committees might however be extended to encompass review of the broad social and ethical impact of research. Scientists engaged in research with real or potential human pathogens or toxins would be required to file with their studies a Maximum Negative Impact Statement (MNIS), an analog to an Environmental Impact Statement, that indicates foreseeable societal consequences of their work in terms of (1) the likelihood of misuse, (2) the probability of environmental or public health harms associated with the conditions of the study, *and* (3) future harms from foreseeable applications.

This may appear to be an arduous and burdensome requirement, but it is morally required. It fulfills a gap in our ethics of experimentation, namely, that we have never required researchers to examine the long-term consequences of their work. (This objective was originally intended to be in the guidelines for human experimentation, but was removed with the understanding that such a review would be conducted where necessary by a Presidential Ethics Committee that never materialized.)

If every scientist were required to perform a causal chain of extrapolation to every imaginable consequence of his or her work, it could paralyze the research effort and lead to absurd consequences. For work involving harmful biological agents, however, it *is* reasonable to require a MNIS where scientists engage in a less extreme version of this exercise to demonstrate the absence or relative absence of probable societal harms from their work, particularly when it is conducted at military installations which have historically supported biological weapons applications.

Scientific Societies

Scientific societies involved with microbiological or toxicological research should prohibit members from participation in work that violates our treaty obligations or contributes to morally unacceptable forms of warfare using biological systems. A clear statement proscribing research that directly aids or abets the biological warfare program would be most desirable. For example, the pledge against the military use of biological research being circulated by the Council for Responsible Genetics commits biologists and chemists "not to engage knowingly in research and teaching that will further the development of chemical and biological warfare agents" (appendix K).

Societal Response

Regulation of scientific research is problematic, since broad proscriptions (e.g., limitations on fetal research) can lead to unforeseen constraints on potentially valuable research programs (e.g., the use of fetal tissue for brain grafts). Similarly, a ban or limitation on toxin research or some other sub-set of biological weapons systems will inevitably constrain bona fide research directed towards public health ends. Thus, the public response must focus on the institutions in which military research in the biological sciences is conducted. They should be accessible to oversight and review, and be part of the international inspection program implied by disarmament treaties. They should be required to publish lists of studies conducted under their auspices, and to disclose the results of all research and development to congressional committees.

9 Conclusions

I have argued in this chapter that all offensive and some forms of ostensibly "defensive" biological warfare research are inevitably unethical to the extent that they have a high likelihood of causing harm to innocent persons, increase the likelihood of use of unlawful agents, and require the participation of scientists in immoral programs that pervert the uses of science. Virtually all research directed to achieving the capacity to conduct such warfare is likewise ethically questionable to the extent that it requires experimentation in cases where there is little or no bona fide scientific or therapeutic rationale. Classified or secret research also violates the internal norms of scientific inquiry that call for the open and free sharing of ideas and data in a community of scholars. A further problem of secret research is that of deception and nondisclosure, in which scientists and potential human subjects alike are kept in the dark about the intended or actual uses of research data.

Even if it could be shown that acquiring the capacity to wage, but not actually to use, biological warfare serves as a deterrent to others to do the same (a highly questionable proposition), the acquisition of the power necessary to conduct an offensive warfare program would be counter to international treaty and human morality. Hence, direct limitations on biological warfare installations and on research and development programs are justified on ethical grounds.

These recommendations are broader than the legal authority defined by the Biological Weapons Convention but consistent with its larger goal of excluding completely the possibility of use of biological agents and toxins as weapons. Scientific studies of immunization, vaccine development protocols, toxin isolation, or protective equipment are justified when conducted openly as part of a public health effort, but are legally and ethically unacceptable when they enhance the capacity to wage biological warfare, no matter how remote the research from field conditions of use.

Research which can be reasonably foreseen to increase the likelihood of biological warfare is unethical. This position drives the calculus of ethical inquiry in biological research in general, and makes void the notion that biological warfare research can be done ethically.

Acknowledgment

The thoughtful and generous contribution of Susan Wright to the organization of the arguments used in this chapter is gratefully acknowledged.

Notes

1. Ann Van Wynen Thomas, and A.J. Thomas, Jr., *Legal Limits on the Use of Chemical and Biological Weapons* (Dallas: Southern Methodist University Press, 1970).
2. Colin Norman, "Biological Defense Defended," *Science* 240 (1988), 981.
3. Statement of Colonel David L. Huxsoll, Commander of the Medical Reserch Institute of Infectious Diseases, Fort Detrick, Maryland, cited in Malcolm W.

Browne, "Defenses to Biological Weapons Tested by Army in China and Argentina," *New York Times* (6 February 1989), 7.

4. Defense Intelligene Agency, *Soviet Warfare Threat*, Publication No. DST–1610F–057–86, 1986, 5.

5. An epidemic of Rift Valley Fever on the Senegal River in West Africa was partially controlled through the use of a vaccine developed by the U.S. Army Medical Research Institute of Infectious Diseases: see John Walsh, "Rift Valley Fever Rears its Head," *Science*, 240 (1988), 1397–1399.

6. Martin Gumpert, *Duvant: The Story of the Red Cross*, Oxford (London, 1938).

7. Oath of Hippocrates, In: "General Codes for the Practice of Medicine," *Encyclopedia of Bioethics*, Warren T. Reich, ed., (New York, the Free Press, 1972), Volume 4, Appendix, 1731.

8. Principles of Medical Ethics (1957) with Reports and Statements, American Medical Association, in *Encyclopedia of Bioethics, op. cit.*, Appendix, 1751.

9. Declaration of Geneva, World Medical Association, in *Encyclopedia of Bioethics, op. cit.*, Appendix, 1749.

10. British Medical Association, *The Torture Report*, (London, BMA, 1986); see also Leonard A. Sagan, "Torture and the Health Profession," in *Encyclopedia of Bioethics, op. cit.*, Volume 3, 1354–1356.

11. Anonymous, "Buenos Aires Oath, April 1988", Professional Ethics Report 1 (3): 1, (Summer 1988), 1.

12. "Final Regulations Amending Basic HHS Policy for the Protection of Human Research Subjects: Final Rule 45 CFR 46," *Federal Register: Rules and Regulations*, 46 (16) (26 January 1981), 8366–8392. See also 45 CFR 46.111 wherein it states, "In evaluating the risks and benefits, the IRB should consider only those risks and benefits that may result from the research (as distinguished from risks and benefits of therapies subjects would receive even if not participating in the research). The IRB should not consider possible long-range effects of applying knowledge gained in the research (for example, the possible effects of the research on public policy) as among those research risks that fall within the purview of its responsibility."

13. Marc Lappé, "Reflections on the Non-Neutrality of Hypothesis Formation," *Chinical Research*, 24 (1976), 56–63.

14. Freeman Dyson, *Disturbing the Universe*, New York: Harper and Row, 1979.

15. Daniel Callahan, "Ethical Responsibility in Science in the Face of Uncertain Consequences," *Annals of the New York Academy of Sciences* 265 (1976), 1–12.

16. Title III, *Superfund Amendments and Reauthorization Act of 1986*, "Emergency Planning and Community Right to Know."

17. Robert M. Veatch, *The Patient as Partner: A Theory of Human Experimentation Ethics*, Bloomington: University of Indiana Press, 1987, 78 ff.

18. D.P. Rennie et al., "An Immunotoxin of Ricin A Chain Conjugated to Thyroglobulin Selectively Suppresses the Anti-Thyroglobulin Autoantibody Response," *Lancet* 2 (10 December 1983), 1338–1340.

19. Personal communications from Dr. Vera Byers, Xoma Corporation, Emeryville, CA, November 19, 1986.

20. Personal communications, September 10, 1969.

21. These subjects include fetuses and pregnant women ("Protection of Human Subjects: Fetuses, Pregnant Women and in Vitro Fertilization," *Federal Register*, 40 (8 August 1975), 33526–33552; the mentally disabled ("Protection of Human

Subjects: Proposed Regulations on Research Involving Those Institutionalized as Mentally Disabled," *Federal Register* 43 (17 November 1978): 53950–53956); and children ("Additional Protections for Children Involved as Subjects of Research: Final Rule: 45 CFR 46 *Federal Register*, (8 March 1983) 9814–9820).

22. See "Final Regulations," 45 CFR 46, 8389, which documents that risks and harms may not be considered. According to Charles McKay of the Office for Protection from Research Risks (personal communication to the University of Illinois IRB office, February 22, 1989), this regulation does not intend to preclude consideration of the long-range benefits of applying human knowledge gained in the research.

III

The Military and the New Biology

5

New Forms of Biological Warfare?

Richard Novick and Seth Shulman

When the Nixon administration unilaterally renounced biological weapons in 1969, the move was predicated on the view that biological agents could have little or no military utility. After reviewing the information available at the time, President Nixon's advisors found biological weapons to be unreliable and unpredictable and subject not only to great variability in attack and survival rates but also to great uncertainty because of their dependence on environmental conditions. Biological agents, the administration realized, could spread out of control and initiate epidemics in civilian populations on either side of an armed conflict and could readily backfire locally; furthermore, their use would be met with universal repugnance and might trigger a nuclear response.

In fact, the case against the military utility of biological weapons was so strong that the Nixon administration even felt confident that stockpiles of biological weapons would be useless as a deterrent, and hence need not be maintained. The rationale for this decision, then, was that neither military capability nor national security would be compromised by the unilateral renunciation of this category of weapons regardless of the policies adopted by other countries. The use of biological weapons would be so risky for any party concerned that the U.S. did not feel threatened by the prospect of giving them up completely. As described elsewhere in this book, the administration policy and its underlying view of biological agents helped to set the stage for the ensuing Biological Weapons Convention of 1972 (chapter 2).

Two decades after Nixon's bold policy decision, the Reagan administration adopted a very different attitude towards the dangers of biological warfare, claiming that biological weapons presented a new threat to national security. As Assistant Secretary of

Defense Douglas Feith told Congress in August 1986: "The prevailing judgment of years ago that biological warfare is not a militarily significant weapon is now quite unsustainable. Biological warfare can be designed to be effective across the spectrum of combat, including special operations and engagements at the tactical level."[1]

Judging from the three-fold increase in military funding for biological weapons research between FY 1981 and FY 1987, and from the accounts given by Feith and others in the administration, it is clear that the Reagan administration believed something in the equation had changed since the 1969 unilateral renunciation of biological weapons. As far as the technology of genetic engineering is concerned, this view would seem reasonable enough at first glance: the Nixon administration's decision to renounce biological weapons just slightly predated the birth of recombinant DNA technology—a virtual revolution in microbiology. In fact 1972, the year that the Biological Weapons Convention was signed, was also the year that the first gene-splicing experiments were performed.[2] Even at that time few fully anticipated the speed and breadth of the far-reaching advances to come in the field of genetic engineering and other areas of biotechnology.

But has the advent of biotechnology made a difference to the military utility of biological weapons, either in actuality or in perception? Could the enhanced power over the behavior and properties of living things provided by genetic engineering be used to produce more effective biological weapons? And, if so, how much more effective?

The answers to such questions must remain speculative. Because of the strong barriers to the development of novel biological weapons, there is presently no publicly available evidence to indicate that these possibilities have been pursued so far. Concerns about the application of genetic engineering and other forms of biotechnology for weapons purposes, however, have been stimulated both by the expansion of military activity in this area and by claims from certain voices within the U.S. government that biotechnology makes it feasible to develop novel—and potentially usable—biological weapons. The purpose of this chapter is to examine these claims.

To be accepted as useful in a war-fighting scenario, a weapon must meet standards of reliability, targetability, and practicality. To understand the way in which biological weapons fit these criteria requires a brief discussion of the different types of conceivable uses for such weapons.

There are two basic types of military scenarios. The first is *strategic*—the waging of war at the international, or intercontinental level. In a strategic scenario, biological agents would be dropped as bombs or released as aerosols from aircraft, or transported by missile to a foreign adversary nation. With biological weapons used in this manner, the target would obviously be predominantly the civilian population; military targets would be irrelevant. As the Nixon administration realized, such a scenario would be senseless because of its unreliability, its inhumanity, and because it could trigger a nuclear response; it could also boomerang—the disease-causing agents spreading back to infect the aggressor nation's population. It is also highly improbable that the capability to launch biological weapons would serve as any sort of deterrent.

In a *tactical* scenario, namely a local theater or battlefield situation, biological agents could be disseminated by troops in a ground conflict, or locally by air or aerosol, with the aggressor's troops protected by specialized, protective clothing and/or vaccines against the agent. Here again, unreliability would be a major detriment; the threat would require troops to wear unwieldy protective clothing which would hamper field operations and lower morale.

Overall, strategic and tactical uses of biological warfare can easily be discounted on grounds of impracticality, as recognized by President Nixon, and it seems absurd to consider any need to possess biological warfare capability so as to respond "in kind" to an attack.

A complete accounting of military uses of biological agents, however, must include the possibility of *covert warfare* where the aggressor would not be identified. Here, an attacker nation would release a biological weapon surreptitiously (for example, in the water system) to undermine an adversary's troops or civilian population. The only practical difference between such a scenario and the open military use of biological agents would be that, theoretically at least, retaliation (such as a nuclear response) could possibly be avoided because the aggressor would remain anonymous. The danger of spread would, of course, remain the same in such a case.

Aside from the above military uses of biological agents, the possibility also exists for paramilitary and terrorist actions involving their use. One such case is in a situation in which overt military action against an adversary would appear unacceptable and subversion is attempted. With biological agents, a small nation, for example, could conceivably be undermined by a larger one desiring to remove or replace that country's government. A biological agent could be used to create an epidemic or to destroy crops or livestock. Here genetic engineering techniques could help to assure that the agent used infected only a specific target or region (conceivably, for instance, an agent might be engineered that was infectious only in a certain climate or environment). Genetic engineering techniques could also be used to help ensure that the agent, when released, would be difficult or impossible to trace.

This last possibility seems to us to be far and away the most likely potential use of biological warfare and most of our thinking is focused on this possibility.

Finally, the possible use of biological weapons by terrorists is certainly a horrifying prospect and one to which no population group would be immune. The possibilities are obvious enough; here, however, one need not be concerned about use of genetic engineering since any imaginable terrorist objective would be very adequately served by existing microorganisms; additionally, it is not likely that most terrorist organizations would have the scientific sophistication necessary to perform gene splicing and then test the results. Whether anything could be done in the way of prevention or defense against such a scenario seems rather doubtful.

Advances in molecular genetics and biotechnology have yielded a variety of new techniques, each of which could, to a varying degree, incrementally remove specific obstacles to the development of potentially more usable biological weapons. While these advances are significant, it is difficult to see how their application could possibly eliminate the fundamental uncertainty and unpredictability of biological agents in open warfare, or how they could diminish the universal horror associated with their use.

At least in the short and medium term these new techniques do little to alter the analysis that guided the Nixon administration's initial renunciation of this form of warfare, especially in strategic or tactical war-fighting scenarios. In short, unleashing disease-causing pathogens, genetically manipulated or not, does not make for an effective or useful military strategy.

As we discuss below, however, the use of biological agents in covert or subversive actions does remain a serious threat. Currently existing microorganisms could be used to cause local human epidemics or to infect crops, livestock, or water supplies. It is also conceivable that the usefulness of such biological agents for these types of application could be substantially improved by either classical or modern genetic manipulation. But the threat of covert or subversive uses of biological agents existed twenty years ago as well and has not been fundamentally altered by the latest techniques. It is more likely, in our view, that modern molecular biology has fired the military imagination and engendered the irrational fear of being outdone by the Russians rather than providing the substantive wherewithal for the creation of more useful biological weapons.

1 Background: Genetic Technology

Deoxyribonucleic acid (DNA) (or in the case of certain viruses, ribonucleic acid, RNA) is the chemical substance of genes, serving the dual function of hereditary transmission and of programming the cell to perform its biological functions. In chemical terms DNA is an exceedingly long, double-stranded linear helical polymer composed of four low-molecular-weight subunits known as nucleotides, namely adenine, thymine, guanine, and cytosine, commonly abbreviated as A, T, G, and C, respectively. A gene consists of up to several thousand of these units, arranged like beads on a string, in an absolutely specific order. The double-stranded structure of DNA entails an explicit and rigid complementarity such that wherever there is an A on one strand, there is a T on the other and similarly for G and C. A-T and G-C are known as base pairs (nucleotides are referred to as bases because they are chemically basic rather than acidic; the acid in deoxyribonucleic acid is the phosphoric acid which serves as the linking group between adjacent nucleotides in the chain) and their complementarity is due to their individual chemical structures.

The specific sequence of nucleotides in any segment of DNA constitutes the genetic information which is contained in that DNA in the form of a three-letter code where each triplet, or codon, specifies one of the twenty amino acids of which all proteins are composed. The code is read out sequentially, with certain codons serving as start and stop signals for the cellular process by which the information encoded in the DNA is translated into the amino acid sequence of a protein. Bacteria, which are free-living microorganisms with a single chromosome and a relatively simple cellular organization, have evolved specific enzymes, known as restriction enzymes, that

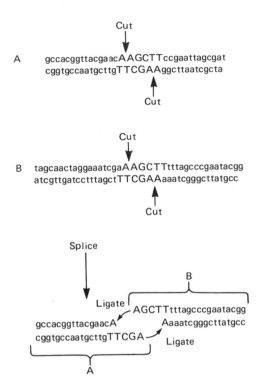

Figure 5.1
Two random DNA sequences, A and B, are shown, each with the 6-base
recognition site for EcoRI restriction enzyme, with the positions of the cutting
sites, staggered by four bases. Below: the left half of sequence A is shown joined to
the right half of B, using the complementary base pairing of the single-stranded
4-base regions generated by the enzyme.

attack the DNA of invading parasites such as bacterial viruses.
These restriction enzymes recognize certain short nucleotide sequences, usually four or six nucleotides, and cut both strands
of the DNA chain wherever such sequences are found. Often, the
cuts on both strands are staggered, leaving two or four nucleotides
protruding on each new end, as shown in figure 5.1. If two unrelated DNA segments, A and B, from different species, possess the
same hexanucleotide recognition sequence, here, AAGCTT, both
will be cut by the same restriction enzyme at this site, as shown. If
this reaction is performed in a test tube and the resulting products
are mixed, they will re-associate in a pairwise manner, with half of
the re-associations producing the A-B hybrid that is shown in the
diagram. Another enzyme, known as ligase, is then added, which

1

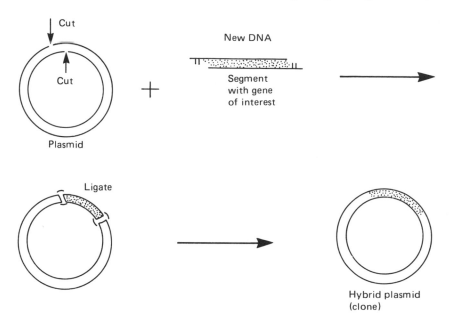

Figure 5.2

Top: the process shown in figure 5.1 is used to join a short DNA segment (a),
prepared from a much larger molecule by cutting with a restriction enzyme, to a
plasmid (b) that has been cut with the same enzyme. Bottom: The ligation process
and the hybrid plasmid produced.

re-attaches the matching ends, establishing chemical continuity.
This simple process is the basis of recombinant DNA, or gene-
splicing technology. Following the cut-and-splice process, which
occurs in the test-tube, one needs a method of returning the spliced
DNA molecule to an intracellular environment so that its coding
function can be used and so that it can multiply. Most commonly
used for this purpose are relatively small, free-living circular DNA
species known as plasmids that inhabit most bacterial cells. These
are easy to isolate and can be used to insert new DNA segments as
shown in figure 5.2. The hybrid plasmid, or clone, can then be
returned to the bacterial cell, where it will multiply and where any
protein encoded by the cloned DNA segment will be produced by
the bacterial cell.

This, then, is the essence of recombinant DNA technology at
its simplest. In actual practice, many highly sophisticated developments have added greatly to the versatility of this technology,
making it possible to clone and modify at will any gene from any

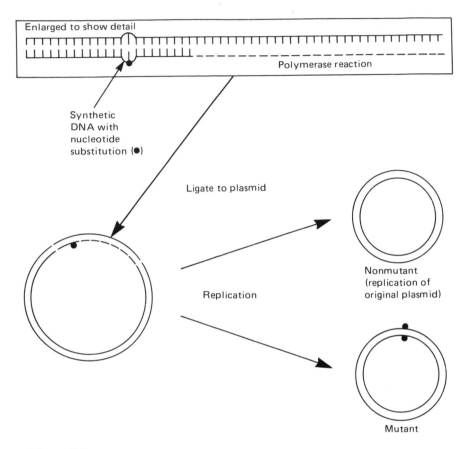

Figure 5.3
A synthetic DNA molecule with one base incorrect is hybridized to a single-stranded preparation of the DNA to be mutated. The synthetic DNA is enlarged by extension with DNA polymerase, using the other strand as template. The extended DNA is then cut with an appropriate restriction enzyme and ligated to a plasmid as in figure 5.2. After replication, one molecule has the mutation on both strands, the other on neither.

organism. One of these developments, namely that of introducing specific mutations, is especially relevant to this discussion. The sequence of nucleotides in a DNA chain can now be determined chemically and it is possible to synthesize chemically a short stretch of DNA (up to 50 nucleotides is quite simple). To create a simple mutation (a change in a single nucleotide) one synthesizes a short DNA segment incorporating the desired change, allows another enzyme, polymerase, to complete the copying, and then attaches the product to a plasmid, as shown in figure 5.3. Here, the desired DNA fragment is prepared, the strands are separated (by heating), the synthetic DNA is allowed to pair, and the rest copied by polymerase.

From this very brief description it should be clear that we now have powerful tools for exchanging genetic material between totally unrelated organisms and for modifying the existing genetic information, especially of microorganisms such as bacteria and viruses, essentially at will.

In some cases, such as mammalian genes for insulin, growth hormone, or interferon, genetic engineering can provide the means of producing large quantities of rare and important substances. In other cases, such as the bacterial genes for botulin toxin, enterotoxin, or diphtheria toxin, these techniques can create a novel organism that produces a specific substance of military interest in large quantities. In still other cases, random segments of DNA from a disease-causing organism could be introduced into a second species and the recombinants tested for the acquisition of disease-causing ability. This latter type of experiment permits the identification of specific genetic functions that are involved in the causation of disease and is thus of major medical interest; since it could also create novel organisms with modified disease-causing potential, it could be of major military interest as well.

From the outset it is important to note that, for biological reasons, it is very unlikely that such a hybrid bacterial organism would be more pathogenic than either of the parental species from which it was derived; rather, it might combine certain desirable characteristics of one species—immunological properties, adaptation to new environment, survival characteristics—with the disease-causing potential of the other and so make a more effective biological weapon.

Because the ability to cause disease is due to a highly complex set of very poorly understood biological traits and because current knowledge does not fully encompass the understanding of these traits for any organism, it is likely that such hybrids could be biologically effective only if constructed from very closely related species. For example, a gene for invasiveness from *Yersinia pseudotuberculosis* has been shown by Falkow and coworkers to function effectively in *Escherichia coli.*[3] This type of hybrid could be of potential interest as a biological weapon. Any attempt to do this with unrelated organisms is likely to interfere adversely with the highly developed and integrated pattern of characteristics that constitute pathogenicity. Aside from the biological obstacles, the value inherent in the construction of hybrid pathogens and their potential value to the military is unclear; the release of any successful hybrid would entail dangers far greater than any possible military advantage could justify.

Given the current nature of genetic engineering, concerns about the creation of new and highly pathogenic diseases are therefore misplaced. More practical and realistic from a military standpoint are modifications of existing biological agents that could potentially allow them to overcome specific obstacles which currently hamper their utility as weapons. We suspect, therefore, that this objective underlies to a considerable extent the renewed interest of the U.S. military in biological research, despite the official position that all current military biological research is solely for defensive purposes.

The biological warfare defense program has directed much energy to the development of vaccines against highly exotic pathogens, such as Marburg and Lassa fever viruses. While humanitarian purposes are surely served, one must nevertheless question the motivations behind such developmental research. As vaccines are generally too slow-acting to be used following an attack, it is unlikely that they could be useful defensive agents unless all troops are vaccinated against all possible agents in advance. There seems to be no intention to do this, so far as an outside observer can tell. Much more useful, however, is the possession of a vaccine against an agent that one may contemplate using as an offensive weapon. Even if this is not the true motivation, it will be perceived as such and will inevitably serve to unbalance the international biological warfare situation, possibly triggering an international biological warfare arms race.

Because, in our view, these efforts could theoretically make biological weapons more usable and thus pose the greatest potential threat to the existing Biological Weapons Convention, we now turn our attention to categorizing possible types of genetic modifications to existing agents, including state-of-the-art research and beyond. It is important to note, however, that many of the following modifications could be achieved, in principle, by conventional microbiological methods and that it is not always obvious how gene splicing could be applied.

2 Genetic Technologies and New Biological Weapons

Modification of Physical Characteristics

The physical characteristics of biological agents often present obstacles to their potential use as weapons. A given biological agent's ability to withstand a broad range of temperature, humidity, and other environmental factors clearly affects its survival during storage and dissemination. Genetic engineering techniques could be used to alter these physical characteristics, increasing (or decreasing) a biological agent's ability to survive in a given environment.

Many examples of such genetic manipulation could easily be imagined, but one important example involves the dispersal of biological agents by means of aerosols; aerosol dispersal is an area of particular interest because it has been a standard scenario in biological warfare and has been widely tested in the past. It is well recognized as a particularly effective means of military dispersal at either the tactical or strategic level. Other types of dispersal of biological agents, such as by insect vectors, seem to be considerably more unwieldy (although these methods have been investigated in some detail and continue to be given serious consideration).[4]

The dispersal of biological agents in aerosol form presents several practical problems. Organisms contained in aerosol particles are sensitive to various adverse environmental factors such as desiccation and radiation. Certain bacteria are highly resistant to radiation and this resistance is due to a relatively small number of genes. These genes could readily be transplanted into a radiation-sensitive pathogenic organism with the intention of improving its ability to survive the radiation it would receive when aerosolized.

Modification of Biological Characteristics

Those interested in the possibility of biological weapons have occasionally expressed an interest in developing a pathogenic organism that was specific for a particular racial type.[5] Clearly if this could be accomplished in any truly reliable way it could pose a heinous, though conceivably more usable biological agent, particularly as a subversive or even overt weapon for use against a genetically homogenous population.

There is clearly no human "racial" subpopulation that is sufficiently homogeneous to be uniformly and uniquely susceptible to any pathogenic organism. Nevertheless, many genes have differing distributions among various subgroups, and a misguided attempt to develop some organism with a preference for one or another subpopulation based on uneven gene distributions is imaginable. Practically speaking, however, any such research would seem quite absurd in the modern world: aside from the improbability (or impossibility) of success, extensive testing of human subjects would be required, and this must be regarded as unthinkable.

Modification of Immunological Properties

As the history of genetic engineering to date has shown, the most soluble problems tend to be those where clearly understood, specific genetic mechanisms are involved. The immunological properties of an organism are based on the number and nature of its antigens, the substances it possesses that are capable of evoking the immune response. Therefore, changes in the antigenic structure of an infective agent may allow it to bypass the natural or acquired immunity of a target population. Changes of this type may be the most attractive application of gene splicing to biological warfare.

Antigenic modification would involve primarily viruses since the substances that evoke protective immunity are usually proteins that are located on the surface of the virus particle and are relatively easy to identify. Here, for example, one could modify the gene for an immunity-evoking surface protein or could replace it with a similar gene from a related virus. This happens spontaneously with influenza virus and is a common and problematic characteristic of this virus. Antigenic variation occurs in HIV, the AIDS virus, and is largely responsible for the difficulty in developing a vaccine for the virus. If the antigenic structure of a virus were modified for biological warfare purposes, it could then bypass any immunity in the target population while the attacker could immunize its own personnel, and conceivably, even its own civilian population.

Another advantage of such a technique would be that many of the highly sensitive methods currently available for detecting and identifying bacteria, viruses, and other infectious agents, such as monoclonal antibodies, radio-immuno assays, etc., rely mainly on the detection of certain specific antigens on the surface of living agents. Modification of antigenic specificity would have the added advantage of making the agent harder to detect and identify and hence more difficult to counter.[6]

While the scenario is surely a frightening one, the uncertainties involved are almost overwhelming and the practical difficulties virtually insurmountable. For a nation even to seriously consider the inclusion of such a weapon in its arsenal much research would have to be done, partly with human subjects, as there would be no guarantee that the modified virus would be infective. Also, given the unpredictable way in which disease can spread, an attacker nation would still risk infecting its own population. Even if all the above criteria could be met, for such a biological agent to be even conceivably usable an attacker nation would have to produce an effective vaccine and immunize its civilian population weeks in advance of an attack. Needless to say, the maintenance of secrecy would be essentially impossible, as would the avoidance of vaccine-related side-effects. In this context, the recent highly unsuccessful attempt at mass immunization against swine flu should be recalled.

Introduction of Toxin Genes into Non-Toxigenic Bacteria

One biological warfare scenario, readily imagined and often heard in discussions, would be to transplant the gene for botulinum toxin into *Escherichia coli*. One could then contaminate the water supply of an enemy with a common organism capable of producing the deadliest poison known. It is fortunately doubtful, or at least highly uncertain, that such an organism would perform as desired, primarily because *E. coli* does not secrete protein products into the surrounding environment and secondarily because toxins are characteristically produced by bacteria only under special conditions—which might not be met in an environment (the *E. coli* cell) that is abnormal for the production of the toxin.

Although in principle such an organism could be used with effect only in a country with poor sanitation and public health practices, no sane government would contemplate releasing it because once released there would be no way to control its spread and it could easily turn up anywhere in the world.

Other possibilities might involve diphtheria toxin, staphylococcal enterotoxins, or ricin and might employ *Streptococcus fecalis*, a fecal organism that can contaminate water supplies and can secrete proteins. As with the other types of experiments that could be contemplated, much laboratory work would be required to establish effectiveness. With toxins however, this research would not require human subjects.

In balance, in military terms, the use of toxin-producing organisms is hardly a particularly effective means of delivering an active dose of toxin to a large number of people in a short time. From this perspective the toxin itself would appear more effective; certainly genetic engineering technology could be used to develop a bacterial strain capable of producing any toxin in much larger amounts than those produced by the native organism. This, however, would provide an advantage only in production.

A more novel approach using toxins would be to create hybrid molecules by genetic engineering. Here, one would splice two or more genes or parts of genes to produce a protein with a desired structure. The possibilities are limitless here: hybrids between toxin and antibody molecules have been constructed with the purpose of targeting the toxin to cells, such as cancer cells, recognized by the antibody.

Here, conceivably, might be an opportunity for the development of an "ethnic" weapon. It would first be necessary to accomplish the improbable feat of identifying a protein specific for a particular population group, developing an antibody against this protein, then connecting this to a toxin by gene splicing. The construction would have to be cleverly engineered so that the toxin would be activated only as a consequence of the reaction between the antibody and the targeted protein. Moreover, the material would probably have to be administered by injection. This idea, at present, would have to be regarded as science fiction; the same objections would hold as for other types of "ethnic" weapons.

Additionally, rumors have been heard from time to time that experimentation was afoot to construct double- or triple-toxin molecules as weapons. While no substantiation of such rumors has been found, there is also no obvious advantage that such molecules might have over the individual toxins.

3 Implications

As the above discussion illustrates, the advent of genetic engineering does offer many new and enhanced options that could be employed in the development of biological weapons. However, none of these techniques can, in the foreseeable future, fundamentally alter the factors that have traditionally caused biological agents to be regarded as virtually useless as weapons for open warfare, namely the unpredictability and uncertainty associated with their use. An additional disadvantage specific for genetically engineered organisms is that they can readily be identified as gene-spliced products.

Covert or terrorist uses of biological warfare must remain a cause for concern in this area. With terrorism, as with defense against any type of unknown biological agent that might be used in any military or paramilitary scenario, genetic engineering can do little or nothing in any real sense to create a true anti-bioweapons defense, despite any government posturing to the contrary. While a good deal of military-sponsored vaccine research is currently underway, it has been pointed out frequently that vaccines would be useful only in the face of positive intelligence with respect to the nature of the hostile agent; treatment with drugs such as antibiotics would be useful only for bacteria and only after the isolation and testing of the organism.

It is virtually inconceivable therefore, that a civilian population could be protected against a surprise biological attack unless one knew with certainty the identity of the agent and could therefore administer the appropriate vaccine well in advance of the attack. The same argument would hold for livestock, and it is unclear that any type of protection or defense could be used for crops or other plant life. This leaves only protective clothing as a truly defensive posture against a possible biological warfare attack.

Meanwhile, because of the power of the new technology of genetic engineering, and because of the fear that it quite naturally engenders about its potential use to design novel weapons, it is perhaps easy to understand how the issue provides fertile ground for inflammatory and near-hysterical rhetoric. Whether in a calculated attempt to justify expanding military activity in this area, or simply out of a lack of understanding of the technical issues involved, such provocative statements have occurred in the U.S. during the Reagan administration.

A good example is the series of articles which appeared in the *Wall Street Journal* and several other newspapers during the spring of 1984.[7] These articles, reportedly based upon secret CIA documents, alleged that the USSR was involved in an extensive program to develop new biological weapons by means of genetic engineering technology. The articles, presumably based on information leaked and "planted" by the U.S. government, appeared shortly before the public announcement that the Reagan administration proposed to build an aerosol-testing facility for biological agents at Dugway Proving Ground in Utah. They must therefore be regarded as fabrications designed as a "weapons gap" ploy, used so successfully with missiles. More recent examples include the inflammatory language in testimony by administration representatives before a congressional subcommittee in 1986. As cited briefly above Douglas Feith, assistant secretary of defense, told members of Congress that the Soviet Union violated not only the Biological Weapons Convention, "but every prohibition in it."

"The scale and seriousness of the Soviet BW program are formidable," Feith stated, adding that at one Soviet facility "a veritable city" of researchers live and work, isolated from the rest of their society.[8] Regardless of what kind of real or specious intelligence reports Feith's comments were based upon, such rhetoric went far to promote the dramatic increase in biological weapons-related funding during the course of the Reagan years, funding which totalled more than $60 million in FY 1988.[9]

If one accepts the argument, outlined above, that effective defenses in the age of genetic engineering are unlikely in the extreme, then one must view any program of research involving potential biological agents of warfare as potentially offensive in nature. This vision is likely to have a severely destabilizing effect at an international level, causing any nation that perceives such programs in the hands of a potential adversary to undertake similar research and leading to a dangerous—and futile—biological arms race.

As we have tried to illustrate, the biological "defense" research build-up initiated by the Reagan administration was misguided, even if the administration's claimed fear of similar Soviet research into biological warfare agents was valid. The overriding unpredictability and genocidal characteristics of biological agents continues to make them a particularly repugnant *global threat* rather than a weapon of war, and because of this the U.S. must continue to abide unflaggingly by its complete renunciation of their production, stockpiling, or deployment. Because no defense against the panoply of possible agents is practicable, the only viable response to the potential threat of terrorist or subversive uses of biological agents is an open dialogue between major powers on the issue to avoid undue suspicion, and a continued forceful renunciation of the use of any such dangerous and unwieldy weaponry.

Notes

1. Testimony by Deputy Assistant Secretary of Defense for Negotiations Policy Douglas J. Feith before the Subcommittee on Oversight and Evaluation of the House Permanent Select Committee on Intelligence, August 8, 1986. Reprinted in *Defense Issues*, vol. 1, no. 60, American Forces Information Service.

2. See, for example, Sheldon Krimsky, *Genetic Alchemy*, (Cambridge: MIT Press, 1982), chapter 2: "A Troublesome Experiment."

3. R.R. Isberg, and S. Falkow, "A Single Genetic Locus Encoded by *Yersina pseudotuberculosis* Permits Invasion of Cultured Animal Cells by *E. coli* K-12," *Nature* 317 (September), 262–264.

4. According to DOD reports, researchers at Fort Detrick conducted experiments concerning animal and insect vectors as early as the 1950s, including major studies on yellow-fever-bearing mosquitoes, plague-infected fleas, ticks with tularemia, and flies carrying cholera, anthrax, and dysentery. See, for example: U.S. Senate, Subcommittee on Health and Scientific Research, Committee on Human Resources, *Hearings, Biological Testing Involving Human Subjects*, 95th Congress, 1st Session, 1977, 177–88; and Erhard Geissler, ed., *Biological and Toxin Weapons Today*, (Oxford: Oxford University Press, 1986), 32.

5. See, for example, *Military Review* (November 1970), 3, and U.S. Army Chemical Corps, "Special Report No. 160: Contamination of a Portion of the Naval Supply System," November 12, 1951 (declassified 1981) as cited in Charles Piller and Keith R. Yamamoto, *Gene Wars: Military Control Over the New Genetic Technologies* (New York: William Morrow, 1988), 99–100.

6. Geissler, ed.., *Biological and Toxin Weapons Today*, 29.

7. William Kucewicz, series of editorials, *Wall Street Journal*, (April 23, 25, 27, and May 1, 3, 8, 10, 18, 1984.)

8. Feith testimony before the Subcommittee on Oversight and Evaluation, 2.

9. DOD, Annual Report on Chemical Warfare-Biological Research Program Obligations for FY 1981 FY 1987.

6

The Hazards of Defensive Biological Warfare Programs

Jonathan King and Harlee Strauss

Introduction

Organisms dangerous to human health and welfare, such as the AIDS agent, influenza virus, dengue virus, *Bacillus anthracis*, and the fungi that produce aflatoxins, already plague human society. There is little doubt, given the fiscal resources available to the military establishments of major industrial nations and the new developments in biotechnology, that new variants of these and many other harmful organisms can be intentionally generated. Article I of the Biological Weapons Convention of 1972 pledges signatory nations "never to develop, produce, stockpile or otherwise acquire or retain . . . microbial or other biological agents, or toxins whatever their method of production, of types or in quantities that have no justification for prophylactic, protective or other peaceful purposes." However, the Convention neither proscribes biological weapons research nor the possession of quantities (not otherwise specified) of biological agents for prophylactic, protective or peaceful purposes. This has been interpreted as allowing research for defensive purposes.

The development of "defensive" BW programs requires the generation and growth of putative BW agents. Such research and development programs represent serious hazards to human health and the environment, even without progressing to the stage of implementation and use. The hazards include: (1) the direct public health danger from research with novel infectious agents directed to military needs, (2) the risks of proliferation of biological weapons defense programs as additional nations follow the leaders, and (3) the long-term danger of destabilization of the treaty regime.

Within both national and international arenas, the legitimacy of the development of a "defensive" biological warfare program rests on two major assumptions: (a) that the content of a "defensive" program differs fundamentally from the content of an "offensive" program, and (b) that it would in fact be possible to "defend" populations of humans, plants, and animals from an adversary bent on utilizing biological agents.[1] Below we outline the arguments which indicate that both of these assumptions are unfounded and fundamentally incorrect. We also discuss briefly the risk of defensive biological warfare programs to human health and the environment, and the danger of the proliferation of these programs.

The Similar Needs for Offensive and Defensive BW Programs

One characteristic of biological weapons that distinguishes them from all other weapons is their ability to reproduce. Starting with very small initial quantities of an infectious pathogen, infections of a small number of susceptible individuals can be transmitted to a substantial fraction of an entire population. This happens periodically among humans with influenza, adenovirus, and chicken pox.

A program to develop variant or nonnaturally occurring viral pathogens for offensive purposes requires development of vaccines against them for protecting troops and others who must handle the organisms. The most common traditional vaccines are inactivated forms of the virus itself. Development of a vaccine generally requires growth of an organism in sufficient quantities to provide the doses necessary to inoculate thousands to tens of thousands of individuals. Thus in the development of BW agents for offensive purposes, the preparation of the infectious agent and the vaccine against it are intimately associated both technically and strategically.

A major component of the defensive programs of a number of industrialized nations is focused on the development of vaccines directed against putative "offensive" agents. For example the current U.S. Biological Defense Research Program is developing, improving, and producing vaccines against a variety of known or suspected pathogens (see table 6.1).

The development of the vaccine will in general involve the isolation, identification, modification, and growth of the potential BW agent. In addition, both the agents and the vaccines have to be tested for efficacy, which means challenging inoculated individuals or animals with the putative BW agent. These steps—the generation of a potential BW agent, development of a vaccine against it,

Table 6.1
Selected vaccines currently under study or produced by the U.S. Army

Agent	Availability
Smallpox[a]	Stockpile
Chikungunya virus[b]	Production
Eastern encephalitis virus[a]	Stockpile
Western encephalitis virus[a]	Stockpile
Venezuelan encephalitis virus[a]	Stockpile
Dengue virus[a]	Under study
Yellow Fever virus[a]	Stockpile
Junin-Machupo virus[b]	Production
Lassa Fever virus[a,b]	Under study
Lymphocytic choriomeningitis virus[a,b]	Under study
Crimean-Congo hemorrhagic fever virus[a]	Under study
Hantaan virus[a]	Under study
Rift Valley fever virus[a,b]	Stockpile
Ebola Marburg virus[a]	Under study
Coxiella burnetti (Q fever)[b]	Production
Bacillus anthracis[a]	Stockpile
Francisella tularensis (tularemia)[a,b]	Stockpile

a. Geissler, E. "New BTW Vaccine Generation" in E. Geissler, ed., *Biological and Toxin Weapons Today (New York: Oxford University Press*, 1986) 60–61.
b. U.S. Army. *Draft Programmatic Environmental Impact Statement for the Biological Defense Research Program*, May, 1988.

and testing of the efficacy of the vaccine—are all components that would be associated with an offensive BW program. It is not that the programs "appear" similar; it is that they have many of the same components.

The vaccines may be prepared from attenuated strains of the virus which are not themselves virulent. However, the development of attenuated strains that yield effective vaccines requires a substantial research program involving the virulent parent that is the target of the attenuation.

The production of vaccines involving only protein subunits of the virus rather than the entire virus is receiving considerable attention. Preparation of such vaccines through genetic engineering reduces the need to grow up large quantities of the infectious agent, although the generation of recombinant strains entails novel hazards of their own. However, such vaccines may have limited use for defensive purposes. For example, these vaccines are unlikely to be effective against variants in which the targeted subunit (the subunit that is the basis for the vaccine) is altered.

A comprehensive defensive program will have components other than just the inoculation of the target population. In order to prepare a defense, whether physical isolation, chemical inactivation, or immunization of targets, all aspects of the biology of a putative biological weapon require study. An infectious organism must possess several characteristics to make possible its conversion into an effective biological weapon. These include: (a) infectivity; (b) virulence; (c) environmental persistence; (d) capability of being grown in large quantities; (e) stability under conditions of storage and of dispersal; and (f) resistance to routine medical countermeasures (chapter 5). A research and development program designed to protect against such putative BW agents would require similar studies. Generally, the argument presented is as follows: In order to develop defenses against such putative BW agents, it would be necessary to: (a) understand the underlying mechanisms of pathogenesis, especially those pertaining to infectivity and virulence; (b) study the mechanisms by which infectious organisms evade the immune system or acquire resistance to common antibiotics; (c) know by which routes different organisms may be dispersed, and the infectivity of the organism by each route. These studies are of course exactly what would be required for the development of a biological weapon.

In order to study the pathogenic organisms that have weapons potential adequately, it would be necessary to have significant quantities of the organism. This would be especially true for studies of means of dispersal, such as aerosolization. Thus, by-products of "defensive" research would be the knowledge and techniques necessary for large-scale production of the organism. Likewise, the study of means of dispersal and the development of effective countermeasures, such as protective clothing, would require special facilities. It may be possible to discern the difference between offensive and defensive intent by the size of the manufacturing, storage, and/ or dispersal facilities, but usually there will be a large grey area where claims of either intent will be equally convincing.

Discerning the intent of research is further complicated by the fact that much of the basic research required to alter an organism for weapons purposes contributes to important, nonmilitary uses.

These include infectious disease, toxicology, and the commercial development of microorganisms destined for environmental release for use in agriculture, mining, pollution control, and so on. For example, the study of mechanisms of pathogenesis and disease immunity has long been a central focus of researchers interested in the infectious diseases of humans, animals and plants. Similarly, research into effective medical countermeasures to diseases, including vaccines and antibiotics, has long been a focus of many health scientists. Fermenter technology and other bioprocessing techniques for both microorganisms and mammalian cell cultures are undergoing rapid development as a consequence of the commercialization of biotechnology. The level of containment of the organisms necessary in commercial settings is quite high to prevent product contamination and to comply with environmental and occupational safety standards.[2] This requirement for high containment allows similar technologies to be useful for both commercial organisms and highly pathogenic organisms with weapons potential.

The development of microorganisms for use in the environment has given impetus to research about the persistence of microorganisms in the environment and how to stabilize them for storage and dispersal.[3] Although the microorganisms being developed for commercial use are quite different from those being examined for their weapons potential, the basic mechanisms and methods for altering persistence in the environment while increasing stability for storage and dispersal purposes are likely to be similar.

In addition to the BW agent itself and protective vaccines, several other processes and associated equipment are important for both offensive and defensive purposes. These include protective clothing, methods of detection, and methods of decontamination. The development of protective clothing and masks is necessary for battlefield protection no matter who initiates an attack. Such protection is necessary for defensive purposes, as vaccines and therapeutic drugs are not likely to be effective. It may also be important following an offensive attack with a known strain of weapon if a protective vaccine is not totally effective.

Reliable, sensitive and specific methods of detection are critical both for offense and defense.[4] A method must be reliable and sensitive in order to determine that an attack has occurred. It must be specific in order to identify the organism and decide upon appropriate countermeasures. (Multiple methods of detection in the field followed by identification of the specific organism in a laboratory might be required in order to fulfill these requirements.) Reliable and sensitive methods of detection are important to the aggressor in order to determine the extent of spread of the biological agent and when an area is safe for the occupation of an unprotected population.

Methods of decontamination are important to rid an area of the harmful organism so it can be reoccupied by an unprotected population. Effective decontamination procedures are also important during the research and development stages of weapon programs in order to clean up after accidental releases of harmful organisms. In general such procedures, whether used offensively or defensively, require an understanding of an organism's ecology, mode of transmission, and the potential resevoirs that will contribute to its persistence. One of the arguments presented in testimony by the Department of Defense in support of expanding test facilities at Dugway Proving Ground was the need to test the effectiveness of decontamination procedures against the actual weapons agent— not a simulant—in the environment.[5]

The blurring of defensive and offensive programs is not limited to research, but extends to development, testing, production and training. Although it may be possible to use the scale of the project as an indicator of the intent at the development stage and beyond, there is a large grey area where offensive and defensive needs will be indistinguishable.

In summary, "offensive" and "defensive" biological warfare research programs, particularly defensive programs that focus on the properties of specific BW agents, share the same components. One has to rely on the stated intent of the program to distinguish between offensive and defensive efforts. Thus a program aimed at defenses against BW agents may easily be misconstrued by adversary nations and is provocative in character.

The Intrinsic Difficulties of Defending Against BW

A critical question in examining biological defense programs is the nature of the population to be defended. Our examination of public documents describing the U.S. Biological Defense Research Program makes clear that this program is designed to defend *troops*.[6] However, in public meetings we find uniformly that the public interprets this as referring to defense of the civilian population, and to

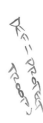

the extent they are supportive of the program, are acting on this understanding. If the basis of public support for the program is the belief in the defense of civilian populations, this needs to be closely examined.

In discussing the possibility of the defense of civilian populations from biological agents, we take as the starting point the current inability to prevent the spread of many infectious diseases in both industrialized and developing societies. Three major strategies are available for preventing or alleviating the effects of an infectious disease: (a) preventing exposure to the agent, (b) rendering the population resistant, and (c) alleviating the effects of the disease by drugs or other therapeutic measures. Our ability to control exposure to many infectious diseases in humans is quite limited;[7] recent world pandemics of influenza, the growing international problem of AIDS, and our everyday experience with the common cold are evidence of this.

Given the inability to control the spread of known agents, even during times of international cooperation, we have to assume that the control of agents introduced intentionally into local environments and ecosystems would also spread. Thus, "defenses" would have to be at the level of rendering the target population resistant or developing effective therapeutic measures.

Biological weapons can be directed against people, livestock or plants.[8] For each of these targets, there is a large collection of viruses, bacteria, fungi and other biological agents known to cause disease. For example, there are more than 200 obligate human viruses with varying degrees of virulence and 8 species of rickettsia that cause human disease.[9] This does not include the multiple variants associated with many of these species, the large number of human bacterial pathogens and their many variants, and the agents that cause disease in plants and animal populations. This enormous diversity of potential biological weapons can now be increased, virtually without limit, by the use of genetic engineering techniques and other new biotechnologies.

Protection from biological agents may be possible if the specific agent is known beforehand. This situation can only be expected to hold for a nation planning to use biological weapons. In this case as noted above, a rational strategy can be developed. But in defending against biological weapons, uncertainty as to the nature of the threatening organism or organisms is the norm.

For humans and livestock, the means of protection include vaccination in the case of viruses and the use of antibiotics in the case of sensitive bacteria. For plants, crops or cultivars resistant to the specific disease would have to be planted or an appropriate fungicide or other pesticide must be available. However, the early knowledge of the exact nature of a biological agent will in general only be available to a nation planning to use the agent in a biological warfare attack.

From the point of view of a target population, the notion of an effective defense against such agents has no basis in existing theory or technology. Neither individuals nor populations can be vaccinated against all possible naturally existing strains and variants of viruses that might be used as weapons.

The application of recombinant DNA technologies to alter viruses limits the possibilities of vaccination even against specific strains. For example, using recombinant DNA technologies, it is possible to identify and then alter the factors that affect the recognition of a virus by the human immune system. This has been the case for influenza, where epidemics have been associated with the occurrence of virus variants that have altered surface proteins. Immunity developed against a previous strain is not effective against new strains.[10] It is now possible to generate variants of influenza and other viruses in the laboratory. Again, immunization against previous outbreaks would not confer resistance against the new strain. Those producing the new strain could, of course, produce a vaccine initially protective against it.[11] Those defending against an altered viral strain would have to know the genetic alteration in order to generate an effective vaccine. However, even if the exact strain of the biological weapon were known, either by good intelligence or rapid detection and identification techniques, it is unlikely that sufficient doses of the appropriate vaccine could be delivered in a timely manner.

A similar problem exists with antibiotics. Bacterial strains can usually be generated that are resistant to most antibiotics in common use.[12] Though one could certainly find an antibiotic to which a BW bacterial agent was sensitive, the likelihood that this would be in mass production or widely available at the time of the challenge is vanishingly small.

Plants are far more susceptible to biological agents because they lack an immune system. In general, it would not be possible to protect food crops from intentional exposure to infectious agents.

Plants are a particularly vulnerable target because of the extensive use of monocultivation in modern agriculture.[13] Often all of the cultivars planted across a vast area are quite uniform. Once planted, the crop cannot usually be rapidly ploughed under or re-planted because of limits on the growing season. In addition, rapid-ly changing the cultivar in use to one resistant to a particular dis-ease would be difficult because of the amount of seed that would have to be produced (assuming that such a resistant strain could even be identified). It is perhaps in recognition of this possibility that the U.S. Biological Defense Research Program does not in-clude protection of plant or animal resources.[14]

In summary, although it may be possible to vaccinate a popula-tion against one or at most a few agents, or to develop crop strains resistant to particular plant pathogens, it is totally unrealistic to expect to protect a population from the great variety of agents that might be developed as potential weapons. Thus, the implicit assumption that "defensive" biological weapon programs can pro-vide reliable defenses of civilian populations against biological weapons is unfounded.

The Public Health and Environmental Risks of Defensive Biological Warfare Programs

An infectious pathogen, no matter how virulent, does not necessari-ly constitute a biological weapon. The military concept of a weapon involves control and specificity; the agent must maximally damage selected targets with minimal damage to friendly forces. It is un-clear whether the application of modern biotechnology will convert infectious agents to biological weapons. However, the failure of such research programs could be more hazardous than their suc-cess. For example infectious agents for which vaccines have not been developed are not useful as weapons. Yet they constitute a grave risk for researchers in the case of laboratory accidents and for domestic civilian populations in case of accidental release.

Thus the development of "defensive" biological warfare pro-grams constitutes a substantial environmental and health risk to the nation conducting the research. These risks are qualitatively dif-ferent from those associated with the development of traditional explosive munitions and with chemical or nuclear weapons develop-ment. In the former cases leaks and accidents may occur during the research and development or testing phase. However, the damage is generally local. These agents cannot reproduce themselves, even though they may cause damage over large areas. In contrast, the "leak" of a biological weapons agent may lead to its reproduction and establishment in some niche in the ecosystem.[15] Unlike the hazardous products or by-products of explosive, chemical, and nuclear weapons, it is not necessarily the case that the hazard of the released microbe or its evolving variant forms will decrease over time.

The defensive programs noted above generally require growing and testing agents thought to be related to potential BW agents. Many of these will be outright pathogens or relatives of them. Even in the absence of an accident, it will be extremely difficult to develop and test the effects of such agents on target organisms under realistic conditions without releasing them into the ecosystem.[16] In addition, as with all organisms newly introduced into an ecosystem, it will be difficult to predict their effects against nontarget organisms or new ecosystems.

Once a pathogen has entered the ecosystem, it may persist for long periods of time, causing significant disruption to the economy and/or public health of the area. For example, *Bacillus anthracis*, the bacterium responsible for anthrax, appears to be capable of establishing itself in a wide range of climates, and spores of the organism are able to persist for more than forty years. Thus the release of BW agents into the environment could lead to the creation of new and permanent reservoirs of disease.[17] A pathogen that has escaped into the environment has the potential to disperse by natural forces such as wind, water or insect vectors. The survival and dispersal properties of such microorganisms are difficult to predict or control.

The Danger of the Proliferation of Defensive Biological Warfare Programs

Because of the ambiguity between defensive and offensive BW research, the existence of military programs aimed at defenses against specific biological warfare agents is likely to generate the impetus for further expansion and proliferation of such programs. The U.S. Department of Defense itself has used the existence of such programs elsewhere as a justification for expanding its own BDRP.[18] A further justification for the program is likely to provoke other nations to initiate or expand similar programs of their own.

The Department's claim that these are purely defensive programs and largely effective against most BW threats may appeal especially to nations that feel threatened by their neighbors. Adversarial neighboring nations at various stages of industrial development exist throughout the globe.

The proliferation of defensive biological warfare programs will pose long-term threats to human health and the environment. For each program, there would be an assessment of what pathogens the adversary might develop into a weapon. Next, it would be necessary to establish research programs to generate these pathogens and to prepare defenses. These worldwide efforts will almost certainly yield as products or side products the development of variant, novel, or prophylaxis-resistant pathogens of plants, animals or humans. If these pathogens escape containment, they may threaten workers at the facility, the surrounding population, and/or the environment. The likelihood of an accidental release from containment will increase as the number of defensive BW facilities increases.

Conclusions

In recent years, there has been a disturbing shift in resources and funding in the biomedical sciences from the civilian to the military sectors. As other chapters show, the U.S. Biological Defense Research Program has grown rapidly in the 1980s (chapters 2 and 7). Some European countries are stepping up their biological defense activities (chapter 15). There have also been reports from American intelligence sources that the Soviet Union is concentrating its biotechnology resources in institutes run by the military.[19] And even within the U.S. military, there has been a shift in funding from general biomedical to defensive biological warfare research. For example, at Walter Reed Army Institute of Research, a memo circulated to personnel in 1985 stated that 31 jobs in the division of surgery would be cut, but that new spaces would be made available if the Institute formed a "credible research group in biological toxin defense."[20]

The danger of these programs is that they are likely to stimulate the very activities they are designed to anticipate and counteract. The presence of a "defense" is fundamentally destabilizing for the reasons explained above and will almost certainly be perceived as a threat, triggering a parallel response. The ensuing interaction is likely to lead to continued accusations of treaty violations and demands for increased funding for biological warfare research. The final result may well be a biological arms race. ⎫

Acknowledgment

This chapter is adapted from Harlee Strauss and Jonathan King, "The Fallacy of Defensive Biological Weapon Programmes" in E. Geissler (ed.), *Biological and Toxin Weapons Today* (Oxford: Oxford University Press, 1986).

Notes

1. H. Strauss and J. King, "The Fallacy of Defensive Biological Weapons Programmes" in E. Geissler (ed) *Biological and Toxin Weapons Today (Oxford University Press*, 1986) 66–73; Jonathan King, "The Threat and Fallacy of a Biological Arms Race," *geneWATCH* 2(2) (1985), 13–20.

2. P. Knight, "Fermentation, Special Report", *Bio/Technology* 9(5) (1988), 505–516; Office of Technology Assessment, U.S. Congress, *Commercail Biotechnology: An International Analysis* OTA-BA-218 (Washington, DC: U.S. Government Printing Office, 1984.

3. Office of Technology Assessment, U.S. Congress, *New Developments in Biotechnology—Field Testing Engineered Organisms: Genetic and Ecological Issues*, OTA-BA-350 (Washington, DC: U.S. Government Printing Office, 1988), 118.

4. United States, Report of the Secretary-General on Chemical and Bacteriological (Biological) Weapons and the Effects of their Possible Use (UN Document A/7575), 1 July 1985; Stockholm International Peace Research Institute, *The Problem of Chemical and Biological Warfare VI: Technical Aspects of Early Warning and Verification* (Stockholm: Almquist and Wiksell, 1975).

5. "Biological Defense Program," U.S. Department of Defense, Report to the Committee on Appropriations, House of Representatives, May 1986.

6. Huxsoll, D., Statement by the Commander, U.S. Army Medical Research Institute of Infectious Diseases, before the Governmental Affairs Committee, U.S. Senate, May 17, 1989. U.S. Army. Draft Programmatic Environmental Impact Statement for the Biological Defense Research Program, May, 1988.

7. J. Westwood, *The Hazard from Dangerous Exotic Diseases* (London: Macmillan, 1980).

8. United Nations, *Report of the Secretary-General on Chemical and Bacteriological (Biological) Weapons and the Effects of Their Possible Use* (New York: United Nations, 1969). Jonathan King, "The Threat of Biological Weapons," *Technology Review* 85 (1982), 10–11.

9. E.D. Kilbourne, "Introduction to Viral Diseases," in P.B. Beeson and W. McDermott (eds.), *Textbook of Medicine*, 14th ed., Philadelphia: W.B. Saunders, 1975 H. Rothschild, F. Allison, Jr., and C. Howe (eds.), *Human Diseases Caused by Viruses* (New York: Oxford Unversity Press, 1978). E.S. Murray, "Rickettsial Diseases" in P. Beeson and W. McDermott (eds.,), *Textbook of Medicine* (Philadelphia: W.B. Saunders, 1975).

10. R.G. Webster, W.G. Laver, and G.M. Air, "Antigenic variation among type A influenza viruses," in P. Palese and D.W. Kingsbury (eds.), *Genetics of Influenza Viruses* (New York: Springer-Verlag, 1983).

11. R.M. Chanock and R.A. Lerner (eds.), *Modern Approaches to Vaccines. Molecular and Chemical Basis of Virus Virulence and Immunogenicity* (Cold Harbor, NY: Cold Spring Harbor Laboratory, 1984).

12. C. Stuttard and K.R. Rozee, *Plasmids and Transposons* (New York: Academic Press, 1980).

13. J. Doyle, *Altered Harvest* (New York: Viking Press, 1985).

14. Huxsoll, 1989.

15. J. King, "New Diseases in New Niches," *Nature* 276 (1978), 47.

16. J. Tiedije, R.K. Colwell, Y. Grossman, R. Hodson, R. Lensiki, R. Mack, and P. Regal, "The Planned Introduction of Genetically Engineered Organisms: Ecological Considerations and Recommendations", *Ecology* 70 (1989), 297–315. H. Strauss, D. Hattis, G. Page, K. Harrison, S. Vogel, and C. Caldart. "Genetically-Engineered Microorganisms: I. Identification, Classification and Strain History," *Recombinant DNA Technical Bulletin* 9 (1) (1986), 1–15; "Genetically-Engineered Microorganisms: II. Survival, Multiplication, and Genetic Transfer," *Recombinant DNA Technical Bulletin* 9 (2) (1986), 67–88.

17. A.H. Westing, "Chemical and Biological Weapons," in Stockholm International Peace Research Insitute, *Weapons of Mass Destruction and the Environent* (London and Philadelphia: Taylor & Francis, 1977).

18. U.S. Department of Defense, "Biological Defense Program."

19. Julian Perry Robinson, "Chemical and Biological Warfare: Developments in 1984," in Stockholm International Peace Research Institute, *World Armaments and Disarmament: SIPRI Yearbook 1985* (London and Philadelphia: Taylor and Francis, 1985), 178–179; The President's Unclassified Report to the Congress on Soviet Noncompliance with Arms Control Agreements, February, 1, 1985.

20. United States Department of the Army, Walter Reed Army Institute of Research, unpublished memorandum SGRD-UWZ (6 December, 1985).

7

The U.S. Biological Defense Research Program in the 1980s: A Critique

Charles Piller and Keith R. Yamamoto

Offense or Defense?

Since 1981 the U.S. Army has greatly expanded its efforts in biological warfare. These efforts are always described as strictly defensive and research oriented. It is the thesis of this chapter that these efforts are highly ambiguous, provocative, and strongly suggestive of offensive goals, calling into question the basic framework and rationale for the efforts.

This conclusion rests on these points:

• The major thrust of the Biological Defense Research Program (BDRP) is based on a policy of medical defense against biological weapons agents. This policy assumes that vaccines and antiviral drugs can form a reasonable medical defense against a potentially infinite array of BW agents and toxins produced using recombinant DNA and other new biological techniques—a premise rejected by virtually every independent scientist who has examined the issue.

• An analysis of more than 300 biological research studies conducted by the Department of Defense (DOD) or its contractors indicates a clear and consistent pattern of potential offensive applications. Further, these studies are in most cases inconsistent with the DOD's stated strategy of medical defense. The work does touch on nearly all aspects of biological warfare research, however, from molecular genetics to dissemination of weapons agents.

• Spending on biological defense rose drastically in the 1980s, enjoying an average increase of 37.1 percent per year in the first five years of the Reagan administration, peaking at $90.6 million in FY 1985, and remaining at a high level thereafter.[1]

• The Army has proposed a new laboratory which would conduct secret research on large volumes of aerosolized, deadly microorganisms and toxins, possibly including agents produced using recombinant DNA technology. Leading scientists regard the lab as unneeded for any plausible defensive research.

• In general, the lines between secret and open research are indistinct, and a consistent lack of openness in response to requests for information on the BDRP lends troubling implications to vaguely defined DOD rules on secrecy.

The Defense Department's program in biological warfare defense has never faced the kind of detailed public scrutiny that many government programs are often subject to. However, a great deal is known about its basic structure, stated goals, and methods. According to DOD sources, most research and development falls into one of five areas: medical defense, protective gear, decontamination technology, ultrasensors and other devices to detect or measure BW agents, and intelligence gathering.

The military says it conducts basic research in the life sciences—such as molecular biology and environmental biology—to maintain a technology base for certain nonmedical aspects of BW defense, including ultrasensors and decontamination. Basic and applied medical researchers investigate well-known and newly discovered organisms or toxins to uncover their properties and dangers. This involves analysis of everything from the genetic make-up and virulence of threat agents, to development of methods for their isolation, large-scale bioprocess reproduction, and dissemination. Ultimately, they aim to create and test vaccines, toxoids, or drugs to counteract or neutralize agents that are seen as threats to U.S. forces. These products are often manufactured on a mass scale. Vaccines for a range of diseases have been produced in the millions of doses.

The Army is the primary military agency for all biological defense work.[2] Its Medical Research Institute of Infectious Diseases (AMRIID) at Fort Detrick is the heart of BW medical defense, while its Test and Evaluation Command runs the physical protection program. The Navy also conducts substantial BW research. All the military agencies involved in BW research contract out a large portion of their work to universities and corporations all over the United States and to a limited extent in allied nations.

In addition to playing a vital role in protecting the nation, leaders of the BW program say their work contributes broadly to society. In 1971, an epidemic of Venezuelan equine encephalomyelitis

(VEE) ravaged northern Mexico and Texas, killing hundreds of horses and infecting scores of people. The vaccine that quelled the outbreak was furnished by the BDRP. "It can be considered a beneficial result of biological warfare research," an Army spokesman said at the time.[3]

And DOD representatives point out that military researchers in the biological sciences have made important contributions to the understanding of fundamental questions of disease transmission. The study of anti-plant and anti-animal weapons has occasionally led to agricultural advances. More effective detection of BW agents has aided in the control of environmental pollutants. These civilian "spin-offs"—though incidental to military goals and far less cost-effective than projects designed to serve civilian goals directly—add a layer of complexity to the justification for biological warfare research. But the fundamental rationale for this massive effort is simple: the Soviet threat.

The U.S. military justifies its actions by the firm conviction that the Soviets are prepared to routinely violate legal and moral standards pertaining to BW. The Biological Defense Research Program has grown robust in the lengthening shadow of this fear (chapters 2 and 9). Any credible analysis of U.S. goals and intent must recognize the far-reaching influence of this fear. The comments of one key BW scientist are a fittingly bellicose preface to a description of the U.S. biotechnology program: "This lab and the [AMRIID] are charged with a very frightening task," according to David Kingsbury, then director of the Naval Biosciences Lab in Oakland, California, in 1984. "We're the two Defense Department labs that are tasked with identifying biological warfare agents. That's one of the most awesome tasks I can think of, coming up with a definitive statement that we've been attacked with a biological weapon, knowing that that statement is probably equivalent to pushing the [nuclear] button. Reagan could always call the Kremlin and ask, 'What the hell did you do that for?' My guess is he wouldn't. He'd tape that message to the front end of a Minuteman missile."[4]

Sifting the Facts

The following analysis is thorough and rigorous—but unfortunately not comprehensive.[5] After describing the DOD's biotechnology program, we explain how the military penchant for secrecy has seeped into areas mandated to be open to public view. The result has been to veil, if not black out, any detailed independent analysis of the BW program—to the peril of U.S. and international security.

We analyzed 329 separate projects funded during the period from 1980 to 1986, for which we obtained clearly identifiable, specific documentation. All were designated by the DOD as directly related to biotechnology. Although this represents the most detailed, comprehensive independent overview of DOD work in biotechnology, it is nevertheless a *nominal* analysis. Several key avenues of research noted in alternate DOD sources are barely mentioned in the Work Unit Summaries that we obtained. Therefore, the 329 projects are unlikely to portray a representative cross-section of the CBW biotechnology effort as a whole.

We did not attempt to infer priorities for specific projects or general topics from the total funds allocated for each—ranging from a few thousand to several million dollars—although that information is included in our data base. This is because cost is not always a good indicator of relative importance in biotechnology, and because the military refused to release the full complement of supporting documentation.

Although the research and development priorities cannot be precisely quantified, when supplemented with more cryptic information from other DOD sources, conclusions can be drawn about the apparent implications of the total body of work. Table 7.1 presents an overview of the 329 core projects.

We also appraised the apparent scientific merit of each project, as well as its potential for offensive use. The process was subjective, especially in view of the limited amount of available information, but it employed well-established standards for assessing the quality and goals for biomedical research. Somewhat to our surprise, the projects fell into three rather simple, overlapping primary categories:

• "Offensive": research that has obvious *potential* for offensive applications. (None of these studies were labeled "offensive" by the DOD, of course. That would be an acknowledgment of violations of U.S. policy and the spirit of the 1972 BW Convention.) This category constituted about one-fifth of contractor projects and fully one-third of in-house military projects.

• "Standard": research similar to projects that might be submitted to the NIH. Many studies in this category, however, appeared inferior to those typically funded by the NIH. This category consti-

Table 7.1
Institutions, goals, and methods of 329 Department of Defense biotechnology projects (1980–1987)

	Total	Percent
Institution Conducting R&D Project		
Total projects:	329	100
DOD In-house lab	143	43
Total contractors	186	57
Academic	166	51
Corporate	16	5
Governmental	4	1
Stated Goals of R&D Project		
Vaccine Development	61	19
Toxin, antigen isolation/characterization	102	31
Development/use of antibodies as therapeutics	36	11
Diagnostics/ultrasensors	66	20
Manipulation of antigens	12	4
Aerosol vaccination	2	1
"Basic" studies related to cell growth, immunity, neurobiology	61	19
Other "basic" studies	46	14
Anti-viral drug development/characterization	9	3
CW antidote development	19	6
Broad-spectrum therapies	12	4
Fellowship/equipment/conference funding	43	12
Clinical research	23	7
Stated Research Methods		
Recombinant DNA	107	33
Monoclonal antibodies	126	38
Microencapsulation	2	1
Manipulation of antigens	3	1
Computer modeling	6	2
Classical biochemistry/cell cultures/genetics	125	38
Bioprocess technology	4	1

Note: some percentages do not total 100 due to rounding and multiple applications for a single study; some study counts exceed 329 due to projects which have multiple applications.

Table 7.2
Potential offensive applications of 86 DOD biotechnology projects

Potential offensive application	Total	Percent
BW agents that defeat vaccines	23	27
BW agents that inhibit diagnosis	14	16
"Supertoxins"[a]	17	20
Aerosol delivery of BW agents	5	6
Biological vectors for BW agents	19	22
Novel BW agents	51	59
Drug-resistant BW agents	3	3
Highly specific ethnic weapons	0	–
"Biochemical (hormone) weapons"	1	1
Increased toxin-production capability	15	17

a. Genetic alterations which could increase the toxicity of an organism's toxin products.
Note: percentage total exceeds 100 and study count exceeds 86 due to multi-application projects.

tuted about seven-tenths of contractor studies and less than half of in-house military work.

• "Poor": research that is poorly conceived or designed, uses confused logic, or addresses problems of questionable significance. This category constituted about one-fifth of contractor work and one-fourth of in-house military projects.

We then created a list of offensive applications of biotechnology (reflected largely in chapter 5). Many studies in the "standard" and "poor" categories had clear potential for offensive application, but we discuss here only the 86 studies that seemed most explicitly "offensive" in nature. This eliminated studies whose offensive applications are obscure, or could be considered extraneous or an abstraction of the overall research goals. It concentrated and refined the sample. These were then categorized by specific applications in table 7.2.

On the basis of this initial review, "offensive" projects appear to emphasize the creation of novel BW agents; agents that defeat vaccines and inhibit diagnosis, new methods of dissemination using living organisms, such as insects, as the carriers (vectors); and the increased production of toxins—especially toxins with enhanced effects.

For example, one well-funded study entitled "Microbial Genetics and Taxonomy,"[6] conducted at the Walter Reed Army Institute of Research, used genetic and recombinant DNA methodology to modify bacteria that grow in the human digestive tract "to produce any desired antigenic structure and level of pathogenicity." Studies contracted to an investigator at the University of Wisconsin were more explicitly focused.[7] Using recombinant DNA procedures, it was shown that the deadly neurotoxic effects of the agent that causes botulism could be separated from its major antigenic structures; new derivatives of the botulism neurotoxin were created whose activities were unimpeded by antibodies made against the naturally occurring forms. Clearly, these studies would be invaluable in the creation of new strains of BW agents. Another series of studies categorized as "Defensive Systems: Exploratory Development"[8] that took place within the Army's biological research program boasted that "a new generation nose-only aerosol exposure system was made operational. For the first time, T-2 mycotoxin was successfully disseminated. The aerosol contained sufficient toxin to kill mice." The report continued, "the Romeo strain of Junin virus was disseminated as a small-particle aerosol and was found to be highly infectious and lethal for guinea pigs." These studies, while described as defensive, are obviously designed to explore the potential use of known pathogens as aerosols—essential for an offensive development program.

At face value, these would be intelligent priorities for an offensive BW program. Regardless of the Pentagon's motives or perspectives on the use of biotechnology, these projects would likely have the greatest chance of short-term success. Defeating vaccines, for example—a frightening BW enhancement that is quite feasible with today's biotechnologies—appears to be an area of intense scrutiny. In contrast, more technologically remote prospects which pose forbidding technical and logistical challenges, such as ethnic weapons, apparently received little attention. To extend the analysis, we then looked at the four *stated goals* appearing most frequently among the 86 studies—vaccine development, toxin/antigen isolation and characterization, development and use of antibodies as therapeutics, and diagnostics and ultrasensors—and compared them to the list of potential offensive applications. The results of these comparisons were fully consistent with the initial observations. More significantly, however, this breakdown gives an important clue about how an offensive program may be "coded"—what each defensive-sounding label on the DOD Work Unit Summaries may represent. Following are the *offensive* applications which may lurk beneath the four major defensive *stated* goals:

- *Vaccine development*
  Novel BW agents
  Defeat vaccines
  Increased toxin production
  Supertoxins

- *Diagnostics/ultrasensors*
  Biological vector delivery
  Novel BW agents
  Defeat vaccines

- *Toxin, antigen isolation/ characterization*
  Novel BW agents
  Defeat vaccine
  Increased toxin production
  Supertoxins
  Biological vector delivery

- *Development/use of antibodies as therapeutics*
  Novel BW agent
  Defeat Vaccines
  Inhibit diagnosis

Although these designations are based on limited data, they show logical applications of the DOD's studies to an offensive program. Therefore, a review body—be it an independent panel of concerned scientists, an official agency of the government, or an international arms-control team—could use these relationships as a point of departure for probing the motives of the overall DOD program in biotechnology as it develops over the next few years.

Using these "codes," some relationships between otherwise dissimilar, geographically and institutionally separated projects seem to emerge. Biotech Research Laboratories, a small company in Maryland, wins a DOD contract to produce monoclonal antibodies to surface antigens of the bacterium *Bacillus anthracis* (the organism which causes anthrax) to "support ongoing studies of infectious diseases."[9] Meanwhile, an investigator at Louisville University obtains contract funds to test the reactivity of "lectins," naturally occurring compounds that can target and bind tightly to specific molecules in bacterial cell surfaces, "to determine if different lectins have different affinities for various microbes."[10] This work showed that *Bacillus anthracis* was selectively bound by certain lectins. While there is no stated relationship between these projects, one wonders whether the bound lectin would block access of the monoclonal antibody to the *Bacillus anthracis* cells. Such a discovery could easily find offensive application, since it would allow potential pathogens to escape detection.

As a second example, Stanley Falkow, a noted Stanford University researcher, obtained an Army contract to clone a gene from a pathogenic bacterium into the innocuous bacterium *E. coli*. The novel *E. coli* strain gained the ability to attack human cells in the same manner seen for the pathogen.[11] In the same period, as noted above, a group at the Walter Reed Army Institute of Research developed methods to genetically modify bacteria such as *E. coli* "to produce any desired antigenic structure and level of pathogenicity."[12] Obviously, joining these projects might yield a new generation of invasive and deadly BW agents.

Thus, even research that may seem harmless or even scientifically meritorious in isolation must be viewed warily considering the possibility that Pentagon planners are combining the fruits of labor from a broad array of work it supports.

Still, some areas, such as aerosol delivery of BW agents and microencapsulation—feasible and logical needs for any offensive effort—were strangely absent from our sample. Does this mean they are being ignored by the military?

Hardly. The DOD Obligation Reports fill in many of the apparent gaps.[13] Here are some areas of research and development—all essential to a well-coordinated offensive program—which are indicated as significant priorities in these reports, but were not well represented in the 329 biotechnology projects:

Microencapsulation

Aerosolization of BW agents and toxins to evaluate offensive potential and protective gear

Mathematical models for aerosol delivery

Aerosol vaccination methods

Aerosol delivery of drugs and nerve agent antidotes

Industrial-scale bioprocess facilities

Vaccine stockpiling in the millions of doses

Broad-spectrum and synergistic antiviral drug development

Insect vectors

And the DOD response to a 1986 lawsuit filed by the Washington, D.C.-based Foundation on Economic Trends, revealed additional studies on target vulnerability in Europe, Asia, and the United States, and on "Biological Agent Delivery by ICBM (intercontinental ballistic missile)."[14]

The Consistency Factor

This range of work clearly indicates pursuit of the most obvious potential offensive research and development applications of the new biotechnologies. Table 7.3 shows how the DOD's current program might fit into a well-coordinated, deliberate strategy to develop an offensive capability.

This pattern of activities is particularly troubling in light of the inconsistency between the DOD's actual research activities and what Col. David Huxsoll, commander of the Army's largest BW lab, calls the cornerstone of the medical defense strategy: broad-spectrum or generic vaccine development.[15] Only nine of the 329 core projects could reasonably be construed as focused on this goal. And available alternate sources mention broad-spectrum vaccines only in passing.

The simplest interpretations of this gulf between stated strategy and actual work are that the military either does not understand its own approach, or that it's lying. MIT biologist Jonathan King suggests an additional explanation for this admixture of checkered quality and suspect intentions: the DOD is "casting a wide net" in order to recruit scientific talent and establish a flexible, broad base of technological support.[16]

This is reflected in the fact that 43 of the 329 core projects—12 percent of the total—provided funding for graduate education fellowships, equipment purchases, and scientific conferences to discuss biotechnology problems of military interest. In many cases, the expectation that contractors would later take on military research was made explicit. For example, the Army funded a University of Washington "Neurotoxin Research Facility" to "make possible or improve research which supports the Army thrusts in CBD (chemical and biological defense)."[17]

"At this stage of the program, it doesn't matter very much what the specific projects are—or even if the work has any intrinsic scientific merit," King said. He cited a personal example: the Office of Naval Research (ONR) attempted to recruit King's department to conduct recombinant DNA studies on marine biofouling—how to use molecular biology to detach barnacles from ship bottoms. "Our department has no experience with or knowledge of marine organisms or environments. However, we are a world center of expertise in genetic engineering and molecular and cellular biology," he said. "The ONR's true goal is to form a reser-

Table 7.3
U.S. BW Program Development—Offensive Development Implications[a]

Stages in the development of an offensive capability[b]	Verified evidence
1 Policy review of pros and cons of offensive BW program[f]	Yes
2 Decision to proceed on offensive program	No
3 Preparation of detailed budgetary estimates for R&D[f]	Yes[c]
4 Voting of R&D budgets[f]	Yes[c]
5 Recruitment of R&D personnel[f]	Yes[c]
6 Organization of in-house research facilities, funding of university/corporate researchers to build flexible technology infrastructure[f]	Yes
7 Selection of BW agent research projects[e,f]	Yes
8 Selection of BW agent development projects[e,f]	Yes[c]
9 Organization of development facilities[e,f]	Yes[c]
10 Development of large-scale agent manufacturing techniques[e,f]	Yes
11 Target vulnerability studies[f]	Yes
12 Selection of munitions/vector projects for research[e,f]	Yes
13 Selection of munitions/vector projects for development	No
14 Standardization of weapons for possible procurement	No
15 Large-scale field testing with simulants, BW prototypes	No
16 Development of theory for battle planning[g]	Yes
17 Preparation, voting of budgets for procurement and maintenance	No
18 Selection of standardized material	No
19 Large-scale manufacture, transport of agents	No
20 Manufacture, bulk transport/storage of munitions	No
21 Munition filling, storage	No
22 Deployment of material in forward areas	No
23 Training of individual troops in offensive techniques[i]	Yes[d]
24 War games including BW exercises[f]	Yes[d]

a. This table refers to activities during the 1980s. Prior to 1969, the United States maintained a large-scale offensive effort which incorporated each component listed here. The earlier offensive program would, in some important areas, obviate the need for extensive development and field testing in a present-day offensive effort.

b. Stages adapted from SIPRI, *The Problem of Chemical and Biological Warfare, Volume V: The Prevention of CBW*, 1971.

c. The DOD has not formally indicated that "development" activities are being conducted. But the pattern of work indicates all aspects of agent weaponization short of standardization and large-scale manufacture. This work is designated "defensive research" by the DOD.

d. Training for offensive use of *chemical* weapons, which is part of the current U.S. regimen, is substantially the same as that of *biological* weapons.

e. Sources: 329 core projects.

f. Sources: Other DOD source materials, including Obligation Reports, other DOD reports and testimony to congressional committees, responses to lawsuits, projects indicated on official DOD lists of rDNA studies but for which no Work Unit Summaries could be obtained, and interviews with BW researchers and administrators.

g. Sources: U.S./NATO war-fighting strategy documents—see text for details.

voir of scientists to help the DOD understand and explore the technology's full potential. Under such circumstances, it would hardly be surprising if much of the research were of mediocre or inferior quality."[18]

Although this effort is described as "defensive," it demonstrates precisely how effective *offensive* efforts to exploit a new technology must begin. In later stages, defensive and offensive activities will diverge. As King also noted, the research focus will narrow sharply when specific offensive military missions are clearly identified. And its quality will markedly improve when weapons are developed and tested. That stage will be the polar opposite of the current, freewheeling program: a few precisely defined goals pursued with exacting, rigorous quality control.

Given the range and depth of the military program and the futility of medical defense against today's BW threat (discussed in chapter 6), it would seem either that the Pentagon's scientists are largely incompetent, or that their work is essentially offensive— albeit at an early stage of development.

The Desert Hideaway Affair

In October 1984 an Army proposal to build a \$1.4 million biological weapons test laboratory in order to conduct secret research on "substantial volumes of toxic biological aerosol agents"[19] was made public. The research would be defensive, like all its BW work, the Army explained, and would be carried out under conditions of utmost safety. The news sparked protests among a host of scientists. The following December, Harvard molecular biologist Richard Goldstein spoke for many colleagues when he said, "In my mind, the opening of this facility substantially escalates the biological arms race."[20] "Whether or not one accepts the hypothesis that the new [lab] is offensive research wearing a defensive cloak," added Richard Novick, director of the New York Public Health Research Institute, "there is no question that it represents a major escalation in biowar activity."[21]

The new lab would be the centerpiece of a planned major modernization and expansion of Dugway Proving Ground in Utah. At the time these plans were announced Dugway was expected to add 309 employees to its payroll[22] and double its CBW testing workload by 1988.[23] In its request to Congress for funding, the Army said the aerosol lab would be used "to evaluate biological defensive readiness and to test protective gear and detection/warning equipment by employing toxic microorganisms and biological toxins requiring a level of containment and safety not now available within the Department of Defense."[24]

The lab would operate under Biosafety Level (BL) 4 containment—the most secure physical protection possible—for experiments with some of the most dangerous pathogens known. Fort Detrick has six large BL4 labs, but it tests only small quantities of pathogenic aerosols in its infectivity studies. The Dugway unit would be the only BL4 lab in the nation devoted exclusively to nonmedical research, and would have by far the largest BL4-level aerosol capacity.

The proposed tests would be of two general types, according to the Army's request: "Biological defensive testing of military equipment and detection devices [and] evaluation of the foreign biothreat. The latter ranges from testing the vulnerability of protective masks or other equipment to assessing the characteristics of biological materials suspected of being used by potential adversaries in military or terrorist situations."[25]

Although proposed appropriations with substantive policy ramifications are normally debated by Congress, the DOD buried the Dugway aerosol lab funding request in a routine application to transfer unspent funds from other Army projects. Typically, the Army asks for "reprogramming" approval to complete such uncontroversial projects as parking lots or offices.

Reprogramming requests are usually rubber-stamped by the ranking Republican and Democrat on the House and Senate Appropriations Committees' Subcommittees on Military Construction. Tennessee Senator James Sasser, ranking Democrat on the subcommittee, initially approved the plan but later took the extraordinary step of withdrawing his assent. In a letter to subcommittee chair Mack Mattingly, Sasser complained that there was no statutory authority for the project, and that it raised "important questions with regard to the potential capabilities for testing and production of offensive lethal biological and toxin weapons."[26] He concluded that the Army sought "to avoid the regular authorization and appropriation process of the Congress."

At Mattingly's urging, however, the other subcommittee members fell into line, and voted to override Sasser's objection.

In a letter to Sasser, Secretary of Defense Caspar Weinberger tried to provide reassurance that the laboratory would not be used to develop offensive biological weapons and that the Defense Department did not intend to violate the 1972 treaty.[27] But many leading scientists questioned the need for this type of lab for purely defensive purposes. Prominent among these was MIT's David Baltimore, a Nobel laureate and one of the most influential molecular biologists in the world. "This is too elaborate a program," he said. It is "too open to ambiguous interpretation, even if [the Army's] intentions are good."[28] Scientists' concerns were based primarily on four issues: The Army's rejection of biological simulants in favor of testing with highly dangerous pathogens; the dangers of experiments with aerosols; the possible testing of genetically engineered organisms; and the admission that some testing would be conducted secretly.

The Army agreed that using simulants—benign organisms that mimic the behavior of pathogens—would be a safer, and therefore preferable method. But the results from simulant tests would be unreliable. "The efficacy of simulants for various testing purposes cannot be determined without exhaustive comparisons between simulants and threat agents," one Army report stated. "Establishing the adequacy of the simulant for a specific test may require more aerosol work with pathogens than the test itself." The Army argued that calibrating ultrasensors and evaluating protective gear and decontamination techniques would therefore be impossible without using the actual threat agents. "Adequate data concerning persistence cannot be developed [using simulants]," it continued.[29]

A few scientists outside the DOD, including Emmett Barkley, safety director at the National Institutes of Health, publicly supported this rationale. But a throng of leading independent scientists disagreed strongly. Harvard molecular biologist and CBW expert Matthew Meselson was among them. Virtually all the toxins and BW agents to be tested in the aerosol lab can be simulated, he said, adding that the use of simulants is a better military strategy. "The characteristics of aerosols important for defensive work are particle size and surface tension, and we've known for a long time how to match these with simulants," he said.[30] A single simulant organism could duplicate the characteristics of many viruses and bacteria. And it could pose a more generic, hardier test of protective gear. "We know a good deal about the likely biological warfare agents, and one can easily choose nonpathogenic or avirulent agents with the same size and molecular properties," said Roy Curtiss, chairman of the biology department at Washington University. "I don't see the need for a [BL4] lab. It's overkill and it's not good science."[31]

"Development of defensive and detection equipment can be performed with absolute confidence and . . . safety by the use of killed organisms," Novick argued. "These will have precisely the same particle size and chemical composition as the live organism and no containment would be necessary; indeed, field conditions could be much better approximated by performing the tests outdoors. Decontamination analysis and tests of persistence do not require aerosols. Additionally, these tests can be performed in complete safety by the use of live attenuated organisms such as those used for vaccines." Novick also pointed out that toxins, which are nonliving and nonpersistent, would not require BL4 containment. Beyond these practical arguments, there is some question whether persistence data has any significant value for defense. Clearly an area would be designated "safe" only after contamination could no longer be detected—regardless of prior persistence data.[32]

"Data such as infectivity, symptomology and lethality can also not be obtained with simulants, should these be required," an Army report also argued.[33] Novick strongly questioned this point. "Experiments with live human subjects would not be permissible," he said. "'Symptomology' is well known for most of the agents under consideration on the basis of natural disease and experiments performed by the Japanese during World War II on human subjects. 'Infectivity' and 'lethality' data . . . would be unnecessary for any imaginable purely defensive purpose."[34]

Critics also cited the inherent dangers of aerosolized pathogens, especially when used in "substantial volumes." Aerosols are "the most dangerous vehicle for dissemination and the most difficult to contain," Novick said. Absolute physical containment is "a theoretical as well as practical impossibility," he added.[35] As few as 10 organisms of the causative agents of tularemia and Q Fever—each planned for Dugway testing—can cause human infection. A single drop of such agents could contain billions of organisms. Even a minute chance of accidentally spreading a deadly disease might be considered excessively hazardous.

The DOD has repeatedly stated that a major goal of its CBW defense program is to verify that combat vehicles are leak-proof and could effectively be decontaminated. Indeed, part of the planned expansion of Dugway is to test *chemical* exposure and decontamination in a facility large enough to hold a tank.[36] But curiously, discussion about *biological* testing on that scale has been conspicuously absent from military documents and statements, although the need for such tests is dictated by Pentagon logic.

"We continue to obtain new evidence that the Soviet Union has maintained its offensive biological warfare program and that it is exploring genetic engineering to expand their [sic] program's scope," Weinberger wrote to Sasser. "Our development efforts in this area are driven by the Soviet threat. To ensure that our protective systems work, we must challenge them with known or *suspected* Soviet agents [emphasis added]."[37]

This statement is consistent with the DOD's longstanding public posture—defense against the Soviet threat. But in this context it lends credence to fears of lab critics that the testing of recombinant prototypes ("suspected Soviet agents") is the actual goal for the lab. "There is no question that this equipment will give the Army the capability to perform genetic manipulations. . . . If they actually begin such work, that would give me cause for concern," Baltimore said. "They should also say that they are absolutely not going to make any new toxins."[38] "The infectious characteristics of most of the 'standard' agents are very well known," Novick said. "The filling of 'knowledge gaps,' suggested to be an important part of the program . . . arouses strong suspicion that new types of agents will be developed and tested for their potential as bioweapons."[39]

DOD officials repeatedly stated that they had no plans to conduct recombinant DNA work at Dugway, and denied they would ever create prototypes. They refused, however, to rule out recombinant DNA work completely, or the use of Dugway facilities to test aerosolized recombinant microbes that had been engineered at other labs. It may be difficult for the Soviets to produce practical BW in the lab, Col. Robert Orton, director of the Army's nuclear-biological-chemical defense division said. "But one surely has to look at all the possibilities and ensure that there isn't an easy way to do it."[40]

Beyond the prototype question, genetic engineering work would present new safety problems. The federal guidelines on recombinant DNA research mandate absolute avoidance of aerosols for any agent requiring BL2 or higher containment. There are no data to support the claim that any existing or contemplated BL4 lab could safely contain high volumes of deadly aerosols. These guidelines also depend on "biological containment"—genetic crippling of potentially dangerous organisms to render out-of-lab survival

impossible. Biological containment, of course, would be antitheti-
cal to the experiments contemplated by the Army.

Critics of the Dugway scheme also question the DOD's plan to
conduct secret research. Secrecy can only feed suspicions of im-
propriety, critics say. Because threat assessment and equipment vulnerability are normally kept secret, DOD spokespersons admitted
that some of the research at the proposed lab inevitably would
be classified.[41] This could include genetic engineering work, they
acknowledged, despite the DOD's self-imposed ban on secrecy in
gene splicing.[42]

After the subcommittee approved funding for the lab, genetic
engineering critic Jeremy Rifkin and retired Navy Admiral Gene
LaRocque, Director of the Center for Defense Information, a liberal defense research group, filed suit to bar construction. They
charged that the DOD had violated the National Environmental
Policy Act by failing to prepare an environmental assessment to
address the above safety concerns.

The suit spotlighted the proximity of Dugway to Salt Lake City
(less than 90 miles), and the fact that Dugway also tests conventional weapons. This raises the concern that deadly microorganisms might be released should a errant projectile hit the lab. These
fears gain credence upon review of Army documents: the proposed
lab site is less than 5 km from a conventional weapons range, while
Dugway's "artillery, missile, and mortar ranges may be used for
firing up to 65 km."[43] Such an accident seems unlikely. But the lax
safety practices of Dugway testing programs during past decades
give pause.[44]

In January 1985, before the lawsuit was heard in court, the Army
agreed to file an environmental assessment. A cursory report was
released in early February.[45] Not surprisingly, the study found no
significant environmental risks in the laboratory plan, largely
reiterating earlier arguments.

The Army did make a surprising shift in its rationale, however.
The original reprogramming request to Congress justified the ex-
penditure as "an urgent requirement . . . to provide an essential
laboratory [which is] the only way to ensure [the] survival of our
armed forces on the biological battlefield."[46] This rhetoric was
toned down substantially in the environmental assessment. The
Army concluded that it did not really need a BL4 lab for current
work after all. It could make due with a more modest containment
facility. Still, the new report stated, a maximum containment lab

should be constructed in anticipation of some hypothetical future threat. "The Soviets are exerting great efforts in this area. Consequently, we must develop appropriate defenses," the report noted. "Conceivably, such studies could involve laboratory operations which require the use of [BL4] containment."[47]

Rifkin and LaRocque immediately reactivated their suit on the grounds that the assessment was inadequate. A hearing was held on April 26, 1986. The Pentagon made a concerted effort to persuade U.S. District Court Judge Joyce Hens Green that an aerosol-test lab would pose no environmental or health threat. It further distanced itself from its original rationale for aerosol testing. No expansion of current testing was planned, DOD spokespersons now insisted, nor was there any clear idea of when a BL4 lab would be needed. It was required, they said, "in anticipation of requirements which may never materialize."[48]

This new stance generated the counterargument that a lab unjustified on emergent national security grounds that stimulated substantial safety and arms-control concerns should not be built. Green sided with the plaintiffs. She slapped an injunction on lab construction pending an adequate environmental assessment.[49]

In a related development, in May 1986, the DOD released a response to questions by the House Committee on Appropriations about the Dugway lab proposal.[50] The report is a surprisingly detailed and elaborate explanation of Pentagon views on biotechnology. Its basic message reverted to the DOD's earlier posture of urgency: the new genetic technologies combined with Soviet arrogance were depicted as leading to unprecedented dangers. Only a major U.S. biotechnology push to develop effective countermeasures can save the nation from a horrible fate, the report stated. And a Dugway aerosol lab, once again, became the key to survival. This report made it clear that a legal setback had not dampened the Pentagon's resolve. After a delay of more than three years, it finally released a full environmental impact statement in February 1988.[51] This was greeted by widespread public and official opposition in the Dugway area and elsewhere.[52]

The Army finally abandoned its pursuit of a BL4 facility as a result of the Foundation on Economic Trends lawsuit and strong citizen opposition in Utah. It announced in September 1988 that it would build a BL3 facility instead, which would ostensibly preclude the testing of agents for which there are no known cures.[53] Whether this facility will ever be approved is unclear. The Army has yet to complete its final environmental impact statement for the lab. But the issues raised in connection with the Dugway scheme— use of BW agents instead of simulants, plans to explore the offensive potential of genetic engineering, and possible classification of research—are likely to persist because they are connected with the expansion of the volume and scope of the program as a whole.

A Tactical Shift

The large biotechnology program in general and the Dugway lab affair in particular seem provocative. But do they in fact reflect a systematic U.S. retreat from its renunciation of biological warfare? There is no certain answer to this question. But an important clue can be found in U.S. war-fighting doctrine—the theoretical framework that dictates military strategy and action in the field.

In August 1982, the Army revised its field operations manual[54] to incorporate two significant tactical changes prompted by new technologies. The first is the "extended battlefield"— the ability to make a "deep strike" behind enemy lines. New electronic technologies have endowed missiles with unprecedented accuracy. Distant targets can be hit with minimal "collateral" or unintended damage. The second change is the "integrated battle field"—the ability to employ conventional, nuclear or chemical weapons interchangeably as required by military conditions.

Instead of offering the dichotomous stalemate of inaction or nuclear holocaust, the new strategies promote a victory-oriented posture. In December 1984, NATO began to adopt this extended battlefield concept, according to a leading West German military analyst, Alfred Mechtersheimer. "'Deep strike' has led unavoidably to a reevaluation of chemical and biological weapons, which were previously neglected in military strategy."[55]

Another aspect of the new offensive plans lends itself well to CBW. "The key factor is no longer destructive capability but rather the capability of rapid advance," Mechtersheimer says. "Ground-winning thrusts presuppose the use of captured weapons and infrastructure. This is a completely new task compared to previous NATO strategy, and along with neutron weapons ["enhanced radiation" weapons which are deadly but do not destroy physical surroundings], chemical and biological weapons are particularly well suited to this task."[56]

Chemical and biological weapons might even be considered superior to nuclear (including neutron) weapons because they offer the requisite intermediate and deep saturation effects, but might be considered slightly less likely to provoke uncontrollable escalation. International law prohibits first use of CW. But in the heat of battle it may be impossible to determine which side used chemicals first.

In any case, a major Army field manual makes the adoption of *chemical* weapons explicit: "Commanders must be prepared to integrate chemical weapons into nuclear and conventional fire plans on receipt of chemical release," it reads, and lists the advantages of chemicals "employed in mass and without warning."[57]

Although NATO commanders are working on plans to integrate CW into their procedures, considerable conflicts remain within the NATO alliance about chemical deployment. In 1986, seven NATO leaders unequivocally rejected stationing new nerve gas weapons on their soil. Others reserved veto power over any decision to deploy.[58] The changes in war-fighting strategy are a long way from becoming institutionalized.

But a doctrine that radically increases the utility of unconventional weapons holds troubling implications. "If political and military leaders show no scruples in preparing for the use of atomic and chemical weapons of mass destruction, why should they dispense with biological weapons if they have military advantages," Mechtersheimer asks, "particularly since they can be produced cheaply, secretly, and on short notice."[59]

NATO and the Warsaw Pact are silent on BW deployment, which is banned by international law. Bellicose speechmaking and devotion to BW research, however, demonstrate unwavering respect for the BW threat. Articles in specialty publications on both sides frequently treat biological and chemical arms as virtually the same. The term "chemical-biological warfare" has increasingly gained currency. An apparent shift in strategy alone, of course, is an ambiguous guide by which to judge U.S. motives and ambitions in the biological sciences. But it adds new questions to the already burdened rationale of defensive research.

A Question of Secrecy

Openness, say independent scientists, is the litmus test of defensive intentions in biological research. Secrecy—whatever the justification—breeds suspicion and skepticism on the part of domestic critics and enemies alike. In biological warfare, the DOD is by no means an impenetrable monolith populated by sinister ideologues. To allay fears regarding genetic engineering, the DOD established a policy in 1981[60] that requires a complete record of each recombinant DNA study to be kept on file at AMRIID. This was part of a multifaceted effort to "ensure that all DOD recombinant DNA research is thoroughly reviewed, properly approved, and can bear the scrutiny of an interested party," the policy reads.

Almost nothing in the medical defense program is classified, says Col. David Huxsoll, AMRIID's commander. "It's a whole lot easier to do the work if it's unclassified," Huxsoll added. "You do not have that barrier to acquisition of good research—whether it's in-house or a contract. . . . I have a personal responsibility to see that [the openness of the research program] continues."[61]

Although the AMRIID labs are within Fort Detrick which, like all Army installations, is reasonably secured, the Institute is no fortress. AMRIID scientists and their cohorts in other military labs conducting research into medical defense against BW are free to publish the results of their studies in the scientific literature. The Army even follows Food and Drug Administration rules and procedures in licensing their vaccines and anti-viral drugs, Huxsoll said. These products are often shared with public health authorities around the world.

Compared to the extreme secrecy in which many military programs are shrouded, Huxsoll's operation might seem to be operating in a fishbowl. But a number of actions, discrepancies and policies cloud the water—and pose serious doubts about the credibility of DOD claims that its medical defense program is completely unclassified.

The "interested party" referred to in the DOD's openness policy has to be possessed of an interest amounting to relentless determination in order to check up on the military. It is a simple matter to obtain from Fort Detrick a list naming its rDNA studies, investigators and their institutions. Information beyond single-phrase descriptions, however, mandates a Freedom of Information Act (FOIA) request. The DOD routinely delays responses to such requests for months beyond the 10-day statutory deadline. The process can involve a considerable time investment even on relatively straightforward petitions.

In analyzing the responses to many FOIA requests filed over a period of four years, we found none of the official lists of recombinant DNA studies to be comprehensive. The lists we obtained in spring and fall 1983 and fall 1986 were either outdated or omitted certain studies. Documents released to us by a wide range of other military agencies prove these discrepancies unequivocally.

No similar list is known to exist for biotechnology work not involving recombinant DNA. So when we sought summaries of biotechnology projects under the FOIA, we made identical requests to several military branches. Because each branch relies on the same central computer system, we could cross-check the responses for accuracy and completeness.

The result was far from reassuring, with major differences between the responses. And as noted in the above analysis of the 329 descriptions received from these requests, portions of the biotechnology program—clearly identified in other unclassified sources—were not represented in the summaries released to us. These included substantial development work in industrial-scale bioprocess technology, and major microencapsulation, aerosol vaccination, and recombinant DNA research projects. It is difficult to know if such "errors" are due to a failure of administrative control or a lack of understanding of the technologies—or are the product of deliberate subterfuge. These are all equally disturbing possibilities.

It may also be misleading to take comfort in the fact that military scientists are allowed to publish in academic journals. CIA researchers who conducted studies on the use of LSD for mind control for the MKULTRA program during the 1950s and 1960s also published their work. "But those long, scholarly reports often gave an incomplete picture of the research," according to *The Search for the 'Manchurian Candidate,'* written by John Marks, the most comprehensive volume on these mind-control activities.[62]

"In effect, the scientists would write openly about how LSD affects a patient's pulse rate, but they would only tell the CIA how the drug could be used to ruin that patient's marriage or memory," Marks commented. This is not to say that AMRIID operates in the same fashion. But this much is clear: the right to publish, per se, is an insufficient test of openness. Indeed, many of the military's primary biological defense researchers do not publish at rates even remotely consistent with the vast resources at their disposal.

The commercial database MEDLINE, compiled by the National Library of Medicine, is the most comprehensive on-line source for worldwide biomedical literature. We tapped MEDLINE for records going back to 1981 on 19 leading investigators from various

DOD units, as indicated on the 329 summaries.[63] The data were startling: seven scientists published only in obscure, poorly distributed, undistinguished journals, such as the Southeast Asian Journal of Tropical Medicine and Public Health. Four investigators—who collectively spent more than $7.8 million dollars from 1982 to 1986—published a total of only seven papers. At $1.12 million per article, these may be among the most wasteful biological research projects in history. Either that, or the touted "open publication" policy is a sham.[64]

Beyond medical defense, much in the BDRP is classified. The problem lies in definition and dual-use research. Just as the parameters of "medical defense" are vague, the technologies used are applicable in many areas. For example monoclonal antibody techniques form the backbone of ultrasensor development. The same methods are the key to creating vaccines. Knowledge gained from examining novel biothreats, which might be classified, has direct vaccine applications. Of course, it may have equally plausible offensive uses, such as precisely targeted toxin weapons.

Most scientists in AMRIID and other military labs conducting unclassified research must obtain security clearance. This requirement has nothing to do with their work, Huxsoll says. It merely allows them to see classified intelligence data. Again, the distinctions blur. If vaccine researchers view classified data involving the experimental analysis of novel threat agents, how does this influence their openness about their own work? The DOD views biotechnology expansively—applying it to everything from barnacle-removal to chemical warfare. Marine biofouling studies probably contain little pressing national security data. But this may not be the case with chemical warfare. The CW program is largely classified, and makes liberal use of biotechnology—for antidotes and weapons development, as well as to gain a better general understanding of chemical effects at the molecular level. By its nature, such research has many applications. What is to prevent the Army from using properly classified CW research in its BW program?

The Pentagon's efforts to allay such concerns are often less than soothing. Military leaders say they are completely open about overall BW issues. "A generalized [biological defense] program—we don't classify any of that," said nuclear-biological-chemical defense chief Robert Orton in an interview. "It's when you get into something that might identify a specific vulnerability of a member of the U.S. forces or of the U.S. forces in larger scale, to something a potential enemy might use, then we would classify it."[65] Translation: any militarily meaningful research finally can be classified at Army discretion. It is difficult, if not impossible, to precisely identify the programmatic distinction between "secret" and "open."

Ambiguity in secrecy criteria aside, the DOD's logic in classifying *anything* in the BW program tends to belie stated defensive intentions, some leading scientists argue. There is no reason to classify detection or protective measures, says Meselson. "It's only through force of habit that they're doing it. With the exception of intelligence work, we've got to be able to say, 'Absolutely everything we're doing, we're doing out in the open.' We must get rid of secrecy. Secrecy is the real threat."[66]

The extent of military illogic in classification was apparent in a 1986 interview with Huxsoll.[67] He freely acknowledged that AMRIID holds, in small quantities suitable for research, dozens of deadly toxins and hundreds of strains of viruses and bacteria. He identified scores of these agents by name in a recorded interview, and gave parameters for the maximum amounts maintained at any time. But Huxsoll would not release a complete list with precise quantities. As a reason for his reluctance, he suggested a terrorist or psychotic might see the list and want to break into a fortified U.S. Army base to steal some BW agents. Presumably only the official list with definitive amounts would tempt a terrorist.

Commercial factors also contribute to medical defense secrecy. AMRIID sponsors a major "Cooperative Antiviral Drug Development Program,"[68] in which private companies work with the Army to develop products which might have both BW defense and civilian applications. Included in the contracts are explicit, broad protections for "proprietary information." AMRIID routinely agrees not to publish or otherwise disclose test data or any other aspect of the studies. Of course, proprietary information is routine in corporate America. But it is still *secret*. "Such relationships are highly susceptible to abuse," said King. "Corporations—particularly small, struggling firms—might recognize tremendous economic incentives to conspire or collude with the Army about how much information to release and when to release it. Protecting proprietary information could act as a cover for classifying defense efforts."[69]

Cutting Off the Source?

In 1984 the Reagan administration reasserted the importance of controlling the flow of biotechnology know-how to the Soviets, and began to press for stringent controls on the export of what Defense Intelligence Agency spokesman John H. Birkner called "keystone equipment."[70] This includes high-containment facilities, large-scale fermentors for growing biological organisms, ultracentrifuges and other equipment which could be used to refine toxic biological products. Corporations that might be tempted to export such devices would confront government officials who are charged with "rooting out all those who would cooperate with the enemy," Birkner warned. "In such a contest," he added ominously, "government would probably prevail."

The problem with such controls is that the international biotechnology equipment trade is already widespread. The tools of biotechnology are accessible to any reasonably advanced nation through domestic production or trade with European countries. Such an embargo, therefore, would have little impact on the Soviets. Arms control may actually be hampered by such restrictions, if other nations interpret them as evidence of heightening U.S. respect for the value of genetically altered BW.

In May 1985, the Defense Department released a new publication for military contractors seeking access to technical data in order to prepare bids.[71] The image on the cover of the document is illuminating—a hammer and sickle with a bold line through it. "Stopping the Soviets' extensive acquisition of military-related Western technology in ways that are both effective and appropriate in our open society is one of the most complex and urgent issues facing the free world today," according to the booklet's opening statement. The document was prepared for the Defense Technical Information Center (DTIC)—the main computer conduit for public access to defense-related information. Since 1985, restrictions have been placed on even *unclassified* information within DTIC. For example, the summaries used for our analysis, once distributed relatively freely, are now restricted to qualified government agencies and contractors, or released only reluctantly and incompletely to investigators willing to assert their rights under the FOIA.

In light of the multitude of loopholes in the DOD's "openness" about biological warfare and biotechnology, the true depth and range of its program may vastly exceed what the public has been allowed to discover.

Decoding Military Spending

The military budget provides the final insight into the breadth and direction of the BW effort and the extent that biotechnology research is being militarized in the United States. Unfortunately, this budget is also a highly complex puzzle replete with ambiguities. Just as the overlap in DOD programs makes it impossible to know how much biological warfare research is kept secret, budget categories also overlap. Medical research in the *chemical* warfare budget, protective equipment development, and general biomedical and environmental research all may include biotechnology studies that could be used to solve problems relevant to *biological* warfare. In this sense the designation "BW defense" for some studies, but not others, is arbitrary.

And because the range of DOD biological research indicates an infrastructure of talent and expertise that identifies with the military and relies on Pentagon support, it would be misleading to focus solely on the "biological defense research" budget to the exclusion of other DOD spending in the life sciences.

The term "biotechnology" has no uniformly accepted definition. Funds spent on "medical defense against biological warfare" include everything from classical biochemical procedures established decades ago to the newest, most sophisticated genetic manipulations. Monoclonal antibody and recombinant DNA technologies are unmistakably part of the bioengineering revolution. But many methods cannot be discretely separated into "classical" vs. "novel." They lie on a continuum, which constantly changes with the field's rapid innovation. For this reason we present overall research figures, although our analysis emphasizes the specific impacts of the new biotechnologies.

Again, interpretation of the data must be tempered: the Pentagon says its entire biological defense budget is unclassified, as mandated by federal law. But the secrecy inherent in military operations and overlap in research categories make it impossible to evaluate that claim with certainty. Each year the DOD budget contains a classified portion known as the "black budget," because it is blacked out in published material and is not publicly accountable. Even Congress may know little about this spending.

Table 7.4
U.S. Biological Defense Research Program Obligations[a]

Fiscal year	Current $M	Inflation index[b]	Constant $M—1982	Percentage change, constant $M—1982
1977–1978	16.5	.6703	24.7	
1978–1979	16.5	.7172	13.0	− 6.8
1979–1980	16.0	.7790	20.6	−10.5
1980–1981	15.1	.8474	17.8	−13.4
1981–1982	21.6	.9321	23.1	29.8
1982–1983	38.8	1.0000	38.8	67.8
1983–1984	62.5	1.0423	60.0	54.5
1984–1985	68.5	1.0827	63.3	5.6
1985–1986	90.6	1.1200	80.9	27.8

a. Obligations refers to funds committed to a specific project.
b. This refers to the Gross National Product Price Deflator index, used by the National Science Foundation to calculate constant dollars for scientific research and development.
Source: DOD, "Annual Reports on Chemical Warfare-Biological Research Program Obligations."

Black-budget requests have tripled during the Reagan years— to $35 billion in the FY 1988 request—according to the Philadelphia Inquirer.[72] Now at 11 percent of the total, secret spending is growing faster than any other defense category. Funds for secret projects may also be hidden in unclassified programs, The New York Times has noted.[73] Therefore, reported figures may be considerably lower than actual spending levels.

As table 7.4 shows, the reported budget for the Biological Defense Research Program has grown rapidly during the 1980s—in contrast to its decline in Carter years (chapter 2). Looking more broadly to the life sciences as a whole, the full impact of the DOD's ascendancy is unmistakable in table 7.5. These data are sobering. Over a period of five years, the Reagan administration shifted $180 million dollars from civilian to military biological research. In medical sciences research, the shift—$129 million—was even more dramatic relative to total federal funding (see figure 7.1). During this period, the federal government spent an average of more than $5 billion a year on life sciences research.[74] In this context, $180 million is hardly an overwhelming shift. But it is a drastic departure from past practice.

The trend is profoundly worrisome. The scale of the Pentagon's biological research enterprise makes it increasingly difficult to oversee—opening the door to abuse. And the diversion of huge

Table 7.5
DOD research obligations, adjusted to reflect average increases for all federal agencies ($ millions — constant 1982)

Fiscal year	Actual DOD funding	Average federal change from previous year	Amount DOD would have received if increased at average for all agencies[a]	Funds allocated to DOD above average for all agencies
All Life Sciences funding				
1980	176			
1981	185	−3.8	169	16
1982	209	−0.3	168	41
1983	214	4.7	176	38
1984	227	4.8	184	43
1985	243	9.2	201	42
Net shift, 1980–1985:				180
Medical Sciences[b] funding				
1980	98			
1981	105	−4.8	93	12
1982	119	2.7	96	23
1983	129	4.3	100	29
1984	135	5.5	106	29
1985	152	9.8	116	36
Net shift, 1980–1985:				129

a. This represents a hypothetical calculation that applies the average increase in funding for all federal agencies to DOD funding, using 1980 as the base year (see text for details).
b. Subset of Life Sciences
Source: National Science Foundation, "Federal Funds for Research and Development," for the fiscal years indicated.

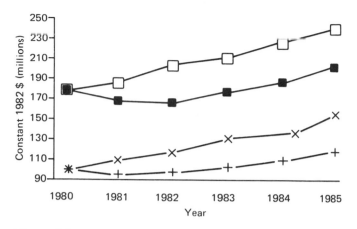

Figure 7.1
Actual and hypothetical DOD obligations for life sciences and medical sciences research.

☐ Actual DOD obligations, life sciences research
■ DOD obligations, if calculated at total federal rate of change
✕ Actual DOD obligations, medical sciences research (subset of life sciences)
+ DOD obligations, if calculated at total federal rate of change

Source: National Science Foundation.

sums from civilian biomedical research weighs heavily on the progress of studies that serve the overall needs of society.

The above data include the most recent year for which firm figures are available. Estimates of more recent years, however, show an increasingly contracted NIH biomedical research budget. As normal sources of funding are reduced, the DOD's funding for biomedical research develops a strong gravitational pull. "I wouldn't be in this field if I hadn't gotten money from the Army," Brigham Young University biochemist Donald Robertson, who is conducting rDNA experiments on anthrax bacteria, told the *Wall Street Journal*.[75] "A bunch of my colleagues who 10 years ago would have looked down their noses at the Defense Department," added Francis Hoskins, a DOD contractor at the Illinois Institute of Technology, "are coming to me now asking how they can get their grants approved."[76] Hoskins' genetic engineering work concerns nerve gas antidotes. In December 1985, Col. Franklin H. Top, director of the Walter Reed Army Institute of Research in Washington, D.C., warned scientists in his biochemistry division that they would soon be out of a job if they didn't form "a credible research group in biological toxin defense."[77]

Conclusions

What can be predicted from this funding trend? The carte blanche enjoyed by the Reagan administration in its early years has ended. But by any measure—budgetary, ideological, strategic or political—the exploitation of biotechnology has been institutionalized in the DOD. Pressure to expand and modernize the BW program will survive in some form no matter who runs the government.

In the past the private sector has wielded considerable clout in CBW development and policymaking. The role of the chemical industry—that stood to lose hefty profits—in scuttling U.S. ratification of the 1925 Geneva Protocol on chemical and biological weapons is perhaps the classic case. A more recent example of the compelling commercial incentives in boosting CBW is Agent Orange. In 1978 a class-action suit was filed on behalf of Vietnam veterans who suffered severe health effects from exposure to dioxin, a contaminant of the herbicide sprayed in Vietnam by the U.S. Army through the early 1970s. This led to disturbing revelations about the chemical's manufacturer's prior knowledge of the toxicity of dioxin. Massive documentation from the suit shows that "Dow, the main supplier of Agent Orange, and other chemical companies knew the toxic dangers of dioxin exposure as early as the mid-1960s," years before it discontinued the product, according to a report by the Southeast Asia Resource Center, a Berkeley, California think tank.[78] The companies may have understood these dangers even as early as the 1950s, the report added. Ironically, they based part of their legal defense on arguments that the government knew as much about the dangers of dioxin-tainted Agent Orange as industry did.

In recent years the chemical industry throughout the developed world has been tethered by growing export restrictions in response to evidence that uncontrolled international trade has contributed to CW proliferation. Iraq, for example, is believed to have established its chemical capability using equipment and CW precursors supplied by European firms.[79]

The stigma associated with the manufacture of Agent Orange and napalm, along with concerns over proliferation, have discouraged some large companies from seeking military contracts for chemical weapons production. This has combined with the recognition that although nerve gas production has once again been authorized, it is an unstable business, prone to curtailment by a recalcitrant Congress. As a result, when the Army requested bids for binary nerve gas production in 1985, the largest companies were not interested.[80]

DOD officials also fear that CBW defense matériel "might never offer a market large enough to attract the industries that could produce it," according to a 1985 congressional General Accounting Office report.[81] "The problem might be particularly acute for medical equipment, because chemical and biological defense drugs would make up a very small share of a pharmaceutical company's business (Army medical officers place the estimate at less than one percent)," the report continued. "Chemical and biological defense drugs are limited production items; DOD might place an order for two production runs followed by none for five years," the GAO noted. Vaccines present similar headaches. "Making firms interested in the diseases of biological warfare is considered difficult, because these diseases are extremely rare in peacetime, making DOD the only customer," said the report. In light of the long lead time and the cost of compliance with elaborate federal regulations associated with drug and vaccine development, many firms reject DOD contracts as unlikely to produce an acceptable return on investment. "For biotechnology applications such as decontamination, development officials say the incentive for major firms is nonexistent," the report added. "Chemical and biological defense is simply too small an area compared to the rest of the commercial potential for biotechnology, and developments outside chemical and biological defense do not transfer easily."

These factors have opened the door to smaller, entrepreneurial firms which are plentiful in the young biotechnology industry. Small firms have more urgent immediate needs for capital and may be less concerned with market potential years down the line than would larger, diversified corporations. Venture capital is still flowing into hundreds of start-up companies. But most industry observers agree that a shakeout is already underway. Some small companies will fail. They will not achieve the breakthroughs that lead to successful products in time to satisfy impatient investors, or they will not be able to compete effectively. As this happens the increases in biotechnology funding from the Pentagon may assume ominous implications that dwarf the dollar amounts involved.

"Struggling biotechnology firms will increasingly turn to the DOD for a bailout if the money is there," King predicts. "Appeals to patriotism and economic desperation combine to create a compelling incentive to accept DOD contracts. But private companies, because of their relative independence from oversight and peer review, may be more willing to bend rules and overlook potentially offensive or illegal research."[82] This phenomenon is already apparent in the failure of several corporate recombinant DNA contractors to register safety committees with the NIH, although DOD rules require such registration.[83]

Military control of biotechnology is on the rise. Each year, it becomes more integral to Pentagon biological defense planning and more integrated into its academic and commercial network. But a parallel oversight process is conspicuously absent. In the face of secrecy, suspiciously ambiguous research implications, vast expenditures, and vague doctrines that defy logic, self-policing in biological-warfare research is a perilous way to keep the arms race in check.

Notes

1. U.S. Department of Defense, *Annual Report on Chemical Warfare—Biological Defense Research Program Obligations,*" FY 1980 through FY 1986.
2. U.S. Department of Defense, Directive Number 5160.5, May 1, 1985.
3. Robert Gillette, "VEE Vaccine: Fortuitous Spin-off from BW Research," *Science* (30 July 1971), 405.
4. John Hubner, "The Hidden Arms Race," *San Jose Mercury News/West,* (14 April 1984), 12.
5. To appraise the role of biotechnology in U.S. biological-warfare research, we reviewed only unclassified information. We used the DOD's "Annual Reports on Chemical Warfare—Biological Research Program Obligations," which contain a broad, though sketchy, overview of trends and priorities. We also used a wide range of technical reports, analyses, and promotional and academic publications generated by the military, press reports, and extensive interviews of DOD officials and independent experts. The analysis also includes more than 300 "DOD Research and Technology Work Unit Summaries," one page forms prepared for each DOD project, obtained under the Freedom of Information Act. They contain brief descriptions of the military objective and technological approach of the researchers, as well as a progress report or final statement.
6. U.S. Department of Defense, "Microbial Genetics and Taxonomy," Form 1498, agency accession number DAOA6436 (1 October 1982).
7. U.S. Department of Defense, "The Study of Toxic and Antigenic Structures of Botulinum Neurotoxins," Form 1498, agency accession number DAOG5087 (15 October 1983).

8. U.S. Department of Defense, *Annual Report on Chemical Warfare-Biological Defense Research Program Obligations*, FY 1983-84, 16-17.

9. U.S. Department of Defense, Form 1498, Agency Accession Number DA300961, (1 March 1983).

10. U.S. Department of Defense, Form 1498, Agency Accession Number DAOG6605, (5 August 1983).

11. Isberg, Ralph R., and Stanley Falkow, "A single genetic locus encoded by *Yersinia pseudotuberculosis* permits invasion of cultured animal cells by *Escherichia coli* K-12," *Nature* (19 September 1985), 262.

12. U.S. Department of Defense, Form 1498, Agency Accession Number DAOA4836, (10 October 1982).

13. U.S. Department of Defense, *Annual Report on Chemical Warfare-Biological Defense Research Program Obligations*," FY 1980 through FY 1986.

14. U.S. District Court for the District of Columbia, Foundation on Economic Trends et al., v. Caspar W. Weinberger et al., Civil Action No. 86–2436, (23 September 1986).

15. Interview with Col. David Huxsoll, 19 November 1986.

16. Interview with Jonathan King, 4 November 1986.

17. U.S. Department of Defense, Form 1498, Agency Accession Number DA302383, (29 March 1985).

18. Interview with Jonathan King, 4 November 1986.

19. U.S. Army, *Military Construction, Army, Reprogramming Request (project 0817300)*, (undated), 3.

20. R. Jeffrey Smith, "New Army Biowarfare Lab Raises Concerns," *Science* (7 December 1984), 1176.

21. Richard Novick, "A New Biological Warfare Laboratory?" (unpublished).

22. U.S. Army, *Military Construction, Army, Reprogramming Request (project 0817300)*, (undated), 3.

23. U.S. Army, *Information Paper. Subject: Modernization of Dugway Proving Ground*, DAMA-PPM-T, (8 November 1984), 5.

24. U.S. Army, *Military Construction, Army, Reprogramming Request (project 0817300)*, (undated).

25. U.S. Army, *Military Construction, Army, Reprogramming Request*, "Response to Congressional Staff Inquiries," 3.

26. James Sasser to Mack Mattingly, October 31, 1984.

27. Caspar Weinberger to James Sasser, November 2, 1984.

28. Smith, "New Army Biowarfare Lab Raises Concerns."

29. U.S. Army, *Environmental Assessment: Construction of a Biosafely Level 4 Facility at Baker Laboratory, U.S. Army Dugway Proving Ground (DPG), Utah* (31 January 1985), 11.

30. Smith, "New Army Biowarfare Lab Raises Concerns."

31. Smith, "New Army Biowarfare Lab Raises Concerns."

32. Richard Novick, "Response to Environmental Assessment of Proposed Dugway Biowar Laboratory," (unpublished).

33. U.S. Army, *Environmental Assessment*.

34. Novick, "Response to Environmental Assessment of Proposed Dugway Biowar Laboratory."

35. Novick, "Response to Environmental Assessment of Proposed Dugway Biowar Laboratory."

36. U.S. Army, Reprogramming Request, Information Paper: Modernization of Dugway Proving Ground, DAMA-PPM-T, Fact Sheet: U.S. Army Dugway Proving Ground, (8 November 1984) 2.

37. Weinberger to Sasser, November 2, 1984.

38. Smith, "New Army Biowarfare Lab Raises Concerns."

39. Novick, "Response to Environmental Assessment of Proposed Dugway Biowar Laboratory."

40. Smith, "New Army Biowarfare Lab Raises Concerns."

41. Smith, "New Army Biowarfare Lab Raises Concerns."

42. Smith, "New Army Biowarfare Lab Raises Concerns."

43. U.S. District Court for the District of Columbia, Civil Action N. 84–3542 (21 November 1984), 15.

44. For examples of lax safety practices in prior Dugway Proving Ground testing, see Charles Piller, "Biological Warfare: Lethal Lies About Fatal Diseases," *The Nation* (3 October 1988), 271.

45. U.S. Army, *Environmental Assessment.*

46. U.S. Army, *Military Construction, Army, Reprogramming Request (project 0817300).*

47. U.S. Army, *Environmental Assessment*, 1.

48. R. Jeffrey Smith, "Court Hears Suit on Biowarfare Laboratory," *Science* (17 May 1985), 827.

49. U.S. District Court for the District of Columbia, Foundation on Economic Trends et al., v. Caspar W. Weinberger et al., Civil Action No. 84–3542, Memorandum Opinion and Order, (31 May 1985).

50. Department of Defense, *Biological Defense Program*, Report to the Committee on Appropriations, House of Representatives (May 1986).

51. U.S. Army, *Draft, Environmental Impact Statement, Biological Aerosol Test Facility, Dugway Proving Ground* (January 1988).

52. Colin Norman, "Biowarfare Lab Faces Mounting Opposition," *Science* (8 April 1988), 135.

53. John R. Cushman, "Army Retreats on Utah Test Site Plan," *New York Times* (20 September 1988).

54. U.S. Army, Headquarters, Army Operations, *Field Manual No. 100–5* (20 August 1982), preface.

55. Alfred Mechtersheimer, "U.S. Military Strategy and Chemical and Biological Weapons," in Erhard Geissler, ed., *Biological and Toxin Weapons Today* (Oxford: Oxford University Press, 1986), 74–75.

56. Mechtersheimer, "U.S. Military Strategy and Chemical and Biological Weapons," 75.

57. U.S. Army, Headquaters, Army Operations, *Field Manual No. 100–5.* (20 August 1982), preface.

58. Lenny Flank, Jr., "The Binary Nerve Gas Shell Game," *The Nation* (21 June 1986), 841; Anonymous, "NATO Leaders Clear Way for Nerve Gas Production," *San Francisco Chronicle* (23 May 1986), 22.

59. Mechtersheimer, "U.S. Military Strategy and Chemical and Biological Weapons," 75.

60. James P. Wade, Jr., "DOD Research Activities in the Field of Recombinant Deoxyribonucleic Acid (DNA)," (1 April 1981).

61. Interview with Col. David Huxsoll, 19 November 1986.

62. John Marks, *The Search for the 'Manchurian Candidate'*. (New York: McGraw-Hill, 1980), 61–62.

63. MEDLINE searches conducted 3 February, 7 March, 2 April 1987.

64. In comments during the meetings of the American Association for the Advancement of Science in San Francisco (17 January 1989) Col. David Huxsoll challenged the publication record we stated for one of his researchers, Dr. Joel M. Dalrymple, in our book *Gene Wars*, from which this chapter is largely excerpted. Huxsoll claimed that his own MEDLINE search yielded many more than the one single paper we found for Dalrymple, who spent at least $1.77 million from 1982 to 1987. To recheck our figures, we ran a new MEDLINE search on 3/5/89, as well as searching several other databases of biomedical research papers. These searches confirmed our original findings on Dalrymple. It is interesting to note that Huxsoll made no effort to contradict the findings of the MEDLINE searches we made about his other researchers. The researchers with some of the poorest publication records, according to our original MEDLINE searches, were from Huxsoll's U.S. Army Medical Research Institute of Infectious Diseases at Fort Detrick, Maryland, and from the U.S. Army Medical Defense Research and Development Command, working at Walter Reed Army Institute of Research in Bethesda, Maryland.

65. Interview with Robert Orton, 24 March 1983.

66. Hubner, "The Hidden Arms Race."

67. Interview with Col. David Huxsoll, 19 November 1986.

68. U.S. Department of Defense, Army Medical Research Institute of Infectious Diseases, "Cooperative Antiviral Drug Development Program," (undated brochure).

69. Interview with Jonathan King, 4 November 1986.

70. Philip M. Boffey, "Biotechnology May be Used Against U.S., Official Says," *New York Times* (28 May 1984).

71. U.S. Department of Defense, *Control of Unclassified Technical Data With Military or Space Application*, DOD 5230.25 (May 1985).

72. Anonymous, "Outlays Soar for Pentagon's Secret Projects," *San Francisco Chronicle* (9 February 1987).

73. Anonymous, "Secret $8.6 Billion in Budget," *New York Times* (27 February 1986).

74. National Science Foundation, *Federal Funds for Research and Development* (FY 1982 to FY 1987).

75. Richards, Bill and Tim Carrington, "Controversy Grows over Pentagon's Work on Biological Agents," *Wall Street Journal* (17 September 1986).

76. Richards and Carrington, "Controversy Grows over Pentagon's Work on Biological Agents."

77. Richards and Carrington, "Controversy Grows over Pentagon's Work on Biological Agents."

78. Joel Rocarmora, "Dioxin: The Persistent Poison," *Southeast Asia Chronicle* (June 1980), 24.

79. John Tagliabue, "Europeans Agree to Chemical Curb," *New York Times* (11 April 1984).

80. Robert Waters, "2 Firms Answer Nerve Agent Call," *Hartford Courant* (9 July 1985), C1.

81. U.S. Congress, General Accounting Office, *Chemical Warfare: Progress and Problems in Defensive Capability*, (July 1986), 56–57.

82. Interview with Jonathan King, 4 November 1986.

83. Verified by Stanley Barban, official of National Institutes of Health Office of Recombinant DNA Activities in interviews, 24 October 1983 and 19 February 1987.

8

The Problem of Interpreting the U.S. Biological Defense Research Program

Susan Wright and Stuart Ketcham

The recent expansion of the U.S. Biological Defense Research Program (BDRP) in the 1980s documented in previous chapters poses an important problem of interpretation. What are the goals of this program? Why is it being pursued at the present time? What is the significance of the military use of biotechnology, initiated in the 1980s?

The difficulty of responding definitively to these questions is underscored by the claims and counterclaims aired with respect to both U.S. and Soviet military research and development in the biological sciences in the 1980s. Department of Defense officials have uniformly asserted that all research and development conducted under the BDRP is aimed only at defense. A characteristic response to queries about the existence of weapons research and development has been that "there is no offensive biological warfare work going on in this country; there are no plans for such work, and, very categorically, there are no plans for anything dealing with recombinant DNA work in regard to an offensive program."[1] In contrast, critics of the program have suggested that the defense rationale is a cover for research aimed at weapons. In a quite similar way, Defense Department officials and conservative analysts have made parallel claims about the Soviet biological defense program which have been denied by the Soviet Union (chapter 9). The problematic character of the evidence about both the Soviet and the American programs is underscored by the fact that the types of Soviet research projects claimed as evidence for a Soviet biological weapons program have counterparts in research in the United States and in other countries.[2]

Clearly, interpretation of the goals, designs, and long-term intentions for military research projects encounters certain ambiguities. These are all the more obscure since evidence concerning such projects is limited. Although the entire BDRP is described as an un-classified program, results of the program are kept secret when the Department of Defense determines that national security interests require such measures.[3] Furthermore, important and relatively ac-cessible sources of evidence about this research—the one-page Work Unit Summaries prepared by military agencies for each pro-ject and the annual reports to Congress on the Chemical Warfare and Biological Defense programs—do not give detailed or nuanced information. What is known about the biological defense programs of other nations is even less detailed.

Interpreting military research is also an exercise that is highly charged, politically and legally. Understating the significance of either the Soviet or the U.S. programs runs the risk of soothing national leaders, the public, and the international community into a possibly unjustified acceptance of a dangerous and ill-conceived program, allowing a military establishment to push ahead with projects that may ultimately undermine the legal regime prohibit-ing possession of biological weapons. On the other hand, overstat-ing the significance of these programs (that is, incorrectly accusing military sponsors of conspiracy to initiate a weapons program under the guise of defense if the charge turns out later to be unjus-tified) might cause cogent criticisms to lose credibility or, if taken seriously, increase international distrust in this area, eventually producing an escalation in the volume and scope of research.

This chapter defines various levels of ambiguity presented by biological research sponsored by the military, especially ambiguity associated with the procedures, observations, and assessments of scientific inquiry on the one hand and with the frameworks and end uses of inquiry on the other. The second section of the chapter examines case studies drawn from the U.S. Biological Warfare Program from 1945 to 1969 and from projects sponsored in the 1980s by the U.S. Medical Research and Development Command. On the basis of our analysis, we argue that while the content and framework of projects aimed at defenses against specific BW agents are ambiguous, this ambiguity is skewed in a manner that favors offensive over defensive applications. The third section explores the reasons why neither present international law nor technical constraints remove the ambiguities associated with content and framework or foreclose the possibility of weapons applications. Finally, the chapter seeks to develop an approach to assessing the content of the present U.S. Biological Defense Research Program that avoids an indefinite suspension of judgment on the significance of ambiguous research.

1 The Ambiguity of Research

Precisely how the ambiguity of scientific results is defined depends partly on the conception of scientific knowledge adopted by the analyst. Until the 1960s, an empiricist conception of science not only dominated assumptions about the nature of science held by scientists themselves but also was deeply entrenched in other disciplines, including the history, philosophy, and sociology of science, and in the general culture.[4] That is, it was widely assumed— despite important undercurrents inside and outside science that persistently raised questions about the validity of the assumption— that the purpose of scientific inquiry was to produce an objective account of a natural world that existed independently of the inquiry; it was further assumed that the application of scientific method, in yielding "plain and unembroidered evidence,"[5] could ensure the progressive elimination of error and bias in a movement towards an ever more complete picture of the natural world.

On this empiricist conception of scientific knowledge, inquiry is an unambiguous attempt to describe regular features of the natural world in terms of natural laws—with the important implication that what scientists do in their laboratories does not engage moral or political issues. Facts and values, description and evaluation, science and morality are thus compartmentalized, following a philosophical tradition that goes back at least as far as David Hume.[6] Ambiguity—and morality—enter the picture only when scientific results are applied—a stage that empiricists assume occurs only after the results have been generated.

Over the last thirty years, this traditional conception of science has been severely challenged by an extensive range of studies on the nature of science and the production of scientific knowledge. The empiricist assumption that observation could be passive and "unembroidered" by prior knowledge has been proven naive by studies in the psychology of perception and the philosophy of science suggesting that sense data are inevitably mediated by preconceptions and that observation is inevitably "theory-laden." Stimulated by Thomas Kuhn's *The Structure of Scientific Revolutions* (1962), which drew attention to the local nature of "paradigms," studies in the sociological tradition emphasized the communal nature of science, concluding that metaphysical and methodological assumptions, criteria for interpretation and evaluation of evidence, and models and metaphors could all be deeply affected by society and culture. The history of science and sociology of knowledge have produced a wide range of case studies documenting the socially and culturally contingent nature of science. Finally, feminist historians and sociologists have also denied the neutrality of scientific inquiry, by showing how this process has been repeatedly conceived and promoted in terms of the categories of sexuality and gender.[7]

A powerful implication of these critiques is that the scientist can no longer be assumed to be cut off from society, engaged in producing a form of knowledge that is morally and socially neutral. The laboratory walls—a symbol for the empiricist of the splendid isolation of the scientist—are now seen as permeable to social and cultural influences. Traditional empiricism has thus been challenged by a position that assumes that social, cultural, and historical circumstances inevitably intervene between the natural world and the scientist's account of it. According to this constructivist conception of science, the natural world may "[constrain] the observations and conclusions of the scientist, but never uniquely determines them."[8]

So effective are these challenges to traditional empiricism that it is rare today to find this position publicly defended. Many scientists would probably agree with Peter Medawar's observation that "there is a mask of theory over the whole face of nature."[9] Yet it should be noted that views of science that derive from an empiricist posture—particularly the assumption of the social isolation of science, its objectivity, and the linearity of scientific progress—are still deeply embedded in the general culture. And they still provide a powerful subtext of most forms of scientific education.

Social constructivists have also challenged a further assumption about the relation between science and technology that is often closely associated with traditional empiricism: the assumption that science and technology are well-defined, separate activities in which discoveries are made first in science and subsequently applied in technology. They perceive no clear boundary separating science and technology and no hierarchical dependence of technology on science (as assumed on the traditional view). According to sociologist Barry Barnes,

We are much less prone to think in terms which subordinate technology to science, and have the former working out the implications of the latter. Instead, we recognize science and technology to be on a par with one another. Both sets of practitioners creatively extend and develop their existing culture; but both also take up and exploit some part of the culture of the other. . . . Technology and science could both survive as forms of institutionalized activity independently of the other, but they are in fact enmeshed in a symbiotic relationship. . . . Cognitively, there is no fundamental distinction to be drawn between the creation of a scientific theory and its subsequent application. Just as the one is the imaginative development and purposive reordering of existing knowledge, so too is the other.[10]

That distinguishing science from technology is problematic is reinforced by studies of science showing that most scientific research today, including research in universities, is conducted in settings where the goals are plainly applied and utilitarian in nature.[11] Recombinant DNA technology, one of the principal fields of biotechnology to be targeted for military development in the 1980s, is an important case in point. The practical potential of genetic engineering was foreseen decades before the feasibility of the techniques was first demonstrated in 1972, was anticipated by the scientists involved in the first efforts to develop techniques for controlled genetic engineering, and was immediately recognized and publicized when the initial successes were achieved. In this field, the practitioners themselves no longer see a distinction between "basic" and "applied" research.[12]

The constructivist analysis opens up new questions about the ambiguity of scientific research. For the empiricist, scientific experiment and observation is a matter of "discovery"—of uncovering something that is already well defined. For the constructivist, on the other hand, the natural world does not *dictate* the content of observations (although on most versions of constructivism, it does *constrain* their content). In other words, on the latter view, results are underdetermined by evidence and there will be considerable flexibility in their production and interpretation.

This analysis suggests that several levels of ambiguity may characterize research. First, there may be ambiguity about the nature of research results whose significance depends, in general, on agreements about measuring techniques, conditions of observation, and standards. Controversies in science often occur at this level. For example, in the case of research on the effects of a toxin, there may be debate about the appropriate animal models to be used for measuring toxicity or about the significance of results produced with a given animal model. Constructivists assume that consensus on the significance of scientific observations is reached when scientists collectively agree on standards of conceptualization and assessment (or at least, when one standard achieves a dominant role in a scientific controversy) so that certain results assume particular significance. Such collective agreements limit interpretation and work to terminate debate about the significance of results, or in other words, to achieve "closure" in a scientific controversy.

Social constructivists have often focused their analysis of flexibility in the production and interpretation of research results at this level.[13] There is, however, a second level at which uncertainty and ambiguity about research results may enter, namely, the level of intention and end use. Is the study of a toxin gene aimed at developing a therapeutic or prophylactic product, or at developing more virulent strains of a potential biological warfare agent, or at understanding the structure and function of a gene? This second level of ambiguity in research has so far received little attention from sociologists and historians of science.[14] Yet clearly it may be important, particularly in the case of research supported by a mission-oriented research agency. The goals of the funding agency or of the scientist—that is, the framework of research—may affect the course of research and the generation of results. For example, the intended end use may produce a preference for the use of certain organisms or a particular sensitivity to the applied potential of freak results.

A distinction between these levels of ambiguity in research, which may be called ambiguities of *content* and *framework* respectively, is largely formal: in practice, since the framework of the research may influence the particular focus of research or the means chosen to pursue it, the content of research may well be affected by larger goals and intentions, and no clear-cut separation of these ambiguities is possible. Like the relation between science and technology, the relation between the content and framework of science is symbiotic in nature, with each aspect of science interacting dynamically with the other. One complication in the case of military research should be noted however: in this case, scientists may be unaware of the goals and intentions of the funding agency, since officials may operate on a "need to know" basis.

In summary, these ambiguities of content and application in research mean that there is ample scope for differing interpretations of research—for the scientist doing the research, for the military agency funding it, and for the observer attempting to evaluate the purpose of military programs. In the case of military research, the ambiguity of framework seems especially important. It may be impossible to decide on the significance of research in this larger sense until the results are incorporated into a final product, or in the most extreme case with respect to military research, used on the battlefield. By this time, authoritative knowledge will have come far too late to be useful for guiding or influencing military policy.

2 The Ambiguity of Biological Warfare Research: Case Studies

Ambiguity in the content, goals, and potential applications of biological warfare research has been recognized by the military at least since the 1940s. A report resulting from a review of the U.S. Biological Warfare Program in 1949 acknowledged the overlap of offensive and defensive preparations. Noting that "[t]he offensive employment of BW is predicated upon the ability to immunize our troops, those of our allies, or other personnel likely to come within range of infection by our own BW weapons," the report went on to comment on the duality of biological warfare research: "Information obtained from research on the defensive aspects of BW is, in the greater part, applicable to offensive problems as well. . . . Defensive BW research has many peacetime applications, particularly in the fields of medicine and public health."[15]

Military awareness of the double-edged nature of research on the vulnerability of American cities to BW attack was also revealed in a 1951 study conducted for the Joint Chiefs of Staff. The report contemplated studying the diffusion of biological simulants (agents whose properties mimic those of biological warfare agents) in mock BW attacks on American cities and noted that the cities chosen for study could be those "resembling Russian targets," and that "the dissemination of hot [biological warfare] agents could be reasonably predicted by the use of sampling stations located throughout the city." As the report noted, the results "would yield valuable information for both offensive and defensive planning. Through the utilization of simulants it should also be possible to work out operational problems, such as handling, storing, and optimum methods of dissemination on all types of targets with complete safety."[16]

The research program did in fact materialize: it was pursued by the Army and the CIA in a collaborative effort as part of the CIA operation MKNAOMI in the period 1952 to 1970 and was later described in some detail in the course of the 1975 Church Committee Hearings and the 1977 Senate Human Resource Committee Hearings (chapter 2). The tests measured the diffusion of biological simulants through a variety of sensitive national systems and institutions—for example, the White House, the Pentagon, and the Manhattan subway system. Results were used both to assess the vulnerability of sensitive American installations as well as to match delivery systems to lethal or incapacitating biological agents. There was nothing in the content of the diffusion tests that dictated a single end use. The same project produced results relevant to both offensive and defensive goals.[17]

Biological research currently supported by the Department of Defense also involves considerable ambiguity. Below, we consider selected examples of research pursued under the U.S. Army Medical Research and Development Command. This command is responsible for the entire Army medical research, development, testing, and evaluation program. As such, it oversees the medical research component of the Biological Defense Research Program as well as general medical and dental activities aimed at protecting and improving the health of Army personnel. Within the Medical Research and Development Command, the U.S. Army Medical Research Institute of Infectious Diseases (AMRIID) at Fort Detrick is responsible for integrating research and development activities, both in military laboratories and under contract in the civilian sector, that are aimed at medical defense against presumed biological warfare threats.[18]

The classification and analysis of projects that pursue this goal pose two general problems. First, the ambiguity of content and of framework discussed in the previous section is reinforced by the fact that many of the pathogens under investigation as potential BW agents are also endemic in various parts of the world. Research aimed at prophylaxis or therapy for the diseases caused by these pathogens may be portrayed both as biological defense research and as public health research, and not untypically, it is portrayed as serving both functions. For example, AMRIID currently sponsors research in Argentina on the development of a vaccine for

Argentine hemorrhagic fever (caused by Junin virus), research in China on treatment of Korean hemorrhagic fever (caused by Hantaan virus) with the drug ribavirin, and research in Liberia on treatment of Lassa fever (caused by Lassa fever virus), also with ribavirin. The ambiguity is captured in a recent statement about research sponsored by AMRIID made by the commander of the agency, Colonel David Huxsoll: "It would be absurd for us to create disease-causing organisms just to test therapies we develop. We therefore conduct tests in cooperation with the host governments of countries where diseases are already claiming victims. It is in the interest of both the United States armed forces and the peoples of other countries to find defenses against lethal or incapacitating diseases that occur naturally but which might also be encountered in warfare."[19]

Although the pathogens currently under study as potential BW agents by the Department of Defense occur naturally in various parts of the world, it is also the case that these pathogens are not generally seen as the causes of major public health problems. Indeed, lists of pathogens identified as potential BW threats and studied by the Department of Defense in the 1980s and pathogens identified in the mid-1980s by the Institute of Medicine as the leading causes of death and disease in developing countries diverge significantly (table 8.1).

Second, the information about the goals of the sponsoring agency provided by the Department of Defense on Work Unit Summaries is often vague. For example, the U.S. Army Medical Research and Development Command sponsors both research aimed at improving the basic health of American soldiers as well as medical research aimed at biological defense. Frequently, this distinction is not made on Work Unit Summaries. There may be nothing in the general descriptors used to classify research to distinguish research aimed at medical applications from research aimed at defense against biological weapons. Precisely which projects fall within the scope of the Biological Defense Research Program and which fall outside is unclear, at least to the external observer. Consequently, we have included in our analysis some examples which, while they may not be formally within the scope of the Biological Defense Research Program, produce results that have varying degrees of relevance to biological warfare.

Throughout this analysis, the central problem faced by military planners engaged in biological defense should be borne in mind:

Table 8.1
Pathogens studied under DOD sponsorship as potential biological warfare agents compared with pathogens identified by the Institute of Medicine as the leading cause of disease in developing countries.

	Organisms studied under Department of Defense sponsorship as potential BW agents in 1980s[a]	Vaccine candidates recommmended by the Institute of Medicine based on potential health benefits in developing countries[b]
Viruses		
Chagres virus	X	—
Chikungunya virus	X	—
Crimean-Congo hemor-rhagic fever virus	X	—
Dengue virus	X	X
Ebola virus	X	—
Equine encephalitis virus	X	—
Hantaan virus (Korean hemorrhagic fever)	X	—
Hepatitis A and B viruses	—	X
Japanese encephalitis virus	X	X
Junin virus (Argentine hemorrhagic fever)	X	—
Kyasanur Forest virus	X	—
Langat virus	X	—
Lassa fever virus	X	—
Lymphocytic chorio-meningitis virus	X	—
Machupo virus (Bolivian hemorrhagic fever)	X	—
Marburg virus	X	—
Mayaro virus	X	—
O'nyong-nyong virus	X	—
Parainfluenza viruses	—	X
Respiratory syncytial virus	—	X
Rift Valley fever virus	X	—
Ross River virus	X	—
Rotavirus	—	X
Sandfly fever virus	X	—
Sindbis virus	X	—
Tick-borne encephalitis virus	X	—
West Nile virus	X	—
Yellow fever virus	X	—

Bacteria

Bacillus anthracis (anthrax)	X	
Intestinal toxin-producing *Escherichia coli*	—	X
Francisella tularensis (tularemia)	X	—
Haemophilus influenzae type B	—	X
Legionella pneumophila (Legionnaires' disease)	X	—
Mycobacterium leprae (leprosy)	—	X
Neisseria meningitidis	—	X
Salmonella typhi (typhoid fever)	—	X
Shigella spp. (bacillary dysentery)	—	X
Streptococcus group A	—	X
Streptococcus pneumoniae	—	X
Vibrio cholerae (cholera)	—	X
Yersinia pestis (plague)	X	—

Rickettsiae

Coxiella burnetii (Q fever)	X	—
Rickettsia tsutsugamushi (scrub typhus)	X	—
Rocky Mountain spotted fever	X	—

Protozoa

Plasmodium spp. (malaria)	—	X

Names of diseases which differ significantly from the names of the pathogens are given in parentheses.

a. Sources: W.C. Anderson III and J.M. King, "Vaccine and Antitoxin Availability for Defense Against Biological Warfare Threat Agents," September 1983 (U.S. Army Health Care Studies Division Report No. 83-002); U.S. Army Medical Research Institute of Infectious Diseases, "Biological Defense, Functional Area Assessment: Overview," 4 January 1985; Work Unit Summaries for research supported by the U.S. Army Medical Research and Development Command, 1980–1987; Naval Biosciences Laboratory, School of Public Health, University of California, Berkeley, *Annual Report*, 1982–1983; Department of Defense, *IBC-Approved Recombinant DNA Research Projects*, 10 February 1984.

b. Institute of Medicine, Committee on Issues and Priorities for New Vaccine Development, *New Vaccine Development, Establishing Priorities, Vol. 2: Diseases of Importance in Developing Countries* (Washington, DC: National Academy Press, 1986).

the development of *specific* prophylactic defenses to provide protection from disease caused by pathogens or toxins is virtually impossible. As noted elsewhere in this book (chapters 4 through 6), vaccines and toxoids are rendered useless by four factors: first, the latency period between vaccination and the immune response (which may be as long as several weeks); second, the time needed to manufacture and deliver adequate doses of an appropriate vaccine; third, the fact that increases in exposure may overcome the protection provided by a vaccine; and finally and most conclusively, the enormous diversity of biological and toxin agents available to an adversary—which becomes virtually boundless if recombinant DNA methods are used to modify natural pathogens. There are no known techniques—and none, as far as we have been able to determine, contemplated for the future—that have any possibility of overcoming this central problem.[20]

Studies of the Lethality of Aerosols of Pathogens and Toxins

In its 1983–1984 report to Congress on the Biological Defense Research Program, the Army describes experiments on aerosols of anthrax, T-2 mycotoxin, and Junin virus, all viewed by the Army as possible BW or toxin warfare agents. The stated goals of this work are "to perform aerosol assessment of microbial organisms or their toxins to determine their danger as biological warfare (BW) threats and develop medical countermeasures."[21]

Tests of aerosols seem to provide no real advances either in assessing BW threats or in developing defenses against them. Procedures for aerosolizing pathogens include many variable parameters that may significantly affect the ability of the pathogen to survive delivery. For example, use of mechanical devices to generate aerosols might impose a variety of mechanical stresses on pathogens. Protective coating (microencapsulation) might provide varying degrees of protection from environmental stresses such as dehydration, sunlight, and freezing. Furthermore, pathogens have varying sensitivities to these stresses. These variables mean that pathogens are not easily assessed as BW threats nor easily eliminated as candidate BW agents. If exposure to an aerosol produces disease in an experimental animal, this result suggests that the mode of delivery is effective. However, if aerosol delivery does *not* produce an effect, this only raises doubts about the effectiveness of one set of parameters but reveals little if anything about the general "threat" posed by the use of the organism in question.

It might be countered that there is a need to test aerosols in order to determine the effectiveness of vaccines against abnormally high concentrations of a specific organism, or to determine whether and how aerosols of a given organism might be most effectively inactivated. Regardless of the results obtained in response to such questions, the usefulness of this knowledge as a basis for a biological defense will always be severely limited by the latency and diversity problems noted above. Furthermore, therapeutic countermeasures may certainly be developed without aerosol tests, and protective clothing may be tested with biological simulants.

In contrast, exploration of the properties of aerosols will reveal information that is useful for offensive purposes, particularly information on the most effective form of delivery.

Research on Vaccines Against Anthrax

In 1986–1987, AMRIID supported at least six projects whose goals, stated in Work Unit Summaries, included producing vaccines against anthrax bacillus components using recombinant DNA methods.[22] Three of the Work Unit Summaries specifically cite the need for defense against possible use of anthrax as a BW agent as the reason for the project.

As in the previous case study, the achievement of specific prophylactic defenses for biological or toxin warfare is a hopeless exercise because of the numerous and unpredictable variables, deriving in part from biological diversity, that render such efforts impossible. Effective protection is possible only if the BW agent to be used is known in advance—a situation that will normally apply only to a potential *user* of biological weapons. Furthermore, although production of vaccines using genetic engineering techniques requires only initial access to a very small amount of a pathogen, subsequent testing of the vaccine requires further quantities of the organism. Such tests, in turn, could generate knowledge of effective delivery methods. Thus development of an anthrax vaccine for military purposes is likely to produce results relevant to offensive application as well as to require supplies of the organism itself.[23] Civilian applications are also possible, for in this case, the organism can generally be anticipated. This project could provide benefits to public health, particularly in countries like the Soviet Union, where anthrax is endemic to certain regions.

Cloning of Genes Coding for Toxin Genes for Vaccine Development[24]

As stated in the Work Unit Summary, the goals of this project, pursued at Fort Detrick, are "to clone, sequence, and express the genes coding for snail conotoxins, scorpion toxins, snake toxins, myotoxin, cobrotoxin, cardiotoxin, crotoxin, taitoxin, and bungaro-toxins," for the purpose of developing novel vaccines for these toxins. For each toxin, the investigator apparently intends to identify the DNA that encodes the toxin in question, to clone this DNA in *E. coli*, and in particular to screen for bacteria that may make the toxin. A toxoid might be produced either in the traditional way, by first inactivating the toxicity of the toxin by heat or chemical treatment, or by genetically engineering a modified toxin gene coding for a protein that lacks toxicity but is sufficiently similar to the original toxin that it stimulates an immune response.

The study is justified in terms of defense against toxin weapons and indeed, it fits well with the Army's strong emphasis on toxin defenses, on which it plans to spend roughly $57 million a year from FY 1987 to FY 1990.[25] However, again, prophylaxis for specific toxin warfare agents seems doomed to failure since a determined adversary would have an enormous array of options available. On the other hand, such research could well generate information useful for offensive purposes. It should be also noted that the research itself may pose substantial laboratory hazards unless special care is taken to avoid expression of entire toxin genes in *E. coli*—a precaution not mentioned in the Work Unit Summary for this project. Public health benefits from this research are likely to be low since these toxins do not pose major public health problems.

Study of Infectious Multiple Drug Resistance in the Enterobacteriaceae

This is a broad study, conducted by Stanley Falkow of Stanford University, of genes located on the bacterial elements known as plasmids that encode for resistance to antibiotics or contribute to the virulence of enteric organisms such as *Vibrio cholera* and *Escherichia coli*.[26] In particular, Falkow investigated the function of a region of DNA in the bacterium *Yersinia pseudotuberculosis* (an organism which causes severe intestinal infections in humans and rodents) associated with the capacity of the organism to enter host cells (a property known as invasiveness). He produced a result of considerable interest to cell biologists—namely, a demonstration of the feasibility of endowing an inocuous strain of *E. coli* with invasiveness.[27] In so far as this result increases understanding of properties that play a crucial role in disease, it may provide a basis for more effective preventive or therapeutic measures. In this sense, Falkow's research has broad medical application.

Because the engineered *E. coli* strain that is capable of invasion does not kill the cells it has invaded or cause disease, this result in itself has no direct offensive application. Only if it were combined with studies of the insertion of other genes into *E. coli K12*—for example, a gene encoding a toxin—would this research raise questions about possible offensive end use.

Characterization and Mass Production of an Opioid-like "Hibernation Trigger"

Perhaps the most surprising studies funded in the 1980s by the Medical Research and Development Command involve "endogenous bioregulators"—a class of substances normally present in the body in minute quantities that appear to be essential for many psychological and physiological functions. An important subgroup of bioregulators are substances known as opioids, whose properties include induction of euphoria and analgesia. AMRIID, recognizing that exposure to higher than normal concentrations of these substances may be harmful, sees them as posing a new biothreat.[28] Apparently the bizarre BW scenario contemplated is the incapacitation of a military force by inducing euphoria, hallucination, or sleep in troops.

A project being pursued at the University of Kentucky, intriguingly entitled "Characterization of an Opioid-like Hibernation Induction Trigger," aims at the isolation and characterization of the gene for a protein called Hibernation Induction Trigger, or HIT, and the mass production of the protein using genetic engineering.[29] HIT, a substance isolated from the blood of hibernating animals, was shown by the same principal investigator and others in earlier studies to induce a hibernation-like state in summer in animals that normally hibernate in winter; they also showed that when the substance is infused into the brains of conscious monkeys, it produces "retching, yawning, mouth-gaping and marked lethargy" followed by the "appearance of an anesthetized state that persisted for 3–5 hours." In some experiments, additional effects included loss of appetite, drop in body temperature, and slowing of the heart rate.[30] (It should be noted that the chemical structure of HIT was not known at the time of this research and that indirect evidence yielded by subsequent studies suggested that HIT might be a "potent *releaser* of endogenous opioids" rather than belonging to this class of substances.[31])

Medical applications have been claimed for this research. While the project is described in the Work Unit Summary as having "civilian-limited potential," elsewhere, the principal investigator has stated that "[t]he clinical potential for a molecule such as [HIT] is vast. It could be used to depress metabolism, lower body temperature, manage cardiovascular function, or reduce food intake."[32] However, the undesirable effects of HIT suggest that medical uses are probably remote at present.

It is difficult to see how mass production of HIT would contribute to biological defense. Offensive application, on the other hand, seems more likely if delivery of HIT as an active agent is achieved. In summary, while the potential for defensive or medical application seems limited, the potential for offensive application seems greater although still remote in the sense that further major developmental steps would be required.

Table 8.2 summarizes the results of this analysis. The case studies are ranked according to the probability of an effective end use for public health, BW defense, or BW offense on a scale ranging from zero to high probability. This scale takes into account first, the likelihood of achievement of an application; second, the effectiveness of an application once achieved. (Thus we assess an anthrax vaccine as quite likely to be achieved but as having extremely limited defensive use and low-to-medium public health application.) The least troubling of the projects analyzed (D) has obvious public health application and remote offensive application. The most troubling projects promise to be ineffective in providing a biological defense but have high potential for generating information and techniques relevant to offensive applications.

These estimates are no more than educated guesses, based on what is generally understood to be feasible with current technology and what is known about the conditions for effective BW defense or offense. Despite the uncertainties in these estimates, however, the analysis underscores an important asymmetry of so-called "defensive" research: while ambiguous with respect to end use, such research is more likely to produce information and techniques useful for offensive application than for an effective defense. This asym-

Table 8.2
Ambiguous research projects sponsored by the Army

Project	Probability of effective end use		
	Public health	Biological warfare Defense	Offense
A. Aerosols of anthrax, T-2 mycotoxin, Junin virus	0	0–low	medium–high
B. Anthrax vaccine	low–medium	0–low	medium–high
C. Cloning of toxin genes	low	0–low	medium–high
D. Virulence factors	medium–high	0	low
E. Hibernation induction Trigger	0–low	0–low	low-medium

metry is particularly important for research that is aimed at exploring the nature of agents designated as a specific "threat" (such as bioregulators) or at developing a defense against a specific pathogen or toxin—all areas selected for special emphasis by AMRIID in 1985.[33] "Defensive" research thus ends in paradox: the greater the volume of defensive research, the higher the probability that offensive applications will ultimately result.

3 Legal and Technical Constraints on Military Research in the Biological Sciences

Especially since the beginning of the 1980s, when renewed military interest in the biological sciences became apparent, there have been attempts to argue that either legal restraints or technical conditions remove the ambiguities of application associated with research in the biological sciences that might allow offensive research to continue under a defensive rationale.[34]

In the first place, it has been argued that the broad prohibitions of the Biological Weapons Convention essentially solve the problem from a legal perspective. For example, this position was widely although not universally adopted at the first Review Conference on the Convention in March 1980.[35] However, as emphasized throughout this book, the Biological Weapons Convention does not address research; furthermore, the qualification in Article I of the Convention, allowing activities that can be justified for "prophylactic, protective or other peaceful purposes," opens up a loophole that allows research and development of a problematic and ambiguous nature (chapters 2 and 11). Nor does the present guideline used by the U.S. Department of Defense further clarify or restrict the nature of research permitted under the Biological Defense Research Program. Indeed, this guideline (appendix H), issued as National Security Decision Memorandum 35 by former National Security Advisor Henry Kissinger in 1969 and intended to define the limits of permissible research following Nixon's unilateral renunciation of biological weapons, reinforces the ambiguities of the Convention. According to the Kissinger guideline, the confinement of the Biological Research Program to research and development for defensive purposes does not "preclude research into those offensive aspects of bacteriological/biological agents necessary to determine what defensive measures are required." In other words, research into offensive aspects of biological agents is allowed as long as this research is performed for defensive reasons. Thus the operative criterion for permissible research concerns the *motives* for research rather than its *product*. As a prominent member of the Recombinant DNA Advisory Committee for the National Institutes of Health stated when the committee considered the question of military use of genetic engineering in 1982, "It is my understanding that any form of basic research, even if it deals with things that might have a weapons implication, is allowed. . . . One can, I guess, do anything for research purposes, as long as it is not something designed to *produce* biological weapons."[36]

A second argument attempts to eliminate concern about the ambiguity of military research on technical grounds. This line of reasoning focuses on what is currently feasible with the present technology, concluding that the advent of biogenetics will have no significant impact on the military attractiveness of the biological sciences because biotechnology can neither render natural pathogens and toxins more lethal nor significantly eliminate their military liabilities. Nature already provides a whole range of lethal pathogens and toxins, so this argument goes, and it is technically unfeasible to produce a biological weapon which would be militarily more effective.

The basic assumption of this argument, that the future of science and technology may be predicted, is questionable. Developed theories that have well-defined boundary conditions for their application may be predictive. However, sciences like molecular biology for which both the conceptualization of living things and the technology of intervention into biological processes is rapidly evolving cannot be addressed as if they already had well-defined boundary conditions. An instructive precedent is the case of the responses of physicists to the discovery of nuclear fission in the late 1930s. Physicists were divided about the implications of fission: some, like Niels Bohr, held that fission could not produce a huge release of energy; others, like Leo Szilard, were so concerned about that possibility that they attempted to persuade their colleagues to keep the results of their research secret.[37] The point is that there was no consensus *in advance* of the demonstration of the amount of energy released by nuclear fission at least in part because the boundary conditions for the process were ill defined. Even a so-called "exact" science that is susceptible to mathematical description and analysis is not predictive until relevant boundary conditions have been well defined. It is impossible to predict the future development of evolving sciences and thus to rule out in advance the emergence of novel weapons applications. Indeed, as military interest in biotechnology has increased, there has been a clear shift in international attitudes toward potential weapons applications from the view that there is no cause for alarm to considerable concern about military development of this field.[38]

4 Avoiding Suspending Judgment

Neither legal nor technical constraints can produce closure on the significance of research now being pursued under the sponsorship of the Biological Defense Research Program. Faced with the ambiguous end uses of many of the research projects currently underway, observers of this program may be tempted to avoid assessment by claiming that the variety of interpretations possible (depending on such factors as the framework and goals of research) requires suspension of judgment until further evidence becomes available. Particularly for military research, however, there is an obvious danger in placing one's judgment indefinitely on hold: "closure" may be defined only at the point of deployment of research results, and in this case a possible outcome is the enhancement of the effectiveness of biological weaponry. At that point, it would almost certainly be too late to influence policy. Those who either make military policy or seek to influence it cannot afford the luxury of an academic retreat from judgment. In the military and political spheres, assessment of the significance of military research may be required long before closure on the significance of individual research projects is possible.

An alternative approach to the assessment of military research and development programs in the biological sciences is to examine the pattern of support for the program as a whole and to ask to what extent this pattern indicates interests in either defensive or offensive goals. In evaluating the content of a military program from this perspective, it is important to recognize that the development of a weapons system generally requires far more than the development and stockpiling of a harmful biological agent. To be developed as a weapon, such an agent would generally need to be integrated first, into a *technological* system that provides the means to mass produce the agent, to store and transport it safely, to deliver it to a target, and (not least) to protect the users; and second, into an *organizational* system that is responsible for maintaining and operating the weapons system and that requires communications and command structures as well as trained personnel. The left-hand column of table 8.3 lists the principal technical and organizational elements that might reasonably be expected for an offensive system. Clearly, however, the precise requirements will vary with the circumstances.[39]

A defensive system on the other hand would be based on generic therapy, detection, decontamination, and protective clothing (categories IV to VIII in table 8.3). As discussed in other chapters in this section, only a generic defense is reasonable in the case of biological warfare because of the enormous range of candidates for biological weapons available to a determined aggressor. It follows that purely defensive work could be pursued almost entirely with biological simulants. Aerosol tests with BW agents would be unnecessary. Similarly, the need for prophylactic measures aimed at specific BW agents (category III in table 8.3) is questionable since it is highly unlikely that these measures could ever provide adequate protection to troops and certainly not to civilian populations. Not even the development of extremely rapid diagnostic and detection techniques could work: an inventive aggressor could overcome such measures by an arsenal of BW agents with varying immunological properties. Indeed, speculation about the form a highly sophisticated defense might take leads quickly to the anticipation of a technological race, with features that parallel that of the nuclear arms race, in which a technological advance on one side is

Table 8.3

Present activities conducted under the Biological Defense Research Program and related activities conducted under the Chemical Warfare Program

	Research/ development	Production/ stockpiling
I. Biological warfare agents		
Stability for storage/dispersal	−	−
Low pesistence in the environment	−	−
High infectivity/high virulence	A	−
Evasion of detection/diagnostic systems	A	−
II. Delivery systems		
Transmission by insects or other arthropods	+	−
Aerosol delivery	A	−
Missile delivery	T	−
III. Prophylaxis for troops and support personnel		
Vaccines	+	+
Toxoids	+	+
IV. Therapy for troops and support personnel		
Antibiotics	+	+
Antiviral drugs	+	+
Antitoxins	+	+
V. Detection		
Detection methods and devices	+	+
Diagnosis methods and devices	+	+
VI. Decontamination		
Methods and devices	+	+
VII. Protective clothing	+	+
VIII. Testing and evaluation		
High-containment facilities for testing BW agents	Available at Fort Detrick	
High-containment facilities for testing detection, decontamination, clothing	Proposed for Dugway Proving Ground	
Large-scale testing of delivery systems	−	
IX. Large-scale manufacture		
High-containment facilities	−	
X. Organizational system		
Command and control	Developed for CW	
Training	Carried out for CW	

Documented projects	+
No documented projects	−
Ambiguous projects	A
Theoretical study	T

neutralized by further advances on the other side—a dangerous progression in which each side strives to achieve an unattainable security.

To what extent do the present activities supported under the U.S. Biological Defense Research Program fit either offensive or defensive patterns of development? The evidence relevant to these activities that is currently available—the annual reports on the BDRP to Congress, the Work Unit Summaries prepared by the Department of Defense for each project and available through Freedom of Information Act requests, the information provided by the Department of Defense in response to litigation, and previous analyses—is summarized in Table 8.3.

In some respects, this pattern confirms claims by representatives of the Department of Defense that present work is oriented towards defense.[40] The evidence suggests a strong emphasis on research and development aimed at prophylaxis, therapy, decontamination, detection, and protective clothing. In addition, certain elements that would generally be expected for developing a weapons system—particularly large-scale testing of delivery systems, high-containment facilities for manufacturing large quantities of lethal biological agents, and research on biological agents that has as its sole purpose increasing their virulence, infectivity, stability, or ability to evade detection—are reassuringly absent.

On the other hand, as we have argued above, the current emphasis of the BDRP on prophylactic measures for specific biological and toxin warfare agents is not merely ambiguous: because of the overwhelming difficulty of producing effective prophylactic defenses, such projects are more likely in the long run to produce results effective for offensive rather than defensive applications. This research has been defended by the commander of AMRIID, David Huxsoll, on the grounds that development of vaccines entails only the lessening of the virulence of the pathogen in question rather than its enhancement. In 1989, Huxsoll claimed on this basis that "defensive research is based on different postulates and hypotheses than is research directed toward offensive ends, and the rationales for data collection and analysis are different."[41] This argument might apply to a specific stage in the development of a vaccine against a naturally occurring pathogen. However, more generally, it will break down at many other points in the research-development-testing-evaluation sequence. It may be possible for the head of a single military research unit to dismiss concerns about the ambiguity of defensive biological warfare research because of the compartmentalization of knowledge within the military; it is impossible to do so for the Biological Defense Research Program as a whole.

In addition, the Department of Defense has proposed projects and facilities that, if approved, would greatly expand the range of ambiguous research and development conducted under the BDRP. The high-containment aerosol facility proposed for Dugway Proving Ground would make it feasible to assess the properties of aerosols of the most lethal organisms and toxins—generating the sort of information for offensive application that was appreciated so well by the Army and the CIA in the 1950s and 1960s. Noticeably, the Department of Defense has never ruled out the possibility that this facility, if constructed, would be used for testing the properties of novel, genetically engineered agents. The proposals made in September 1985 by the Chemical Warfare Commission to "address the chemical and biological threats of the future as well as the present," in May 1986 by the Department of Defense to counter the "threat" posed by the use of biotechnology to develop novel biological weapons, and in July 1987 by the Army Science Board to assess the use of molecular genetics and biotechnology "by potential adversaries to modify, enhance or greatly alter the pathogenicity, survival capacity, dissemination potential, susceptibility to detection, and identification of viable BW agents" all reflect growing military interest in the investigation of the offensive potential of biological warfare under a defensive rationale.[42] It seems safe to assume that these public indications of the future direction of military research in the biological sciences have been reinforced by more detailed proposals that are safely sheltered from public scrutiny.[43]

In summary, the present orientation of the U.S. Biological Defense Program is provocative in its general character and the emphases of its current research and development activities as well as in the political and military postures associated with its promotion. It has rapidly expanded since 1980, particularly in the use of the new biotechnology; it remains partially secret, classifying policy documents and some research results; and it indicates repeated military interest in exploring dimensions of biotechnology that an outside observer could reasonably construe as having potential for offensive application.

The impulse to expand the Biological Defense Research Program was a product of the bellicose posture towards the Eastern bloc and the swollen military budgets supporting massive growth in military arsenals and research and development programs that character-ized Reagan's first term. Now that a significant relaxation of superpower tensions has been achieved, it would be ironic if the expansionary momentum of the BDRP was allowed to continue and if ambiguous and provocative research and development were allowed to undermine progress towards strengthening the legal reg-ime supporting chemical and biological disarmament. No matter how vocal President Bush's support for the CBW regime may be, his assurances cannot be persuasive if at the same time the United States pursues ambiguous CBW research and development activi-ties that send a mixed signal about American intentions to other nations.

To initiate a reversal of the biological warfare policy initiated by President Reagan in his first term, an important step would be a comprehensive review of the BDRP that asks first, to what extent current projects actually promote defense against bioweaponry; second, whether some projects are so ambiguous that they are like-ly to stimulate offensive research in other countries; and third, to what extent the Department of Defense is funding legitimate re-search in public health and basic molecular biology. This review should be followed by the elimination of all projects that do not have clear justification for defense and the transfer of responsibility for oversight and support for public health and basic research to civilian agencies such as the National Institutes of Health. In this way, all research aimed at prophylaxis and therapy would be open to the full exercise of the Federal Administrative Procedures Act, the Freedom of Information Act, and the Federal Advisory Com-mittee Act, unmitigated by claims of the need to protect "national security." The public could then be reasonably assured that the ambiguities of this research could be clarified and that any applica-tions that resulted could be publicized and distributed.

Acknowledgments

We would like to thank Richard Falk for drawing attention, early in the gestation of this chapter, to the political and legal implications of misrepresenting the significance of military research, and Robert Sinsheimer for his very helpful response to a draft of the chapter.

Notes

1. Dr. William Beisel, former director of BW research at Fort Detrick, quoted in Howard Zochlinski, "Army DNA Researchers Try to Shed Biowarrior Image," *Genetic Engineering News* 1 (September/October 1982), 31–33.

2. See William Kucewicz, "Beyond 'Yellow Rain': The Threat of Soviet Genetic Engineering," *Wall Street Journal* (April 23, 25, 26, 27, May 1, 3, 8, 10, 18, 1984) and letter of Elkan R. Blout, "Research, Pestilence and War," *Wall Street Journal* (May 24, 1984).

3. U.S. Army Medical Research and Development Command, *Final Programmatic Environmental Impact Statement: Biological Defense Research Program*, April, 1989, 2–2. According to this document, "[t]hose results which impinge on national security may be classified in accordance with Army Regulation (AR) 380–86, Classification of Chemical Warfare and Chemical and Biological Defense Information."

4. Useful descriptions of the traditional empiricist view of science are given by Peter Medawar in *The Art of the Soluble* (London: Methuen, 1967), 131, and Michael Mulkay in *Science and the Sociology of Knowledge* (London: George Allen and Unwin, 1979), 19–21.

5. Peter Medawar, *The Art of the Soluble*, 147.

6. Max Black, "Is Scientific Neutrality a Myth?" Lecture given at the annual meeting of the American Association for the Advancement of Science, January 27, 1975.

7. For guides to the literature on these challenges to the empiricist conception of scientific knowledge, see Ron Johnston, "Contextual Knowledge: A Model for the Overthrow of the Internal/External Dichotomy in Science," *Australian and New Zealand Journal of Sociology* 12 (October 1976), 193–203; Steven Shapin, "History of Science and its Sociological Reconstructions," *History of Science* 20 (1982), 157–211; Michael Mulkay, *Science and the Sociology of Knowledge*, chs. 2–4; Karin Knorr-Cetina and Michael Mulkay, *Science Observed: Perspectives on the Social Study of Science* (London: Sage Publications, 1983); and Sandra Harding, *The Science Question in Feminism* (Ithaca: Cornell University Press, 1986), ch. 1.

8. Michael Mulkay, "Knowledge and Utility: Implications for the Sociology of Knowledge," *Social Studies of Science* 9 (February 1979), 63–80. For an extreme version of social constructivism which holds that scientific descriptions (and the social and cultural assumptions embedded in them) are *constitutive* of reality, see Steve Woolgar, "Irony in the Social Study of Science," in Karin Knorr-Cetina and Michael Mulkay, eds., *Science Observed* (London: Sage, 1983), 239–266.

9. Peter Medawar, *The Art of the Solbule*, 131.

10. Barry Barnes, "The Science-Technology Relationship: A Model and a Query," *Social Studies of Science* 12 (1982), 161–169.

11. Ron Johnston, "Contextual Knowledge," 198.

12. Susan Wright, "Recombinant DNA Technology and Its Social Transformation," *Osiris* 2 (1986), 303–360.

13. See, e.g., Bruno Latour and Steve Woolgar, *Laboratory Life: The Construction of Scientific Facts*, 2nd ed. (Princeton: Princeton University Press, 1986); Harry Collins, ed., "Knowledge and Controversy: Studies of Modern Natural Science," *Social Studies of Science* 11 (1981).

14. So far, social constructivists have tended to concentrate on the analysis either of forms of scientific inquiry for which applied goals are relatively remote, or of technology: see, e.g., Wiebe E. Bijker, Thomas P. Hughes, and Trevor J. Pinch, eds., *The Social Construction of Technological Systems* (Cambridge, MA: MIT Press, 1987), 17–50.

15. U.S. Office of the Secretary of Defense, "Report of the Secretary of Defense's Ad Hoc Committee on Biological Warfare," July 11, 1949 (declassified June 25, 1986), 12.

16. "Memoradum by the Joint Advanced Study Committee for the Joint Chiefs of Staff on Biological Warfare," September 21, 1951 (JCS 1837/26). The phrase "American cities resembling Russian targets" is somewhat ambiguous, but the word "resembling" if used accurately, suggests that the author intends "Russian cities targeted by the United States." We thank Rodney McElroy for making available a copy of this document.

17. U.S. Senate, Select Committee to Study Government Operations With Respect to Intelligence Activities, *Final Report: Foreign and Military Intelligence* (April 26, 1976), 360. See also U.S. Army, *U.S. Army Activity in the U.S. Biological Warfare Programs* (February 24, 1977) in U.S. Senate, Committee on Human Resources, *Hearings: Biological Testing Involving Human Subjects*, 95th Cong. 1st Sess. March 8 and May 23, 1977, 34.

18. U.S. Army Medical Research Institute of Infectious Diseases, *Biological Defense: Functional Area Assessment, USAMRDC Medical Defense Program* (January 4, 1985), C2–C3.

19. Malcolm W. Browne, "Defenses to Biological Weapons Tested by Army in China and Argentina," *New York Times* (February 6, 1989), 7.

20. These problems are noted in W.C. Anderson III and J.M. King, "Vaccine and Antitoxin Availability for Defense Against Biological Warfare Threat Agents," September 1983 (U.S. Army Health Care Studies Division, Report #83–002) but the overwhelming difficulty of effectively responding to them is not addressed.

21. Department of Defense, *Annual Report on Chemical Warfare and Biological Defense Program Obligations for the Period 1 October 1983 Through 30 September 1984*, 46–47.

22. See, e.g., U.S. Army Medical Research Institute of Infectious Diseases, "Basic Studies on Conventional Agents of Biological Origin and Development of Medical Defensive Countermeasures," (Performing Organization: U.S. Army Medical Research Institute of Infectious Diseases; Principal Investigator: J.M. Dalrymple; Project Number DAOG1522; December 10, 1986).

23. For a more detailed development of this argument, see chapter 6 and Erhard Geissler, ed., *Biological and Toxin Weapons Today* (Oxford: Oxford University Press, 1986), chapter 4 and appendix 7.

24. U.S. Army Medical Research Institute of Infectious Diseases, "Cloning of Militarily Relevant Toxin Genes for Novel Vaccine Development," (Performing Organization: U.S. Army Medical Research Institute of Infectious Diseases; Principal Investigator: L.A. Smith; Project Number: DA306147; December 10, 1986).

25. U.S. Army Medical Research Institute of Infectious Diseases, *Biological Defense: Functional Area Assessment, USAMRDC Medical Defense Program* (January 4, 1985), C6–C8, C11, C27.

26. Walter Reed Army Institute of Research, "Infectious Multiple Drug Resistance in the Enterobacteriaceae," (Performing Organization: Standford University; Principal Investigator: Stanley Falkow; Project Number; DAOG9398; April 1, 1983).

27. Ralph Isberg and Stanley Falkow, "A Single Genetic Locus Encoded by *Yersinia Pseudotuberculosis* Permits Invasion of Cultured Animal Cells by *Escherichia coli* K-12," *Nature* 317 (September 19, 1985), 262–264.

28. U.S. Army Medical Research Institute of Infectious Diseases, *Biological Defense: Functional Area Assessment, Overview* (January 4, 1985), 17; *USAMRDC Medical Defense Program* (January 4, 1985), C6.

29. U.S. Letterman Army Institute of Research, "Characterization of an Opioid-like Hibernation Induction Trigger," (Performing Organization: Unviersity of Kentucky; Principal Investigator: P.R. Oeltgen; Project Number: DA312580; May 4, 1987).

30. W.A. Spurrier, P.R. Oeltgen, and R.D. Myers, "Hibernation 'Trigger' From Hibernating Woodchucks (*Marmota monax*) Induces Physiological Alternations and Opiate-like Responses in the Primate (*Macacca mulatta*)," *Journal of Thermal Biology* 12 (1987), 139–142.

31. See, e.g., P.R. Oeltgen et al., "Kappa Opioid U69593 Did Not Induce Hibernation But Blocked HIT-Induced Hibernation in Summer-Active Ground Squirrels," *Federation Proceedings* 46(3) (March 1, 1987), 839; and D.S. Bruce et al., "Summer Hibernation in Ground Squirrels (*Citellus tridecemlineatus*) Induced By Hibernation-Induction Trigger (HIT) From Torpid Black Bears Is Blocked By Naloxone," *Federation Proceedings* 46(3) (March 1, 1987), 839.

32. Spurrier, Oeltgen, and Myers, "Hibernation 'Trigger' from Hibernating Woodchucks."

33. U.S. Army Medical Research Institute of Infectious Diseases, *Biological Defense: Functional Area Assessment. Overview*; USAMRIID, *Biological Defense: Functional Area Assessment: USAMRDC Medical Defense Program*.

34. See, e.g., Martin Kaplan, "Another View," *Bulletin of the Atomic Scientists* 39 (November 1983), 27.

35. Report of the Preparatory Committee for the Review Conference of the Parties to the Convention on the Prohibition of the Development, Production and Stockpiling of Bacteriological (Biological) and Toxin Weapons and on Their Destruction (February 8, 1980), U.N. Document BWC/CONF. I/5. But also see *Views of States Parties on New Scientific and Technological Developments Relevant to the Convention* (February 29, 1980), U.N. Document BWC/CONF. I/6.

36. David Baltimore, transcript, meeting of the National Institutes of Health Recombinant DNA Advisory Committee (June 28, 1982), 36 (emphasis added).

37. Spencer Weart, "Scientists with a Secret," *Physics Today* (February 1976), reprinted in Spencer Weart and Melba Phillips, eds., *History of Physics* (New York: American Institute of Physics, 1985), 123–129.

38. See, e.g., briefing papers by Sweden, the United Kingdom, the Soviet Union, and the United States for the Second Review Conference on the 1972 Biological Weapons Convention: U.N. Documents BWC/CONF. II/4 (August 18, 1986), BWC/CONF. II/4/Add.1 (August 29, 1986) and BWC/CONF. II/Add. 2 (September 8, 1986).

39. The main components of an offensive biological warfare system are discussed in *Report of the Secretary General on Chemical and Bacteriological (Biological) Weapons and the Effects of Their Possible Use* (U.N. Document A/7575/Rev. 1) July 1969, 9–10, and in Stockholm International Peace Research Institute, *The Problem of Biological Warfare V: The Prevention of CBW* (Stockholm: Almqvist and Wiksell, 1971), 141–43. Clearly, these components will vary somewhat with the circumstances and will be less demanding for a small-scale operation.

40. See, e.g., David Huxsoll, "Defensive Biological and Toxin Weapons Research in the United States and the Soviet Union," Annual Meeting of the American Association for the Advancement of Science, San Francisco (January 1989).

41. David L. Huxsoll, testimony, U.S. Senate, Committee on Governmental Affairs and Permanent Subcommittee on Investigations of the Committee on Governmental Affairs, *Hearings on Germ Wars: Biological Weapons Proliferation and the New Genetics*, May 17, 1989.

42. Walter Stoessel et al., *Report of the Chemical Warfare Review Commission* (Washington, D.C.: U.S. Government Printing Office, June 1985), 69–71; Department of Defense, "Biological Defense Program," Report to the Committee on Appropriations, House of Representatives, May 1986; Department of the Army, Army Science Board, "Final Report of the Ad Hoc Subgroup on Army Biological Defense Research Program," July 1987.

43. The following documents may provide further information about Defense Department intentions for those with security clearances: Charles A. Fowler, Final Report of the Defense Science Board on Chemical Warfare and Biological Defense, September 11, 1985 (secret); U.S. Army Chemical Research and Development Center, Aberdeen Proving Ground, MD, "Technologic Changes Since 1972: Implications for a Biological Warfare Convention," March 1986 (secret).

IV

Charges of Violation of the Biological Warfare Legal Regime

9

Sverdlovsk, Yellow Rain, and Novel Soviet Bioweapons: Allegations and Responses

Leonard A. Cole

Ronald Reagan assumed the presidency in 1981 on a rigidly anti-Soviet platform. His attitude toward the Soviet Union was reflected in his insistence that its leaders could not be trusted to adhere to international treaties. This belief was ostensibly validated throughout most of Reagan's tenure, as the United States accused the Soviets of violating a series of weapons agreements. Among those cited from the outset were the 1925 Geneva Protocol, which prohibits the use of chemical or biological weapons, and the 1972 Biological Weapons Convention, which prohibits the development, production, or stockpiling of biological or toxin weapons.

The purported violations of these two agreements arose from three sets of allegations: that an illegal biological weapons facility exploded in Sverdlovsk in 1979, that the Soviets or their surrogates used "yellow rain" toxins as weapons in Southeast Asia and Afghanistan during the late 1970s and early 1980s, and that the Soviets were developing novel biological weapons through recombinant DNA techniques.

The administration's allegations took on different emphases over time. As the evidence for one drew substantial skepticism, the government shifted emphasis to another. Doubts about the Sverdlovsk charges surfaced soon after they were made in 1980. By the end of 1981, yellow rain overtook Sverdlovsk as the focus of U.S. claims about Soviet biological treaty violations.

As questions mounted in the early 1980s about the validity of the yellow rain allegations, the United States added yet another charge. In 1984, the administration announced suspicions that the Soviets were developing weapons through genetic engineering. Thus, whether by design or not, the Reagan administration gave the appearance of searching for issues to validate its presumptions about Soviet untrustworthiness. When the evidence for each issue was challenged, the administration, without abandoning its earlier charges, claimed new infractions.

After reviewing the alleged violations, I shall assess their reception by the American public and by other nations. The evidence suggests that the administration had little success in convincing either audience that the Soviet Union had violated the legal regime prohibiting chemical and biological warfare. At the same time, however, the charges were influential in Congress in helping to justify the expansion of the chemical warfare and biological defense programs.

1 The Alleged Violations

Anthrax in Sverdlovsk

Taking the lead from a Russian-language magazine published by émigrés in Frankfurt, several European tabloids reported in late 1979 that a bacteriological accident had occurred in the Soviet Union. The magazine later indicated that hundreds had been killed, and that the accident took place in Sverdlovsk, situated in the Urals, about 900 miles east of Moscow. In March 1980, U.S. State Department officials expressed concern that a lethal biological agent apparently had caused an epidemic in Sverdlovsk, a city of 1.2 million people, the previous year. Hundreds of residents reportedly died of anthrax during a one month period. In June, after briefings from the CIA, State Department, and Arms Control and Disarmament Agency, the House Intelligence Committee suggested that the epidemic was linked to the accidental release of anthrax bacilli from a military facility. If true, this could have meant that the Soviet Union had violated the 1972 Biological Weapons Convention.[1]

The Soviets informed U.S. officials that the outbreak had been caused by anthrax-contaminated meat, and had nothing to do with biological warfare. Within months after Reagan became president, however, administration officials made clear they regarded the incident as a violation of the 1972 Convention. Although the United States did not issue formal charges, government officials have never retreated from the presumption that the Sverdlovsk epidemic resulted from illegal biological warfare activities.

The Reagan administration's position was based on a variety of inferences. They included claims by Soviet émigrés that an illegal biological weapons plant was located in Sverdlovsk; that the victims suffered from respiratory rather than gastric forms of infection, suggesting that the disease was spread by air rather than through the distribution of tainted meat; and that the Soviet Defense Minister visited Sverdlovsk two weeks after the outbreak began.

The first émigré to make the claim to U.S. officials was, reportedly, Mark Popovsky. A science writer, Popovsky had left the Soviet Union in 1977, and was in the United States in 1979 when the Sverdlovsk incident occurred. He testified before the House Select Committee on Intelligence in 1980 that Soviet underground sources had informed him that a secret biological warfare facility was situated in Sverdlovsk.[2] His allegations and those of other émigrés were expanded upon in a series of *Wall Street Journal* articles in 1984. The newspaper cited the émigrés as the main basis for its presumption that the epidemic resulted from a "spectacular accident at a biological weapons facility."[3]

The *Journal* named only one émigré beside Popovsky but claimed that others confirmed the allegation. None of the émigrés had witnessed biological weapons activities at Sverdlovsk. Their claims rest on second- or third-hand accounts and cannot be regarded as hard evidence.

The United States contended that the anthrax epidemic was caused by inhalation of airborne spores released during an explosion. The Soviets said that the spores were ingested and the infections were gastric in origin. The U.S. position assumed that pulmonary and gastric anthrax infections yield distinctive symptoms. However, the medical literature on anthrax suggests that these symptoms are not easily distinguished, and that both may cause pneumonia-like symptoms. Moreover, gastric anthrax is so rare in the West—U.S. experts had never seen a case—that no one can be entirely sure what its symptoms are.[4]

The visit to Sverdlovsk by Defense Minister Dmitri Ustinov two weeks after the outbreak began is cited by the United States as further evidence of a military connection to the epidemic. Several large military facilities are indeed located in Sverdlovsk. Whatever the cause of the outbreak, its possible effects on military personnel might well have interested the Defense Minister and could explain his personal investigation. Yet if there had been a spectacular accident, it hardly seems likely that he would have waited two weeks before traveling to the scene.

Skepticism about the U.S. position was later buttressed by an American physics professor, Dr. Donald E. Ellis, who was residing in Sverdlovsk on a scientific exchange during the time of the anthrax outbreak. Ellis had been allowed to move freely in and around the city. He noticed no particular precautions, no efforts to quarantine or decontaminate. He said he traveled with his wife close to the site of the purported accident: "I don't exclude the possibility that something may have occurred. But [if it did] I think I or my wife would have sensed some effort to protect us from it."[5]

The Soviets *could* have been more forthcoming and allowed investigation by outsiders immediately after suspicions were raised. But their refusal does not in itself signify culpability. Although consultation and cooperation among states are urged in the 1972 Convention, provisions for verification are absent. The Soviets maintained initially that the incident was a matter of public health and not subject to the requirements of the Convention. Their reluctance to invite foreigners to the area, while regrettable, was not a treaty violation.

In keeping with moves toward openness under the leadership of Mikhail Gorbachev, Soviet spokesmen offered more information about Sverdlovsk at the Second Biological Weapons Convention Review Conference in the fall of 1986. Several U.S. scientists said after briefings by Soviet public health officials that they considered the Soviet explanation of the epidemic "credible" and "plausible."[6]

Even more revealing was information provided in 1988 to American scientists by Soviet physicians who had treated the Sverdlovsk victims. After the Soviets made a presentation at the National Academy of Sciences, many listeners expressed doubts that the U.S. allegation was correct. Among those who attended, unequivocal support for the U.S. position came only from two American military officers[7] who reiterated the Defense Department's view, expressed months earlier in its 1987 annual report on *Soviet Military Power*. The nature of the events in Sverdlovsk, the report said, provided "a very strong contradiction of the Soviet position that the anthrax outbreak was just a public health problem resulting from the sale of contaminated meat."[8]

Yellow Rain

The accusation that the Soviets or their surrogates were using mycotoxins as weapons, specifically toxins from the fungus Fusarium, was first made by Secretary of State Alexander Haig in September 1981. Two months later, Richard Burt, Director of the Bureau of Politics and Military Affairs for the State Department, graphically described the government's case. Before a Senate Foreign Relations Subcommittee, he testified that planes had released clouds described as yellow rain over defenseless people in Laos, Kampuchea, and Afghanistan. The exposed people "would experience an early onset of violent itching, vomiting, dizziness, and distorted vision. Within a short time they would vomit blood tinged with material, then large quantities of bright red blood. Within an hour, they would die of apparent shock and massive loss of blood from the stomach."[9]

Burt indicated that the presence of toxins (trichothecenes derived from fungi) had been confirmed in three yellow rain samples obtained by intelligence sources from alleged attack sites in Laos and Kampuchea. Government investigators concluded that they were toxin warfare agents because trichothecenes cause the symptoms that Burt described and are not found naturally in the combinations identified in the southeast asian samples. Further, Burt claimed that the toxins produced all the symptoms reported. "The fit," said Burt, "was perfect."[10]

Several scientists received this contention with skepticism. Harvard molecular biologist, Matthew Meselson, testifying at the same hearing, argued that the government's supposed facts were speculations. Contrary to the government's assertion, Meselson contended that "there is, to my knowledge, not even a single study of whether these mycotoxins do or do not occur naturally in Southeast Asia." He noted, however, that mycotoxins were known to occur in warm climates similar to those of Southeast Asia. Meselson also questioned whether trichothecenes disseminated in coarse particles or droplets as claimed by the government could produce the rapid and massive hemorrhage and death described by Burt. Citing a study showing that mycotoxins did not always produce these symptoms, Meselson concluded that claims about a "perfect fit" between symptoms and exposure to mycotoxins did not seem justified.[11]

The State Department in March 1982 presented a lengthy report on the subject that sought to fortify the government's contentions.[12] Ignoring the arguments of skeptics, Deputy Secretary of State Walter J. Stoessel, Jr., in a briefing about the report, claimed categorically that "the Soviet Union and its allies are flagrantly and repeatedly violating international laws and agreements."[13] His uncompromising tone reflected that of the report, which declared that "the conclusion is inescapable that the toxins and other chemical warfare agents were developed in the Soviet Union, provided to the Lao and Vietnamese either directly or through the transfer of know-how, and weaponized with Soviet assistance in Laos, Vietnam and Kampuchea."[14]

Meselson remained unconvinced. As well as his question about the symptoms of supposed victims, he had doubts about the nature of the samples. He had reviewed reports by investigating teams from Thailand, Canada, Australia and the United Nations, each of which had indicated that the yellow rain samples contained pollen. In November 1982, U.S. government investigators publicly confirmed this observation. Meselson discussed this with his Harvard colleague, Peter Ashton, a specialist in southeast asian botany, who wondered if bees might be involved. Ashton contacted Thomas Seeley, a Yale biologist who had studied bees in Southeast Asia. Seeley quickly identified the yellow rain spots as bee droppings.[15]

The idea that yellow rain was bee feces was dismissed by scientists who had previously identified trichothecenes in some of the samples. "Childish," "absurd," said University of Minnesota botanist Chester Mirocha, the plant pathologist at the University of Minnesota responsible for the analysis of the first samples obtained by the U.S. government. The high concentration of toxins in the samples "indicate to me that they had to be put there by the intervention of man."[16] Sharon Watson, the government's original proponent of the toxin-weapon hypothesis, dismissed the bee-feces proposition as amusing. In her view, the Soviets purposely mixed pollen and some kind of solvent with the toxins. The solvent would enhance the toxin's "going through the skin," according to Watson. Whatever remained on the surface would dry, and with the help of the pollen become aerosolized, inhaled, and "retained in the bronchi of the lungs." This toxin-pollen-solvent combination Watson called a "very clever mixture."[17]

Questions about the origin of yellow rain simmered during the following months as the Army laboratories continued to analyze a backlog of samples. By the end of 1983, two phenomena had become clear. First, virtually all yellow rain samples contained pollen from plant families common to Southeast Asia. Second, trichothecene toxins were absent from all the samples from Southeast Asia that were being tested in U.S. government laboratories. This strongly suggests the possibility that the original positive reports, which had come from an outside contractor, were in error.

The United States position was forcefully challenged early in 1984 in an article by Lois Ember in *Chemical and Engineering News*. Ember, a senior editor of the journal, reviewed every piece of alleged evidence cited by the government through 1983—from physical samples through the testimony of alleged victims and eyewitnesses. Her conclusion: "The U.S. simply has not proved that toxin warfare has taken or is taking place in Southeast Asia or in Afghanistan."[18]

Ember first outlined the core of the government's case: that trichothecene toxins do not occur naturally in Southeast Asia, and that the combination of these toxins found in physical samples and in samples of the urine, blood, and tissues of purported victims came from man-made (Soviet) weapons. Yet, more than 90 percent of all the samples tested revealed no traces of toxins. Indeed, the U.S. Army's own Chemical Systems Laboratory failed to detect any trichothecenes at all in any of the approximately 100 samples that it tested. In Ember's words, "the grand total of positive physical evidence gathered by the U.S. is slight: five environmental and 20 biomedical samples (including some tissues from an autopsy) from Southeast Asia, plus one contaminated gas mask from Afghanistan."[19]

Ember reviewed the results reported for each of the five samples from Southeast Asia, and found they were not "scientifically impressive." A sample allegedly from an attack in Kampuchea in March 1981, for example, was split into two sections that gave different readings. The sections differed not only in amounts of various trichothecenes, but in ratios of one toxin to another. A separate sample from the alleged attack showed still different combinations of toxins, and some of the trichothecenes found in the previous sample were entirely absent from this one. The other samples also revealed dissimilar ratios and contents. Ember found it difficult to believe that every positive sample of ostensibly Soviet-manufactured toxin should vary so much from the other in ratio and content.[20]

Beyond the properties of the samples, Ember examined two other causes for skepticism: inconsistencies in the statements from alleged attack victims, and the improbability of the use of trichothecenes as a weapon in view of the availability of far more effective agents.

She consulted social scientists and Southeast Asia experts who read the "150 to 200 reports" compiled by the State Department about purported yellow rain attacks among the Hmong tribesmen of Laos. They noted that virtually all the reports came from a refugee camp in Thailand whose leadership included former members of the old CIA-backed secret army in Laos. Almost no other Hmong made claims about being subject to chemical or biological warfare attacks. Moreover, individual accounts varied widely from one person to the next, and even by the same person over time.[21]

In assessing the manner of interviews and the refugees' responses, Ember reported the views of several of the social scientists and Southeast Asia experts. Each concluded that the refugee reports seemed unreliable, and that the refugee accounts did not make the case for the government's claim. They pointed out that the U.S. interviewers did not take into account cultural differences between themselves and the Hmong interviewees. Individual stories were not cross-checked for accuracy, and interviewers often asked leading questions. Furthermore, Jeanne Guillemin, an anthropologist at Boston University, suggested that the willingness of the Hmong to attribute illness and death to chemical attacks might have a political explanation. According to Guillemin, the American interviewers apparently "didn't appreciate the vulnerability of the people being interviewed, that they were refugees who did not want to spend their life in a camp in Thailand. Of course they are going to be accommodating. Who wouldn't?"[22]

Finally, Ember argued that if the Soviet Union wanted to use chemical or biological warfare agents, trichothecenes would be a poor choice. If the intent were to annihilate an enemy, many more potent agents were available. If it were to terrorize people and make them ill, more controllable agents, such as the riot gas CS that was employed by U.S. troops in Vietnam, could be used.[23]

By mid-1984, the yellow rain debate had become further clouded by the facts that the purported physical evidence was growing older, and that the U.S. government had produced no new samples since 1982. Rather than retreat from its position that the Soviets were still using illegal weapons, the government merely surmised that they had switched to less potent agents.[24]

In assessing the arguments for and against the yellow rain thesis, Philip Boffey, a science reporter for *The New York Times*, questioned whether trichothecenes were accurately identified in the first place:

When the United Nations conducted an investigation in 1981, it sent specimens of yellow powder and vegetation from Laos to three top laboratories in three countries. At the same time, it sent samples that were known to be spiked with trichothecenes and samples that were known to be blank. Two of the laboratories failed to find any trichothecenes, even in the spiked samples. The other laboratory said it found trichothecenes in all of the samples, including the blank.[25]

Official thinking in Washington remained unchanged. In a 1984 report on *Soviet Military Power*, issued about the same time as Boffey's analysis, Secretary of Defense Caspar W. Weinberger stated unequivocally that the United States had "strong evidence of the actual use of chemical and toxin weapons by the Soviet Union and its client forces in Afghanistan, Laos and Kampuchea." In support of this contention, the secretary wrote that a "group of agents, known as mycotoxins, has been identified in the laboratory from samples collected in Afghanistan."[26]

In fact the only physical sample from Afghanistan that showed trichothecenes was a single gas mask; the environmental samples were from Southeast Asia. In addition to misidentifying the origin of the contaminated samples, the secretary failed to mention that the overwhelming majority of samples from areas supposedly under toxin attack showed no mycotoxins. Nor did he note the inconsistencies in virtually every other category of purported evidence.

The most dramatic challenge to the government's yellow rain thesis was offered in a 1985 report by five scientists—Thomas Seeley, Joan Nowicke, Matthew Meselson, Jeanne Guillemin, and Pongthep Akratanakul.[27] Three of them, Seeley, Meselson, and Akratanakul, visited Southeast Asia in March 1984 to undertake a field study in Thailand of honeybee nesting areas. They found large swaths of yellow-spotted vegetation which they determined to be fecal deposits. At one point they were actually caught in a fecal shower.

We were visiting a region known for bee trees in which an unusually large number of nests are suspended. In the village of Khua Moong, about 24 kilometers south of Chiang Mai in Thailand, we examined the area around two such trees, one bearing about 30 nests and the other more than 80, hanging from 20 to 50 meters above the ground. As we observed the second tree through binoculars from a clearing about 150 meters away, we saw a lightening in the color of several nests. Hundreds of thousands of bees were suddenly leaving their nests. Moments later drops of bee feces began falling on and around the three members of our party. About a dozen spots fell on each of us. We could neither see nor hear the bees flying high above us. . . .

Our observation showed that showers of honeybee feces do indeed occur in the Tropics of Southeast Asia; moreover, the showers and spots closely resemble the showers and spots said to be caused by yellow rain.[28]

The three scientists later visited the Ban Vinai refugee camp where most of the interviews with witnesses of the alleged yellow rain attacks had been conducted. One of the three (Akratanakul) speaks Lao, and the scientists were able to question 16 groups at random. After showing the groups leaves spotted with bee feces, 13 "concluded they did not know what the spots were, although some people said they had seen such spots before." Two groups, totaling 15 people, said the spots were "kemi," their term for the chemical/biological warfare poison. One group of three people also agreed that the spots were "kemi," although one of the members initially thought the spots might have been insect feces. The authors concluded that the Hmong refugees from Laos do not "generally recognize honeybee feces for what they are," and that some think the feces are agents of chemical or biological warfare.[29]

The scientists' findings represented a culmination of growing skepticism about the government's view of yellow rain. It prompted Nicholas Wade, an editorial writer for *The New York Times* who specializes in science affairs, to write that "yellow rain is bee excrement, a fact so preposterous and so embarrassing that even now the Administration cannot bring itself to accept it."[30]

The tenuousness of the government's proposition was further highlighted in 1987 by Julian Robinson, Jeanne Guillemin, and Matthew Meselson. They cited recently declassified documents showing that Defense and State Department officials had recognized inconsistencies in the government's position that were never publicly acknowledged (chapter 10). The documents indicated that in 1981, when the government first announced its charges, its only physical evidence was a single leaf-and-stem sample that supposedly contained trichothecenes identified by Sharon Watson. Not until October 1982 did the Army develop careful analytic techniques to determine the presence of trichothecenes. It then analyzed more than 80 samples but found trichothecenes in none. One of the samples included a yellow powder in which Chester Mirocha had previously identified trichothecenes. Furthermore, the documents showed that in 1984 and afterward, British and Canadian scientists found trichothecenes in blood samples from people in Thailand who were never near an alleged attack. This seemed to confirm the natural presence of these mycotoxins in Southeast Asia, despite U.S. claims to the contrary, while at the same time it raised doubts that trichothecenes were commonly present in yellow rain samples.[31]

The government's investigators also found in 1984 that earlier interviews by alleged victims of yellow rain attacks failed to distinguish between first-hand observation and hearsay. The victims had confused dates and locations of alleged attacks. The investigators learned further that army medical specialists sent to Thailand in 1979 had reported on the medical consequences of the attacks—but they had relied on verbal accounts, not medical examinations.[32]

None of this altered the official United States position. In his *Report to the Congress on Soviet Noncompliance with Arms Control Agreements* issued at the end of 1987, President Reagan said again that "the Soviet Union has been involved in the production, transfer, and use of trichothecene mycotoxins for hostile purposes in Laos, Cambodia, and Afghanistan in violation of its legal obligation under international law as codified in the Geneva Protocol of 1925 and the Biological and Toxin Weapons Convention of 1972."[33] No amount of evidence seemed sufficient to induce the government to acknowledge that its position was questionable.

Genetic Engineering

By 1984, contentiousness about the purported 1979 anthrax accident in Sverdlovsk had dissipated, and although the yellow rain debate continued, no new trichothecene attacks had been alleged for more than a year. At this point, the government issued a roundhouse accusation against the Soviets in another area, claiming that hitherto secret intelligence information showed them engaged in a program to create biological weapons through recombinant DNA techniques. The administration's charges were summarized in Secretary Weinberger's annual report on Soviet military power:

Soviet research efforts in the area of genetic engineering may also have a connection with their biological warfare program. There is an apparent effort on the part of the Soviets to transfer selected aspects of genetic engineering research to their biological warfare centers. For biological warfare purposes, genetic engineering could open a large number of possibilities. Normally harmless, non-disease producing organisms could be modified to become highly toxic or produce diseases for which an opponent has no known treatment or cure. Other agents, now considered too unstable for storage or biological warfare applications, could be changed sufficiently to be an effective agent.[34]

Despite the hypothetical tone, the remarks left little doubt about the government's position. The same suppositions were amplified in a series of eight articles in *The Wall Street Journal* during April and May, titled "Beyond 'Yellow Rain,' the Threat of Soviet Genetic Engineering."[35] Written by William Kucewicz, an editorial writer for the newspaper, the articles purported to show that the Soviet Union was engaged in a vigorous biological warfare program. They provided an overview of all the alleged Soviet activities that had previously been known, and many that had been secret. Because of their scope, and the extraordinary amount of space provided by an influential newspaper, the articles themselves were an event. They unvaryingly reflected the Reagan administration's position.

According to Kucewicz, claims that the Soviets were developing biological weapons through genetic engineering rested "foremost" on the word of émigrés to the United States.[36] As with the claims about Sverdlovsk, the émigrés had not seen or participated in such activities. Yet their word was central to the *Journal*'s contention that "the Soviet Union has never halted its biological weapons program."[37]

For the *Journal*, the clinching argument that genetic engineering is "a natural and almost inevitable next step in the Soviet biochemical weapons program" came from a passage in the 1983 edition of the Soviet *Military Encyclopedia*. The author of the series was so impressed by the passage that he referred to it in three of the articles and offered identical quotations in two: "Achievements in biology and related sciences . . . have led to an increase in the effectiveness of biological agents as a means of conducting warfare."[38] Why Kucewicz thought this passage proves that the Soviets are engaged in biological weapons development is hard to fathom. It is merely a statement of fact.

The thrust of the *Journal* series was to justify expanding U.S. biological defense activities, some of which might be interpreted as coming close to violating the 1972 Convention. The final installment of the series concluded with an admonition that everyone should "come to grips with the Soviet genetic warfare program."[39]

Soon after, the columnist Jack Anderson reported CIA findings that the Soviets had mastered "gene-splicing techniques as ominous as the atom-splitting discoveries that led to the nuclear bomb." The information, Anderson wrote, came largely from "a key Soviet source who defected." Once again, if Anderson's attribution is accurate, the United States was making presumptions about novel Soviet bioweapons on the word of an unnamed source whose basis of information was left to the reader's imagination.[40]

Several American specialists who are familiar with Soviet scientific work challenged *The Wall Street Journal*'s and the government's contentions about Soviet activities. Dr. Elkan Blout of the Harvard Medical School dismissed Kucewicz's claim that the many papers in the Soviet scientific literature dealing with the chemical components of toxins imply biological warfare activity. Blout, who works in the same scientific area, wrote that "a similar article could have been written by a Soviet editorial writer about my research and that of. . . 60 other laboratories [which] are clearly not involved in biological warfare research." He deplored "guilt 'by implication' journalism."[41]

Dr. David Dubnau, a molecular biologist at the Public Health Research Institute in New York, was similarly skeptical. In an interview in 1985, Dubnau, who had made several visits to Soviet laboratories, rejected the possibility of greatly advanced work being done in secret. "You can't just do sophisticated work in one secret laboratory. You need a broad infrastructure in your universities and basic research labs which can inform the work being done in that particular laboratory." He concluded emphatically, "The Soviets don't have it."[42]

2 Effects of U.S. Accusations

The effects of the United States allegations about Soviet violations of the 1972 Biological Weapons Convention may be assessed in terms of popular attitudes, responses by other nations, and U.S. biological warfare activity. Among the U.S. allegations, only that of yellow rain was attributed to direct evidence. Moreover, the yellow rain charges received more media coverage over a longer period than those of Sverdlovsk or genetic engineering. Thus the yellow rain issue provides the core of discussion about popular and international reaction to U.S. contentions about Soviet violations.

Popular Attitudes

Doubts about the evidence for yellow rain came from a few scientists soon after the United States issued charges in 1981. Although their skepticism received considerable newspaper attention, the media in general reflected support for the government's contentions during the first years of the debate.

About 50 articles, editorials, and cartoons on the subject that had appeared through mid-1983 were reproduced in an 85-page special edition of *Current News*, a publication by the Air Force for the Defense Department. The great majority endorsed the view that yellow rain was a Soviet chemical-biological weapon.

Articles contending that the Soviets were responsible for yellow rain were reproduced from *Discover, Foreign Affairs, Nature, Science,* and major newspapers including *The New York Times, The Washington Post,* and *The Wall Street Journal.* The items may not have been an unbiased sample—criteria for inclusion were not specified. But the number of articles supporting the government's claim was impressive, far outweighing those representing perspectives critical of the official position.[43]

How much the public was influenced by government claims and by media coverage is a tantalizing question. In August 1982, a Gallup Poll commissioned by *The Wall Street Journal* surveyed popular attitudes about yellow rain and chemical and biological warfare. This was the only occasion that a major polling organization inquired into attitudes about yellow rain and biological warfare treaty violations.

Although the survey was conducted before scientific challenges to the U.S. position had been sharpened, even then many respondents were unconvinced by the government's allegations. The contention that the Soviets were using yellow-rain-toxin weapons had been highly publicized for a year. Nonetheless, only 22 percent of the respondents named the Soviet Union when asked: "To the best of your knowledge, have any countries engaged in biological or chemical warfare since World War II?" Sixteen percent cited Vietnam as having engaged in such activities, and 11 percent the United States."[44] (Presumably the United States was mentioned because of its use of defoliants and riot control agents during the Vietnam War.)

Responses to another question were interpreted by the editors of the *Journal* to mean that the government's yellow-rain accusations were causing Americans to be more skeptical about arms control agreements in general with the Soviet Union. The question:

Since 1925, several international treaties signed by the Soviet Union have banned the use of biological and chemical warfare. If the charges about yellow rain are true, the Soviet Union has broken a treaty. Which of the following options comes closest to your opinion of what the U.S. should do? Suspend nuclear arms reduction talks with the Soviet Union until it abides by the chemical and biological warfare treaty? Or, not let the yellow rain issue interfere with nuclear arms reduction talks because of the importance of slowing down the arms race?

Thirty-six percent of the respondents favored suspension, while 49 percent opposed letting the yellow rain issue interfere with nuclear arms talks. The interest of about half the respondents in seeing arms talks continue despite alleged Soviet violations may seem surprising. But the *Journal* quotes the Gallup Organization as interpreting this to mean that the purported violations had an effect: "From a polling perspective, this is a relatively large number voting against talks with the Russians. Almost all questions which suggest talks with the Russians receive strong public support: that less than half would favor continuing talks is indicative of a strong reaction to the 'yellow rain' charges."[45]

This analysis seems strained in view of the speculative character of the question. It includes the qualifying phrase, "if the charges are true." But few apparently believed the charges were true; as noted, only 22 percent thought the Soviets had been engaged in biological or chemical warfare. Since opinions on continuing negotiations were not correlated with belief in yellow rain, nothing can be said definitely about the effect of the latter.

Nevertheless, the *Journal*'s editors concluded that the poll showed that "confusion exists in the public's mind over the precise nature of the yellow-rain issue." They made clear their hope that the U.S. government will "mount an effective campaign" to gain public support for its position.[46] Two of the newspaper's editors later wrote that yellow rain had brought arms control in general to a "dead end"—implying that every arms control agreement was now worthless.[47]

Most of the public never became convinced by such contentions. The Reagan administration's influence in 1982 on public attitudes about alleged Soviet activities was modest. In the following years, as more weaknesses in the government's case were demonstrated, public support dwindled further. In September 1986, on the eve of the first Reagan–Gorbachev summit, 79 percent of the respondents in a Louis Harris poll favored "an agreement with the Russians on [the] outlawing of chemical weapons and warfare." Only 19 percent opposed.[48]

This 1986 survey did not ask about violations of existing treaties, but the respondents' answers imply little concern about the administration's claims concerning yellow rain or other allegedly illegal Soviet activities. If people believed the Soviets were violating agreements on biological weapons, it seems unlikely that they would overwhelmingly support a treaty outlawing chemical weapons. This is true especially because many people (mistakenly) fail to distinguish between chemical and biological weapons.

Another survey suggests minimal concern about a different area of purportedly illegal Soviet activities. In 1984, the United States asserted that the Soviet Union might be engaged in genetic engineering research to develop offensive weaponry. Few science policy leaders seemed worried, however. Six hundred and thirty such leaders were asked in a 1985 survey to choose risks that "come to mind" from a list of five concerns related to recombinant DNA research. The list included ecological hazards, creation of undesirable organisms, negative effects on humans, ethical issues, and use as a weapon in warfare. The item cited by the fewest respondents (5 percent) was use as a weapon in warfare. This figure did not reflect doubts that undesirable organisms could be created, because 73 percent considered that a risk.[49] But if the administration's concerns about Soviet military-genetic engineering activities were taken seriously, more science policy leaders would likely have reacted.

The Congress seemed more responsive to the administration's charges than the public or scientists who had been surveyed. Several members of each party in both houses announced their belief that the Soviets were violating the Geneva Protocol and the Biological Weapons Convention. A Senate resolution noting "accumulated evidence" of illicit Soviet activity in Southeast Asia and Afghanistan passed without dissent in February 1984. The issue was not equally salient for all, however. No such resolution reached the floor of the House of Representatives, and after 1984 few members in either house raised the matter. Nevertheless, appropriations by Congress for chemical and biological defense programs grew through most of the 1980s, suggesting at least tacit acceptance of the administration's position.

Attitudes of Other Nations

In 1982, the British determined that "information released to us by the United States Government has now led us to believe that chemical weapons, probably including mycotoxins, have been used in Southeast Asia." The British, like most other friends of the United States, did not initially conduct their own inquiry but rather based their conclusions on information provided by the United States.[50] The Canadians were an exception. A scientific group headed by Dr. H.B. Schiefer of the University of Saskatchewan reported to Canada's Department of External Affairs in 1982 that chemical/biological warfare agents had been used in Southeast Asia.[51]

Paradoxically, the Schiefer group's report praised a United Nations team that had just determined that the data to support such accusations were inconclusive. The U.N. report contained some "minor misinformations [sic]," the Schieffer group concluded, but "by and large, is a respectable piece of work." Moreover, "although the U.N. experts were of the opinion that their report was inconclusive, one has to admire the thoroughness and objectivity of the approach."[52] Here, embedded in the most supportive statement by a foreign source for the U.S. position, lay generous praise for a report that could not find evidence that the Soviets were culpable.

By the mid-1980s, doubts about the nature of yellow rain grew. In May 1986, the Canadian government reported that the environmental samples it tested contained only traces of trichothecenes, comparable to the levels of naturally occurring toxins measured elsewhere. Furthermore, a Canadian government survey of 272 Thai who did *not* claim to be victims of yellow rain attacks revealed trichothecenes in the blood of five participants in the survey, while samples from ten people who did claim exposure to yellow rain were all negative.[53] In the same month, the British government also acknowledged that its Chemical Defence Establishment Laboratory at Porton Down had been unable to detect trichothecenes in any of its environmental samples. Tests by the French and Swedish governments were similarly negative (chapter 10). Canada and other previously supportive countries became more equivocal. Only the United States remained steadfast in its accusations about yellow rain.

The mood of uncertainty was reflected in statements in 1986 at the Second Review Conference of the Parties to the Biological Weapons Convention. The Canadian representative's remarks at the Review Conference still came closer than other nations to the U.S. position. But even his was ambiguous. Canada's own investigations, said the delegate, "did not in themselves provide conclusive proof but nor did they refute the allegations of violations." He thought it unfortunate that a thorough examination had been impeded, in part because investigators were denied access to the sites of alleged yellow rain attacks. Uncertainties, therefore, "had not been resolved."[54]

Most other nations either noted without taking a position that there was controversy about yellow rain, or failed to mention the subject at all. The delegate from Ireland contended, for example, "that unless means were found to deal objectively with such allegations, erosion of the authority of the Convention might well be inevitable."[55] From the Australian delegate: "Two events had occurred since the entry into force of the Convention that had focused on its effectiveness. The first was the outbreak of anthrax among people living in Sverdlovsk. . . . The second event involved allegations that toxin weapons had been used against civilians and resistance fighters in Laos and Cambodia." After regretting that outside investigators were denied entry to either location, the delegate merely said, "Australia had discussed those allegations in an informal manner with a number of States Parties."[56]

The French delegate first appeared to scold those who would not allow on-site investigation in Sverdlovsk and Southeast Asia. He regretted the absence in the 1972 Convention of a "procedure which would help to resolve the problem in such situations." But he implicitly included the United States in his criticism of "the parties concerned." "They did not seem," said the delegate, "to have done everything in their power to demonstrate their good faith."[57]

The United States delegate courted no ambiguity. "Despite the lack of stringent verification provisions," he said, the United States determined "that the Convention had been violated."[58]

It is only possible to speculate about the effect that the perceptual gap about yellow rain might have on relations between the United States and its friends. But if no other nation can share the United States' unambiguous conclusions, confidence in this country's judgment is hardly likely to be enhanced. As the validity of claims about Soviet violations becomes more doubtful and the U.S. position remains rigid, the motivation for the claims becomes suspect.

3 Concluding Assessment

The Reagan administration's accusation that the Soviets were violating the Biological Weapons Convention faced increased skepticism in the late 1980s. A portion of the public embraced the official U.S. position in the early 1980s; Britain and Canada initially gave it lukewarm support. But by 1987, the evidence was viewed largely as ambiguous or improbable, except by officials in the administration.

From the administration's standpoint its most patent success was its ability to generate increasing amounts of money for biological defense projects. The growth was steady through the mid-1980s. It occurred, paradoxically, while doubts about the validity of the administration's allegations were also growing. The financial and programmatic increases seemed to take on a life of their own, propelled along with increasing annual military budgets through most of President Reagan's tenure.

Every allegation about Soviet violations—Sverdlovsk, yellow rain, genetic engineering—was open to question. Few nations, including America's closest friends, remained convinced that the Soviet Union was culpable. Nor did the American public. Yet the Pentagon continued to seek more funding and more programs in the name of countering a Soviet biological weapons threat. U.S. biological warfare policy in the 1980s seems to have been driven less by sound evidence than by ideology.

Notes

1. Elisa Harris, "Sverdlovsk and Yellow Rain: Two Cases of Soviet Noncompliance?" *International Security* 11, No. 4 (Spring 1987), 45–47.
2. U.S. House of Representatives, Subcommittee on Oversight of the Permanent Committe on Intelligence, 96th Congress, 2nd Session May 29, 1980, 3–4.
3. William Kucewicz, "Beyond 'Yellow Rain,' the Threat of Soviet Genetic Engineering," *The Wall Street Journal*, May 3, 1984, 28. The article was part of a series of eight by Kucewicz on the subject. The others appeared on April 23, April 25, April 27, May 1, May 8, May 10, and May 18, 1984.
4. Harris, 52; Leslie H. Gelb, "Keeping an Eye on Russia," *The New York Times Magazine*, November 29, 1981, 52; R. Jeffrey Smith and Philip J. Hilts, "Soviets Deny Lab Caused Anthrax Cases," *The Washington Post*, April 13, 1988, A-1, A-4.
5. Gelb, 66.
6. "Biological Weapons: Debate on Anthrax Incident Flares," *Chemical and Engineering News*, Vol. 65, No. 14 (April 6, 1987), 4.
7. John H. Cushman, Jr., "Russians Explain '79 Anthrax Cases," *The New York Times*, April 14, 1988, A-7.

8. U.S. Department of Defense, *Soviet Military Power, 1987* (Washington, DC: Government Printing Office, 1987), 111.

9. U.S. Senate, Subcommittee on Arms Control, Oceans, International Operations, and Environment of the Committee on Foreign Relations, 97th Congress, 1st Session, November 10, 1981, 14.

10. Senate Subcommittee on Arms Control, Oceans, International Operations, and Environment, 15.

11. Senate Subcommittee on Arms Control, Oceans, International Operations, and Environment, 29–31.

12. U.S. Department of State, *Chemical Warfare in Southeast Asia and Afghanistan*, Special Report No. 98, Report to the Congress from Secretary of State Alexander M. Haig, Jr., March 22, 1982.

13. *The New York Times*, March 23, 1982, A-1.

14. *Chemical Warfare in Southeast Asia and Afghanistan*, 6.

15. Eliot Marshall, "Bugs in the Yellow Rain Theory," *Science* 220 (June 24, 1983), 1356–1358.

16. Marshall, 1358.

17. Lois R. Ember, "Yellow Rain," *Chemical and Engineering News* 62, No. 2 (January 9, 1984), 22.

18. Ember, "Yellow Rain," 34.

19. Ember, "Yellow Rain," 10.

20. Ember, "Yellow Rain," 16–18.

21. Ember, "Yellow Rain," 29.

22. Ember, "Yellow Rain," 32.

23. Ember, "Yellow Rain," 26.

24. Philip M. Boffey, "Evidence is Fading as U.S. Investigates Use of 'Yellow Rain'," *The New York Times*, May 15, 1984, A-1.

25. Boffey, B-6.

26. U.S. Department of Defense, *Soviet Military Power 1984*, (Washington, DC: Government Printing Office, 1984), 70.

27. Thomas D. Seeley, Joan W. Nowicke, Matthew Meselson, Jeanne Guillemin, and Pongthep Akratanakul, "Yellow Rain," *Scientific American* 253, No. 3 (September 1985), 128–37. See also Peter Ashton et al., "Origins of Yellow Rain," *Science* 222 (28 October 1983), 366–368; Joan Nowicke and Matthew Meselson, "Yellow Rain—A Palynological Analysis," *Nature* 309 (17 May 1984), 205–206.

28. Seeley et al., "Yellow Rain," 137.

29. Seeley et al., "Yellow Rain," 137.

30. Nicholas Wade, "Rains of Error," *The New York Times*, August 30, 1985, A-24.

31. Julian Robinson, Jeanne Guillemin and Matthew Meselson, "Yellow Rain: The Story Collapses," *Foreign Policy* 68 (Fall 1987), 108–112.

32. Robinson et al., "Yellow Rain,"

33. The President's Unclassified Report on Soviet Noncompliance with Arms Control Agreements, to the Speaker of the House of Representatives and to the President of the Senate, December 2, 1987 (mimeographed), 14.

34. *Soviet Military Power*, 1984, 73.

35. Kucewicz, see note 3.

36. Kucewicz, April 23, 1984, 30.

37. Kucewicz, May 10, 1984, 34.

38. Kucewicz, April 23, 1984, 30; April 27, 1984, 28; and May 18, 1984, 26.

39. Kucewicz, May 18, 1984, 26.

40. Jack Anderson, "Soviets Push Biological-Weapons Work," *The Washington Post*, December 2, 1984, B-15.

41. Elkan R. Blout, "Research, Pestilence and War," Letter to the Editor, *The Wall Street Journal*, May 8, 1984, 35.

42. Interview, March 27, 1985.

43. *Current News*, Special Edition on "Yellow Rain," October 4, 1983, prepared by the Air Force for the Department of Defense.

44. *Wall Street Journal*, September 15, 1982, 30.

45. *Wall Street Journal*, September 15, 1982, 30.

46. *Wall Street Journal*, September 15, 1982, 30.

47. Robert L. Bartley and William, P. Kucewicz, communication in *Foreign Affairs*, reproduced by *Current News*, 40.

48. Survey by Louis Harris and Associates, September 4–7, 1986, on file at Roper Center, Storrs, Conn.

49. Jon D. Miller, "The Politics of Emerging Issues: An Analysis of the Attitudes of Leaders and Larger Publics Toward Biotechnology," paper presented at the Annual Meeting of the American Political Science Association, August 30, 1985, 27.

50. "Yellow Rain," (Washington, DC: United States Information Agency, c. 1983), 16. In 1986, the British government reported that ever since it began testing in 1982 it had never found trichothecenes in yellow rain samples. See Robinson et al., "Yellow Rain," 110.

51. Canada. "An Epidemiological Investigation of Alleged CW/BW Incidents in S.E. Asia," prepared by Directorate of Preventive Medicine, Surgeon General Branch, National Defence Headquarters, Ottawa, August 1982, 12; based on H.G. Schiefer Toxicology Group, University of Saskatchewan, "Study of the Possible Use of Chemical Warfare Agents in Southeast Asia," A Report to the Department of External Affairs, Canada, 1982.

52. Schiefer Toxicology Group, 11, 42.

53. Lois Ember, "New Data Weakens U.S. Yellow Rain Case," *Chemical and Engineering News* (9 June 1986), 23.

54. Second Review Conference of the Parties to the Convention on Bacteriological (Biological) and Toxin Weapons and on their Destruction. Final Document, Geneva, 1986, BWC/CONF. II/SR. 4, p. 3.

55. Second Review Conference, Final Document, /SR 6, p. 10.

56. Second Review Conference, Final Document, /SR 8, p. 4.

57. Second Review Conference, Final Document, /SR 8, p. 6.

58. Second Review Conference, Final Document, /SR 3, p. 4.

10

Yellow Rain in Southeast Asia: The Story Collapses

Julian Robinson, Jeanne Guillemin, and Matthew Meselson

In September 1981 the Reagan administration charged that Soviet-backed forces in Southeast Asia were waging toxin warfare. The Soviets flatly denied the charge, but the administration continued to make the accusation and, in 1984, incorporated it into the president's first *Report to the Congress on Soviet Non-Compliance with Arms Control Agreements*. Subsequent noncompliance reports reiterated the charge, claiming that the use of toxins continued at least into 1983. Most recently, in the 1987 report, the administration repeated its conclusion that "the Soviet Union has been involved in the production, transfer, and use of trichothecene mycotoxins . . . in violation of its legal obligation under international law as codified in the Geneva Protocol of 1925 and the Biological and Toxin Weapons Convention of 1972."[1] According to the administration, the attacks generally were conducted by aircraft spraying a yellow material that fell like rain and that contained trichothecene toxins, causing illness and death to thousands of victims. In presenting its case, the administration relied heavily on three kinds of evidence. First, there were interviews with alleged victims and eyewitnesses—most of them Hmong tribespeople from Laos living in Thai refugee camps, others Khmer Rouge soldiers near the Thai–Cambodian border.[2] Second, there were actual samples of the suspected CBW agent handed in by alleged witnesses. Finally, there were chemical analyses reporting the presence of the trichothecene toxins in samples from alleged attacks.

The administration's scenario and its supporting evidence were presented authoritatively in two special reports to Congress from the State Department.[3] The March 1982 report of then Secretary of State Alexander Haig, Jr., stated that "beginning in the fall of 1978, the majority of the attacks were carried out by aircraft spraying a yellowish substance which 'fell like rain.'" And again, in the November 1982 report of Secretary of State George Shultz: "Descriptions of the 1982 attacks have not changed significantly from descriptions of earlier attacks. Usually the Hmong state that aircraft or helicopters spray a yellow rain-like material on their villages and crops." The Shultz report also stated, "We now know that the yellow rain contains trichothecene toxins and other substances that cause victims to experience vomiting, bleeding, blistering, severe skin lesions and other lingering signs and symptoms."

The Haig and Shultz reports were presented with obvious political authority and appeared to be based on conclusive evidence. Nevertheless, in various parts of the U.S. government, investigation of the chemical warfare allegations did not stop. To the contrary, the laboratory and field studies became more systematic, replacing the more improvised procedures that had been relied on initially. As investigations broadened both within the government and outside and in other countries, key elements of the evidence upon which the administration's case rested could not be confirmed. In addition, scientists made an unexpected discovery that was altogether at odds with the administration's scenario. As traced in the following description, compiled in part with documents only recently declassified and to date unreported, these developments effectively destroyed the case for treaty violation presented by the administration. Nevertheless, the allegation itself is still made at the highest level of government.

In September 1978 the U.S. embassy in Bangkok, Thailand, sent its first telegram to Washington reporting interviews conducted by its personnel with Hmong refugees who claimed to have witnessed chemical and biological warfare in Laos. The telegram said that refugees claimed to have been attacked by aircraft with rockets, bombs, stones and "medicine from the sky."[4] As refugee claims of chemical warfare continued to come in, the State Department dispatched a Foreign Service officer to Thailand to conduct more interviews. He and another officer went to Thai camps where they interviewed, through interpreters, 22 Hmong refugees in June 1979. Nineteen of the refugees told of a CBW agent that was yellow. Two of them handed in samples, leaves on which there were yellow spots a few millimeters in diameter. The following October, four U.S. Army medical and toxicological specialists went to refugee camps in Thailand where they completed 38 more interviews with Hmong who claimed they had witnessed attacks.[5] The army interviewers also were given a sample—small yellow spots on pieces of bark from a village rooftop.

By early 1983, Hmong refugees claiming to have witnessed attacks had turned in dozens of samples of the alleged CBW agent to American, Australian, British, Canadian, French, Thai, and other investigators. These samples displayed a striking uniformity. Virtually all of them were yellow spots or powdery yellow scrapings. In what probably was the first published use of the expression, an English-speaking Hmong soldier was quoted by the writer Stanley Karnow in the August 13, 1979 issue of the *Baltimore Sun* as describing an allegedly poisonous spray delivered by jet aircraft in Laos as "yellow rain."[6]

When tested for standard chemical warfare agents, the samples yielded negative results. But in the interviews, investigators thought they discerned a constellation of symptoms—skin irritation, dizziness, nausea, and bloody vomiting and diarrhea—that eventually pointed them in the direction of toxins, including the trichothecenes. In July 1981, a leaf and stem sample from the area of a supposed attack in Cambodia, near the Thai border, was sent to a University of Minnesota laboratory for testing for trichothecenes. The report came back positive. Soon after this, during a September 13 speech in West Berlin, Haig announced that the United States now had "physical evidence" of toxin warfare in Southeast Asia. This physical evidence, Haig said, had "been analyzed and found to contain abnormally high levels of three potent mycotoxins—poisonous substances not indigenous to the region and which are highly toxic to man and animals."[7]

Subsequently, the Minnesota laboratory would report trichothecenes in four more environmental samples from Southeast Asia and in samples of blood, urine, or tissue from about 20 Hmong refugees and Khmer Rouge soldiers and civilians, collected between March 1981 and March 1983. A laboratory at Rutgers University in New Jersey reported trichothecenes in a sample of yellow powder from Laos. A gas mask from Afghanistan was also reported to have traces of trichothecenes on its surface. A substantial body of evidence was thus accumulating. Further, government officials claimed that they had secret intelligence data that confirmed the specific dates of CBW attacks reported by refugees. Congress seemed to be persuaded. Impatient with those who still questioned the administration's charges, an editorial in the February 15, 1984

Wall Street Journal contended flatly, "Among men of affairs the 'yellow rain' debate is closed."[8]

A Hitch in the Scenario

But already in 1982 an unexpected discovery began to move the investigation of yellow rain into an altogether new direction. The administration never claimed that more than four samples of the yellow material contained trichothecenes. Even in these the toxins reportedly made up less than a few hundredths of a percent of the sample. What was the remaining 99.9 percent? From 1979 until the beginning of 1982, U.S. government laboratories had performed various tests on the growing collection of yellow spots and powders without discovering their principal component. Then, in January 1982, a British government scientist at the Chemical Defence Establishment at Porton Down put a sample of yellow rain under an ordinary microscope and discovered that it consisted largely of pollen. Soon afterward, the same discovery was made independently by scientists in Thailand and Canada. The British finding was passed on to the United States and was confirmed with many additional samples by scientists at the Army Chemical Systems Laboratory in Aberdeen, Maryland. It also was confirmed at defense establishments in Australia, France and Sweden. Altogether, more than 50 samples of yellow spots and powders from alleged attacks in Laos and Cambodia were examined under the microscope, and every one of them consisted mainly of pollen.

The possibility that the pollen was merely a coincidental contaminant of the samples could be rejected quickly. The concentration of pollen hardly varied from one sample of yellow rain to another and was thousands of times too high to have resulted from the general presence of pollen in the environment. The finding that the yellow rain was mainly pollen created great difficulties for the U.S. scenario. The administration's response was to argue that the Soviets deliberately added pollen in manufacturing yellow rain. At a November 1982 press conference to release the Shultz report, the senior State Department intelligence officer investigating yellow rain, Gary Crocker, said, "It contains pollen, and not wind-borne pollen, but pollen that would be commercially collected or is collected, if you will, by insects, the type of thing . . . a honeybee would take from flowers." An Army medical intelligence analyst who was present, Sharon Watson, described the presumed combination of pollen and toxins as a "very clever mixture," explaining that after the drops of yellow rain became dry, wind could disperse the material as toxic dust that could be inhaled. But this theory could be dismissed for a number of reasons, not the least of which was that the samples of yellow rain had no such tendency to disperse.

Nevertheless, in a December 1982 address to the first Committee of the U.N. General Assembly, Kenneth Adelman, then U.S. deputy representative to the United Nations, announced: "We are now, however, able to isolate the components of yellow rain. . . . There is good evidence for the presence of commercially-prepared pollen as a carrier and to help ensure the retention of toxins in the human body." A year later a U.S. official, quoted in the January 9, 1984 issue of *Chemical and Engineering News*, referred in a background briefing to "an association of bee-pollen collecting facilities near the confines of a chemical weapons facility in the Soviet Union."[9] When asked why there should be pollen in every sample of yellow rain, Deputy Assistant Secretary of State for Politico-Military Affairs John Hawes replied: "I have no idea how the Soviets produce this stuff. We've not been in their factory."[10]

The notion that the Soviets collected pollen from honeybees and added toxins to make yellow rain taxed the imaginations of many, both in and out of government. But if the pollen was not part of a CBW agent, what was its origin? The answer, at first put forward only tentatively, was that yellow rain was not a CBW agent at all, but a phenomenon of nature: the feces of wild honeybees. This suggestion was made by Thomas Seeley, a Yale University honeybee expert, and first presented at a meeting of the American Association for the Advancement of Science in May 1983.[11] It was greeted with derision by administration officials, yet it provided for the first time an alternative to the administration's theory that yellow rain was a weapon, an alternative that could be subjected to simple and reliable scientific tests.

The spots of yellow rain and of honeybee feces proved indistinguishable in size, color and general appearance. And, like bee feces, the yellow-rain samples were composed almost entirely of pollen. Moreover, the pollen grains in yellow-rain samples were merely empty husks, like those digested by honeybees. The match extended to the fine level of detail revealed by the electron microscope. Analyses done at the Smithsonian Institution in Washington and in other laboratories specializing in pollen identification in France, Great Britain, and the United States showed that the pollen in yellow-rain samples was from plants indigenous to Southeast Asia and was composed of precisely the kind of pollen gathered and eaten by wild honeybees in the region's forests. In short, no sample of the yellow material from alleged attacks in Laos and Cambodia was found to be anything other than honeybee feces. This included even the yellow-rain samples reported positive for trichothecenes.

At the time, many aspects of tropical Asian honeybee behavior had not been closely studied. In particular, entomologists did not know whether these bees defecated collectively, producing showers that could be mistaken for sprays from aircraft. But in Thailand in March 1984, two American university scientists and a Thai colleague discovered that wild honeybees, flying too high to be noticed, do indeed conduct collective cleansing flights, lasting several minutes and covering areas of an acre or more with hundreds of thousands of yellow spots.[12] Although one might think that people living in the Southeast Asian countryside would recognize bee feces for what they are, Hmong refugees and Thai villagers shown spots of bee feces on leaves usually did not recognize them. Indeed, some of the Hmong identified the spots as "kemi," a term they have come to use for chemical weapons.

The mistaken identification of bee feces as poison from the sky was not limited to the Hmong, although the administration was not familiar with this fact. In 1976 in China, strange, sporadic showers of yellowish material were noticed in different parts of Jiangsu province. The local people, who actually called the showers "yellow rain," associated them with serious threats to their well-being. Some saw the yellow showers as "air-dropped poison" and would not consume water or food that might have been exposed to it. University scientists examined local inhabitants and scrutinized local medical records for any abnormal incidence of clinical disease, which they did not find. They subjected samples of the yellow substance to chemical analysis, which revealed nothing out of the ordinary. But under the microscope they saw pollen, and this led them, by the same route previously described, to conclude that the yellow material was bee feces.[13]

The discovery that the yellow rain in Southeast Asia was honeybee feces directly contradicted the administration's allegations of chemical warfare. If the yellow rain was just bee feces, the administration's identification of the supposed toxic material was invalidated. Nor could the two other main categories of supporting evidence—interviews and trichothecene analyses—remain unaffected. The discovery that yellow rain is bee feces meant that the testimony of many who claimed to be eyewitnesses was greatly compromised. How could they have seen CBW attacks intense enough to kill scores of people without noticing any material substances but honeybee feces? Certainly bee feces could not cause such effects. Yet it was the testimony of Hmong refugees that had directed attention to the yellow materials in the first place—the same testimony from which the symptomology and much of the circumstantial evidence described in the Haig and Shultz reports had been drawn. Did this mean that these parts of the Washington scenario were now only precariously supported, or was the refugee testimony still to be regarded as a bulwark of the administration's case? Likewise, was it possible that the toxin reports were in error or that, if trichothecenes were indeed present in some of the samples, their origin was natural, not artificial?

The Pressure Mounts

To students of CBW, the trichothecenes were another bizarre aspect of the Washington scenario. Naturally occurring poisons of other types—bacterial and algal toxins, for example, but not fungal toxins—are known to have been developed for weapons purposes, not least by the United States prior to President Richard Nixon's renunciation of toxin weapons in 1970. But from what was reported in the scant literature on trichothecenes, they seemed improbable CBW agents. Their aggressive characteristics, such as their ease of distribution and their lethality, appeared inferior to those of more familiar military poisons, making it difficult to imagine military situations in which they would be preferred. Nonetheless, their very implausibility as CBW agents seemed to suggest that the Reagan administration must have had strong evidence for charging that they were being used. This, it is now known, was not so. The early reports of trichothecenes in the samples were totally unverified, and the corroboration that emerged later was tenuous and unreliable.

At the time of Haig's speech announcing the trichothecene findings to the world, the evidence consisted of no more than a single uncorroborated analysis of a leaf and stem sample from Cambodia. The source of the crucial sample was ambiguous. In March 1981 a Thai army chemical officer had given a sample of vegetation to an American embassy official.[14] Reportedly, it came from an area in Cambodia where Khmer Rouge soldiers had fallen ill after drinking the water and also after passing through a region with a strange, perfume-like smell. Khmer Rouge officials could not explain how a poison might have been disseminated: they had seen no aircraft spraying nor any artillery firing chemical rounds. The State Department's regional medical officer, Dr. Henry Wilde, went into Cambodia and examined patients allegedly affected by these incidents. He concluded in a March 1981 report that their illness could be ascribed to "chronic malaria and/or other natural diseases as well as possible battle fatigue."[15]

The vegetation sample was sent to the Army Chemical Systems Laboratory, where it was divided into several portions. One of these, a leaf and stem sample, was provided to Watson at the U.S. Army Medical Intelligence and Information Agency (AMIIA) in Fort Detrick, Maryland, with a notation that "mold and other biological growth" had been observed on it.[16] Then, in July 1981, this portion was sent by means of an intermediary contractor to the Minnesota laboratory. On August 17, in a then secret message to the rest of the U.S. intelligence community, Watson announced the positive report of trichothecenes.[17]

While interagency discussion of the need for corroborating the finding proceeded, pressure mounted to present this new and potentially dramatic information to the public. On August 31, Watson received a telephone call from the office of Richard Burt, then director of the State Department's Bureau of Politico-Military Affairs, asking that the August 17 message be prepared for public release. She and others at the AMIIA thought the request "ill-advised" because of the lack of corroborative tests. But as her now declassified August 31 memorandum on the telephone call noted, "Despite these concerns, it was decided to release the information since we were told that it would break anyway with or without our permission."[18]

The same day, Burt sent a memorandum to Haig summarizing the toxin finding and urging that "we need to be prepared to move quickly to ensure that the administration is recognized as being on top of this important turn of events."[19] But apparently the State Department's objective went well beyond projecting an informed public image. In a September 3 briefing memorandum, Burt cautioned Haig to withold the trichothecene report from the press for the time being, "in order not to preempt our strategy for securing the maximum impact from this issue."[20] On September 11, Haig sent President Ronald Reagan a memorandum telling him about the trichothecene report and informing him that, "In order to ensure that the administration is recognized as being on top of this important development, I plan to present this new information publicly at the earliest opportunity, which will be my September 13 speech in Berlin."[21]

Following the speech, U.S. government scientists sought to replicate the findings. The task ahead was no easy one. To analyze small samples of a natural substance for quantities of other organic chemicals is extremely difficult. Samples of the kinds being sent in from Southeast Asia presented major risks of getting analytic results either falsely positive or falsely negative for trichothecenes. In October 1981 the Army approved the plans of its Chemical Systems Laboratory to develop an adequate analytic capability of its own for trichothecenes. Abroad, in Britain, Canada, France and Sweden, the West Berlin speech had stimulated government agencies to do likewise.

Not until October 1982 did the Chemical Systems Laboratory satisfy itself that it had developed a method of the requisite reliability. The Army then began a series of new analyses, examining more than 80 samples from alleged attacks in Southeast Asia. In one of these, a pollen-rich yellow powder from Laos known as C-168-81, relatively large amounts of trichothecenes had been reported from the Minnesota laboratory one year previously. The Chemical Systems Laboratory found no trichothecenes in this or in any of the other samples it examined from Laos and Cambodia.

The fact that the Army was failing to provide verification was slow to emerge, and was for a while obscured by the publicity accorded to positive findings from two unofficial investigations. The first of these findings, in December 1981, was in a yellowish powdery material from Laos acquired by ABC Television News for the purposes of a documentary. It was reported by a chemist in New Jersey, at Rutgers University. Subsequent electron-microscopic examination of the powder, however, showed it to be to indistinguishable from bee feces.[22] The other findings were reported in April 1984 from a laboratory at a university in Belgium, but rested, it later transpired, on an unreliable analytical method.[23]

Simultaneously, the government laboratories abroad were coming on stream. They all used analytic methods that basically were the same as the one the army had chosen, less stringent versions of which had been used in the Minnesota and New Jersey laboratories: an elaborate and powerful technique combining gas chromatography and mass spectrometry known as GC/MS. No other methods were likely to be reliable; even GC/MS, without rigorous precautions,[24] could easily yield false positives.

The largest of these overseas activities was at Porton Down. Starting in March 1982, Porton analyzed about 50 environmental samples and about 20 samples of blood and urine for trichothecenes. These samples were furnished by a British collection effort in Thailand and from allies, and included a portion of the C-168-81 sample provided by the U.S. Army. On June 7 of that year the British government stated, in a reply to a parliamentary question in the House of Lords, that it had been led to "believe that chemical weapons, probably including mycotoxins," had been used in Southeast Asia. But four years passed without any release of Porton's analytic findings and it came to be asserted, both in internal documents of the U.S. Government and in the press, that Britain was deliberately witholding confirmatory data to avoid disrupting British-Soviet relations.

Finally, in May 1986 the British government, in a written statement to the House of Commons, confirmed that Porton had found no trichothecenes at all in any of its samples from supposed CBW attacks in Southeast Asia.[25] Nor had any such samples yielded positive results in the French or Swedish defense laboratories where GC/MS had been used. The large-scale effort to verify the analyses of the nongovernment laboratories was careful and skilled. Set against this international laboratory endeavor, the positive reports of trichothecenes stood out as peculiarities: the two American non-government laboratories reported five positives out of six environmental samples, contrasting with no positives out of more than 100 such samples examined in government laboratories. Contrasted with so many nonconfirmatory results and lacking the rigorous precautions taken in the governmental laboratories, the initial positive test reports no longer could be considered reliable.

The reliability of the evidence from the Soviet gas mask found in Afghanistan was also in question. Although the Shultz report claimed that three different laboratories had found traces of trichothecenes in a sample swabbed from its surface, the data were never published. It was the only claim of a positive finding for the numerous samples retrieved from Afghanistan; though two others had been mentioned in the Shultz report, they were never again cited by the Administration. At least one part of the U.S. Government, a panel of the Department of Defense Science Board, reportedly found the evidence for mycotoxin warfare in Afghanistan to be dismissable.[26] The British government, whose agencies had also examined samples from Afghanistan, stated only that it believed "some form of incapacitating agent" to have been used there.[27] Tear gases are "incapacitating agents" in official British terminology.

There remained to consider the possibility that, in rather unusual circumstances, trichothecenes could occur naturally. The incidence and behavior in tropical regions of the molds that are capable of producing the toxins are not yet well known. Nevertheless, from the time of the West Berlin speech, the administration adamantly maintained that trichothecenes did not occur naturally in Southeast Asia. Under that assumption, now known to be incorrect, the occurrence of trichothecenes near a war zone might be construed as evidence of their use as weapons. A case in point is an episode in February 1982 at Ban Sa Tong, a Thai village ten kilometers from the Cambodian border. The episode involved a sighting by villagers of an aircraft flying at high altitude and the appearance of numerous spots of yellow material on surfaces in a small area of the village. Neither deaths nor any abnormal incidence of clinical illness were associated with the episode.[28] Under appropriate examination, the yellow spots later were shown to consist almost entirely of pollen. Some samples also showed very low levels of trichothecenes.[29] A report by the Canadian government stated that the quantities found in the yellow-spot material were "comparable to the levels reported worldwide for natural occurrences of trichothecenes on stored cereal."[30] In other words, there was a possibility that what had been measured in these samples was not residue but a background level of mycotoxin attributable to toxin-producing molds in the natural environment.

In August 1985 Canadian government investigators reported that a leaf sample collected at the site of the Ban Sa Tong episode was found to have a trichothecene-producing mold on it.[31] Moreover, in May 1986 the Canadian government confirmed that two years earlier its investigators had undertaken an extensive collection of blood samples in Thailand. Blood was taken from 270 individuals and analyzed for trichothecenes. Measurable levels of trichothecenes were found in the blood of five persons who had not claimed exposure and had not been in the vicinity of any alleged attack. Most recently, in April 1987, British government scientists

at Porton reported the natural occurrence of trichothecenes in samples of food crops from Thailand.[32] Despite what the U.S. government had previously asserted, these various findings indicated that
trichothecenes do occasionally occur naturally in Southeast Asia.

The Defense-State Team

With the administration's explanation of yellow rain seen as insup-
portable, it remained to examine the meaning of the many cases
of personal testimony that linked yellow rain to debilitating symptoms. Until late 1983, interviews with Hmong refugees and Khmer
Rouge soldiers who claimed to have experienced CBW came from
three sources. Personnel from the American embassy in Bangkok
conducted interviews part-time; State Department and Army investigators were sent out from Washington for several weeks in 1979;
and, from 1981 to 1983, a retired U.S. Air Force doctor and a British nurse-midwife interviewed alleged witnesses. There also were
forays by the Canadian government, the United Nations, journalists, and others. By 1983 these various arrangements had produced
a large volume of information—testimony that embassy officials
regarded as variable and perhaps of dubious quality. The embassy
repeatedly requested and Washington eventually supported a more
systematic, full-time approach by specialists; a joint Defense-State
CBW team was created in 1983. Consisting of an army chemical
corps officer, an army medical officer (later replaced by a navy doctor), and a Foreign Service officer, the CBW team operated in
Thailand for nearly two years, from November 1983 until October
1985. When the CBW team began its investigations, the Assistant
Secretary of State for Legislative and Intergovernmental Affairs explained, "Our 'yellow rain' investigation effort has necessarily
progressed from ad hoc arrangements to more formally established
procedures, particularly as the debate over the evidence turns
increasingly on its scientific reliability."[33]

Before the Defense-State CBW team arrived in Thailand, almost
all of the refugees interviewed were selected for having said they
witnessed chemical attacks. Individuals from the same area of Laos
who might have allowed independent cross-checking of chemical
warfare stories were not sought out. The supposed witnesses and
the interpreters, often refugees themselves, generally knew in advance that the purpose of the interviews was to gather information

about chemical warfare. The accounts were taken at face value; there was little attempt to double-check the stories by reinterviewing or to appreciate cultural differences between interviewers and respondents.

Documents recently declassified show that when the Defense-State CBW team began to address these matters, it discovered serious problems with the reliability of the previous interviews.[34] For example, earlier interviews had failed to distinguish between firsthand observations and hearsay. Characteristic of the more careful approach taken by the CBW team was a report telegraphed back to Washington in January 1984.[35] A Hmong man graphically told in an interview that he had seen "with his own eyes" chemical attacks on a village in Laos, had witnessed six deaths, and had suffered medical symptoms. But when reinterviewed by the CBW team and asked about how he knew so much about attacks on the village while he was a resistance fighter in the distant jungle, he changed his account to say that he "did not personally see the attacks but rather had received accounts of the attacks from others." In another example, the team was able to locate a Hmong woman previously interviewed by the nurse-midwife. In that earlier interview, the woman was represented as saying that she had experienced a chemical attack and become very ill from it. When reinterviewed by the team, the woman gave a different account: she confirmed that airplanes flew over her village every two or three days at high altitude but she denied ever having experienced chemical warfare. The team also interviewed a Hmong man who, when in a group, "told of gassing attacks but denied its reality when the interviewer talked to him alone outside."

The members of the CBW team also questioned people who had not been interviewed before. In May 1984 they interviewed a former resistance leader who had recently led a group of 93 other Hmong to Thailand. He had commanded about 40 men and their families living since 1975 on the slope of Phu Bia, the highest mountain in Laos. According to the reports of Haig and Shultz, most of the more than 200 chemical attacks said by refugees to have occurred in Laos were in the vicinity of Phu Bia. But the CBW team reported in a telegram to Washington that "he denied ever having experienced a CBW attack nor ever having seen any evidence of CBW use. When questioned why many other Hmong refugees related accounts of CBW attacks and he as a resident of

Phu Bia for eight years had seen nothing, he stated that he was an educated man who related what he saw and not what he felt. He added that other Hmong are different in that they relate what they hear and feel."[36]

A grave problem came to light about the precision of dates specified in Hmong accounts. Many of the interviews relied upon in the Haig and Shultz reports specified the exact day of attacks, and secret intelligence intercepts were proclaimed to have confirmed the timing of these events. But, for example, when the CBW team reinterviewed three family groups from the same village in Laos, they could not agree on the date within a four-month period, or on the location of a yellow rain incident to which they had testified earlier. In an April 1984 telegram, the CBW team recognized the obstacle to resolving conflicting details: "The Hmong culture does not compartmentalize units of time as tightly as we who have broken our lives into seconds, minutes, hours and days. Their time blocks are by seasons and as a result any effort to confirm a specific date of a given incident is usually frustrated."[37] Had earlier interviewers and interpreters helped the Hmong to stipulate Gregorian calendar dates? And, if so, what would this imply for the re-evaluation of information still classified?

Medical evidence to confirm Hmong and Khmer Rouge claims of chemical warfare was equally elusive. The Army medical specialists sent to Thailand in 1979 relied on verbal accounts, not on medical examinations. In 1981 the embassy's regional medical officer examined purported Khmer and Hmong chemical warfare victims, but he found no clear evidence to support the allegations. Some doctors who had contact with refugees and Khmer Rouge soldiers noted various signs and symptoms that they thought possibly had resulted from exposure to toxic materials, but others interpreted them as indications of known tropical diseases, such as fungal infection, tuberculosis, or malaria, or attributed them to the effects of conventional warfare. At no time, then or later, was any case documented in which diagnostic examination or autopsy provided clear evidence of exposure to chemical warfare agents.[38]

This left the statements of Hmong refugees and Khmer Rouge soldiers claiming to have witnessed chemical warfare as the primary source of medical information. According to the Haig report, the interviews revealed a common symptomatology suggestive of trichothecene exposure. But simple examination of the Army and

State Department medical interviews shows that only two of the 60 alleged witnesses interviewed reported that particular constellation of symptoms. Over time this ratio did not increase. In a total of 217 interviews accumulated by 1984, only five matched the constellation of medical symptoms described in the Haig report.

The medical investigations of the Defense-State CBW team in Thailand revealed no clear cases of exposure to chemical attack; its negative reports were nevertheless illuminating. Between December 1983 and May 1984, at least a dozen suspected chemical warfare attacks were reported to the team, but none yielded confirmatory evidence. For example, on several occasions the team investigated claims that Khmer Rouge soldiers had been gassed in combat. In a typical instance, cited in a February 1984 telegram to Washington, an extensive medical workup on an alleged victim who had complained of dizziness, nausea, and vomiting blood yielded this conclusion: "[His] symptoms, which he reported to be due to 'toxic gas exposure' could be easily explained by the clinical course resulting from the blast effects alone."[39] In another case, in response to Bangkok newspaper stories that chemical attack victims had been admitted to a Khmer Rouge hospital, the team's chemical and medical officers went to investigate. Five patients complained of dizziness, vomiting, chest pains, and temporary unconsciousness, which they attributed to chemical attacks. After examining them, however, the team reported in a telegram to Washington, "We conclude that their symptoms were as a result of battle fatigue, smoke inhalation, heat stress, or a combination of these effects."[40] A few days later,the Royal Thai Ministry of Defense Supreme Command Headquarters notified the CBW team that additional chemical casualties had been admitted to the same hospital. The CBW team returned the next day accompanied by a Royal Thai Navy physician. This time there were four patients, complaining of the same symptoms as had the others. After investigating, the CBW team telegraphed Washington with the Thai physician's diagnosis that "all four victims suffered smoke inhalation and there was insufficient clinical evidence to support a finding of chemical weapons use."[41]

The CBW team also investigated incidents closely resembling those investigated by Canadian physicians at Ban Sa Tong in 1982. In February, 1984, four yellow-spot incidents were reported inside Thailand near Cambodia. Although Thai military officers and local villagers thought the events were CBW attacks, the team concluded otherwise. Its report to Washington stated, "In the team's opinion the lack of evidence of an explosive device, the small size of the area affected, and the seemingly selective distribution of spots [means] the incident appears to have been caused by insects or some other natural phenomena."[42]

In sum, the administration's claim of toxin warfare rests on evidence that, over the past several years, has been discredited. In large measure, it was the systematic efforts of American government investigators that undermined the administration's case. The careful analytic work by U.S. Army chemists did not validate the initial reports of trichothecene toxins. Extensive and meticulous attempts by government laboratories in other countries also failed to confirm toxin warfare. The investigative work of the Defense-State CBW team in Thailand cast doubt on the entire body of evidence adduced from interviews with supposed witnesses. And the yellow-rain samples turned out to be the innocuous excrement of honeybees.

In retrospect, it is easy to see how the administration came to be in its present predicament. The U.S. intelligence community departed from established procedures for verifying laboratory and field information and instead supported a conclusion that should have been regarded as only a hypothesis. Scientific issues obviously were central. Yet the administration ignored—indeed bypassed—the available institutional arrangements for obtaining high-level scientific advice. The president's science advisor, the Department of Defense Science Board, and the National Academy of Sciences were not asked to evaluate the evidence before policy was set. Instead, without carefully checking the claims of supposed witnesses, without obtaining independent corroboration of the toxin analyses, and without ascertaining the composition of the yellow rain, the Reagan administration chose to pursue a strategy of maximum public impact. The secretary of state's dramatic announcement in West Berlin in 1981 then locked the administration into a political position from which it has yet to extricate itself.

Acknowledgment

Reprinted with permission from *Foreign Policy* 68 (Fall 1987), with additions. Original article copyright 1987 by the Carnegie Endowment for International Peace.

Notes

1. Most of today's arms control in the field of chemical and biological warfare (CBW) rests on these two treaties. The Protocol outlaws use of CBW weapons while the Convention outlaws possession of germ and toxin weapons, treating all naturally occurring poisons as toxins. Tricothecenes of the type referred to by the president fall within the scope of both the Convention and the Protocol because they are mycotoxins, poisonous substances generated by certain molds or fungi.

2. The Hmong are an ethnic group of the southeast Asian highlands, many of whom fought during the Vietnam war in the CIA-supported army of General Vang Pao until it was disbanded in 1975. Some of them continued to resist the Communist government of Laos and about 100,000 of the Hmong subsequently fled from Laos across the Mekong to Thailand.

3. United States Department of State, Special Report No. 98, "Chemical Warfare in Southeast Asia and Afghanistan," 22 March 1982; and Special Report No. 104, "Chemical Warfare in Southeast Asia and Afghanistan: An Update," 11 November 1982.

4. Bangkok telegram 25420, U.S. Embassy to Department of State, 2 September 1978, subject: Hmong Refugees Escape Description.

5. U.S. House of Representatives, Committee on Foreign Affairs, Hearing before the Subcommittee on Asian and Pacific Affairs, "Use of Chemical Agents in Southeast Asia Since the Vietnam War," 96th Congress, 1st session, 12 December 1979.

6. Stanley Karnow (From Loei, Thailand), "The Meos' tragedy: America should help," *The Sun* (Baltimore), 13 August 1979, A13.

7. The speech was made before the Berlin Press Association on 13 September 1981. The text has been published by the State Department as No. 311 in its series *Current Policy*.

8. "Science and Windmills," *The Wall Street Journal*, 15 February 1984, 30.

9. Quoted in Lois Ember, "Yellow Rain," *Chemical and Engineering News* 62 No. 2 (January 1984), 22.

10. Quoted in Robert Bazell, "Bees Did It," *New Republic*, February 1987, 10.

11. P.S. Ashton, M. Meselson, J.W. Nowicke, J.P. Robinson and T.D. Seeley, "Comparison of Yellow Rain and Bee Excrement," (paper presented at the annual meeting of the American Association for the Advancement of Science, Detroit, Michigan 31 May 1983).

12. T.D. Seeley, J.W. Nowicke, M. Meselson, J. Guillemin and P. Akratanakul, "Yellow Rain," *Scientific American* 253, no. 3 (September 1985): 128–137; and Bangkok telegram 25935, U.S. Embassy to Defense Intelligence Agency, Washington, 21 May 1984. Subject: CBW Sample; TH840515–1MS, etc.

13. Zhang Zhongying et al., "A Study of the Origin and the Pollen Analysis of 'Yellow Rains' in Northeast Jiangsu" (in Chinese), Kexue Tongbao 22, no 1 (1977): 409–412; and Zhang Zhongying, "Yellow Rain" (in Chinese), Ziran Zazhi 9, no. 2 (February 1986): 122–125.

14. Bangkok telegram 15629, USDAO to JCS/DIA, 20 March 1981, subject: Forwarding of Possible CW Samples.

15. Trip report by Regional Medical Officer, U.S. Embassy, Bangkok, dated 18 March 1981, subject: Report on Visits to Democratic Kampuchea Hospitals.

16. DRD-RAI-C, letter dated 20 April 1981 addressed to SGMI, subject: Vegetation Sample.

17. Message DTG 171800Z Aug 01 from CDRUSMIIA, subject: Analytical Results on Possible CW Samples.

18. Memorandum for record dated 31 August 1981 from SGMI-SA, subject: Telephone Conversation with Fred Celec, State Department.

19. Memorandum to the Secretary from Richard Burt, 31 August 1981, subject: Handling of New Intelligence on Reported Use of Chemical Weapons in Afghanistan and Southeast Asia.

20. Briefing Memorandum to the Secretary from Richard Burt, 3 September 1981, subject: Your Interview This Afternoon with Gwertzman.

21. Memorandum for the President from Alexander M. Haig, Jr., 11 September 1981, subject: New Evidence on Use of Lethal Toxins in Southeast Asia.

22. Joan W. Nowicke and Matthew Meselson, "Yellow Rain—A Palynological Analysis," *Nature* 309 No. 5965 (17–23 May 1984), 205–6.

23. See Lois R. Ember, "Yellow Rain Controversy Remains Unresolved," *Chemical and Engineering News* 62 No. 26 (25 June 1984), 25–28.

24. Such as those described by P. Begley, R.M. Black and coworkers in *Journal of Chromatography* 367 (1986), 87–101 and 103–115.

25. *House of Commons Official Report*, Vol. 98, No. 117, Col. 92, written answers to questions, 19 May 1986.

26. See the discussion in Elisa D. Harris, "Sverdlovsk and Yellow Rain" *International Security* 11, No. 4 (Spring 1987), 91.

27. *House of Lords Official Report*, Vol. 481, No. 159, cols. 781–2, written answers to questions, 29 October 1986

28. The fullest account of the episode is to be found in the report of a Canadian team that investigated it. See: G.R. Humphreys and J. Dow, "An Epidemiological Investigation of Alleged CW/BW Incidents in SE Asia," Directorate of Preventive Medicine, Surgeon General Branch, National Defence Headquarters, Ottawa, 1982 (DSIS 83–0592).

29. One of these laboratories, Canadian, also found traces of trichothecenes in another type of sample as well, a plastic bag with brown powder and yellow spots on its surfaces that had been produced by one of the villagers a fortnight after the episode and which the villager said had fallen from the aircraft. The bag, though it looked like an ordinary kitchen bag and bore no burn or explosion marks, has been portrayed by some commentators as a CBW agent delivery device. Its association was uncorroborated, however, and no such bags have been handed in from any of the scores of other yellow rain episodes. For particulars, see the Canadian reports cited in the two adjacent footnotes.

30. J.J. Norman and J.G. Purdon, "Final Summary Report on the Investigation of 'Yellow Rain' Samples from Southeast Asia," *Defense Research Establishment Ottawa Report*, no. 912 (Ottawa, Canada, February 1986).

31. R. Greenhalgh, J.D. Miller, G.A. Neish, and H.B. Schiefer, "Toxigenic Potential of Some *Fusarium* Isolates from Southeast Asia," *Applied and Environmental Microbiology* 50, No. 2 (August 1985), 550–552.

32. R.M. Black, R.J. Clarks, and R.W. Read, "Detection of Trace Levels of Trichothecene Mycotoxins in Environmental Residues and Foodstuffs Using Gas

Chromatography with Mass Spectrometric or Electron-Capture Detection," *Journal of Chromatography* 388 (1987), 365–78.

33. W. Tapley Bennett, Jr., letter dated 8 March 1984 addressed to Congressman Hamilton Fish, Jr.

34. These problems had at the time been remarked by anthropologists and sociologists outside government. See especially Grant Evans, *The Yellow Rainmakers*, (London: Verso, 1983).

35. Bangkok telegram 00656, U.S. Embassy to Defense Intelligence Agency, Washington, 5 January 1984, subject: Alleged Use of CBW/Yellow Rain Against Hmong. See also Bangkok telegram 27244, U.S. Embassy to Defense Intelligence Agency, Washington, 30 May 1984, subject: CBW Samples: TH-840523-1DS Through 7DS, which states, "The Hmong leadership itself has been more than forthcoming in cautioning USG representatives on total acceptance of Hmong accounts of CBW incidents. The present Ban Vinai camp leader, [Name Deleted], has told every member of the CBW team that he doesn't know whether the gassing stories result from cal [chemical] warfare or beefeces but that he would like the team to find out. . . . The former head of the Ban Vinai camp [Name Deleted] informed a U.S. mission officer in December, 1980 that the last reliable gassing report that he had heard concerned an incident which occurred in September, 1979 (Ref B). The fifteen month period between 9/79 and 12/80 contained many accounts of CBW use and [Name Deleted] apparently felt obliged to communicate his own skepticism of their accuracy. The question is not whether Hmong refugees lie but whether Hmong refugees are accurate reporters of reality. Generally, we have not found them to be so and believe that their stories must be supported by external and, if possible, objective means."

36. Bangkok telegram 24354, U.S. Embassy to Defense Intelligence Agency, Washington, 10 May 1984, subject: Interview Summaries of Hmong Refugees regarding CBW.

37. Bangkok telegram 21367, U.S. Embassy to Director, Armed Forces Medical Intelligence Center, 25 April 1984, subject: CBW Sample Report from Ban Vinai Interview Follow-up.

38. C.J. Stahl., C.C. Green and J.B. Farnum, "The incident at Tuol Chrey: pathologic and toxicologic examinations of a casualty after chemical attack," *Journal of Forensic Sciences* 30, No. 2 (April 1985), 317–37. And see Lois Ember, "Autopsy is Ambiguous in 'Yellow Rain' Case," *Chemical and Engineering News* 63, No. 38 (23 September 1985), 22–23.

39. Bangkok Telegram 08848, U.S. Embassy to Defense Intelligence Agency, Washington, 17 February 1984, subject: CBW Samples TH-840211-1MS/2MS and TH-840212-1MS/2MS.

40. Bangkok telegram 20177, U.S. Embassy to Defense Intelligence Agency, Washington, 19 April 1984, subject: Alleged Chemical Attack at Ban Sa Ngae on 15 April 84.

41. Bangkok telegram 21018, U.S. Embassy to Defense Intelligence Agency, Washington, 24 April 1984, subject: Alleged Chemical Attacks at Ban Sa Ngae on 17–18 April 84.

42. Bangkok telegram 11615, U.S. Embassy to Defense Intelligence Agency, Washington, 6 March 1984, subject: CBW Sample TH-840209-1DL through TH-840209-11DL Supplemental Record.

V

The International Legal Regime on Biological Warfare

11

Inhibiting Reliance on Biological Weaponry: The Role and Relevance of International Law

Richard Falk

Strengthening international law restraints on recourse to biological warfare is certainly useful, but an exclusive focus on the importance of such restraints can be misleading. Unfortunately, experience in wartime suggests that weapons options are determined primarily by considerations of military effectiveness. The state as the nexus for military policymaking is basically a power system with relatively little independent disposition to constrain state behavior by showing respect for moral and legal norms, however firmly established. This attitude, often associated with a realpolitik orientation, is especially pronounced in foreign affairs during periods of armed conflict, when considerations of "military necessity" are rarely contested. At such times, there is a tendency for statesmen to invoke ultimate concerns about "sovereignty" and "survival" to the extent that they even feel inclined to justify official behavior. Normative thinkers have reinforced such tendencies by drawing a distinction in international affairs between "moral man" and "immoral society," or by speaking of the bad fit between "a Lockean nation" and "a Hobbesian world." In any event, whether or not such "realism" is still "practical," given the character of modern warfare and weaponry, it would be misleading not to presume the persistence of a geopolitical ethos that is skeptical about the propriety of restraining foreign policy, especially on the battlefield, out of respect for international law. The admiration accorded Henry Kissinger as a diplomat *par excellence* was a tribute to his embodiment of statist "realism," partly as measured by his scornful attitude toward normative restraints.

This skepticism about legal restraints is reinforced by certain additional factors. Legal rules are almost impossible to draft without allowing parties some degree of latitude in interpreting their scope. Unresolved disputes about substance that arise during treaty negotiations often produce "deliberate" ambiguities that show up in the language of a final agreement. Since compliance is, in the first instance at least, dependent upon self-interpretation by governments, there is plenty of room for maneuvering within the four corners of virtually every international agreement. In the war/peace area, states are especially reluctant to accept third-party procedures for resolving disputes about alleged treaty violation.[1] Such allegations are difficult to substantiate, further eroding the distinction between genuine treaty violations and hostile propaganda. The "yellow rain" controversy is a recent illustration of this structural dilemma.[2] The allegations were given prominence by those eager to justify a harsh approach on East-West relations; reassurances flowed from viewpoints favoring strategic moderation. The merits of the controversy were never seriously or objectively addressed by either superpower, and public understanding has depended on the efforts of dedicated and respected scholars to examine available evidence.[3] The withering away of the yellow rain allegations seems to reflect both an inability by the U.S. government to back up its accusations with convincing evidence and a growing acceptance among scientists that benign explanations of what was reported were persuasive. But at the same time the very existence of a controversy implying Soviet willingness to use toxic weaponry sowed seeds of doubt about the feasibility of a restraining regime.

A related difficulty is that of *tu quoque*, that is, the basic notion that whatever the other side does or might conceivably do can, with propriety, be offset by comparable capabilities and contingency plans. Suspicions that the Soviet Union is embarked upon a biological weapons program powerfully encourages those voices that favor an expanded program of research and development activities by the United States both for deterrent and retaliatory roles, as well as for possible defensive measures (such as protective clothing, immunization, and the like).[4] Governmental secrecy is so strong in this kind of setting that "national security" makes governmental units and civil servants unresponsive to inhibiting normative restraints, even if written into international law in the most explicit manner, and accepted as binding upon national policy. (See section 3, below.)

The most disturbing of all these developments is Iraq's widespread reliance on chemical weapons in the latter stages of its 1980s war against Iran.[5] Both countries were bound by the unconditional prohibition on CW use embodied in the 1925 Geneva Protocol. Iraq reportedly used chemical weapons extensively and recurrently (Iran evidently retaliated in kind, but briefly and without great effect); according to some interpretations, their use affected the course of the war. It is not only that the legal regime failed in a blatant manner but that the wider community response, while vigorous at a rhetorical level, was feeble and futile operationally. A thoughtful journalist sums up the effect of Iraq's reliance on chemical weapons as follows: "But the war's legacy is that Iraq turned the tide and now doesn't apologize for its use of chemical weapons. According to U.S. officials, Iraqis say they were fighting for their survival. Under such conditions, the Iraqis asserted, they don't see the West's moral distinction between killing with bullets and killing with chemicals."[6] And, in fairness, it is doubtful if the West would retain the moral distinction if confronted with the sort of threat posed by invading Iranian armies.

The failure of law to restrain Iraq's reliance on chemical weapons reinforces the basic image of international relations as a system governed by "the law of the jungle." It also casts a shadow across efforts to protect ourselves against the prospect of biological weaponry by erecting ever higher legal barriers. Biological weapons are viewed as complements to chemical weapons, and experience with the latter bears on our analysis of how to prevent the development and use of the former. At the same time, there is some danger in overinterpreting the Iraqi breakdown. No legal regimes, even in conditions of well-ordered domestic societies, can effectively inhibit illegal behavior in periods of perceived crisis. International law seeks, above all, to establish a common framework that discourages certain forms of behavior. Further, the moral and legal inhibitions on BW exceed those on CW, and prospects for effective use seem far less for the foreseeable future. Finally, the reaction of leading states and international institutions is important. The Iraqi experience can either add a dimension of urgency to ongoing negotiations on the text of a comprehensive treaty of prohibition on chemical weapons, or it can reinforce cynical views that the only reliable protection is a superior capability of one's own.

In effect, then, the Iraqi experience provides an historical frame for our inquiry. It suggests, above all, the inability of legal regimes to provide ironclad assurances. Iraq's violation of the Geneva Protocol may also stimulate the design of *more inhibiting legal regimes*, which may strengthen the disposition in the BW context to reach back to the development stage, and possibly even to restrict research. Of course, the case for strengthening legal regimes in this manner will raise demands for adequate verification. Whether such demands can ever be met is an open question; it places another type of limit on a legal approach in a world of sovereign states that enter into bargains about national security issues on the basis of presumed mistrust. This is a time when clear analysis will help uncover pitfalls as well as opportunities as we try to protect ourselves against the potential menace of biological warfare.

These introductory comments are not meant to denigrate the international legal regime's efforts to inhibit certain forms of behavior under wartime conditions. Its purpose is to locate inquiry and appraisal in an intermediate zone between legalism (taking the law as determinative of official behavior) and cynicism (regarding unscrupulous and unrestrained displays of force as inevitable in international relations).[7] Identifying the conditions under which international law effectively regulates behavior is a complicated endeavor that is quite context-dependent. In general, given the absence of centralized sanctioning capabilities, international law works best when the governments that enter agreements or subscribe to customary rules perceive mutual and reciprocal interests in upholding legal expectations. Respect for ambassadorial immunity is a favorite instance. Governments rarely encroach upon this legally protected zone of autonomy for diplomats because the interest in sustaining it is strong and even a minor state is well-situated to retaliate. The prohibition on biological weaponry has *potentially* these features, but it is important to clarify the interest of governments in a widely respected regime and to avoid, at all costs, the *misperception* of noncompliance. It is very damaging to law-abidingness in international relations, especially between adversaries and particularly on matters that touch upon national security, if they *wrongly* suspect a violative course of conduct, since it sets in motion a retaliatory chain of actions and reactions.

My additional concern is to emphasize the importance of tendencies by modern states to claim absolute control and emergency powers (including an implied discretion to ignore binding legal constraints) in relation to the conduct of national security. The Iran-contra disclosures and hearings (1986–1987) were both an extreme instance of these tendencies and a confirmation of broader "normal" patterns of governmental behavior. Because of this characteristic behavior of governments, almost regardless of their ideological orientation toward democratic principles of operation, it is important for citizens to realize that implementing normative restraints depends heavily on their direct action, both in encouraging bureaucratic compliance and in invigorating representative institutions.[8] Putting this emphasis differently, the prospects for effective international law is less a matter of devising and tinkering with existing texts of rules and agreements than it is in creating a compliance-oriented political climate at home. This dependence on civic action and awareness poses special challenges in those countries, such as the Soviet Union, where virtually no tradition of opposition to official policy, and no governmental responsibility to keep the citizenry informed, exists.

1 The Setting

There is no evidence available that suggests any disposition on the part of the U.S. government to back away officially from President Richard Nixon's 1969 unconditional repudiation of biological warfare and his unprecedented unilateral undertaking to destroy then existing stockpiles of biological weaponry. By 1973 the United States Government announced that it had completed destruction of biological and toxin agents that had been in its possession at the time of Nixon's statement. Furthermore, the 1972 Biological Weapons Convention, with its sweeping prohibition on development, production, and stockpiling of biological weapons, has been ratified by the Soviet Union, the United States, the United Kingdom, and most other major states. In this respect, the illegal status of biological weapons is more widely and significantly established than for any category of dubious weaponry or tactic, including chemical and nuclear.[9]

Of late, however, a variety of indications of renewed concern about the possibility of biological weaponry has surfaced. Advances in genetic engineering could spur efforts to overcome some of the earlier practical difficulties of dissemination and delivery that seemed to limit the military appeal of biological weapons, thereby creating a potentially attractive option from a strictly technical standpoint of military planning and effectiveness[10] Considering the economic burdens associated with the acquisition of advanced arms, and given the prospects for further improvements in delivery and dissemination, biological weapons cannot be ruled out as a temptation for the desperate, or even the ambitious. Additionally, the attractiveness of a type of weaponry that kills and incapacitates without doing physical destruction is likely to enter the political calculations of military establishments. More speculatively, but not without some relevance in this period of nuclear stalemate, global antagonism, and the search for nuclear defense systems, is the pressure to shift attention to non-nuclear weapons of mass destruction. Suppose it became possible to immunize friendly populations while contaminating the enemy, or even the leadership of the enemy country? Such a scenario is surely remote. But the powerful drive to avoid unanticipated vulnerability from any type of technological advance may cause governments to authorize covert "defensive" activities that are then perceived and interpreted via rival intelligence operations as potentially "aggressive," as well as "illegal," warranting denunciation, counter-measures, or both.

In addition, tangible displays of activity have caused serious concern. In the first half of the 1980s, the United States Government stepped up noticeably its support for research in the BW area, especially for research that includes experimentation and "development" for biological agents possessing a medical rationale, but could serve directly or indirectly for development of a weapons system (see chapters 2 and 7). Pentagon funding of the Biological Defense Program increased considerably in the 1980s in comparison to earlier periods, leveling off at about $60 million per year. These activities have been partly justified by a claim that the Soviet Union is investing heavily in research and development with an intention to achieve a biological weapons arsenal, or, more alarmingly, to circumvent the nuclear stalemate by way of seeking a first-strike BW capability. These suspicions seemed confirmed by the 1979 outbreak of anthrax in Sverdlovsk that resulted in many deaths apparently caused by the release of anthrax spores into the atmosphere, an interpretation contested from the outset by Soviet sources. Until the Second Review Conference in 1986 Soviet reassurances on Sverdlovsk were not of a serious factual nature. Whether American suspicions about Sverdlovsk were genuine or deliberately manipulated, the incident definitely encouraged alarmist views about a Soviet willingness to explore the strategic potential of biological warfare, thereby providing an occasion for prudent explorations by the United States as well. In the background of this alarmism on the American side is the contention, partly inferred from alleged Soviet activities, that a closed society could immunize its own population and then threaten or actually use a biological agent that would spread a disabling or lethal disease throughout the enemy society. To avoid the overall effects of alarmist interpretations of adversary conduct, it is highly desirable that governments recognize the extent to which it is in their interest to provide prompt and convincing reassurances about Sverdlovsk-type incidents.

As with other aspects of arms competition, such suspicions are used to rationalize the acquisition of a neutralizing capability elsewhere. This, in turn, arouses fear, and an alarming arms race based on imperfect knowledge and maximum suspiciousness can easily be generated. It is important to appreciate that perceptions are as crucial as behavioral patterns in international relations, and that, therefore, a treaty regime could be undermined as directly by misperceptions as by the reality of noncompliance. To the extent that there is a commitment to making a treaty effective it is appropriate for parties to remove the suspicions of others and to avoid irresponsible accusations. Here, it is the interaction between governments distrustful of one another that could lead to a result disastrous for all, as each claims it is acting to deter the other from taking advantage of an illicitly achieved biological weapons capability. In this setting, pressures supporting the proliferation of biological weapons in a variety of states and beyond, to other non-state political actors, could be anticipated. The relative ease of production and of sustaining secrecy, together with low capital requirements, could make the lure of biological weapons considerable for governments seeking to acquire or neutralize strategic threats, especially if their security is threatened by weapons of mass destruction, or by rivals with superior overall capabilities.

Finally, in the background of current, renewed concern may be an insidious unraveling of the diffuse cultural support for banishing biological weaponry. Nuclear weaponry has greatly weakened the notion of strategic victory (despite some continued evidence of a Pentagon quest for "first-strike" capabilities).[11] The idea of using biological agents as weapons for specific purposes has been present in some form since ancient times.[12] However, with the apparent exception of Japanese efforts during World War II, biological weapons have not generally been highly regarded for strategic missions even within military circles. They were thought to be difficult to control and unpredictable in effect. Indeed, it was hard to conceive of a rational mission for major states outside the limited, if abhorrent, setting of "covert operations." There are fairly substantial charges that the CIA's destabilization efforts against Castro's Cuba included projects to infect poultry and induce pig fever through an African swine virus, previously unknown in the hemisphere.[13] If it occurred, such a use of biological agents would be especially significant as it was evidently subsequent to Nixon's repudiation of 1969. It suggests that law-abidingness cannot be taken for granted in the BW context. Visions of the nature of BW from the 1980s are more grandiose.[14] Journalist William Kucewicz charged in 1984 that the Soviet Union is embarked on a search for biological weapons agents for which no credible defense is possible: "It now appears such weapons are being developed in earnest by the Soviet Union, and that threat may someday rival even nuclear war."[15] Such a prospect, however speculative, engenders a climate of opinion favorable to the sort of deterrence posture that has taken hold in the chemical area, that is, to treaty-denying "development" activities.[16]

These dimensions of BW debate point to several features that affect current attitudes toward biological weaponry. First of all, distrust in an East-West setting tends toward arms-racing as long as security is linked to those forms of deterrence that rely on matching specific weapons systems (i.e. nuclear, conventional, chemical, and so forth). Secondly, if restraints on a specific type of warfare or weapon between the superpowers erode, then prohibited forms of behavior are likely to spread rapidly throughout the state system as a whole, especially if the type of warfare and weaponry involved is inexpensive and possesses strategic advantages. Thirdly, these instabilities can be aggravated by either faulty intelligence or by hostile propaganda that represents a rival state as engaged in threatening behavior relative to the legal prohibitions at stake.

2 The Existing Legal Regime

The basic international law prohibition directed at biological warfare is contained in the 1925 Geneva Protocol and the BWC (appendices 2 and 3). The full name of the Geneva Protocol is "Protocol for the prohibition of the use in war of asphyxiating, poisonous or other gases, and of bacteriological methods of warfare." It continued an earlier effort by international law to ban poison gas as a weapon, and was preoccupied with this goal. Biological warfare was incidental to this principal treaty objective and not even mentioned in the Preamble of the Protocol, which begins:

"Whereas the use in war of asphyxiating, poisonous or other gases and of all analogous liquids materials or devices, has been justly condemned by the general opinion of the civilized world. . . ." The preamble goes on to assert an international law obligation "binding alike the conscience and the practice of nations."

The operative clause of the Protocol, in effect, reaffirms a pre-existing prohibition on poison gas that arguably was superfluous. In this regard, the status of BW was quite different. No definite prior legal tradition of prohibition existed. The treaty rule established the prohibition. In the language of the Protocol, "the High Contracting Parties . . . extend this prohibition [on poison gas] to the use of bacteriological methods of warfare."

There are several problems with the Protocol, despite wide adherence and the general view that it embodies a customary rule of international law, at least with respect to CW.[17] This view has been endorsed by the UN General Assembly.[18] The first problem, exemplified by the U.S. use of herbicides and nonlethal gases (tear gas) during the Vietnam War and more recently by Israel's extensive reliance on a variety of nonlethal chemicals to carry out its belligerent occupation of the West Bank and Gaza, concerns the absence of a consensus as to the range of toxic agents covered by the prohibition.[19] Julian Perry Robinson has noted that the Vietnam precedent is damaging, not because tear gases or herbicides in themselves present any abnormal threat to international security, but because no unambiguous distinction can be drawn between these agents and other clearly "poisonous . . . materials specified in the Protocol: their legitimation therefore risks impugning the entire body of law that stems from the Protocol."[20] U.N. General Assembly Resolution 2603A, passed in 1969, does reassert an extensive view of the Protocol to include nonlethal chemicals, but the resolution, while passed by an 80–3 vote, is only recommendatory, and is further weakened by 36 abstentions and 7 absentees, including most of the close allies of the United States. Since Vietnam, herbicides have been used in Portuguese Africa and in the Horn of Africa without arousing international controversy under the Protocol, and Israeli practices have only received selective criticism. The relevant point here is that a sovereign state can make its own self-serving interpretation of international law obligations, especially during a war, and there is very little under most circumstances that can be done about it. Neither the political will nor an enforcement mechanism exists. As well, the organized international community is rarely united enough to take a strong coherent stand. Such an ambiguity may also pertain to biological weapons.

GA Resolution 2603A interprets the Geneva Protocol as prohibiting any chemical agents of warfare, whether gaseous, liquid, or solid, employed for direct toxic effects on persons, animals, or plants. The same resolution also construes the Protocol as prohibiting all biological agents of warfare intended to cause death or disease in persons, animals, or plants. The United States has dissented from this interpretation of the Protocol, at least as it pertains to CW. Presumably its position on BW closely corresponds with the interpretation made by the resolution, although some disclosures about CIA retention of toxic biological agents seem to express an official unwillingness, at least on the part of a bureaucratic subunit to comply fully. We do not know whether this unwillingness was in response to presidential wishes or a betrayal of them. Nor can we be even sure that the leadership of the CIA approved or knew about the retention of BW agents, and if so, on the basis of what rationale.

A second problem with the Protocol is that it has been interpreted, by some parties, as merely a no-first-use agreement. Countries have either made a reservation to this effect, or their practice has emphasized the development of stockpiles available for retaliatory use as necessary.[21] In fact, the overall nonuse of poison gas during World War II has been generally understood as reflecting this deterrent structure, that is, fear of retaliation, as well as the sense by military commanders that no decisive advantages could be achieved.[22] Italy used poison gas against Ethiopia (1935–1936) and Japan used it in China (1937–1945). In both instances, the victim states lacked either protection or an in-kind retaliatory capability.

A third weakness of the Protocol is that it only prohibits use. It does not even clearly forbid threats to use. It makes no effort to prohibit research, development, and possession. As a consequence, despite the Protocol, a chemical arms race is almost inevitable, is under way. The treaty prohibition remains a factor in policymaking, but it must increasingly compete with considerations of military necessity. Once stockpiles for retaliation exist, under wartime conditions other uses will be contemplated. It is reliably reported, for instance, that Winston Churchill advocated large-scale recourse to gas attack on Germany during World War II, and was dissuaded by tactical reasoning and by retaliatory prospects, not by legal inhibitions.[23]

A final dramatic weakness, already discussed, is the breakdown of the Protocol in the Iran/Iraq War during the 1980s. This breakdown consisted of several elements:

• extensive recourse by Iraq to chemical weapons both against its external enemy, Iran, and against the Kurdish civilian communities within Iraq;

• perceived battlefield effectiveness as a result of such recourse;

• ineffectual responses by way of ritualistic censure, but no serious effort at an international level to impose sanctions on Iraq;

• general reaction by public opinion and political leaders that such weaponry could be tempting to the military establishment and that it is necessary to deter its use by others through the possession of a capability to retaliate.

Some of these weaknesses evident in relation to CW do not pertain to BW. Others are addressed in the 1972 Biological Weapons Convention (BWC) which entered into force in 1975 (for text see appendix C). The Convention was signed simultaneously in Washington, London, and Moscow in 1972.

The Preamble to the Convention places the BWC in the wider setting of "achieving progress toward general and complete disarmament, including the prohibition and elimination of all types of weapons of mass destruction." It also explicitly builds on the Geneva Protocol and augments its prohibition on use, a feature reiterated in Article VIII. The Preamble also asserts that a regime prohibiting development, production, and stockpiling of biological weapons is "a first possible step" toward the establishment of a comparable regime for chemical weapons, a consideration reiterated as Article IX. The linking of BW and CW regimes is important, and applies in a negative (deterrence regimes, arms races), as well as a positive (comprehensive regimes of prohibition) sense. Finally, the preamble asserts the goal of the BWC to be "to exclude completely the possibility of bacteriological (biological) agents and toxins being used as weapons" and insists "that such use would be repugnant to the conscience of mankind." Note here, particularly, that societal attitudes are invoked as a ground for the effort of statesmen to achieve an effective legal regime, and that effectiveness is understood to involve development and possession, as well as actual use. This extension of the Geneva Protocol to stages prior to use is a practical recognition that inhibiting use in an atmosphere of armed conflict requires a stable regime of nonpossession.

Article I formulates the basic treaty obligation. Parties agree "never in any circumstances to develop, produce, stockpile or otherwise acquire or retain: (1) Microbial or other biological agents, or toxins whatever their origin or method of production, of types and in quantities that have no justification for prophylactic, protective or other peaceful purposes." (As will be discussed later, this prohibition is of limited value because the qualification upon it is so uncertain and vague.) Article I also seems to use language that encompasses the circumstances described in Section III pertaining to retention and use of biological weaponry by intelligence operations, especially the reference in Article I(2) to "hostile purposes" as well as to "armed conflict." There seems to be no reasonable way to interpret this language that does not encompass the role of the CIA and analogous intelligence agencies, or in fact, any entity directly or indirectly related to the government.

Article II of the Convention pledges parties "to destroy, or to divert to peaceful purposes" all biological agents, including delivery equipment. Article IV imposes on parties the important obligation to assure that "necessary measures" are taken to prevent any "development, production, stockpiling, acquisition or retention of the agents, toxins, weapons, equipment and means of delivery" within its territory. Such obligation imposed on governments requires domestic regulation of activities by individuals, universities, and corporate groups. Article V is an undertaking by parties "to consult . . . and to cooperate" in solving problems arising under BWC. Article VI(1) allows a party to file a complaint with the U.N. Security Council if it finds that the other party is "acting in breach of obligation" under the convention, while Article VI(2) obliges parties "to cooperate" in carrying out a U.N. Security Council investigation of allegations.

Article X involves the agreement of parties to share fully in peaceful uses arising from "further development and application of scientific discoveries in the field of bacteriology (biology)." Article XI provides a procedure by which to amend the treaty, whereas Article XII calls for periodic review that explicitly includes consideration of "new scientific and technical developments" that are relevant to the treaty. Article XIII(1) states that the BWC "shall be of unlimited duration" but Article XIII(2) reserves a right of withdrawal from the treaty obligations if a party "decides that extraordinary events related to the subject matter of the Convention have jeopardized the supreme interests of the country."

The signal achievement of this BWC should not be overlooked, nor should its contents be too easily deprecated. Both superpowers have legally committed themselves to forego possession, as well as use. As a result, no retaliatory use is contemplated or permissible, and renunciation is unconditional. Furthermore, according to Article II existing stockpiles of biological weapons were obliged to be destroyed within nine months of entry into force (as of 1975). On its face, then, the BWC seems to provide a comprehensive repudiation of BW that does not depend on deterrence or enforcement.

Research associated with "defensive" purposes, as well as peaceful applications, is allowed under the BWC. Yet given developments in biological capabilities and in the attitudes of states toward such weaponry, the BWC is no longer sufficiently reassuring. First of all, "peaceful" applications cannot be reliably distinguished from potential military applications. The Article I limitation on *developmental* activities is restricted to biological agents or toxins "that have no justification for prophylactic, protective or other peaceful purposes." This is a potentially troublesome loophole since many provocative, militarily relevant research and development activities can be reconciled with treaty commitments so long as they are not dedicated openly to weapons applications. Since much biogenetic research has dual civilian/military applications, there is an inevitable buildup of knowledge and experience that could be either covertly diverted to biological warfare application or could be redirected in the event of a shift of policy or as a result of a breakdown of the treaty regime. Similarly, the Article II obligation to destroy stockpiles exempts any biological agent or toxin that is diverted to peaceful purposes, which again allows a particular state an alarming degree of discretion; when taken together with the absence of verification procedures, this makes compliance almost depend on good faith and self-interest. Second, "defensive" research (to protect populations by immunization and other methods) cannot be reliably disengaged from "offensive" research, even if such a political will existed (chapters 6 and 8). Third, a veil of secrecy covers activities in this area, arousing suspicions and making it difficult to distinguish innocent from sinister activity on the part of foreign states. Malicious propaganda cannot easily be distinguished from disturbing revelations. Fourth, suspicions about violative behavior are, as a practical matter, impossible to verify by the procedures set forth in the Convention. Parties are not cooperative, tending to dismiss allegations as propaganda; the Security Council cannot operate if a Permanent Member exercises its veto. Furthermore, the Convention lacks any reliable enforcement mechanism. Fifth, evidence exists suggesting a disturbing failure by government agencies such as the CIA to abide by an overall national policy apparently respectful of the BWC. Sixth, there is a deep cultural tendency in both science and the military to explore any research that might enhance mastery over nature or the extent of state power.

These problems are not surprising, and at least until recently their correction has seemed difficult to achieve either through recourse to the available amending process within the treaty framework or through the development of a further protocol. Particularly problematic has been the fact that states have been reluctant to forego "peaceful applications" to increase reassurance that military developmental activities are not taking place. At the same time, principal states have rejected the idea of establishing an impartial, external monitoring procedure over national research activities capable of providing high levels of verified compliance. The BWC complaint and investigative procedures—including, ultimately, recourse to the Security Council—seemed unlikely to be useful and, in fact, have not yet been used despite the accusatory atmosphere of the early 1980s.

However, the relaxation of superpower tensions since the November 1985 summit may indicate new orientations towards arms control. The Soviet shift toward the Western view on verification in arms control settings creates a far better framework for negotiations and for agreed procedures to verify compliance. Encouraging tangible expressions of this positive trend were exhibited at the Second Review Conference on the BWC, as well as in the ongoing negotiations for a Chemical Weapons Convention and through the adoption of verification mechanisms in the INF Treaty, properly hailed as the most elaborate form of verification in the history of arms control.

A protective, holding-the-line posture toward BWC seems less necessary than a few years ago. The pressures on the U.S. side to withdraw in light of suspicions about Soviet "developmental" activities seem less intense and credible than earlier; they have, however, not altogether disappeared.[24]

Under these circumstances, the prospects for strengthening the BWC by informal as well as formal means have begun to seem brighter. A greater effort should be made to induce Israel, as well as other states currently not parties, to give their adherence. In an era where conditionality is relied upon to influence internal economic policies of foreign countries receiving IMF credits and loans, where adherence to human rights standards is used to control foreign aid policies, where retaliatory practices are legislated in the event that international prohibitions on whaling are not respected, it seems reasonable to condition economic support on adherence to crucial arms control treaties, including the BWC. The strength of the unconditional prohibition on BW will be increased by each step toward universality of adherence to the treaty regime. If possible, an intergovernmental select body of experts should be established to investigate the general directions of biological research and to set forth guidelines to sustain and strengthen existing prohibitions on military development.

It may even be possible now to propose, by treaty amendment, that the Article I prohibition be reformulated in a more restrictive manner. For instance, the wording of "have no justification" in relation to peaceful uses could be replaced by "do not have as their overwhelming and unambiguous justification." Restrictions might also be introduced to limit or prohibit research with serious military applications. In addition, particularly if negotiations for the parallel chemical weapons convention are completed, it may also be possible to initiate negotiations for a protocol to the BWC that creates independent verification and compliance machinery. Such a process of augmenting the control side of the BW legal regime will not be easy to agree upon, nor to design, and may not make such an important contribution either by way of confidence of the parties in the treaty or actual verification capabilities. Along such reformist lines, it may also be desirable to constrain research by treaty amendment, either by way of a general or limited prohibition on *any* military use of genetically modified material, including "defensive" purposes. The weaknesses of legal regimes of this sort is not fortuitous. They express the state-centered quality of international relations, and the persisting attachment of governments to sovereign rights. Therefore, a rationalist insistence on closing treaty loopholes so as to move toward greater effectiveness remains naive, unless it is reflective of political tendencies. Legal effectiveness is never more than one factor embedded in an overall political context.

3 A Note on CIA Activities

Rarely discussed is the relation between prohibited weaponry and the activities of intelligence agencies carried on beneath the rubric of "covert operations." This relation could be used to circumvent treaty restrictions, or at least to make a violation more difficult to discern, on some occasions even by a government that would like to uphold relevant treaty obligations. "Covert operations" sometimes depart from the apparent boundaries imposed on national policy; they are covert, in fact, precisely in order to obscure or disguise the real dimensions of national policy. In this section some attention is given to this problem in light of prior disclosures of CIA retention of biological weapons in defiance of national policy.

Over the years there have been several allegations of crop and animal destruction by the CIA, undertaken with biological and chemical agents as part of destabilization programs. Covert operations of this sort are properly conceived as military or paramilitary activities that should be regarded as "bacteriological methods of warfare" falling clearly within the prohibition of the Geneva Protocol. The issue arose directly during the 1975 Church Committee Hearings that inquired into the CIA's retention of biological weapons long after President Nixon had issued an order for their destruction. Senator Mondale then questioned a CIA official, Nathan Gordon, about the failure of the agency to carry out the order, especially with respect to 11 grams of shellfish toxin and 11 milligrams of cobra venom, both substances retained for possible use as weapons:

Senator Mondale: So what the CIA was involved in was not military?

Mr. Gordon: The CIA is not a military organization. It is not, nor has ever been charged with the functions of Department of Defense. Yes; it is not a military organization.[25]

There seems here to be a kind of bureaucratic rationale useful for evading national and international obligations, either by regarding only military organizations as obliged or by transferring military activity to nonmilitary entities within the government, or by characterizing certain toxic substances as nevertheless falling outside the prohibition.

There are also revealing exchanges with William Colby, director of the CIA. In his prepared statement before the Senate Select

Committee Colby indicated a fairly comprehensive CIA role in relation to BW. He referred to four "functional categories" of activity by the CIA:

a. maintenance of a stockpile of temporarily incapacitating and lethal agents in readiness for operational use,

b. assessment and maintenance of biological and chemical disseminating systems for operational use,

c. adaptation and testing of a nondiscernible microbio inoculator (a dart device for clandestine and imperceptible inoculation with BW/CW agents) for use with various materials and to assure that the microbio inoculator could not be easily detected by later examination of the target, and

d. provision of technical support and consultation on request for offensive and defensive BW/CW.[26]

Throughout the hearings there is a disturbing failure by CIA officials to acknowledge any legal (or normative) inhibition on the use of biological agents, even for offensive purposes. Colby referred to the Office of Strategic Services (OSS), the predecessor to CIA, relying on BW materials to incapacitate a Nazi leader during World War II as establishing "[t]he need for such capabilities."[27] Of the toxic substances in the CIA's possession in violation of Nixon's destruction order, Colby said forthrightly, "there is no question about it. It was also for offensive reasons No question about it."[28]

Among those biological agents held by the CIA at Fort Detrick were materials "designed to induce tuberculosis." Here is the exchange at the Hearings:

Senator Huddleston: What application would be made of the particular agent?

Mr. Colby: It is obviously to induce tuberculosis in a subject that you want to induce it in.

Senator Huddleston: For what purpose?

Mr. Colby: We know of no application ever being done with it, but the idea of giving someone this particular disease is obviously the thought process behind this.[29]

As the Chairman of the Select Committee, Frank Church expressed his concern, "The particular case under examination today involves the illegal possession of deadly biological poisons which were retained within the CIA for 5 years after their destruction was ordered by the President and for 5 years [sic] after the United States had entered into a solemn international commitment not to maintain stocks of these poisons except for very limited research purposes."[30]

These concerns indicate deep-seated issues involving making law effective for the internal functioning of the modern state in the national security context.

There are several salient features of these CIA hearings that are worthy of note. First of all, the relative openness of American society, especially in the post-Vietnam setting of Congressional opposition to the Executive Branch, enabled such an inquiry into this secret, sensitive subject matter and exposed the broader structural problem. That is, there is every reason to suppose that the patterns, practices, and attitudes of the CIA—basically, nonaccountability—are to some extent present in the intelligence services of all major states. Second, the expectations of law-abidingness are mainly associated with domestic compliance (obeying the Nixon Memorandum); no serious emphasis was placed on issues of compliance with international law. Third, the political language of the civil servants shows almost no sensitivity whatsoever to the existence or importance of international legal constraints. What seemed important to these government officials was obedience to "superior orders" within the government and maximum policy flexibility for the CIA in relation to *any* future mission. Fourth, these overall attitudes also infused the Congressional orientation toward its inquiry. No serious effort during extensive questioning was made by the Senate Select Committee to assess the manifested indifference to international legal obligations to which the United States has given its assent. Note how this attitude contrasts with evidence and allegations of noncompliance directed at rival states.

In other words, evidence suggests a disturbing failure by subdivisions of government to abide by a national policy respectful of international commitments or to feel constrained by law. These concerns raise fundamental issues of state-civil societal relations, and indicate the difficulty involved in making the law effective in the internal functioning of the modern state in the national security context. What do we expect from government? How should "checks and balances" function in relation to compliance and accountability in the national security area? What is the relevance of international law to this process?

The presumed standard operating procedure of governments is to meet evidence, or even suspicion, of noncompliance with compensating noncomplying behavior. Interactions of this sort are likely to induce some form of BW arms race, a result that in its overall effects is almost certain to be worse for all parties than a continuing effort to discourage threat or use of biological weaponry. It is indispensable, of course, that these strong interests in sustaining the BWC regime be understood within governmental circles, as well as among governments.

Ways of discouraging deliberate noncompliance might underscore a kind of whistle-blowing ethos as part of what it means to accept professional responsibility in the area of biotechnology. A creative initiative to reinforce such duties could offer asylum and relief for anyone who divulges under oath information on noncompliance and on irresponsible allegations to this effect. Scientific organizations possibly on an international basis, could provide the means whereby individuals could present information anonymously; the organization would then evaluate the allegations, provide the relevant government with an opportunity to respond, and decide whether publication of the allegations is warranted. Building confidence in compliance would probably require a special protocol to the BWC devoted exclusively to verification; this protocol could establish procedures and institutional mechanisms for assessing allegations and fashion responses in the event that violations are verified. Short of this, the treaty regime can be critically strengthened through building of confidence that some degree of verification can be obtained through a combination of informal investigation and a cooperative attitude by treaty members, with or without formal procedures. The effectiveness of the BWC is dependent on two elements: the perceived unattractiveness of a biological weapons option and a related conviction that reassurance and confidence are needed to avoid an "accidental" biological weapons arms race (that is, a *perceptual* dynamic arising out of allegations and perceptions rather than a *behavioral* determination to obtain military advantage through a deliberate decision to go for a biological weapons capability). The objective would be to confront those who contemplate undermining the BWC with the prospect that their conduct will be detected and repudiated, as well as its effects contained. Of course, a reconciliation of legal obligations and the practice of intelligence agencies would require restricting the latter to intelligence-gathering, thereby eliminating any mandate for military research and development, or any temptation toward reliance on BW applications in the context of "covert operations."

4 Strengthening the Setting of the Legal Regime

The reasons for normally sustaining confidence in the Biological Weapons Convention of 1972 even in a situation where suspicions exist can be summarized. As earlier suggested, unleashing a BW arms race is likely to increase tensions and risks, as well as to add a new dimension of uncertainty to international relations. Perhaps more pertinent, any significant weakening of the BWC is likely to add greatly to the danger of horizontal proliferation, with the hazard that unscrupulous individuals and unsophisticated governments might develop biological weapons for their blackmail potential or to achieve greater power status cheaply and quickly. In such an atmosphere, the access of terrorist groups to BW might increase dramatically, as would the temptation to threaten or use.

In other words, the inhibitions built into the BWC are intimately associated with upholding even the existing poor quality of international order. In the context of their wide web of commitments, sustaining the BW legal regime seems especially helpful for both superpowers. The rational basis for cooperation seems strong, but not strong enough to do away altogether with paranoid apprehensions; these take on added vitality by being linked to profitability for industry and arms production. To offset a BW lobby it is essential that public interest groups show high levels of concern across the spectrum of biogenetic activities.

The stress placed here is upon reassurance about the effectiveness of the BWC as an inhibiting regime. It is foolish to demand or expect an assured framework of near-perfect verification. If that expectation is maintained, especially in a context of unfounded allegations and special interest lobbying, a crisis of confidence in the adequacy of the treaty regime is sure to develop. The statist reflex would be to act upon the worst case scenario, treating the principal enemy as though it were determined to acquire a crippling BW capability that would give it a decisive edge in the future. A complementary danger is associated with exaggerated self-criticism, as when critics of U.S. policy overstate the evidence that the Pentagon is intent upon circumventing treaty prohibitions by exploiting the defensive research loophole.[31] Here, the problem is that the Soviet elites could easily be misled by such accusations, and goaded by their own military advisers to take offsetting steps that would then induce an escalating spiral of fears and perceptions on all sides. The prevention of political and military vulnerability, standard reasoning goes, requires a neutralizing capability and this implies a superior attack capability.

Although this spiral of escalating in preparations rarely contributes to the security of a state, the mixtures of realist mindset and bureaucratic pressures are difficult to resist. Because such a series of developments could easily engulf the BWC regime and would be particularly disastrous, it is of extreme importance to do whatever possible at this time to strengthen prospects for upholding and even extending the treaty.[32] Fortunately, after a discouraging period in the early 1980s when Reagan's national security approach emphasized self-reliance and great distrust of Soviet motives and intentions, especially relating to arms control policy, the atmosphere has started to change. In the aftermath of the INF treaty prospects are more hopeful, but depend on vigilance and continuing efforts. There are several promising lines of development.

Professional Support for the BWC

Respected nongovernmental groups and scientists in the West have brought a healthy skepticism to bear on anti-Soviet allegations and raised the overall awareness level regarding the general benefit of sustaining the BWC regime. This skepticism is also appropriately directed at those who charge that the Pentagon is undermining the treaty regime by its "research" activities. Of course, there is the possibility that such allegations are accurate; it then becomes important to assess such evidence of noncompliance and to encourage a return to the framework of the treaty regime. Even if violative behavior is verified, the ground exists to appeal *within* the treaty framework rather than to take self-help measures *outside* of this framework. Treaty supporters are working actively to offset those who support an active BW developmental program for the U.S. as a geopolitical tactic. It is essential that bioengineers and associated scientists throw their professional weight behind whistle-blowing canons of responsibility, disclose deviant behavior, and refuse work that seems to undermine treaty obligations. As elsewhere, secrecy breeds suspicions and suspicions justify noncompliance by others; noncompliance, in turn, could feed an escalatory spiral culminating in a dreaded BW arms race. It is also important to persuade other governments and their scientific communities, especially in the

Soviet Union, to offer convincing reassurances about their commitment to live within the four corners of the treaty.

Governmental Commitment to the BWC Regime

It is especially crucial that the main governments manifest their commitment to the viability of the BWC and to its desirability. Such a posture of seriousness and sincerity can be expressed in several mutually reinforcing ways. First of all, the appropriate legislation should make the provisions of the BWC binding under domestic law, imposing penalties for violative conduct (including entrepreneurial activity in the private sector that services a potential BW black market). On the basis of past behavior, it would be helpful to explicitly extend these obligations of compliance to the CIA and similar entities. Second, countries should maintain openness with respect to biotechnical undertakings that are funded directly or indirectly by military or intelligence sources. Third, they should share information at international meetings, especially to help offset an impression of noncompliance. Recent Soviet efforts to provide reassurance about the Sverdlovsk outbreak of anthrax are especially encouraging. Fourth, government officials should make it their overriding concern to uphold the treaty regime by carefully screening irresponsible allegations and avoiding any disinformation activities that bear on BW. Fifth, no research program should be undertaken that is "provocative," i.e. implies a possibility of offensive capabilities being developed under the guise of purely defensive activities.

The outcome of the Second Review Conference of the parties to the BWC in Geneva in 1986 was extremely encouraging; it not only demonstrated the willingness of participating nations to adopt specific measures designed to increase confidence in the operation of the treaty, but also disclosed a new appreciation of the treaty regime on the part of governments, including both superpowers (see appendix G). On the American side, there was a more constructive attitude evident, possibly expressing a general shift in the Reagan Administration on arms control arrangements. On the Soviet side, there was an acknowledgment that secrecy pertaining to suspicious activity was inconsistent with confidence in the regime, and that reassurances about compliance had to be convincing and could not rest on mere ritual denials of noncompliance. The commitment to periodic consultation on problems of compliance and exchanges of information in several principal areas of concern—activities taking place in high containment facilities, unusual outbreaks of disease that suggested the possibility of covert BW developmental activity, and biotechnological innovations—was especially impressive.

Overall, this renewed confidence in the inhibiting potential of the BWC engenders hope for the future while it underscores the importance of closing up remaining loopholes, sustaining positive momentum, and reinforcing cultural attitudes that reject reliance on biological weaponry as an acceptable form of warfare. With the expansion of biotechnical operations as a private sector activity, domestic implementation legislation seems important to reduce the risk that a fanatical political commitment or a high commercial premium will induce development and production of biological warfare agents for nongovernment political groups.

At the same time, the threat from revolutionary groups engaged in armed struggle may not be as great as commonly assumed in the counter-terrorist literature. In fact, terrorist groups have refrained from poisoning water supplies and air ducts, and generally do not rely on tactics that produce large numbers of casualties. The typical terrorist undertaking seeks to induce shock through symbolic violence that spreads fear and brings anguish and death to those who are targeted.

The pattern of focused violence by terrorist groups suggests a lack of interest in weapons of mass destruction (at least for the time being). The main danger, at present, seems to be that principal states could set a pattern of exploration of weapons potential of the new biotechnologies (for "defensive" purposes), generating models of development that are copied elsewhere. For these reasons it is desirable to reinforce the cultural rejection of biological weaponry with a stronger regime of prohibition, with the goal of removing the idea from political consciousness as much as possible.

The advantageous situation of the BW legal regime should be appreciated—cultural revulsion tied to a framework endorsed by all major governments, political ideologies, and social institutions, that prohibits possession and development of biological weaponry, as well as their threat or use. Furthermore, leading states possess an overriding geopolitical incentive to avoid opening the BW Pandora's box given the severe instabilities that could follow, including widespread proliferation, sabotage, and terrorism. This incentive is not by itself sufficient. BW developmental pressures and prospects are increasing at a rapid rate. It becomes especially important at this time for citizen groups with knowledge and anxiety about the menace of biological warfare to add their own transnational efforts to uphold and build upon the BWC. These can include the development of procedures whereby suspicious information can be disclosed, but assessed (to avoid either complacency or alarmism in evaluating by informal means, including inducing the cooperation of the accused), concerning the activities pertaining to biological research and development that could be militarily relevant. As suggested throughout, it is important to strike this balance between remaining silent and fostering unfounded suspicions.

Acknowledgment

This chapter benefits from my collaboration with Susan Wright who has acted as mentor on the more technical, nonlegal sides of this subject matter.

Notes

1. For discussion of this reluctance, especially relating to the United States government's refusal to respect the decision of the International Court of Justice in the setting of its policies toward Nicaragua during the Reagan presidency, see Thomas M. Franck, *Judging the World Court* (New York: Priority Press Publications, 1986); for a different view see Falk, "Strengthening the Rule of Law in Foreign Policy," in Marcus Raskin and Chester Hartman, eds., *Winning America: Ideas and Leadership for the 1990s* (Boston and Washington, D.C.: South End Press, 1988), 317–325.
2. See inclusive report of the Secretary General investigating these charges, U.N. General Assembly A/37/259, 1 December 1982, and the gradual abandonment of allegations by the United States government.
3. Julian Robinson, Jeanne Guillemin and Matthew Meselson, "Yellow Rain: The Story Collapses," *Foreign Policy*, 68 (Fall 1987), 100–117, reprinted in this book as chapter 10.
4. For alarmist treatment of these issues embodying an extreme cold war worldview see Joseph D. Douglass, Jr. and Neil C. Livingstone, *America the Vulnerable: The Threat of Chemical/Biological Warfare: The New Shape of Terrorism and Conflict* (Lexington, MA: Lexington Books, 1987).
5. The wider context that is delimited by Iraqi reliance on chemical weapons is well explored in an editorial, "That Hellish Poison: Still Intolerable," *New York Times*, Aug. 8, 1988, A-16.
6. Robert S. Greenberger, "Iraq Opened Dangerous Pandora's Box by Using Chemicals in War with Iran," *Wall Street Journal*, August 1, 1988, 12.
7. For a similar orientation see Myres S. McDougal and Florentino P. Feliciano, "International Coercion and World Public Order: The General Principles of the Law of War," *Yale Law Journal* 67: 771–845, esp. 771–779; Falk, "The Relevance of Political Context to the Nature and Functioning of International Law," in Karl

W. Deutsch and Stanley Hoffmann, eds., *The Relevance of International Law* (Cambridge: Schenkman, 1968), 133–152.

8. For analysis in a parallel setting see Falk, *The Promise of World Order*, (Philadelphia: Temple University Press, 1987), 196–219, 299–318.

9. See generally, SIPRI, *The Law of War and Dubious Weapons*, (Stockholm: Almqvist and Wiskell, 1976).

10. Very persuasively documented in Susan Wright and Robert L. Sinsheimer, "Recombinant DNA and Biological Warfare," *Bulletin of the Atomic Scientists*, November 1983, 20–26.

11. Robert C. Aldridge, *First Strike! The Pentagon's Strategy for Nuclear War* (Boston: South End Press, 1983).

12. For helpful background see Seymour M. Hersh, *Chemical and Biological Warfare: America's Hidden Arsenal* (New York: Bobbs-Merrill, 1968), esp. 1–8; and Ann Van Wynen Thomas, and A.J. Thomas, Jr., *Legal Limits on the Use of Chemical and Biological Weapons: International Law 1899–1970* (Dallas: Southern Methodist University Press, 1970).

13. Noam Chomsky and Edward S. Herman, *The Washington Connection and Third World Fascism* (Boston: South End Press, 1979), I., 379, fn. 94.

14. Charles Piller, "DNA—Key to Biological Warfare," *The Nation*, December 10, 1983, 595, 597–601.

15. *Wall Street Journal*, April 23, 1984.

16. Note that activities involving weapons development and production are legal in the chemical area. For argument in support of the extension of a deterrence approach to chemical weaponry see Joseph D. Douglass, Jr., "Chemical Weapons: An Imbalance of Terror," *Strategic Review*, X (1982). 36–47.

17. For a contrary view that the United States was not legally inhibited with respect to BW prior to the 1975 adherence to the Geneva Protocol see Major William H. Neinast, "United States Use of Biological Warfare," *Military Law Review* (April 1964), 1–46

18. See United Nations General Assembly Res. 2603A, 16 December 1969.

19. Especially in the period of the intifada, it has also been contended that Israeli use of these "nonlethal" substances has had lethal effects when used indoors or in extremely confined circumstances or if employed against the very young, the very old, and the infirm, and that Israeli troops have made frequent use of the these substances under these conditions, causing civilian deaths and severe injury.

20. Julian Perry Robinson, "The Changing Status of CB Warfare," in SIPRI Yearbook 1982, 321.

21. For list of Parties that expressly reserve right to retaliate in kind see Table 10, 1, SIPRI Yearbook 1982, 318.

22. Adam Roberts and Richard Guelff, eds., *Documents on the Laws of War* (Oxford University Press, 1982), 138; SIPRI, *The Problem of Chemical and Biological Warfare* I (Stockholm: Almqvist and Wiksell, 1971), 294–335.

23. Barton Bernstein, "Churchill's Secret Biological Weapons," *Bulletin of the Atomic Scientists*, 43 (1987), 46–50.

24. See Douglass and Livingstone, *America the Vulnerable*.

25. Hearings on Intelligence Activities, "Unauthorized Storage of Toxic Agents," Select Committee of U.S. Senate to Study Governmental Operations with Respect to Intelligence Activities, September 16–18, 1975, 71. Mr. Gordon also questioned

the characterization of shellfish toxin as a biological rather than as a chemical agent, 64–73.

26. Hearings, 11.

27. Hearings, 10.

28. Hearings, 17.

29. Hearings, 27.

30. Hearings, 2; see also Mondale statement, 20.

31. See Charles Piller and Keith R. Yamamoto, *Gene Wars: Military Control Over the New Genetic Technologies* (New York: Beech Tree Books, 1988).

32. For useful discussion of means to strengthen BWC see Eric J. McFadden, "The Second Review Conference of the Biological Weapons Convention: One Step Forward, Many More to Go," *Stanford Journal of International Law*, Fall 1987: 85–110.

12

The Second Review Conference on the Biological Weapons Convention

Nicholas A. Sims

The Second Review Conference on the Biological Weapons Convention, held in Geneva in September 1986, was a surprising success. It did much to arrest the seven-year decline in credibility of the comprehensive ban on biological weapons achieved by the "world's first disarmament treaty." That treaty regime had never been robust, and it had suffered an alarming erosion of confidence, particularly in the United States. The Convention is still not as strong a treaty as its original sponsors (from the British government of 1968–1969 to those scientists in the United States and elsewhere who all played a crucial role in campaigning for a treaty banning biological weapons) had hoped it would be. Its verification procedures are minimal; its consultative mechanisms are underdeveloped; it is not equipped with regular scientific advice, let alone with any permanent institutions or secretariat. It lacks resources, but at least governments at the Second Review Conference committed themselves to a course of treatment which should set the ailing Convention on the road to recuperation.

This chapter summarizes the principal achievements of the Second Review Conference and analyzes the reasons for its success. In addition, it discusses the implementation of the important agreements on information exchange reached at the conference. Finally, this chapter evaluates the implications of the outcome of the review process for the maintenance of the BW legal regime and more widely, for the achievement of the long-sought Chemical Weapons Convention.[1]

The Achievements of the Second Review Conference[2]

The Final Declaration of the Second Review Conference adopted on September 26, 1986 (see appendix C) confirmed the "common interest in strengthening the authority and the effectiveness of the Convention."[3] Why is it significant that "strengthening" the treaty became a leading theme of the 1986 meeting? Because at the First Review Conference, held in Geneva in March 1980, the very word had been virtually taboo. That conference had been held under less propitious circumstances, just ten weeks after the Soviet invasion of Afghanistan and with storm clouds gathering rapidly over the Sverdlovsk anthrax outbreak of 1979. Despite this unpromising conjuncture, by dint of skilful diplomacy the conference had made a modest beginning, all the same, in clarifying the terms of the Convention and specifying a consultative procedure. But talk of strengthening the treaty regime was smothered by the complacency of those governments, led by the Soviet Union, that insisted all was well and resisted the more far-reaching improvements identified with the reformist party led by Sweden.

By 1986, however, military and scientific-technological apprehensions had transformed the situation. Any residual complacency was supplanted by a common concern for the Convention's health. The questions facing the Second Review Conference had to do with selecting the best prescription—and with how, and when, to administer it to the patient.

The proposals most widely supported flowed from Article Five (obligation to consult and cooperate in resolving problems, such as compliance issues) and Article Ten (peaceful uses) of the Convention. Some elaborated the formula of a "consultative meeting at expert level open to all states parties," accepted by the First Review Conference as a first step in developing the potential of Article Five, so as to render it a more reliable contingency mechanism for multilateral compliance diplomacy in future. It was a question of filling in the gaps left in 1980, when to agree on the Article Five formula at all had been a considerable achievement of tenacious diplomacy.[4]

Why this claim for the Article Five formula? Because to declare "the right of any State Party subsequently to request that a consultative meeting open to all States Parties be convened at expert level"[5] was the first, all-important clarification of Article Five, ensuring that a government that remained dissatisfied after trying to resolve a problem bilaterally could bring it before the collectivity of States Parties, represented by their experts in a veto-free setting.

Henceforth a state which suspected another of illicit activity involving BW or toxins, or which simply wanted an ambiguous situation cleared up, could bring the matter to the bar of international opinion by availing itself of this pre-arranged procedure. It would no longer face the stark choice between bringing a formal complaint to the Security Council (under Article Six) where even its consideration, let alone investigation and findings, might well be prevented, and making accusations subject to no organized international scrutiny . . .

This important clarification had the further virtue that it offered an institutional means whereby problems could be aired, and their resolution attempted, by states concerned for the implications of any secret BW or toxin rearmament—without, however, bringing the very treaty regime which banned such rearmament crashing down around their ears . . .

What was achieved at the First Review Conference was, then, a double success. New multilateral procedures were agreed straight away for making Article Five work; and it was further recognized that these did not go far enough for the reform party, who were accordingly granted the right to reopen the whole question later.[6]

Other proposals[7] developed the notion of North-South cooperation in the spirit of Article Ten and sought to make it more systematic and beneficial to developing countries. Yet others linked the two Articles, by encouraging relevant exchanges of scientists, research findings, and data on high-containment facilities (e.g., laboratories handling dangerous pathogens) and unusual outbreaks of disease. It was argued that, by enhancing the openness of their societies in these respects, and in particular by promoting contacts between scientists and information on research activities, governments could "prevent or reduce the occurrence of ambiguities, doubts and suspicions" and at the same time "improve international cooperation in the field of peaceful biological activities."

This quotation, too, is taken from the Final Declaration adopted on September 26, whose nine pages record agreement on all the proposals just mentioned as well as several others.

The path to adoption of the Final Declaration was not without incident. On September 15 the veteran Soviet delegation leader, Ambassador Viktor L. Issraelyan, startled many delegates by proposing the subsequent negotiation of a Supplementary Protocol that would institute stronger procedures for verifying compliance with the Convention.[8] His language was reminiscent of the Swedish resolution, adopted by the U.N. General Assembly (in spite of Soviet opposition) in 1982, which called for a special conference of States Parties to elaborate compliance procedures. (These were to be "flexible, objective, and nondiscriminatory."[9] Was the Soviet Union suddenly outbidding the reformist party? Was it calling the bluff of those who had been loudest in deploring the paucity of verification provisions in this particular treaty, and its consequent vulnerability to violation with impunity? Or was this proposal merely the logical outcome of a determination to strengthen this treaty regime which the Soviet government had—in a phrase to which the United Kingdom drew attention[10]—already put on record back in 1984?[11]

Whatever its motivation, the Issraelyan proposal signalled a marked reluctance on the part of the Soviet Union and its allies to allow further obligations to be tacked onto the Convention without fresh negotiations. In Geneva that week I found some apprehension lest this reluctance, perfectly reasonable in itself, be taken so far as to block the inclusion in the Final Declaration of immediately operative measures that many considered permissible within the existing terms of the Convention. The danger then perceived was that rival proposals—*either* political commitments now, *or* legally binding obligations later—might cancel each other out, leaving only the disappointingly insubstantial lowest-common-denominator of an agreed text.

Fortunately, that "double minimum" outcome was avoided. Instead delegates wisely took the long view and combined their proposals. The result was an impressive Final Declaration, bubbling over with bright ideas.

Proposals for exchange of information and other cooperative measures developing Articles Five and Ten were approved, to be implemented through the U.N. Secretariat straight away. An Ad Hoc Meeting of Scientific and Technical Experts, to be held in Geneva from March 31 to April 15, 1987, was scheduled to develop standardized forms for notifying high-containment facilities and unusual disease patterns, and other details. But the governing principles, and some of the specifics, were already accepted in September 1986.

A much expanded framework of international cooperation in peaceful applications of microbiology, including the prevention of disease and the promotion of biotechnology, was also agreed upon in a long text that worked out the implications of Article Ten. India had led the campaign for a new organization for this purpose; however an Australian compromise formula left it uncertain whether a special secretariat would be required or not.

Another substantial section of the Final Declaration was devoted to Article Four, on the importance of national legislation to give effect to the Convention's obligations. Here, as on Article Five, the Second Review Conference built on an initiative taken at the First Review Conference of 1980 by the United Kingdom to draw out possibilities latent in this Article which might likewise strengthen the treaty regime.[12]

All these measures are voluntary in the sense that they rely on the authority of a solemn political commitment expressed in the Final Declaration. What future, then, for the Soviet proposal of September 15, 1986 that favored legally binding obligations arising from subsequent negotiations among the contracting parties? This Issraelyan initiative was criticized by some delegates for leaving unclear the desired content of the obligations the USSR envisaged for stronger verification of compliance. It was followed up on September 22 by Ambassador Harald Rose of the German Democratic Republic. On behalf of the GDR, USSR and Hungary, he asked that the job of preparing the way for such negotiations should be among the tasks of an experts' meeting to be held in March 1987.[13] This request was successfully amended (and the experts' mandate narrowed down to working out, as noted above, the modalities of data exchanges already agreed) so as to defer to the Third Review Conference[14] consideration of "whether or not further actions are called for to create further cooperative measures in the context of Article Five, or legally binding improvements to the Convention, or a combination of both."[15] So all options are kept open.

In the light of experience under the significantly strengthened regime introduced by the Second Review Conference on the foundations laid by the First, the Third Review Conference will need to be persuaded that additional obligations are necessary. If the newly agreed cooperative measures prove sufficiently reassuring, and States Parties are satisfied that compliance concerns can be resolved through the consultative procedures already provided for, then the Convention may be judged adequate as it stands. Alternatively, if a Chemical Weapons Convention (CWC) has been concluded in the meantime, toxins will have been subjected to the much tougher verification provisions of the CWC. Encompassed by both Conventions, toxins will then constitute a "bridge" between them; there may well be moves to adapt some of the CWC control machinery, as deemed appropriate, to the somewhat different requirements of biological disarmament.[16]

Skillful diplomacy and an encouraging international climate enabled this Second Review Conference to avert largely the temptations of mutual recrimination, and to pool constructive ideas from all quarters instead. The outcome, a tribute to the hard work of the delegates most involved, was a Final Declaration of some distinction.

Factors Favoring the Success of the Second Review Conference

The Second Review Conference benefited from six positive factors, some less and some more immediate. Here they are listed in ascending order of immediacy.

1. The First Review Conference had laid the foundations for reform. In particular, the clarification of Article Five achieved in March 1980 pointed the way to further elaboration of a reliable consultative mechanism.

2. Scientific concern about the advent of new potential techniques for biological and toxin warfare gave the issue of openness greater salience after 1980 than it had enjoyed in the 1970s. Although the "revolution" in genetic engineering had occurred in the early 1970s, it was several years before increasing popular awareness of the possibilities it opened up, and in particular a rising chorus of warning voices within the scientific community, was sufficiently strong to be translated into policy proposals. Recombinant DNA techniques and their military applications had been the subject of some concern during the First Review Conference, certainly, but the deliberate organization of a concerted diplomatic response to changing scientific assessments was much more noticeable in 1986 than it had been in 1980.[17]

3. A reform program already existed. First, there was the "unfinished business" of 1980.[18] The clarification of Article Five had been left incomplete, and the special conference of States Parties which should have taken place (in accordance with the Swedish resolution 37/98C adopted by the UN General Assembly on December 13, 1982) had not yet been convened. Then there were also, by 1986, a good many proposals accumulating among the members of that invisible college, the "friends of the Convention."[19] A good example is the set of proposals for information exchange, in order to

generate a reassuring openness among States Parties, which Dr Robert P. Mikulak had put forward at the AAAS on May 26, 1984 in his paper on "Possible improvements in the Biological Weapons Convention."[20] These had been taken up and commended by others,[21] and given steadily wider circulation before the Review Conference opened in September 1986.

4. The "new political thinking" in the Soviet Union associated with the ascendancy of Mikhail Gorbachev was beginning to make an impact on the style and content of Soviet disarmament policy, notably in respect to changing Soviet attitudes to on-site inspection and other aspects of verification and openness. The Second Review Conference was one of the first opportunities for the Soviet Union to conduct its conference diplomacy in line with the "new political thinking." Hence the contrast between the startling proposals put forward by Ambassador Issraelyan in September 1986 and the very different, "traditionally Soviet" line he had pursued in March 1980.

5. A fortunate coincidence of conferences gave rise to the "Stockholm factor." The first (1984–86) phase[22] of the Stockholm Conference on Confidence and Security Building Measures (CSBMs) and Disarmament in Europe was just drawing to an end as the Second Review Conference began. Unprecedented measures of openness in military matters, including even inspection on challenge, were being accepted as CSBMs by the Soviet Union. These went far beyond what had been negotiated by the same 35 states (participants in the "Helsinki Process" of the Conference on Security and Cooperation in Europe) at Helsinki in 1975. Extension of CSBMs had proved impossible at the CSCE follow-up meetings held at Belgrade in 1977–1978 and Madrid in 1980–1983, and even in the first two and a half years at Stockholm in 1984–1986. Then everything changed. Suddenly, it seemed, the impasse was about to be resolved. The pace of progress at Stockholm made a powerful impression on participants, especially European participants, in the Second Review Conference. The Stockholm Document,[23] enshrining the new mandatory CSBMs, was completed over the weekend preceding the final week of the Review Conference at Geneva.[24] Psychologically the timing could hardly have been better. The Final Declaration of the Second Review Conference was taking shape, and the "Stockholm factor" encouraged European delegates to include as many provisions for greater openness and information

exchange as they could negotiate through the Drafting Committee in the remaining one week.[25]

6. The sixth and most immediate factor in the success of the Conference was the skill and goodwill which delegates in key positions contributed to its committee work and in particular to the drafting of the Final Declaration. In this they made good use of advice from government scientists and nongovernmental specialists (some drawn from the scientific community), who had been pondering the problems now on their agenda over many years beforehand and in some cases formulating tentative recommendations. It would be invidious to compliment the individual diplomats and scientists responsible. Suffice it to say that they grasped the opportunities that the five preceding factors, and a perceptible improvement in the international climate compared with the worst of the preceding years, offered for strengthening the BWC treaty regime in September 1986.

The Ad Hoc Meeting of Scientific and Technical Experts, April 1987

The Second Review Conference delegated to an Ad Hoc Meeting of Scientific and Technical Experts, to be held in Geneva from March 31 to April 15, 1987, decisions on the details of the exchange of information and data established in the Final Declaration.[26] This Ad Hoc Meeting took place "as an appendix to the Review Conference"[27] which saved time working out a fresh apportionment of costs. Although it met under the authority of the President of the Review Conference (Ambassador Winfried Lang of Austria), who opened the proceedings, the meeting was chaired by Dr Bo Rybeck, Director-General of the National Defense Research Institute (FOA) of Sweden. Thirty-nine States Parties[28] took part, many with the same defense scientists to reinforce the diplomatic personnel of their Geneva delegations as were at the Review Conference itself; many had their delegations headed by Deputy Representatives or Counsellors, instead of their Ambassadors, in deference to the customary manner of marking the "expert" status of disarmament meetings at Geneva.

A major purpose of the meeting was to define the scope of the data exchange regarding high-containment facilities. (The precise criteria had been left unsettled at the Review Conference, which had adopted the rather general formula "research centres and laboratories that meet very high national or international safety standards established for handling, for permitted purposes, biological materials that pose a high individual and community risk or specialize in permitted biological activities directly related to the Convention.") Under this heading the meeting "agreed that data should be provided on each research centre or laboratory, within the territory of a State Party, under its jurisdiction or under its control anywhere, (a) which has maximum containment unit(s) meeting the criteria for a 'maximum containment laboratory' as specified in the 1983 WHO Laboratory Biosafety Manual, such as those designated as Biosafety Level 4 (BL4) or P4, or equivalent standard; or (b) which has containment unit(s) and specializes in research or development for prophylactic or protective purposes against possible hostile use of microbial and/or other biological agents or toxins."[29] An appropriate form for governments to complete was also agreed upon. This invited answers to seven questions:

1. Name(s) of the research center and/or laboratory.

2. Responsible public or private organization or company.

3. Location and postal address.

4. Source(s) of financing of the reported activity, including indication if the activity is wholly or partly financed by the Ministry of Defense.

5. Number of maximum containment units within the research center and/or laboratory, with an indication of their respective size (m^2).

6. If no maximum containment unit, indicate highest level of protection.

7. Scope and general description of activities, including type(s) of microorganisms and/or toxins as appropriate.

A second form was devised to implement the agreement on the exchange of information on all unusual outbreaks of disease. The meeting also recorded two definitions of *outbreaks*. As to what might make an outbreak unusual, it went on to state: "Since no universal standards exist for what might constitute a deviation from the normal pattern, States Parties are encouraged to fully utilize existing reporting systems within the WHO, and to provide background information on diseases caused by organisms which meet the criteria for risk groups III and IV according to the classification in the 1983 WHO Laboratory Biosafety Manual, the occurrence of which, in their respective areas, does not necessarily constitute a deviation from normal patterns."

Exchange of data on outbreaks deviating from the normal pattern was stated to be particularly important in the following cases:

• when the cause of the outbreak cannot be readily determined or the causative agent (understood as including organisms made pathogenic by molecular biology techniques, such as genetic engineering) is difficult to diagnose;

• when the disease may be caused by organisms which meet the criteria for risk group III or IV;

• when the causative agent is exotic to a given region;

• when the disease follows an unusual pattern of development;

• when the disease occurs in the vicinity of research centers and laboratories subject to exchange of data;

• when suspicions arise of the possible occurrence of a new disease.

The meeting added that, in order to enhance confidence, an initial report "should be given promptly after cognizance of the outbreak and should be followed up by annual reports." In a last echo of the international reverberations following the anthrax outbreak at Sverdlovsk in 1979, the meeting stated: "In order to improve international cooperation in the field of peaceful bacteriological (biological) activities and in order to prevent or reduce the occurrence of ambiguities, doubts and suspicions, States Parties are encouraged to invite experts from other States Parties to assist in the handling of an outbreak, and to respond favorably to such invitations."

In the next section of its report, the meeting addressed the Review Conference's encouragement of publication of scientific findings. Taking up a proposal which had featured in the Committee for Responsible Genetics' petition in 1984, as well as in Robert Mikulak's AAAS paper the same year,[30] the meeting recommended "that basic research in biosciences, and particularly that directly related to the Convention, should generally be unclassified; and that applied research, to the extent possible, without infringing on national and commercial interests, should also be unclassified." [Punctuation added.] States Parties were encouraged to provide information on their publication policies, including publication of results of research carried out in those research centers and laboratories, and on those outbreaks of disease, subject to the agreement on exchange of information. Finally they were encouraged to provide information on relevant scientific journals and other publications.

Under the heading "active promotion of contacts" the meeting encouraged States Parties to provide information "on planned international conferences, seminars, symposia and similar events dealing with biological research directly related to the Convention," as well as "on other opportunities for exchange of scientists, joint research or other measures to promote contacts between scientists engaged in biological research directly related to the Convention." Once again the twin aims of "preventing or reducing the occurrence of ambiguities, doubts and suspicions" and "improving international cooperation in the field of peaceful bacteriological (biological) activities" were invoked, thereby perpetuating the beneficial linkage of Articles Five and Ten which the Second Review Conference accentuated. That linkage provides the context in which these agreed measures of openness can flourish, and binds them firmly to the treaty regime which they are designed to strengthen.

A deadline of October 15, 1987 was set for the first submission of information under these agreements to the U.N. Department for Disarmament Affairs. Thereafter, it was agreed that information would be submitted annually, on April 15.

Further proposals, including the submission of information about field studies of aerosols of microorganisms and toxins and about outbreaks of major animal and plant diseases, and abstention from discriminatory practices that might restrict international cooperation in biological research or international trade in related products were considered but not acted upon. It was assumed that these possibilities, along with the general question of the effectiveness of cooperative measures, would be taken up at the Third Review Conference to be held no later than 1991.

Finally, the meeting also reminded States Parties of the consultative options open to them under Article Five. It even added the possibility that these might include investigation of possible BW use, or outbreaks of disease giving rise to related suspicions, by experts assisting the U.N. Secretary-General.[31]

At last the treaty regime was beginning to regain some of the assets of which it had been deprived in the 1971 negotiations, which watered down the Convention from the original British conception.

At that time, no direct reference was allowed to the Secretary-General's potential role. The nearest the Convention came to such an allusion was in Article Five, which envisaged consultation and cooperation among States Parties. This might include the use of "appropriate international procedures within the framework of the United Nations and in accordance with its Charter." As in 1980, that phrase turned out to be the most promising source of compliance-diplomacy mechanisms, designed to strengthen the verifiability (or at least the consultative procedures) of the Convention, mechanisms that could be utilized by those who were concerned to restore as much as possible of the strength of the original conception to the treaty regime of biological disarmament.[32]

The First Declarations under the Initial Information Exchange

On October 16, 1987 the Department for Disarmament Affairs of the U.N. Secretariat circulated the first declarations received under the agreed initial information exchange.[33] Nine States Parties were represented, contributing seventy-nine pages: thirty-three from the Soviet Union, ten from the United States, eight from the United Kingdom, and declarations of similar length from Sweden and the Federal Republic of Germany. Shorter declarations came from Finland, New Zealand, Norway and Poland.

The submission of these declarations is an encouraging sign. It indicates a willingness to move towards a greater degree of openness and this in turn is important in generating international confidence and reducing the potential for trouble, whether arising from genuine alarm at suspicious activities and ambiguous events, or from mischief-making by enemies of the Convention.

The Department for Disarmament Affairs followed up this compilation by issuing addenda,[34] comprising the declarations of Australia (October 23, 1987); Czechoslovakia, Netherlands and Spain (November 6, 1987); Canada, Denmark and Hungary (November 19, 1987). By June 29, 1988, including declarations submitted for the year 1987 as well as the initial declarations, twelve Western, six Soviet bloc, four neutral states, and nonaligned Togo had declared their high-containment facilities (if any), the purposes for which they are now used, how they are financed and administered, and the biological agents studied in these facilities. The results for the United States and the Soviet Union are summarized in table 12.1. These submissions are an encouraging sign of international support

Table 12.1
Facilities declared by the United States and the Soviet Union in 1987

Facility name	Sponsor and DOD/MOD funding	Location	Containment	Diseases studied
United States				
Plum Island Animal Disease Center	Department of Agriculture	Plum Island, NY	P3/P4	Animal diseases not occurring in the U.S., such as foot-and-mouth disease
National Institutes of Health	Public Health Service	Bethesda, MD	P4	AIDS virus
National Cancer Institute	Public Health Service	Fort Detrick (Frederick, MD)	P4	Herpes simplex type 1, polyoma virus, diphtheria toxin-melanocyte hormone (gene cloned in *E. coli*)
Army Medical Research Institute of Infectious Diseases	Department of Defense	Fort Detrick	P4	Examples: anthrax; Junin, Hantaan, Ebola, Marburg, Rift Valley Fever, and Venezuelan equine encephalitis viruses; Q-fever; botulinum toxin and saxitoxin
Center for Infectious Diseases of the Centers for Disease Control	PHS (approx. $200,000 per year of research for DOD)	Atlanta, GA	P4	Viral research, especially in hemorrhagic viral diseases
Government Services Division	Salk Institute (wholly DOD-funded)	Swiftwater, PA	P3	Examples: Rift Valley Fever, Venezuelan equine encephalitis, Chikungunya viruses; Q fever rickettsiae; tularemia

Table 12.1
(*Continued*)

Facility name	Sponsor and DOD/MOD funding	Location	Contain-ment	Diseases studied
Soviet Union				
All-Union Research Institute for Molecular Biology	Ministry of the Medical and Microbiology Industry	Novosibirsk	P4	Hepatitis A and B, foot-and-mouth disease, tick-borne ence-phalitis, hemorrhagic fevers, influenza, AIDS
Scientific Research Institute Vaccines and Serums	Ministry of the Medical and Microbiology Industry	Tomsk	P3	Tick-borne encephalitis, Venezuelan equine encepha-lomyelitis
Antiplague Scientific Research Institute of Siberia and the Far East	Ministry of Health	Irkutsk	P4	Anthrax, plague, tularemia, Marburg and Ebola fevers
Research Institute for Viral Preparations	Ministry of Health	Moscow	P4	Pox viruses
Antiplague Research Institute	Ministry of Health	Volgograd	P3	Glanders and melioidosis
Microbe All-Union Anti-plague Scientific Research Institute	Ministry of Health	Saratov	P3	Plague, cholera
Georgian Antiplague Institute	Ministry of Health	Tbilisi	P3	Hemorrhagic fever with renal syndrome, W. Nile fever, tick-borne encephalitis
State Antiplague Institute	Ministry of Health	Rostov-on-Don	P3	Plague, cholera and cholera-type diseases
Ivanovsky Institute for Virology	Academy of Medical Sciences	Moscow	P4	Venezuelan equine encephalo-myelitis and arboviruses, AIDS

Institute	Agency	Location	Containment	Pathogens
Gamaleya Institute for Epidemiology and Microbiology	Academy of Medical Sciences	Moscow	P4	Legionnaires' disease, exanthematous typhus, tularemia
Scientific Research Institute for Poliomyelitis and Viral Encephalitis	Academy of Medical Sciences	Moscow	P4	Hemorrhagic fevers (with renal syndrome, Congo-Crimea), Arena viruses
All-Union Scientific Research Institute for Foot-and-Mouth Disease	USSR State Comm. for Agricultural Industry	Vladimir	P3	Foot-and-mouth disease and herpetic stomatitis
Veterinary Scientific Research Institute	USSR State Comm. for Agricultural Industry	Kazan	P2	Anthrax, glanders, brucellosis
Research Institute for Epidemiology and Microbiology	Belorussian Ministry of Health	Minsk	P4	Hemorrhagic fevers, particularly those caused by Machupo and Lassa viruses
Scientific Research Institute for Military Medicine	Ministry of Defense	Leningrad	P3	Tularemia, typhus, tetanus
Scientific Research Institute for Microbiology				
Virology Sector	Ministry of Defense	Zagorsk	P3	Plague, cholera, tularemia, melioidosis, glanders, typhus viral encephalitis, hemorrhagic fevers
Field Laboratory for Scientific Testing	Ministry of Defense	Aralsk	P3	
Microbiology Research Institute	Ministry of Defense	Kirov	P3	
Military Epidemiology Sector	Ministry of Defense	Sverdlovsk	none	No pathogens; study of the mechanisms by which disease is communicated

Source: Table prepared by Gordon Burck, based on declarations of research in high-containment facilities by the United States and the Soviet Union, submitted to the U.N. Department for Disarmament Affairs in 1987. U.N. Doc. DDA/20–87/BW/I.

for the BWC. They are likely to provide some degree of reassurance about intentions. And they may encourage enhanced international cooperation among scientists—for example, conferences, seminars, symposia and scientific publications.

At the same time, Gordon Burck has made the point that the present reporting requirements do not allow close examination of compliance with the Biological Weapons Convention.[35] The information requested for the data exchange is limited to the names of facilities that either handle high-risk biological agents or "specialize in permitted biological activities directly related to the Convention."[36] Details of facilities handling lower-risk biological agents and doing civilian as well as military research are not asked for. Thus the list provided by the United States is restricted to high containment facilities and facilities that are entirely committed to military projects.

In addition, there is no direction as to the detail required for responses to question 7, on the "scope and general description of activities." Because of the generality of the reporting requirements, the submissions do not necessarily give an accurate picture of the extent and scope of military research programs or of their use of the new techniques of biotechnology. For example, according to Burck, the noncommittal lists of containment facilities and of the use of microorganisms and toxins in research provided by the United States give little sense of the size of the Biological Defense Research Program, the expanding civilian infrastructure for this program, or the extent of its use of biotechnology, that emerges from the U.S. Department of Defense's annual reports to Congress, its Environmental Impact Statements, or its responses to requests under the U.S. Freedom of Information Act (chapters 2 and 7).

The declarations relating to high-containment facilities are of the greatest immediate interest. (No unusual outbreaks of infectious disease have been reported yet.) They may set the scene for enhanced international cooperation among scientists, to which other aspects of the initial exchange of information—on conferences, seminars, symposia and scientific journals published—are especially relevant.

The paucity of initial and 1987 declarations is disappointing: at the end of 1988 79% were still awaited. It is to be hoped that the April 15, 1989 deadline for submission of annual declarations in respect to 1988 will be met by many more. Even those governments (probably the vast majority of the 110 States Parties) with nothing substantive to report can usefully follow the example of New Zealand and demonstrate their conscientious performance of an agreed-upon duty, now incumbent upon all States Parties, by sending a "nil return" to the Department for Disarmament Affairs.

It would also be useful if some way could be found to publish this documentation. The U.N. Secretariat, laboring under the well-known financial crisis of the Organization, is restricted to supplying the information in the form (and language) received, in one copy for each State Party and the WHO. There is a strong case for bringing together, in a more readable format and with intelligent editorial commentary to provide coherence, the documentation of the Second Review Conference and the Ad Hoc Meeting, the initial declarations, and the subsequent annual exchange of information.

The scientific community, non-governmental organizations active on disarmament issues, politicians and opinion-formers need to be made aware of the good news of 1986–1987. Reforms, long advocated by "friends of the Convention" in and out of government, are now firmly on the agenda and are beginning to be put into effect. At last the treaty regime of biological disarmament is starting to promote, and to benefit from, a deliberate program of international cooperation in greater openness and mutual reassurance.

Significance of the 1986–1987 Outcome

This chapter has traced a number of positive developments through the Second Review Conference and its follow-up. The pace may be slow but at least the movement is in the right direction. This is of great significance, not only for biological disarmament, but beyond.

For biological disarmament the significance lies in the widely shared perception of the 1972 Convention as something to be cherished, and the treaty regime it inaugurated as something to be nourished. Governments have recoiled from the alternative. Faced with the choice between an imperfect treaty constraint on biological and toxin weapons and no constraint at all, it makes sense to choose the former and set to work on alleviating its various imperfections. The reform party is no longer crying in the wilderness. It has seen a useful range of measures adopted. It has witnessed a commitment to consider further proposals at the Third Review Conference, not later than 1991. Many of these further proposals are already in the public domain[37] and can be discussed and elaborated before the next Review.

By building so successfully on the foundations laid by the First Review Conference and on subsequent proposals for reform, the Second Review Conference has encouraged a cumulative process from which the Third Review Conference can only benefit. The new emphasis is on finding common ground among all the possible ways in which the treaty regime might be further strengthened; turning general statements of principle into specifics; and making sure that specific agreements are given practical implementation.

For the time being, this process has been accomplished by exploiting the possibilities latent within the existing Convention. Formal amendments or supplementary protocols have not been used. In the future, biological disarmament will continue to need sustained care and attention. Like all treaty regimes, it will always be susceptible to debilitating erosion of confidence, as well as to direct assault. But at least at present, it has been rescued from the erosion caused by suspicion and distrust, and some confidence has been restored.

The wider significance of the 1986–1987 outcome lies in its exemplary effect. It shows that a disarmament regime can survive many tribulations and come through strengthened. It demonstrates the value of the review process. It points up the recovery potential of endangered agreements, as treaty regimes wax and wane and endure all the vicissitudes arising from international contention. The experience of biological disarmament reveals *this* treaty regime, at least, as an organism capable of adapting to changes in its environment. It also gives those who may have been inclined to write off the 1972 Convention as a total failure reason to think again. Critics of the wisdom of negotiating a comprehensive ban on chemical weapons must henceforth take account of the 1972 Convention as clarified in 1980 and strengthened in 1986–1987.

The Chemical Weapons Convention, far from being rendered an impossibility in the light of the BWC experience, is a very necessary complement to the BWC (and to the Geneva Protocol of 1925); it should build on the foundations of that pioneering treaty regime of disarmament, improving on its provisions by all means while seeking to retain its strengths. That pattern has been evident in the Conference on Disarmament, which has taken us a long way towards the conclusion of an effective Chemical Weapons Convention.[38] An appreciation of the significance of the 1986–1987 outcome for the BWC should encourage Geneva delegates and their instructing governments as they work to bridge the gaps that remain and bring the negotiation of the Chemical Weapons Convention to a successful conclusion, thereby fully honoring their solemn treaty obligation under Article Nine of the BWC.

The momentum of 1986–1987 must be maintained, if the achievements of the delegates who made the Second Review Conference a success are to yield their full value. It is now up to their governments (and indeed the governments of all States Parties)[39] to carry the process forward, supported—critically, if need be—by an informed public opinion and in particular by the scientific community. Governments must honor their new commitments, and must organize themselves to meet in full the requirements of openness, consultation, exchange of information and other cooperative measures flowing from the review process and the 1987 follow-up. Nor can the "friends of the Convention" afford to relax their concern for its health. Greater resources must henceforth be devoted to the treaty regime of biological disarmament if its present promising signs of recovery are to be sustained. It remains the unique safeguard of our permanent freedom from the threat of biological and toxin weapons.

Notes

1. Other issues associated with the Second Review Conference are addressed elsewhere. For discussion of paths to strengthening the Biological Weapons Convention, see "Banning Germ Weapons: Can the Treaty be Strengthened?" *ADIU Report* (University of Sussex) 8 (5) (September/October 1986), 1–4. For analysis of the moral dimension of the BWC obligation, see "Morality and Biological Warfare," *Arms Control* 8 (1) (May 1985), 5–23. For analysis of diplomatic responses to changing scientific and technological developments relevant to the BWC, see "Diplomatic Responses to Changing Assessments of Scientific and Technological Developments Relevant to a Disarmament Regime: The Second Review Conference of the 1972 Convention on Biological and Toxin Weapons, Geneva 1986," in Hans Günter Brauch, ed., *Military Technology, Armaments Dynamics and Disarmament* (London: Macmillan; New York: St. Martin's Press; 1989), 92–111.
2. This section draws largely on my article "Biological and Toxin Weapons: The 1986 Outcome," *Bulletin of the Council for Arms Control* 29 (November 1986), 6–7, by kind permission of the Council for Arms Control, London.
3. Preambular paragraph 5 of the 1986 Final Declaration: BWC/CONF. II/13, Part II (appendix G).
4. Nicholas A. Sims, *The Diplomacy of Biological Disarmament: Vicissitudes of a Treaty in Force, 1975–85* (London: Macmillan; New York: St. Martin's Press; 1988), chapters 8 and 9.

5. Article V section of the 1980 Final Declaration; BWC/CONF. I/10, Part II, 8.

6. Nicholas A. Sims, *Biological and Toxin Weapons: Issues in the 1986 Review*, Faraday Discussion Paper No. 7 (London: Council for Arms Control, 1986), 10–11.

7. BWC/CONF. II/9, Annex and Addendum, reproduced in BWC/CONF. II/13. Fifty-four proposals made at the Second Review Conference are set out in full, identified by the state(s) sponsoring each proposal, and grouped according to the BWC Article (or Preamble) to which they relate.

8. BWC/CONF. II/SR. 7, paragraph 59.

9. GA Res. 37/98C (13 December 1982).

10. BWC/CONF. II/SR.3, paragraph 7.

11. In a Diplomatic Note circulated to States Parties.

12. Article IV sections of the 1980 and 1986 Final Declarations: BWC/CONF. I/10, Part II, 7, and BWC/CONF. II/13, Part II, 4–5. The significance of national legislation in consolidating the treaty regime, examples of pre-1980 legislation, and the British initiative on Article IV at the First Review Conference, are treated in Sims, *The Diplomacy of Biological Disarmament*, 79–90 and 136–137.

13. BWC/CONF. II/SR. 9, paragraph 10, and BWC/CONF. II/9/Add. 1, 4.

14. The 1986 Final Declaration provides (BWC/CONF. II/13, Part II, p.10) for the Third Review Conference to "be held in Geneva at the request of a majority of States Parties not later than 1991." Since there is insufficient time for the Conference to be organised for 1989, and 1990 is already committed to the Fourth Review Conference of the Nuclear Non-Proliferation Treaty, 1991 is much the most likely year to be chosen.

15. Article XII section of the 1986 Final Declaration: BWC/CONF/II/13, part II, 10.

16. Article XII section of the 1986 Final Declaration: BWC/CONF/II/13, part II, 10.

17. Sims, in Brauch, ed., *Military Technology*.

18. Sims, *The Diplomacy of Biological Disarmament*, 199–225.

19. Sims, *The Diplomacy of Biological Disarmament*, 307–309.

20. Robert P. Mikulak, "Possible Improvements in the Biological Weapons Convention," paper presented to the Symposium on Biological Research and Military Policy at the Annual Meeting of the American Association for the Advancement of Science, May 26, 1984 (mimeo).

21. For example, in Sims, *Biological and Toxin Weapons: Issues in the 1986 Review*, 8–9, 16–17; Raymond Zilinskas, "Verification of the Biological Weapons Convention," in Erhard Geissler, ed., *Biological and Toxin Weapons Today* (Oxford: Oxford University Press, 1986), 82–107.

22. Stockholm 1984–86 was the first phase of the Conference on CSBM and Disarmament in Europe. The CSCE Madrid Mandate of 1983, under which it was established, envisaged a further phase of the Conference as a possibility, but left this for decision of the 35 CSCE states at their Vienna Meeting opening in late 1986, in the light of the outcome of the first phase which was limited to the period January 1984–September 1986. The second phase opened at Vienna on March 9, 1989.

23. *Document of the Stockholm Conference on CSBM and Disarmament in Europe*, reproduced in (*inter alia*) *SIPRI Yearbook 1987*, (Oxford: Oxford University Press, 1987), 355 ff.

24. By dint of stopping the clock, the Stockholm Conference was able to claim that it had achieved this success within the time limit it had set itself, Friday, September 19; in fact it was two days later that the Stockholm Document was finally agreed.

25. Non-CSCE governments represented at the Review Conference, e.g., African, Asian and Latin American delegations, would probably not have accepted the *language* of CSBM however congenial they found the underlying concept. The concept had to be expressed in other phrases (such as voluntary measures, international co-operative measures, etc.), partly because the proposals agreed by the Review Conference differed in substance from the Stockholm CSBMs and partly because of sensitivity to the risk of European and North American participants' CSCE vocabulary dominating the text of the Final Declaration.

26. The Final Declaration had mandated this 1987 meeting to determine "the modalities for the exchange of information and data by working out, *inter alia*, appropriate forms to be used by States Parties for the exchange of information agreed to in this Final Declaration, thus enabling States Parties to follow a standardized procedure." BWC/CONF. II/13, Part II, 6.

27. Ad Hoc Meeting of Scientific and Technical Experts from States Parties to the Convention on the Prohibition of the Development, Production and Stockpiling of Bacteriological (Biological) and Toxin Weapons and on Their Destruction, BWC/CONF. II/EX/2, p.2.

28. At this meeting there was also a World Health Organization presence, something long advocated but frequently elusive (because of WHO's wariness of the supposed risk of "political" involvement) in the earlier life of this treaty regime. Dr K. Uemura, Director of WHO's Division of Epidemiological Surveillance and Health Situation & Trend Assessment, provided the meeting with relevant information at its invitation.

29. BWC/CONF. II/EX/2, 4.

30. Committee for Responsible Genetics, *Petition Concerning the Military Use of Biological Research*; Robert P. Mikulak, "Possible Improvements in the Biological Weapons Convention."

31. All quotations and paraphrases are from/of BWC/CONF. II/EX/2, 2–13. (This report was issued by the U.N. on April 21, 1987.)

32. On the origins and significance of this formula, see Nicholas A. Sims, "Consultative committees as 'appropriate international procedures' in disarmament-related treaties," *Transnational Perspectives* (Geneva), vol. 4, nos. 1–2 (1978), 15–19. On the clarification of Article V by virtue of this formula, see reference 4 above.

33. U.N. Doc. DDA/20–87/BW/I.

34. U.N. Docs. DDA/20–87/BW/I/Add. 1, Add. 2, Add. 3, respectively. The annual declarations in respect of 1987 are contained in U.N. Docs. DDA/16–88/BW and Addenda. Of particular note subsequently are the initial declarations of France and China, issued on May 12, 1989, in U.N. Doc. DDA/16–89/BW.

35. Gordon Burck, "Confidence Building for the Biological Weapons Convention," (unpublished ms. 1988).

36. BWC/CONF. II/EX/2, 1.

37. BWC/CONF. II/9, Annex and Addendum, reproduced in BWC/CONF. II/13, Part III; BWC/CONF. II/EX/2, 12–13.

38. For developments associated with the Chemical Weapons Convention negotiations, see *Chemical Weapons Convention Bulletin*, published quarterly by the Federation of American Scientists Fund.

39. The Second Review Conference was attended by 63 of the "more than 100" States Parties as of 1986. It issued, under the Article XIV section of its Final Declaration, "an urgent appeal to all States Parties . . . which did not participate in its work, to give their effective co-operation and take part more actively in the common endeavour . . [and] in the future work envisaged in this Final Declaration."

VI

Strengthening the Barriers to Biological Warfare

13

Legislative Needs

John Isaacs

Since the United States signed the Biological Weapons Convention in 1972 (appendix C), there have been several attempts to enact domestic legislation that would make the terms of the treaty binding on all individuals and private institutions under U.S. jurisdiction and require severe penalties for violations. For a variety of reasons, however, no final action on this implementing legislation has ever been taken. There is, however, renewed cause for optimism in 1990.

Normally, the United States and other countries follow up their ratification, or formal approval, of an international treaty with legislation designed to conform domestic law with the new international undertaking. Such legislation is required for almost all treaties, including the INF Treaty (Intermediate-Range Nuclear Forces Treaty), the Panama Canal Treaty and the Biological Weapons Convention. Implementation legislation can provide funds to pay for verification teams, append new restrictions in U.S. law, or transfer American assets to another jurisdiction. Unquestionably, 17 years after the signing of the Convention, the United States biological implementation legislation is long overdue.

The United States formally completed its ratification of the Convention in 1975, three years after the Treaty was signed. Upon entering into force, the treaty prohibited the United States Government and its officials from developing biological weapons. On the other hand, there were no penalties in this country for private individuals—to say nothing of terrorists—developing biological weapons. A private research assistant working for a biotechnology company or an independent scientist engaged in experiments in new biological weapons technologies would not necessarily face sanctions under U.S. law.

The United States' lethargic attitude toward this international obligation cannot be ascribed to lack of awareness. Article IV of the Convention requires that each signatory state "take any necessary measures to prohibit and prevent the development, production, stockpiling, acquisition, or retention" of biological agents and toxins designed for nonpeaceful purposes. The United Kingdom, France, Belgium, Australia and other countries have taken such measures. But the U.S. has so far failed to do so.

To prod the U.S. and other countries to take action, the second Biological Weapons Convention Review Conference in 1986 specifically called upon all parties to the treaty "which have not yet taken any necessary measures in accordance with their constitutional processes, as required by the Article [IV], to do so immediately." That call to action has been ignored by the United States. The delay in enacting legislation has now lasted through four U.S. presidencies and is now extending into President Bush's term.

Implementation legislation was first drafted by the State Department when the Biological Weapons Convention was submitted to the Senate in 1973. Because of the delays in completing the Senate's treaty approval process, the implementation legislation was never acted upon at that time. In 1980, during the first Biological Weapons Convention Review Conference, President Carter submitted to Congress the required implementation legislation, legislation which was formally introduced by the Chairman of the House Judiciary Committee, Peter Rodino (H.R. 7977, 96th Congress, Second Session). However, Congress failed to take action during the remainder of Carter's term in office; the Administration, fighting for its political life, lacked time and attention to back the legislation vigorously.

President Reagan displayed little interest in the legislation, failing to resubmit it after taking office in 1981. In fact, a few Reagan Pentagon appointees appeared more interested in exploiting the Convention's ambiguities to expand "defensive" biological weapons research than in strengthening the treaty. After waiting several years for Administration action, Chairman Rodino, together with the highest-ranking Republican on the Committee, Hamilton Fish (R-NY), introduced the implementation legislation in July 1986, but no further action was taken that year. In January 1987, the pair resubmitted the bill, H.R. 901, which they entitled the Biological Weapons Act of 1987.

Rodino explained when submitting the bill that H.R. 901 would impose stiff fines and prison terms up to life for "anyone—whether a private individual, a corporation or a government official—who knowingly develops, produces, stockpiles, transfers, acquires, retains or possesses any agent, toxin, or delivery system for such purpose." Additionally, the bill authorized the Attorney General to seize and destroy biological agents, toxins and weapons, and to seek injunctions in court against anyone planning to produce or use such contraband. While the Toxic Substances Control Act and the Arms Export Control Act cover certain aspects of the problem, at present no uniform statute exists prohibiting private citizens from making biological weapons.

After some intense pressure on the Judiciary Committee— including from the Committee for Responsible Genetics and others interested in preserving and strengthening the Biological Weapons Convention—Representative Roman Mazzoli's House Judiciary Subcommittee on Immigration, Refugees and International Law scheduled a hearing on the bill in March 1988. However, the hearing was cancelled when State Department officials withdrew, citing their involvement with a visit to Washington, D.C., by the Soviet foreign minister Shevarnadze as the reason. Ironically, the last-minute cancellation was a repeat performance; a hearing in late 1986 was planned but then postponed when the immigration reform bill was revived.

In the Senate there was no action at all. Approached to sponsor the legislation, several Senators, including David Pryor (D-Ark.), Patrick Leahy (D-Vt.), Joseph Biden (D-Del.), and Paul Simon (D-Ill.), declined to take the first step. Reasons for the inaction include the difficulty in finding a Republican cosponsor of the proposed bill to help ease the passage of the legislation through the Senate, a "full plate" of other legislative priorities, the press of various election campaigns, and the desire to wait for the House of Representatives to take the first step of approving the legislation.

By and large, it is unlikely that any organized opposition can be held responsible for the long holdup in Congressional action. Rather, the delay in adopting the implementation legislation should be attributed to normal bureaucratic procrastination as well as to different and more pressing arms control priorities, particularly during the Ford and Carter administrations. It is clear that the best opportunity for action on the implementation legislation would have been at the time of the ratification of the Convention itself. For a long period of time, the follow-on legislation has been becalmed in a bureaucratic backwater.

There is little evidence of substantial opposition in any part of the political spectrum. Many American public health, religious, and arms control organizations have endorsed the bill and urged its passage. While some questions have been raised by the American Society for Microbiology concerning the provision dealing with the seizure of property and injunctions, these and other questions about the specifics of the language can be worked out in the congressional hearing and mark-up process.

Within the Reagan administration, interagency disagreements on the bill possibly added to the bureaucratic delay. In part, this may have stemmed from the hostility of some in the administration to arms control agreements negotiated by past administrations (e.g., the 1972 Anti-Ballistic Missile Treaty and the 1979 SALT II Treaty). The Reagan Administration also adopted a highly critical posture towards the Biological Weapons Convention, claiming that the treaty was flawed and insisting that it provided no effective means to verify and to enforce compliance.

The delay may also have been influenced by Pentagon attitudes towards the dramatic advances in the past decade of genetic engineering and other new fields of biotechnology. Twenty years ago, there was widespread acceptance of the notion that biological agents could not be turned into effective military weapons. Modern weapons technology has moved in the direction of more sophisticated and "smart" weapons. In theory, the user has a high degree of confidence that the weapons will perform as intended. A "smart bomb," for example, can be targeted to hit a military barracks while missing nearby civilian targets—if it performs according to specifications. Biological weapons, on the other hand, are the very antithesis of "smart," in that their consequences are highly uncertain and may damage the user as much as the target. Moreover, toxin weapons cannot destroy enemy equipment, such as tanks and airplanes. Overall, use of biological weapons can have unpredictable and potentially uncontrollable consequences, including global epidemics and damage to the health of future generations. Any army wants to have a clear idea how its weapons will work. Many doubt the usefulness of biological agents as effective military tools; nonetheless, there is a temptation to explore new possibilities. As described in other chapters, new military interest in biotechnology has led to an expanded Pentagon budget in the area and a request for funds to construct a new biological weapons defensive testing facility in Dugway, Utah (chapters 2 and 7). The expanded program, in turn, may have helped to foster an ambivalent Reagan administration position on the Biological Weapons Convention.

As recently as October 1985, the State Department, in a letter to Representative Fish, reaffirmed its support for the implementation legislation. The Deputy Assistant Secretary for Politico-Military Affairs wrote: "The State Department continues to recognize the need for implementation legislation."[1] But the next year, the Department began backing away from its long-held position. In an indication of internal bureaucratic disagreement, the Department refused to comment on the latest implementation bill, deferring a response pending an inter-agency review of the issue.[2] During the second Biological Weapons Convention review conference in September 1986, the United States submitted a background document suggesting that current American legislation was sufficient to bar private actions inconsistent with the Convention. It listed such legislation as the Arms Control Export Act, the Export Administration Act, the Hazardous Material Transportation Act, the Toxic Substances Control Act, the Public Health Service Act, and the Federal Insecticide, Pesticide and Rodenticide Act.

Yet detailed analyses of current law, including that by Francis A. Boyle, Professor of International Law at the University of Illinois, indicate that existing statutes do not apply to many of the relevant biological agents.[3] As Chairman Rodino said when introducing his legislation in January 1987, "Remarkably, there presently is no federal statute that directly prohibits and punishes those who would use biological weapons to wreak devastation on the United States."

Notwithstanding the bureaucratic hedging, the legislation remains necessary for a number of reasons. In the first place, in signing and ratifying the Convention, the United States accepted an international obligation under Article IV of the Convention. It is time for the United States to fulfill its commitment. The United States should not expect other nations to live up to other international obligations when we neglect our own responsibility.

Passage of legislation is a significant way to signal the continued American commitment to the Biological Weapons Convention. The Pentagon's renewed interest in the potential uses for biological agents, American suspicions raised about Soviet biological weaponry research and use, and the vague Reagan administration attitude toward implementation legislation all point to the need for an unambiguous endorsement of domestic legislation required under Article IV. An interested administration could also ease concerns over its views by urging international efforts to strengthen the Convention (i.e., strengthen verification procedures, further open scientific exchanges, adopt new ways to handle charges of illegal activity). As the world leader in new biotechnology, the U.S. has a special obligation to act.

Moreover, it is important to the United States' own national security interests for the Government to close the loophole that provides no uniform penalties for terrorists or other nongovernment individuals who might consider working on illegal biological agents. There is always the possibility that some individual might engage in biological weapons research that risks accidents that could endanger the public. Even treaty-permitted biological research in this area can pose serious health hazards due to accidents or sabotage, and may produce agents that could fall into the hands of terrorists or spawn unpredictable, abhorrent consequences.

In an era of flourishing advances in biotechnology, corporations engaged in lawful research need legislation to clarify what kind of research is legitimate and what is outlawed. Such a law, by establishing legal guidelines, would facilitate important scientific research into the potential beneficial uses of biotechnologies.

1989 may finally prove the year of a breakthrough in the long struggle to pass implementation legislation. With speed totally unanticipated by supporters of this legislation, the prospects for passage improved from bleak to promising. This shift has resulted from a confluence of three factors: a freshman Senator who developed an interest in the issue, renewed concern about the convention within the Bush administration, and a new House Judiciary Subcommittee chairman.

The first breakthrough came when freshman Democratic Senator Herbert Kohl of Wisconsin decided to take on the issue as one of his first pieces of legislation. Senator Kohl had been appointed to the Senate Judiciary Committee, the committee which must initiate implementation legislation in the Senate. On May 16, 1989, Senator Kohl, along with several other senators, introduced S. 993, an implementation bill that he entitled "Biological Weapons Anti-Terrorism Act of 1989." It was the first time such legislation had ever been advanced in the Senate.

Two months later, Senate Judiciary Committee Chairman Joseph Biden (D-DE) authorized Senator Kohl to hold a hearing on S. 993 in anticipation of further action at a later date. The July 26, 1989 hearing provided a deadline for the Bush administration to thrash out its position on the legislation.

During its first six months in office, the Bush administration had conducted what it called a thorough review of U.S. arms control and national security policies. This review focused primarily on nuclear and conventional arms control negotiations, but also included a focus on biological and chemical weapons issues as well. Administration officials working on the latter two issues were cognizant of the fact that during the presidential campaign, Bush spoke frequently of his desire to rid the world of biological and chemical weapons. He closed his second debate with Michael Dukakis on October 13, 1988 with, "I'd love to be able to say to my grandchildren, four years after my first term, I'd like to say, 'Your grandfather, working with leaders of the Soviet Union, working with leaders of Europe, was able to ban chemical and biological weapons from the face of the Earth."

Reflecting this high-level interest, the Bush administration formally endorsed the implementation legislation at the July 26 Kohl hearing. This changed attitude was a significant breakthrough after the ambivalence of the Reagan years. Testifying for the Department of Justice, Ronald K. Noble, deputy assistant attorney general in the criminal division, stated: "We believe that S. 993 represents a sound approach to regulating biological weapons, without jeopardizing legitimate research, and that, with relatively minor modifications, some of which I shall suggest below, it would be an effective new tool that would fill a gap in our current statutory arsenal against potential terrorist activities."[4]

On behalf of the State Department, H. Allen Holmes, Assistant Secretary for Politico-Military Affairs, added: "We find useful the efforts of the Congress to formulate domestic criminal legislation against those who would develop or produce biological weapons or assist foreign nations to acquire them . . . We feel that passage of such legislation at this time would give a clear signal to the world that the United States is serious about controlling the proliferation of biological weapons. It would signal to terrorists that we are deadly serious about keeping such weapons out of their hands. The legislation is timely and important, and we are grateful to the congress for bringing it forward."[5]

The third new factor was the election of Rep. Bruce Morrison (D-CT) as chairman of the House subcommittee that would first initiate House action on any implementation legislation. He replaced Representative Romano Mazzoli (D-KY), who had never evinced much interest in the Rodino-Fish bill. Morrison cosponsored legislation (H.R. 237) that was identical to the previous Rodino-Fish bill and was introduced by Representative Robert Kastenmaier (D-WI) in January 1989. In addition, shortly after his selection, he agreed to hold a hearing on the legislation after completing other priority bills. He turned this support into a formal commitment when the testified in favor of implementation legislation at the July 26 Kohl hearing, "It is my urgent hope that 1989 will be the year that the Biological Weapons Convention implementation legislation is enacted into law. I will do all in my power to move the legislation through the House of Representatives so that both the House and the Senate are prepared to send legislation to the President before the end of this Congress."[6]

On November 21, 1989, the last day of the congressional session for the year, the Senate by unanimous voice vote approved the implementation bill introduced by Senator Kohl (appendix I). There is an excellent chance that the similar House bill introduced by Representative Kastenmeier will be adopted early in 1990. A major stimulus for this new action is the heightened interest in both chemical and biological warfare in the U.S. Congress and in the world community. Following evidence of heavy chemical weapons use in the Iran-Iraq war, and charges that U.S. and other Western companies had aided the efforts of a number of Third World countries to develop chemical weapons, Arizona Senator John McCain charged that Iraq may have obtained from the United States deadly bacteria that it may be using to develop biological weapons.[7] The highly respected Arizona Republican pressed his views on the need to take action in a January 25, 1989, statement on the Senate floor: "I strongly support the efforts of the Reagan and Bush administrations to attack the problem of the proliferation of chemical and biological weapons by strengthening the Geneva protocols, and the 1972 treaty on biological weapons. I believe that we need to press all nations to ratify such treaties and agreements, that we need to move toward international inspection, and that we need to halt or minimize any "defensive" research whose true purpose could be the production of chemical and biological weapons."[8]

The breakthroughs of early 1989 have the potential to end the 17-year stalemate on passage of implementation legislation. Success on implementing the ban on biological weapons would demonstrate the continued U.S. conviction that biological weaponry is a danger to mankind. The Second Review Conference held in the fall of 1986 renewed an international commitment to strengthen the Convention and to take the required legal action in various countries (chapter 12). Some of the constraints against research into or use of weapons of mass destruction have, unfortunately, been eroded in recent years. Heavy chemical weapons use in the Iran-Iraq war, use that has been well documented by international observers, has served to arouse new interest in chemical weapons. As described elsewhere in this book, there is also grave concern about the implication of expanded research for chemical warfare and biological defense in the United States and elsewhere. Reductions or limits on these programs, combined with passage of implementation legislation, would demonstrate continued U.S. commitment to strengthening the international regime banning chemical and biological warfare.

Notes

1. Letter to Rep. Hamilton Fish, Jr., from Robert Dean, Deputy Assistant Secretary, Bureau of Politico-Military Affairs, October 22, 1985.
2. Letter to Chairman Peter Rodino from J. Edward Fox, Assistant Secretary for Legislative and Intergovernmental Affairs, September 8, 1986.
3. Boyle, Francis A., *Analysis of Existing Laws With Respect To The Biological Weapons Convention*, unpublished paper, April 1, 1987.
4. Testimony of Ronald K. Noble, Deputy Assistant Attorney General, Criminal Division, U.S. Department of Justice, before the Senate Judiciary Committee, July 26, 1989.
5. Testimony of H. Allen Holmes, Assistant Secretary for Politico-Military Affairs, Department of State, before the Senate Judiciary Committee, July 26, 1989.
6. Testimony of The Honorable Bruce A. Morrison, Chairman, House Judiciary Subcommittee on Immigration, Refugees and International Law, before the Senate Judiciary Committee, July 26, 1989.
7. "Probe Begins on Whether Iraq Got Deadly Bacteria From U.S.," *Washington Post*, January 29, 1989.
8. *Congressional Record*, p. S 216, January 25, 1989.

14

Verification of Compliance with the Biological Weapons Convention

Barbara Hatch Rosenberg and Gordon Burck

1 The Need for Verification

The question of verification of compliance with the Biological Weapons Convention (BWC) has emerged as an important issue in the 1980s as confidence in the effectiveness of this treaty has declined. This chapter examines issues and problems associated with verification of compliance with the BWC and develops specific proposals for the procedures, standards, and institutions required for effective verification.

During the last decade the rapid development of biotechnology increasingly attracted military attention by its potential for greatly facilitating production of biological agents and toxins and for engineering novel agents with certain militarily desirable characteristics (chapters 2 and 7).[1] As a result, suspicions arose that the new technology was being misused under the guise of defense. These suspicions, together with allegations of treaty violations (chapter 9), generated a widespread sense of the inadequacy of the Convention as it now stands. The European Parliament, in a resolution passed on September 8, 1986, expressed its concern that the development of biotechnology had rendered the provisions of the BWC no longer adequate to guarantee its goals. That concern pervaded the Second Review Conference of the BWC, which opened on the same day. Ambassador Winfried Lang, president of the Conference, wrote afterward, "In the light of repeated statements to the effect that the treaty regime was in trouble and that its vulnerability could not be overlooked any longer, the Conference was challenged to strengthen the treaty".[2]

In the discussions of the Committee of the Whole, comprising the 67 States Parties attending the Review Conference, "most delegations agreed that the verification of compliance and complaints procedures required improvement. It was generally recognized that. . . [this] would promote confidence among States Parties in the provisions of the Convention, . . . In the view of some delegations the complaints and verification procedures should be strengthened to ensure that any doubts and suspicions regarding compliance were satisfactorily resolved."[3] The United Kingdom and the Federal Republic of Germany cited the need for further efforts regarding verification. Formal proposals for negotiation of a supplemental protocol with measures to strengthen verification were put forth by the following States Parties: Pakistan, The German Democratic Republic, the Soviet Union, and Ireland; and a joint proposal was presented by the German Democratic Republic, Hungary, and the Soviet Union. Sweden also proposed drawing up new protocols or annexes to the Convention, but suggested that the procedure not be set in motion until soon after the Chemical Weapons Convention (CWC) negotiations were concluded. The United States and a number of other countries supported postponement on the grounds that the stringent verification provisions under negotiation for the CWC would provide a precedent and model for BWC verification; concurrent negotiations would inevitably involve many of the same negotiators and would delay completion of the CWC. At that time it was projected that the CWC might be signed by 1988. Postponement carried the day, and the Final Declaration (appendix G) states:

The Conference, noting the differing views with regard to verification, decides that the Third Review Conference shall consider, *inter alia*:
  • . . . the relevance for effective implementation of the Convention of the results achieved in the negotiations on prohibition of chemical weapons,
  • the effectiveness of the provisions in Article V for consultation and co-operation and of the co-operative measures agreed in this Final Declaration, and
  • in the light of these considerations and of the provisions of Article XI [on amendment of the Convention], whether or not further actions are called for to create further co-operative measures in the context of Article V, or legally binding improvements to the Convention, or a combination of both.

While postponing the elaboration of legally binding measures, the conferees agreed on an unprecedented extension of the interpretation of Article V of the BWC (on cooperation and consultation) to include a voluntary exchange of information that constitutes a first step toward a verification regime. The President of the Second Review Conference noted that for the first time a review conference went "beyond the traditional function of scrutinizing the past performance of a treaty. . . . it had to innovate . . . it had to strengthen an ailing treaty regime without the possibility of major surgery."[4] As a result, information on the location, scope and general description of activities of high-containment facilities and on unusual outbreaks of disease is now exchanged annually (see the Final Declaration of the Second Review Conference [appendix G] and the Report of the Ad Hoc Meeting of Experts set up by the Conference to finalize the modalities for the exchange of information).[5]

Throughout the discussions at the Second Review Conference on politically and legally binding measures for verification and confidence-building it was evident that the less developed states parties had a strong interest in the adoption of measures that would increase openness and thereby make it possible to maximize cooperation and exchange in the burgeoning field of biotechnology (see, for example, proposals by Colombia, Argentina, and Nigeria, as well as the large number of proposals aimed at promoting international cooperation and technical assistance under Article X of the Convention[6]. The linkage between these issues is also noted elsewhere.[7]

There is now some doubt that the CWC will be signed before the Third Review Conference of the BWC is convened, not later than in 1991. But, after a five-year delay, the negotiation of legal BW verification measures should not be postponed any longer. The technology is advancing rapidly, and the threat of BW proliferation is growing; the 1989 Paris Conference on the Geneva Protocol illustrated international concern on this point. The 1991 Review Conference should build on that concern, state its intention of adopting verification procedures, and set the process in motion. This in itself would be a powerful confidence-building measure.

The Conference should convene an ad hoc assemblage of States Parties to draft the text of a new protocol that will elaborate means of complying with Article V of the BWC, in which the States Parties "undertake to consult one another and to cooperate in solving any problems which may arise in relation to the objective of, or in the application of the provisions of, the Convention."

Nicholas Sims points out that the amendment of arms control and disarmament treaties has proved too formidable or too divisive a device to be used at all.[8] There seems to be unanimity among experts that opening the BWC to amendment would jeopardize the Convention and the consensus it represents. A separate protocol, ratified separately, is needed. The 1974 Protocol to the bilateral 1972 ABM Treaty, the only precedent, unfortunately offers no prognosis as to the difficulty of obtaining multilateral ratification.

The drafting of a new protocol will take time. The initial considerations might be the general principles on which biological verification will be based and the elaboration of details only for provisions peculiar to biological as opposed to chemical weapons. Provisions applicable to both types of weapons could be adapted later from the CWC when it has been completed. In this way double negotiations would be avoided and a biological weapons verification protocol could be ready for signing soon after the CWC is signed. BW negotiations might also help to speed the CW negotiations by addressing measures appropriate for toxins, which differ from other chemical agents but are covered by both conventions.

Incentives to sign the protocol must also be considered, especially in view of the fact that there will undoubtedly be financial costs.[9]

2 The Basis for BW Verification—Comparison with CW Verification

The requirements for verification of compliance with the BWC are, like those for the CWC, intrusive because of the potential for clandestine development and production of biological and chemical weapons. Consequently, many procedural and organizational provisions already drafted or planned for the CWC will be directly applicable to verification of compliance with the BWC as well. The establishment of the CWC provisions will greatly simplify the task of negotiating BWC verification measures. At the same time, there are marked differences in the requirements for BW and CW verification.

According to the February, 1988, rolling text of the draft CWC, permitted activities will be monitored primarily through the following: production controls; limits on amounts and sites; and logging of precursor production, transfers and purposes. This approach is not possible for the BWC because the relevant amounts of biological weapons agents are much smaller and they are to be found primarily in the laboratory rather than the factory. According to the U.S. Department of Defense, warfare quantities of biological agents could now be produced rapidly from research stocks in small, easily disguised facilities.[10] The techniques and quantities of agents involved in permitted research may be sufficient for breakout potential.

Although the small scale of BW activities is a complicating factor for biological compared to chemical verification, there are also simplifying factors. Biological weapons agents play a much smaller role in world industry than do chemical weapons agents or their precursors. The global scope and commercial secrecy of the chemical industry greatly complicate chemical controls. Furthermore, the declaration and destruction of biological weapons facilities, stockpiles, and delivery systems, unlike those for chemical weapons, do not need to be addressed, for they have been prohibited since the treaty came into force in 1975.

For biological verification, the necessary focus on research rather than production requires the monitoring of *all* activities involving biological agents and the possession of *any* amount of such agents. High-containment and aerosol-generating facilities are important candidates for controls, as are the testing of BW defenses and the training of troops in their use. Any activity with offensive potential must certainly be monitored; for BW this includes many activities carried out for defensive purposes[11] and even sometimes for civilian purposes. Because of this overlap, full disclosure is the only guarantee of defensive intent. Secrecy in defense programs raises suspicions of treaty violation and could generate escalating cycles of military response, all under the guise of defense. If a verification regime is to provide security, it must require and enforce total openness; at the same time it will obviate the need for secrecy by constituting a better deterrent than any secret defense program. Total openness means true transparency, without any efforts to obscure the facts or make them difficult to ascertain.

The necessity for monitoring activities at the research level, something not needed for other weapons controls, has generated anxieties because of its perceived difficulty. We believe that the difficulty has been overstated. Furthermore, one must not overlook the later stages of BW development, which are more accessible to verification. The U.S. Army maintains, "Even if. . . research of an offensive nature could be concealed in the U.S., then production surely could not, and neither could the integration of such weapons into military training and doctrine."[12] Under questioning by Senator Herbert Kohl at a recent Senate hearing, Dr. B. Richardson, Acting Deputy Assistant Secretary of Defense for Chemical Matters, stated that the development of a biological weapon would require about twenty steps beyond research including scale-up, control, and dissemination, and that this would probably take several years.[13]

Regarding controls at the research level, at the Second Review Conference Sweden proposed reporting information on the orientation of relevant research programs as a confidence-building measure; Pakistan suggested reporting the location and purpose of *all* biological research facilities and opening them to interested scientists.[14] Geissler has suggested imposing an explicit ban on any relevant research not for prophylactic, protective, or other peaceful purposes (i.e., on offensive biological research, which is not explicitly banned in the Convention).[15] This would not, however, solve the defense/offense overlap problem. In the approach taken here, measures are proposed to ensure the openness of *all* biological research, whether civilian or military, and to restrict the most provocative research activities. An effort has been made to eliminate distinctions based on intent, which is difficult to establish. To be enforceable, verification provisions have to apply without distinction to military and civilian activities. Consequently, there can be no requirements that are not acceptable for civilian purposes.

No verification regime can cover everything. Adequate verification will deter violation of the Convention, make illegal actions difficult and limit their scale, and provide workable means for international investigation of concerns that may be raised through national intelligence. For the major powers at least, national intelligence will remain central even after an international biological verification regime is adopted. It will have to be utilized as an integral part of the process of verification, much as it is for bilateral treaties, which rely entirely on national intelligence for this purpose. Even prior to the BWC, President Richard Nixon stated that his unilateral renunciation of biological weaponry would not "leave us vulnerable to surprise by an enemy who does not observe these rational restraints. Our intelligence community will continue to watch carefully the nature and extent of the biological programs of others."[16] The capacity of U.S. intelligence to monitor early developments (by such means as electronic reconnaissance, a National Technical Means, or human intelligence) is indicated by the fact that it has predicted every Soviet ICBM *before* it was tested.[17] In his book *Verification: How Much is Enough?* Allan Krass points out that the capability of the United States and presumably of other nations to intercept and monitor virtually all of the communications of other states must act as a powerful inhibiting factor on any attempts to carry out clandestine activities.[18] In this sense, national intelligence is already contributing to the effectiveness of the BWC. Any precautions to circumvent interception would have to be elaborate and expensive and would themselves be likely to arouse suspicion. Whether or not the United States is adequately applying its intelligence capabilities to monitor compliance with the BWC is a different question.[19]

An international verification regime ought to be designed to take advantage of and maximize the intelligence assets of its parties. Extensive annual reportage requirements and routine inspections can establish a baseline against which nations can check any evidence for clandestine activities that they may acquire. Opportunities for the voluntary transfer of confidential intelligence to the international verification body and for international investigation of suspected violations in a nonpolitical atmosphere need to be provided. Some possibilities will be presented here; no doubt others could also be devised.

3 Clarification of the Interpretation of the BWC

The Second Review Conference of the BWC has already broken ground in defining more clearly the scope of the treaty.[20] The Third Review Conference could build on this precedent to clarify several ambiguous concepts in the BWC so that violations and permitted activities could be clearly differentiated. As things now stand, there are some dangerous and suspicious activities that are not explicitly violations of the Convention but would tend to undermine it (chapters 5–8).[21] Any meaningful verification regime must address these activities.

It would be important to clarify the following points before verification measures are addressed:

The Creation of Novel Agents
Many commentators[22] have felt the need for a more complete definition of the activities permitted under the BWC: activities carried out for "prophylactic, protective or other peaceful purposes." Some have wished to draw a clear line between defensive and offensive activities. Desirable as this would be , it does not seem feasible, for in many cases the difference is indeed purely a

matter of intention. We prefer, therefore, to use the criterion of openness as a distinguishing feature.

One activity, however evokes preeminent concern and could in itself constitute a global threat: the creation of novel biological warfare agents. These can be defined as pathogens (organisms or toxins) that possess a particular combination of properties conferred by scientific manipulation (including genetic engineering by recombinant and classical methods and *in vitro* synthesis) that might increase their usefulness as weapons agents or in the development of weapons agents. Some examples are the combination of pathogenicity with drug resistance, altered antigenicity, altered stability, additional pathogenic factors, altered host range or tissue specificity, altered invasiveness, and properties that would result in evasion of detection or of proper identification (chapter 5).[23] The definition requires careful thought and could probably be simplified and generalized.

The creation or construction of novel warfare agents could have no *net* prophylactic or protective purpose, even if carried out for defensive reasons such as threat assessment or the development of specific defenses. No defense that might be developed could protect civilians (as opposed to troops) from an attack. Moreover, experience with other biological agents shows that once novel warfare agents have been created, sooner or later they are almost certain to escape (whether by accident, intention, human error, theft, or sabotage); the consequent threat of the establishment of a new disease (probably a particularly recalcitrant one) and the possibility of a global epidemic would outweigh any intended defensive (protective) purpose. A different kind of defense against novel agents is needed: a verifiable ban. Since the creation of novel BW agents would not be justified for any purpose, the BWC can reasonably be interpreted to exclude this from the category of permitted activities.

Furthermore, the BWC forbids States Parties "to develop . . . microbial or other biological agents or toxins, whatever their origin or method of production, of types or in quantities that have no justification for prophylactic, protective or other peaceful purposes." The key word is "develop." This word has often been interpreted as if it were in juxtaposition to "research," but that is not the ordinary use of the word. Webster's *Third New International Dictionary* (1971) gives the following relevant definitions: "to make actually available or usable (something previously only potentially available or usable); to cause to unfold gradually; conduct through a succession of states or changes each of which is preparatory for the next; to acquire." These definitions fit the creation of novel agents by, for example, genetic engineering techniques. The Convention therefore can be interpreted as prohibiting such activity.

Biochemical Agents as Toxins

The definition of "toxin" has never been well established. Almost everything is toxic at some level. If toxins are defined as toxic substances that are produced by living organisms, then a great many biochemical substances have to be included under the definition when nonphysiological or abnormal doses are considered. In its Programmatic Environmental Impact Statement of April 1989 covering the U.S. Biological Defense Research Program, the U.S. Department of Defense lists representative toxins under study and adds, "Physiologically active compounds, particularly peptide hormones and neuromodulators, are included for consideration in the toxin category because excesses of these compounds can cause physiological imbalances similar to those caused by some toxins."[24]

Under its Program Element 0601102, Project BS12 (Science Base/Medical Biological Defense), the U.S. Army conducts medical research on "emerging threats such as low molecular weight toxins and endogenous bioregulators." Under this project it was demonstrated in 1988 that the hormones insulin and interleukin-1 are effective in aerosol form in basic pulmonary absorption studies (thus, in overdose, they would constitute potential warfare agents).

As these examples show, biochemical agents (sometimes called "agents of biological origin") with a potential for weapons use can be categorized and studied as toxins; conversely, toxins are clearly biochemical agents. Both classical toxins and other biochemicals are emerging as important CW agents because it has recently become possible to produce them rapidly and cheaply, in quantity, by cloning their genes in bacteria. As weapons they are closely similar to each other and to biological weapons, and differ from other chemical weapons in terms of production, quantity, dosage, methods of use, and the measures required for their prohibition and verification. By the same logic of similarity and convenience that led Nixon to include toxins in the U.S. renunciation of biological weapons in 1969–1970,[25] biochemical agents should be included in the toxin category.

The CWC negotiators have not yet made adequate provisions for dealing with emerging CW agents such as toxins and biochemicals; according to U.S. Ambassador Max Friedersdorf, this is one of the major remaining problems.[26] As discussed earlier, the CW verification provisions now under negotiation are directed toward large-scale industrial chemicals, not toward biological substances. Coverage of toxins (in this expanded sense of the term) under the CWC is important, not only to ensure that this class of substances is never weaponized but also to provide a direct connection between the two treaties. Coverage under the BWC is equally important because of the opportunity to provide verification provisions more closely tailored to fit biologically-produced substances. By defining "toxin" to include biochemical agents and initiating BWC verification negotiations, the Third Review Conference could remove an obstacle to the completion of the CWC while making possible a simpler and more secure regime for the control of these new potential weapons agents than is currently foreseen under the CWC.

Investigation of Compliance Questions by the Secretary-General

The concept of using the Secretary-General of the U.N. to investigate allegations and report any violation of the BWC has been evolving steadily. The BWC States in Article V that "consultation and cooperation . . . may also be undertaken through appropriate international procedures within the framework of the United Nations and in accordance with its Charter." The Second Review Conference considered mentioning the Secretary-General explicitly but finally skirted the issue, stating in the Final Declaration that "any State party may request specialized assistance in solving any problems which may arise in relation to . . . the Convention through, *inter alia*, appropriate international procedures within the framework of the United Nations" (appendix G). A proposal at the Second Review Conference by Australia, Belgium, the Federal Republic of Germany, France, and the United States, spoke more directly of the right of any party to solve compliance concerns by requesting the Secretary-General to conduct a timely fact-finding inquiry; a similar proposal was made by Nigeria.[27] The Report of the Experts Meeting following the Second Review Conference draws attention to the availability of the Secretary-General to investigate "with the assistance of qualified experts, following procedures available to him," any questions of the use of biological weapons, and states that "this possibility covers outbreaks of infectious diseases and similar occurrences caused by toxins. . . ."[28] At the Paris Conference of January 1989, 149 states affirmed their support for the Secretary-General in investigating alleged violations of the Geneva Protocol, and "for the United Nations in the discharge of its indispensable role, in conformity with its Charter". The Third Review Conference should be able to agree on a statement similar to the proposal submitted in 1986 by Australia et al.; this would provide a means of resolving serious problems at least until verification measures have been drawn up and adopted—a process that is likely to take many years.

If these interpretations can be established at the Third Review Conference they will bear on any verification regime that may be drawn up; they could be restated in the legal document on verification. But even without a legal document they would carry weight as a part of "subsequent practice" as defined by the Vienna Convention on The Law of Treaties.

4 Verification Measures Concerning Permitted Activities

The measures assembled here will be further evaluated in the subsequent section.

Schedules of Agents to be Controlled

In a schedule of pathogens to be controlled (Schedule 1), it would be appropriate to include all human and animal pathogens of World Health Organization (WHO) risk groups II, III and IV,[29] given the breadth of possible military interest (ranging from temporary incapacitants to highly lethal agents, with or without a high probability of transmission); all classical toxins (except those used for pest control, provided that they are not toxic to vertebrates) with an LD_{50} below some maximum value (say, 10 mg/kg in the most sensitive species known); all serious pathogens and certain pests of major crops; and all agents of any kind that are quarantined or limited in any way, anywhere, for environmental or health reason. Most important, the schedule should include any and all plant, animal, and human pathogens that have not yet been fully described in standard texts; and all recombinants involving a pathogen (or any genetic material orginally derived therefrom) as donor or recipient, with the exception of established in recombinants that have been fully characterized and described in the literature and found to pose no risk.

In order for the measures that follow to work, all agents that are handled similarly to the types mentioned above have to be included in Schedule 1, not just those of particular military interest.

A second schedule (Schedule 2), listing biochemicals with weapons potential, would be desirable. Provisions for revising the schedules would be needed.

Restrictions

In addition to the prohibitions clearly embodied in the BWC, the following restrictions would enhance confidence and/or facilitate verification:

a. *A maximum limit on the total amount of each agent in Schedule 1* possessed by each State Party, beyond which there could be no justification in terms of prophylactic, protective or other peaceful purposes. The vagueness of the Convention on this point contributes to lack of confidence, as noted by Sweden at the Second Review Conference. Transfer of Schedule 1 agents to non-States-Parties should be prohibited, as in the draft CWC.[30]

b. *A maximum number of facilities (per State Party) handling Schedule 1 agents.* This would include government, private, commercial, medical, or any other type of facility carrying out research, development, production, testing, treatment, or any other activity. Limits are necessary in order to avoid overloading the verification capacity. Sublimits might also be set, e.g., on the number of BL4 facilities or toxin facilities. The relevant facilities would have to be licensed by domestic authorities. Since the permitted number would have to be fairly large, consideration could be given to a sliding scale based on population. It would undoubtedly be necessary for some States Parties to centralize certain activities, much as, under financial constraints, research in some areas of physics is conducted at centers such as the Brookhaven National Laboratory or CERN, the European organization for nuclear research.

c. *A requirement for appropriate containment for Schedule 1 agents* based on the WHO criteria and other appropriate international criteria. Standards also need to be set for new, unknown, recombinant, and other novel agents. Since pathogens do not respect national boundaries, global security requires international standards. Open-air release of any Schedule 1 agent should be prohibited. This would mean that field testing and training with defensive matériel would be limited to the use of simulants.

d. *A prohibition on BL3 and BL4 aerosol generation and containment facilities beyond a small, specified size* minimally adequate for medical testing (e.g., as required for nose cones for small animals). The offensive potential of aerosol facilities requires limitation, even if it should be at the expense of defensive needs, in order to fulfill the goal of the BWC, as expressed in the preamble: "to exclude completely the possibility of bacteriological (biological) agents and toxins being used as weapons . . . no effort should be spared to minimize this risk." Aerosols of simulants would still be available for larger scale use in lower containment, for defensive purposes; therefore, the restriction would not actually limit the development of defenses (although it might require changes in methodology). The U.S. Army currently conducts its laboratory development and testing of detection and decontamination systems, personal protective matériel, detector methodologies, and rapid identification and diagnosis methodologies using low hazard organisms or non-infectious materials such as purified protein antigens, receptors or toxoids in BL1 or BL2 facilities.[31]

Some restrictions at the BL1 and BL2 level may also be necessary in order to prevent the use of toxins and other lower-risk agents or plant pathogens as aerosols on a large scale. Such use would have serious offensive potential.

Annual Declarations
Declarations play a role in verifying restrictions and building confidence in compliance. The information provided would deal with permitted activities, most of them carried out for peaceful purposes unrelated to the BWC but in facilities or with agents that might have military potential; therefore, if unreported, such activities could give rise to suspicions. Most of the activities referred to are at the research level; few, if any, involve production. Providing the specified information, which is similar to that required for grants and contracts, should cause no hardship, as long as confidentiality is maintained where necessary. A technical secretariat would be needed to compile and evaluate the declarations and request additional information when insufficient data were supplied. Current information should be reported, together with any expected changes in the coming year, as envisaged in the draft CWC. The procedures for carrying out the reportage (definitions, guidelines,

data checklists, time, limits, and so forth) could be similar to those that have been or will be developed for permitted activities in the draft CWC, Article VI and its Annex,[32] including measures for safeguarding proprietary information.

a. *All facilities containing Schedule 1 agents.* It would be appropriate to declare the name, location, size, auspices, sources of funding, types of equipment, scope, and general description of activities (including those not relevant to the Convention); number, level and size of any containment units (BL2,3,4); whether encapsulating protective clothing is used; which Schedule 1 agents are involved, their total amounts and sources, any transfers, and a description of any agents, including recombinants, that have not been fully described in the literature. The purpose, sources of funding, and general description of activities involving Schedule 1 agents should be specified.

With respect to personnel, the declarations should include any prophylactic measures, any restrictions imposed (e.g., on movement or on publication), and any requirements for secret clearance.[33]

b. *All facilities for work with aerosols.* Information as above would be appropriate, including number, size, containment level, and technical description of the aerosol chambers, whether Schedule 1 or 2 agents are handled as aerosols, and if so which ones and for what purpose.

c. *All BL4 facilities* Report information as in (a) including the number and size of BL4 units, whether and which Schedule 1 or 2 agents are involved, and the purpose. This declaration has already been adopted as a confidence-building measure.[34] It may also be desirable to report all BL3 facilities (assuming that BL3 facilities are not widely used for purposes not involving Schedule 1 agents) as proposed by France at the Second Review Conference and several nations at the following Experts Meeting. Unreported high-containment facilities can be sources of insecurity and suspicion, especially if under military or government jurisdiction.

d. *All facilities engaged in research, development, or production of large-scale bioprocessing equipment or methodology* appropriate for WHO risk group III or IV agents. A similar proposal was made at the 1987 Experts Meeting.[35]

e. *All facilities conducting research related to BW delivery systems or activities relating to disease vectors.* Report information as in (a), including type of system or vector. Note that research related to delivery systems is not explicitly excluded by the BWC, although the actual development and construction of a delivery system is prohibited.

f. *All facilities concerned with the toxic properties of Schedule 2 agents*, such as the effects of nonphysiological doses or protection from or treatment for overdose. Report information as in (a), including the agents studied and the purpose.

g. *All former sites for open-air field testing or training involving BW agents or simulants; all present sites for field testing or training using simulants; and all sites for any type of training in BW defense.* A similar proposal was made by Sweden at the Second Review Conference, and the exchange of information on facilities engaged in field aerosol experiments was considered at the Experts Meeting. Some of these activities would be amenable to monitoring by national technical means.

h. *The time and site of any open-air dissemination of a permitted agent (simulant) for military purposes (testing equipment or training), and of any open-air military training operations* using matériel for defense against BW. This information should be provided in advance in order to permit monitoring by national technical means and on-site inspection. The significance of such declarations would be greatly enhanced if CW and smoke-screen operations were also included; [36] perhaps that will ultimately be possible. The advance reportage and monitoring of maneuvers has a precedent in the CSCE process, which evolved from the Final Act of the Conference on Security and Cooperation in Europe, 1975.[37]

i. *Evidence that BW techniques are not included in military training and tactical theory.* This could be provided by submission of military field manuals, for example.[38]

j. *All human and animal vaccines and toxoids possessed, beyond a defined experimental quantity, and their locations; and all vaccination programs*, beyond a defined size for experimental purposes. This would include vaccination of the general public and livestock as well as components of the armed forces. The latter was proposed by Finland at the Second Review Conference and also (specifically in the context of an investigation) by France. Others have proposed similar measures.[39]

k. *All outbreaks of infectious diseases and similar occurrences caused by toxins that seem to deviate from the normal pattern.* This declaration is already part of the present information exchange.[40] To this could be added all unusual occurrences involving the nature or distribution of vectors.[41] Disease outbreaks among animals and plants as well as humans should be included. This information should be provided soon after the outbreak is recognized (within 5 days, for example), and should include the location, type of disease, and suspected agent(s). More complete information should be provided as it becomes available.

Inspection and Monitoring

On-site inspection, especially if routine, can reduce operational confidence in deriving military gains from clandestine activities, and can also increase their economic and political costs.[42]

a. *Routine on-site inspection* of declared facilities and stocks as established in the draft CWC. In order to verify declarations inspection could be carried out at random, without prior notification, by an inspectorate established for the purpose. Facilities and sites reported in Declarations (a)–(g) would be included (there will undoubtedly be considerable overlap in the categories). Stocks and records of the quantities and disposition of Schedule 1 agents would be examined. Inspection of vaccine stocks and records, Declaration (j), would also be carried out wherever they might be located.

Inspection protocols would be needed; it would be desirable to begin drafting proposals and carrying out intramural trial inspections now. SIPRI has published a model protocol that includes access to records on the health, training, and experience of personnel and consultants, and inspection of security measures.[43]

Many procedural specifications for inspection and for the inspectorate could be taken from the draft CWC and its future elaboration. This would include provisions for maintaining the confidentiality of information. A precedent is provided by the International Atomic Energy Agency (IAEA), which carries out inspections and administers "safeguards" for materials accounting. Other models are provided by the inspection of industry by national agencies such as the U.S. Environmental Protection Agency (EPA).

Remote monitoring using surveillance devices (e.g., the RECOVER concept) is a possibility that should be considered. Research is needed on its applicability for BWC verification. The IAEA uses closed circuit television for surveillance.[44]

b. *Routine monitoring of announced open-air dissemination of BW simulants, BW defense training operations, and unusual outbreaks of disease* as covered in declarations (h) and (k). This would be done by on-site inspection. Research is needed on the possible use of satellites to monitor some of these activities. Satellite photographs can now be commissioned commercially; perhaps they could be solicited as contributions from States Parties.

c. *On-site inspection on challenge.* Inspection cannot be limited to declared sites if the verification regime is to inspire confidence. Challenge inspection may be of limited value in resolving disputes[45] but it is at least symbolic of the mutual desire of the parties for stringent verification. In the provisions under consideration for the CWC each State Party has the right, upon presentation of evidence suggesting noncompliance, to request that the inspectorate undertake a fact-finding mission at any site on short notice, without right of refusal by the party to be inspected and without any screening of requests.[46] This CWC provision could probably be taken over without change for biological verification.

To help limit abuse of the right of challenge, a maximum frequency of challenge could be considered, a restraint used in the INF Treaty. The Treaty of Tlatelolco (1967), which prohibits nuclear weapons in Latin America, requires that the costs of special inspection be borne by the requesting state; this is, however, unfair to the poorer states.

A possible way of limiting the political costs of challenge inspections would be to require that the inspectorate carry out at least one challenge per year; if no challenge is mounted by a State Party, the inspectorate would choose a site (based, perhaps, on its assessment of international suspicions).

d. *Ad hoc inspection.* The CWC negotiators are considering *ad hoc* inspections "to resolve indicated irregularities."[47] These are presumably questions raised in the course of routine inspection and reportage or by information that reaches the secretariat through informal means. The proposal comes from the chemical industry, which looks upon it favorably.[48] The inspection would only have to be thorough enough to determine whether any illicit activity were occurring; systematic invasion of trade secrets might be avoidable. The concept could be elaborated into a means of inspecting undeclared sites with a minimum of political difficulty. The inspectorate could be given the power to inspect any site anywhere at its own discretion, on the basis of information available to it but held confidentially. The purpose could be to demonstrate compliance as well as to investigate non-compliance; in this way no stigma need be attached to the inspected party. The inspectorate would of course have to be rigorously nonpolitical and governed by a director commanding universal respect.

Provisions could be made for the inspectorate to receive confidential communications from States Parties, nongovernmental organizations (NGOs), and private citizens in a way that would protect the identity of the informer and thus avoid political repercussions. The inspectorate would thereby be provided with a global network of intelligence in which any person could participate. This intelligence, together with the information gathered from declarations and inspections and the inspectorate's own evaluation of the political climate, would enable the inspectorate to act as it saw fit to increase confidence in the BWC. States Parties would thus have the possibility of clarifying questions raised by national intelligence without compromising sources or precipitating political problems. These provisions would provide a critical element of reassurance.

Internship Program

The technical secretariat/inspectorate could run a program for "BWC Fellows" for which researchers and biological defense specialists from all States Parties would b eligible. Such a program would have a quadruple purpose: it would provide training and experience, which would of particular interest to less-developed countries and would therefore serve as an incentive for participating in a verification protocol; it would serve as a confidence-building measure; it could be used to extend and deepen the information available to the inspectorate; and the Fellows, or interns, would constitute a future recruitment pool for inspectorate and technical secretariat personnel and consultants.

The Fellows could be assigned, according to their expertise, to declared facilities; with the approval of the relevant State Party they could also be assigned to undeclared ones. Facilities of all types, including government, university, and industry, in all relevant fields including microbiology, biochemistry, medical research and treatment, biotechnology, and biological defense technologies would be involved.

Fellows could be trained by the inspectorate. It would be understood that they would serve as international rather than national representatives. Each assignment would run long enough for the Fellow to become trained and fully integrated into the work of the host facility (perhaps one year); it would be agreed that no special restrictions would be placed on Fellows by their hosts. To permit comparison, it might be advantageous for each Fellow to experience two different assignments. Fellows might serve in teams of two, with members drawn from different countries appropriately selected with respect to the location of the assignment.

In the course of their work it is likely that Fellows would become cognizant of the various activities in progress at their assigned facilities. During and at the completion of their assignment, Fellows could report any relevant observations and impressions to the inspectorate. All scientists and citizens ought to consider it a duty in the interest of the common good to report any evidence for violation of an international treaty that may come to their attention. This information would form part of the intelligence on which decisions regarding ad hoc inspections would be based.

While working at their assigned facilities, the Fellows could be supported by the host countries in compensation for their work. Other expenses could be covered by the inspectorate. The cost per Fellow to the inspectorate would probably be much less than the cost of a regular full-time employee.

Complete confidentiality of all proprietary or other sensitive information obtained under the internship program would be essential; guarantee of financial compensation, funded by requiring that the Fellow's nation of origin put up a bond in advance, might be useful. In certain instances, Fellows might be barred from taking a competitive position for a certain period after service; serious lapses by Fellows or members of the inspectorate might be made subject to criminal prosecution. (Personnel of the U.S. Environmental Protection Agency are subject to this stricture for wrongful disclosure of officially obtained information.)[49] The program would be largely equivalent to the post-doctoral fellowship system, in which research fellows routinely move freely into positions at other institutions around the world without incident.

The complete openness that such a program would entail would obviate any problems that might otherwise arise from the spread of expertise relevant to BW and BW defense. Most importantly, it would provide a high degree of assurance regarding compliance with the BWC.

Dr. Robert Mikulak, senior scientist at the U.S. Arms Control and Disarmament Agency (Bureau of Multilateral Affairs), has said, "There can be no justification for secret military biological research laboratories or classified biological defense research programs."[50] At the same time he proposed voluntary programs of reciprocal, balanced, and mutually beneficial visits to facilities reported under the present information exchange, in order to promote transparency. Similarly, Yuriy Antipov, counselor at the Permanent Mission of the USSR to the United Nations, has reported that the USSR favors openness in research relevant to the BWC; he expects that the USSR will invite and exchange experts.[51]

Visiting scientists from a number of countries already participate in parts of the U.S. biological defense program. The Federation of American Scientists under Dr. Matthew Meselson, an expert on CBW control, has urged the United States and the Soviet Union to open all their recently-declared defense facilities to reciprocal scientific exchange.[52] SIPRI suggested such an exchange long ago.[53] Dr. Erhard Geissler, of the GDR Academy of Sciences and SIPRI, has pointed out that such an exchange would also help to fulfill Article X of the BWC by enhancing international peaceful cooperation.[54] The plan proposed here would enable specialists from *all* States Parties to participate in an *internationally*-administered program, with commitment primarily to global rather than national interests.

5 Evaluation of Measures

In order to set concrete standards for a verification regime, explicit interpretation of the BWC and specific restrictions or prohibitions on relevant activities are needed. Detailed annual declarations concerning the restricted activities will be necessary as evidence of openness and of resolve to comply with the treaty. Beyond that the national intelligence of other States Parties and any international inspection regime that may be adopted will provide pressure to keep the declarations honest and complete.

Inspection of preannounced open-air testing or training for defensive purposes and surveillance for unannounced activities of this sort are particularly important; these events could provide information relevant to later stages in weapons development, which are difficult to carry out clandestinely. These inspections, which would probably not be very frequent, could probably be carried out by a roster of experts who would be called upon as needed, without requiring a standing inspectorate. At present, surveillance for unannounced activities would have to be left to the States Parties that now possess (and are often reluctant to share) the capacity for surveillance.

Experience has shown that a mechanism for resolving serious allegations is essential. Two possible mechanisms present themselves: challenge inspection by an established inspectorate, and investigation on request by the U.N. Secretary-General. The latter procedure would be simpler; to put it into practice would require only some additions to the list of qualified experts and laboratories available to the Secretary-General to undertake investigations of possible violations of the Geneva Protocol or of the relevant rules of customary international law (as established by U.N. General Assembly Resolution 37/98D in 1982). On the other hand, acceptance of challenge inspection has become symbolic of full commitment to a treaty. The availability of both procedures would provide flexibility for adaptation in differing circumstances.

Routine inspection to verify declarations would require a rather large, established inspectorate. If this is judged to be too costly, a combination of ad hoc inspection and an internship program might be considered adequate. They could be carried out by a relatively small permanent staff and would be considerably cheaper than routine inspection. The internship program might be welcomed as an opportunity to "inspect" as well as to be inspected. The interns would develop greater familiarity with facilities and programs than an inspector would, but they would not have the same access to comprehensive and detailed information.

Ad hoc inspection would provide the possibility for investigating problems at undeclared sites without the political price demanded by other methods. It would require a small permanent inspectorate, preferably one with ongoing inspection experience. If routine inspection is not feasible, the ad hoc inspectorate could be charged with carrying out continuous random inspection of declared sites as well as occasional inspection of undeclared sites; comprehensiveness would not be possible, but the ability to act on confidential information would help in focusing on potential sources of conflict.

6 The Verification Organization

The similarity and overlap of the BWC and its proposed verification protocol with the draft CWC would make it reasonable to adopt an organizational structure similar to that outlined in Article VIII of the CWC rolling text.[55] The Consultative Committee (General Conference), composed of all States Parties, elects a Chairperson, an Executive Council, and a Director of a Technical Secretariat. The Executive Council oversees the Technical Secretariat in implementing the verification provisions. For reasons of economy and efficiency it would make sense for both the BW and CW conventions to utilize the same technical secretariat (note that verification of four different treaties is assigned to the IAEA).[56] This would mean that the Director of the Secretariat would have to be approved by the parties to both treaties. Ideally, they would also share the Executive Council. A way of doing that would be to merge the two Executive Councils into one when overseeing the Technical Secretariat, or to conduct joint elections. The Executive Council might be composed of the Chairpersons of the two Consultative Committees, plus one or several individuals who are universally trusted as being above national interests. The Chair of the Scientific Advisory Council considered in the draft CWC would be a possible candidate. We suggest that a Scientific Council, either joint or one for each Convention, be appointed from nominees proposed by international scientific societies (such as the International Council of Scientific Unions and its member unions) and U.N. scientific organizations (such as WHO and FAO).

A Technical Secretariat would be needed to receive and evaluate annual declarations, to run an internship program and accept reports from the interns, to manage open-air inspections, and to maintain an inspectorate. The Secretariat would compile and provide factual information to the other bodies but, in order to safeguard its objectivity, would make no judgments regarding violations. Nor should the question of violation be politicized by submitting it to the States Parties for a vote. If such decisions are to be made, they would best be delegated to a body considered impartial, possibly the World Court. Other decisions, such as where to conduct ad hoc inspections, would be made by the Director of the Technical Secretariat.

In many situations, confidentiality will be an important consideration. For the CWC it will be even more important because of the necessary intrusion on the gigantic chemical industry. Fortunately, world industry is contributing to and is supportive of the CWC arrangements now under negotiation, and it can be anticipated that the arrangements will be more than adequate for biological verification.[58] This and many other painstaking details will not have to be renegotiated for biological purposes.

An important function of the Technical Secretariat and the Executive Council that would provide an additional incentive to sign a BW verification protocol would be assistance to States Parties threatened or endangered by BW or by any violation of the treaty.

The Technical Secretariat could conclude agreements with appropriate States Parties to maintain standing contributions of specified matériel and services to be supplied immediately upon request. It could routinely solicit, collect, and supply all available information on BW defenses, write reports on the state of the art, hold symposia, conduct training programs, and promote international cooperation on the development of defenses, including vaccines. Proposals along these lines were made by SIPRI in 1971[59] and are now under consideration for the CWC.[60]

The Technical Secretariat could be given the authority to establish an international research center on BW and CW defense at some time in the future. This center could perhaps be organized along the lines of CERN, the European organization for nuclear research, with financial support primarily from nations already engaged in CBW defense research (the extent of their engagement will be obvious from the annual declarations) but with facilities open to all States Parties (another incentive). Research on vaccines, drugs, and medical treatments subject to the "orphan drug problem" could be conducted at such centers and thereby removed from military control without sacrificing defensive needs. Detectors could be developed and tested. The ultimate goal would be to transfer all defensive research and development to international auspices, with results available to all parties.

The question of punitive action in case of violation has to be addressed. For the CWC, imposition of a collective trade embargo has been proposed by Pakistan.[61] Universal agreement on sanctions would be highly desirable, but experience shows that this is difficult to achieve. Revoking privileges under the Convention (voting rights, appointment of interns, right to challenge or call upon the Secretary-General, or use of the services of the Technical Secretariat) for a period of time might be more easily agreed upon and carried out. The mere exposure of incontrovertible evidence of violation would undoubtedly provoke considerable political pressure.

7 Cost

The cost of maintaining a verification organization and carrying out its functions would not be negligible. In the context of the CWC, Venezuela has warned that if the cost is too high, many states would be unwilling to become parties and the effectiveness of the convention would be correspondingly limited; it suggested that the developing countries, especially those not possessing CW, should bear a lesser burden than the developed ones, as is the case in financing the IAEA safeguards.[62]

The cost of verification, however high, must be balanced against the advantages gained and the savings realized—for example, in reliable CBW intelligence (which is particularly hard to obtain) and in BW defense expenditures; the gain in security and warning time, should there be a breakout, would be substantial. The trade-offs have recently been discussed by Herbert Beck.[63]

The IAEA Safeguards Division routinely inspects 400 facilities a year and sporadically inspects many more, with a staff of 200–300 and a budget of $30–40 million per year; an inspectorate of this size is thought to be the maximum that would be politically acceptable for the CWC.[64]

Some experts estimate the total budget for CWC verification at more than $100 million per year (after all CW stocks have been destroyed). Beck has done a careful study of costs for the CWC and estimates the annual budget (after destruction) at $40 to 140 million, depending on the strictness of the regime, with a probable value of about $50 million, covering 136 inspectors and 650 inspections per year.[65] The additional cost for a BW verification regime could probably be kept well below these figures, perhaps in the $15 to 25 million range.

8 Preliminary and Interim Actions

Aside from starting the procedure to draw up a verification regime, the way is open for the Third Review Conference to agree on an interpretation of the BWC that would permit some important measures to take effect immediately. Prohibition of the creation of novel agents of potential BW use could be made clear, and every State Party could be given the right to call upon the Secretary-General to investigate any suspected violation of the BWC. In addition, the Conference could adopt further cooperative measures beyond those already agreed upon. These actions would provide an interim regime until a legal verification protocol is adopted. New cooperative measures could be chosen as trials for future annual declaration requirements. In addition to declarations, steps such as opening declared facilities to reciprocal visits would be useful both for increasing confidence and for identifying issues that should be addressed when setting up inspection procedures. Nikita Smidovich of the USSR Ministry of Foreign Affairs has suggested that instituting visits to declared sites would help smooth the way toward a verification agreement.[66]

The time is now ripe to exchange bilateral invitations. Several members of Congress are interested in forming a delegation to visit the Soviet Union to discuss BW issues; they could issue an invitation to their Soviet counterparts to visit the United States. Further, an exchange of expert personnel to work in biological defense facilities could be arranged now, without waiting for the Review Conference.

In preparation for the Third Review Conference in 1991 the BWC depositary nations, the United States, the United Kingdom, and the Soviet Union, should now begin to hold preliminary discussions on questions relevant to BWC verification—how best to reassure one another of compliance. Matthew Meselson suggests that States Parties could unilaterally decide what information they would want a verification regime to provide about other nations via declarations and inspections, and then begin to carry out internal trial inspections to determine how such information can be obtained with minimal intrusion and disruption. British trials of this sort for the CWC have shown that inspection can be considerably less painful than anticipated.[67]

Nongovernmental experts from various backgrounds should begin drawing up proposals for biological verification measures and inspection protocols. The important role being played by the consortium of North American, western European, and Japanese chemical industry representatives in the CWC negotiations shows that a similar group will be needed when biological verification is negotiated, and in fact is needed now to help address the issue of toxin control in the CWC.

Research on possible remote detection, surveillance, and monitoring devices for national intelligence and international verification relevant to BW has, at least in the United States, been neglected and should be pursued. Both governmental and nongovernmental experts need to look into the possible use of satellite reconnaissance to identify high-containment and aerosol facilities, open-air testing with aerosols, testing of delivery systems and training that involves BW defenses. Radar imaging as well as visible light, UV, and infrared photography and LIDAR (laser) technology are now available. Radar can pierce cloud cover and camouflage. LIDAR detects aerosols (but clouds interfere). Military satellites now have a resolution of about 10 cm, adequate to identify bulky protective clothing.[68] A resolution of 10 m would suffice for viewing roads and ground facilities and determining the operational state of a plant.[69] Eventually it will be feasible for a multilateral treaty organization to make use of satellite reconnaissance for verification purposes, as shown by Canadian research on the PAXSAT Concept. Development of the necessary resolution and coverage is expected to take place during the next decade.[70]

9 Conclusions

President Ronald Reagan was fond of quoting an "old Russian proverb": "Trust, but verify." The present ban on biological weapons rests only on trust. In a report to Congress on December 1, 1988, Reagan noted with respect to biological weapons that "the United States believes that verification provisions are of unprecedented importance in U.S. efforts to rid the world of these weapons of mass destruction."[71] The commitment of President George Bush to "ban chemical and biological weapons from the face of the earth" is well known. He has pledged to make that a priority, and he has emphasized the need for intrusive verification.[72] President Bush is in a position to provide timely leadership on this urgent issue.

Despite essentially universal concern and recognition of the need for BWC verification, there has been little consideration of specific measures beyond those proposed or undertaken for confidence-building purposes. We hope this chapter will help catalyze the debate and discussion necessary for legal action on verification.

Notes

1. For a discussion of the BW potential of biotechnology, see also *Biological and Toxin Weapons Today*, Erhard Geissler, ed. (New York: Oxford University Press, 1986).
2. Winfried Lang, "Taking The Pulse of the Biological Weapons Regime," *Disarmament X* (Winter 1986–7) No. 1, 44–51.
3. Final Document, Second Review Conference of the Parties to the Convention on the Prohibition of the Development, Production and Stockpiling of Bacteriological (Biological) and Toxin Weapons and on their Destruction, Geneva, 30 September, 1986 (BWC/Conf. II/13).
4. Lang, "Taking the Pulse of the Biological Weapons Regime."

5. Report of the Ad Hoc Meeting of Scientific and Technical Experts from States Parties to the BWC, April, 21, 1987 (BWC/Conf. II/EX/2). For an evaluation of the initial information exchanges and suggestions for additional measures, see E. Geissler, ed., *Strengthening the Biological Weapons Convention by Confidence-Building Measures*, SIPRI Chemical and Biological Warfare Studies, no. 10 (London: Oxford University Press, 1990).

6. Final Document, Second Review Conference.

7. Nicholas A. Sims, "Diplomatic Responses to Changing Assessments of Scientific and Technological Developments Relevant to a Disarmament Regime: The Second Review Conference of the 1972 Convention on Biological and Toxin Weapons, Geneva 1986," in *Military Technology, Armaments Dynamics and Disarmament*, H.G. Brauch, ed. (New York: St. Martin's Press, 1988), and B.H. Rosenberg, "Updating the Biological Weapons Ban," *Bulletin of the Atomic Scientists* 43 (Jan./Feb. 1987), 40–43.

8. Sims, "Diplomatic Responses to Changing Assessments."

9. Pablo Macedo, a Mexican delegate to the Conference on Disarmament, has pointed out that for countries like his which do not feel threatened, a commercial carrot is necessary to justify the expenses of verification (U.N. NGO Forum on Chemical Weapons, 27 October, 1988).

10. U.S. Department of Defense, *Biological Defense Program: Report to the Committee on Appropriations, House of Representatives*, May 1986, chapter 1, page 9: "Impacts [of Biotechnology] on BW Agent Production Requirements."

11. A report to the U.S. Biological Warfare Commission on purportedly defensive German BW research states, "development of defensive measures against BW necessitates thorough knowledge and investigation of offensive possibilities" (G.W. Merck, W.M. Adams, G.W. Anderson, H.I. Cole, W.B. Sarles and L.A. Baker, *Summary and Estimate of Enemy Intentions and Capabilities in Biological Warfare*, 16 May 1945, quoted by E. Geissler in a paper delivered to the American Society of Biochemistry and Molecular Biology, 31 January, 1989). More recently, Lt. Col. Wyatt Colclasure, a staff officer in the U.S. Army's chemical and biological defense division, replied to a question about the offensive potential of defensive research: "You do get information, and like a lot of information, you can put it to different uses" (*Science* 226 [1984], 1178). Many authors have described the defense/offense overlap and the fact that an adequate defense is a prerequisite for offensive use of BW. See chapter 6 and E.J. McFadden, "The Second Review Conference of the Biological Weapons Convention: One Step Forward, Many More to Go," *Stanford Journal of International Law* 24 (1987), 85–109.

12. U.S. Department of Defense, Final Programmatic Environmental Impact Statement, Biological Defense Research Program, April 1989, pp. A15–137.

13. Hearing before the Senate Governmental Affairs Committee and its Permanent Subcommittee on Investigations on "Germ Wars": Biological Weapons Proliferation and the New Genetics, May 17, 1989.

14. Final Document, Second Review Conference.

15. E. Geissler, ed., *Confidence-Building Measures*.

16. From "Statement on Chemical and Biological Defense Policies and Programs. November 25, 1969", *Public Papers of the Presidents: Richard Nixon, 1969* (Washington, DC: GPO, 1971), 968–969.

17. D. Hafenmeister, J.J. Romm and K. Tsipis, "The Verification of Compliance with Arms-Control Agreements," *Scientific American* 252 (1985), 39.

18. A.S. Krass, *Verification: How Much is Enough?* (Lexington, MA: Lexington Books, 1985), 79 82.

19. Report of the Chemical Warfare Review Commission, Walter J. Stoessel, Jr., Chairman, June 1985 (Washington, DC: GPO), 67–71.

20. Lang, "Taking the Pulse of the Biological Weapons Regime."

21. See also Marie I. Chevrier, "Verification and the Biological Weapons Convention," unpublished paper, 1988.

22. See chapter 6 of this volume; E. Geissler, ed., *Confidence-Building Measures*; and McFadden, "The Second Review Conference."

23. Standard cloning vehicles could be specifically exempted, and possibly certain medically important procedures as well (for example, the conjugation of toxins with tisue-specific factors as anticancer agents). A verification regime would have to impose requirements of reportage and containment on these and also on the manipulation of plant, insect and other pathogens.

24. Department of Defense, Final Programmatic Environmental Impact Statement, Biological Defense Research Program, April, 1989, pp. A4–9.

25. Robert Mikulak, Ph. D. (Senior Scientist, Bureau of Multilateral Affairs, U.S. Arms Control and Disarmament Agency), personal communication.

26. Ambassador Max Friedersdorf, U.S. negotiator at the Geneva CWC negotiations, comments delivered at the U.N. NGO Forum on Chemical Weapons, 27 October, 1988.

27. Final Document, Second Review Conference.

28. Report of the Ad Hoc Meeting of Scientific and Technical Experts from States Parties to the BWC, Section II, E3.

29. World Health Organization, *Laboratory Biosafety Manual*, (Geneva, 1983).

30. Report of the Ad Hoc Committee on Chemical Weapons to the Conference on Disarmament, 2 February 1988 (CD/795), Appendix I, Preliminary Structure of a Convention on Chemical Weapons. The text is revised several times a year.

31. Department of Defense, Final Programmatic Environmental Impact Statement, Biological Defense Research Program, April, 1989, pp. 2–6; pp. A4–11; pp. A4–14.

32. Report of Ad Hoc Committee on Chemical Weapons to the Conference on Disarmament, 2 February 1988 (CD/795), Appendix I.

33. Proposed in SIPRI, *The Problem of Chemical and Biological Warfare*, Vol. VI: *Technical Aspects of Early Warning and Verification* (Stockholm: Almqvist and Wiksell, 1975).

34. Report of the Ad Hoc Meeting of Scientific and Technical Experts from States Parties to the BWC.

35. Report of the Ad Hoc Meeting of Scientific and Technical Experts from States Parties to the BWC.

36. SIPRI, *The Problem of Chemical and Biological Warfare*, Vol. V: *The Prevention of CBW* (Stockholm: Almqvist and Wiksell, 1971).

37. See Krass, *Verification: How Much is Enough*, 239–240.

38. Proposed by Gordon Burck in "Confidence Building for the BWC," Federation of American Scientists CBW Paper No. I, 1988.

39. See E. Geissler, ed., *Confidence-Building Measures*.

40. Report of the Ad Hoc Meeting of Scientific and Technical Experts from States Parties to the BWC.

41. See E. Geissler, ed., *Confidence-Building Measures.*

42. S.N. Graybeal and M. Krepon, "The Limitations of On-Site Inspection," *Bulletin of the Atomic Scientists* 43 (Dec. 1987), 22–26.

43. SIPRI, *The Problem of Chemical and Biological Warfare*, Vol. VI: *Technical Aspects of Early Warning and Verification* (Stockholm: Almqvist and Wiksell, 1975).

44. Krass, *Verification: How Much is Enough*, 96–97.

45. S.N. Graybeal and M. Krepon, "The Limitations of On-Site Inspection." *Bulletin of the Atomic Scientists*, December 1987, 22–26.

46. Report of the Ad Hoc Committee on Chemical Weapons to the Conference on Disarmament, 12 September 1988 (CD/874), Appendix II, documents presenting work in progress on the draft CWC: On-Site Inspection on Challenge.

47. Report of the Ad Hoc Committee on Chemical Weapons to the Conference on Disarmament, 2 February 1988 (CD/795), Appendix I, p. 109.

48. Kyle B. Olson, "The Proposed Chemical Weapons Convention: An Industry Perspective," *CWC Bulletin* no. 2 (Autumn 1988), 1–3.

49. Environmental Protection Agency, 40 CFR, Chapter 1 (7-1-86 edition), p. 46, Part 2, Subpart B, Section 2.211.

50. R. Mikulak, statement to the American Society for Microbiology Round Table on Defense-Related Biological Research, Miami, FL, on May 11, 1988.

51. Y. Antipov, Commentary on Verifying International Agreements, at the Friedrich Ebert Foundation Roundtable Discussion on The International Control of Chemical and Biological Weapons, New York, on February 10, 1989.

52. Federation of American Scientists, "A New Approach to Compliance with the CBW Treaties," *F.A.S. Public Interest Report* 41, no. 7 (September, 1988).

53. SIPRI, *The Problem of Chemical and Biological Warfare*, Vol. V: *The Prevention of CBW.*

54. E. Geissler, Address to meeting of the U.N. NGO Committee on Disarmament, New York, on February 2, 1989.

55. Report of the Ad Hoc Committee on Chemical Weapons to the Conference on Disarmament, 2 February 1988 (CD/795), Appendix I.

56. Krass, *Verification: How Much is Enough*, 230.

57. Proposed by France, March 1987 (CD/747) and April 1989 (CD/916).

58. Kyle B. Olson, "The Proposed Chemical Weapons Convention: An Industry Perspective," *CWC Bulletin* No. 2 (Autumn 1988), 1–3.

59. SIPRI, *The Problem of Chemical and Biological Warfare*, Vol. V: *The Prevention of CBW.*

60. Report of the Ad Hoc Committee on Chemical Weapons to the Conference on Disarmament, 12 September 1988 (CD/874), Appendix II, Article X.

61. J. Goldblat, "Chemical Disarmament: From the Ban on Use to a Ban on Possession," Canadian Institute for International Peace and Security, Background Paper no. 17, February 1988.

62. J. Goldblat, "Chemical Disarmament: From the Ban on Use to a Ban on Possession."

63. Herbert Beck, *Verifying The Projected Chemical Weapons Convention: A Cost Analysis*, AFES-Press Report No. 13 (Mosbach, FRG: AFES-Press Verlag, 1989).

64. Lois R. Ember, "Fashioning a Global Chemical Weapons Treaty," *Chemical and Engineering News*, March 28, 1988, 7–17.

65. Herbert Beck, *Verifying The Projected Chemical Weapons Convention: A Cost Analysis*, AFES-Press Report No. 13 (Mosbach, FRG: AFES-Press Verlag, 1989).

66. N.P. Smidovich, talk on Soviet Policies and Initiatives, at Experts' Workshop on the Control of CBW: Strengthening International Verification and Compliance (sponsored by the Working Group on International Surveillance and Verification), Toronto, on April 5, 1989.

67. Conference on Disarmament Document 921 (CD/CW/WP. 245), June 14, 1989; and M. Meselson, personal communication.

68. Walter H. Dorn, "Peace-Keeping Satellites: The Case for International Surveillance and Verification," *Peace Research Review* X, nos. 5 & 6 (Dundas, Canada: Peace Research Institute—Dundas, 1987).

69. R. Trapp, "Verification of an International Agreement Banning Chemical Weapons—The Possible Role of Satellite Monitoring," in *Satellites for Arms Control and Crisis Monitoring*, B. Jasani, ed.) SIPRI (New York: Oxford University Press, 1987).

70. "PAXSAT Concept: The Application of Space-Based Remote Sensing for Arms Control Verification," Verification Brochure No. 2, Department of External Affairs, Canada (1987).

71. The President's Unclassified Report on Soviet Noncompliance with Arms Control Agreements, December 2, 1988.

72. George Bush, Republican Convention acceptance speech, August 18, 1988; speech at the University of Toledo, October 21, 1988; and other presidential campaign statements.

15

Preventing a Biological Arms Race: New Initiatives

Richard Falk and Susan Wright

The present situation with respect to the future military use of biological warfare is precarious. Assessments of the strength of the international regime banning biological and chemical weapons have fluctuated, depending on perceptions of the intentions of the two superpowers and more recently, of Third World nations. Greatly reduced confidence in the regime in the early 1980s that accompanied the intensification of the cold war was followed in the later 1980s by a renewal of confidence—a reflection of the thaw initiated by the November 1985 summit meeting between Ronald Reagan and Mikhail Gorbachev. However, as concerns about a Soviet biological and chemical warfare "threat" waned in the late 1980s confidence in the CBW regime again began to erode, this time a result of fears of the spread of chemical and biological weapons to other nations, particularly in the Middle East. In part these concerns rested on solid evidence of Iraq's demonstrated possession and use of chemical weapons as well as of the availability of precursor chemicals for production of chemical agents from European and other countries and the interest of certain Middle Eastern nations in acquiring these substances. In part, however, fears were fanned by exaggerated and premature claims of advanced global proliferation of chemical and biological weapons, which escalated in the late 1980s.[1]

In the United States, each new round of charges was used to justify increasing support for the chemical warfare and biological defense programs.[2] Military support for the use of the biological sciences in these programs rose steeply in the 1980s. As earlier chapters have shown, the biological sciences, particularly the new biogenetic techniques, have been deployed in the development of new vaccines and toxoids, exploration of recently discovered bioregulators, development of rapid detection devices, the study of the action of pathogens, toxins and lethal chemicals, and other military uses. The ambiguity of these activities and uncertainty about their true character has in turn generated concern about U.S. intentions. Furthermore, they provide a model and stimulus for military development of biotechnology elsewhere.

The most general concern, raised repeatedly in this book, is that the synergistic interaction of accusations directed toward biological and chemical warfare activities in other countries, military development of the biological sciences (justified in terms of countering perceived "threats" elsewhere), and other nations' perceptions of those activities could lead to a dangerous and destabilizing arms race in which new advances in biotechnology would be directed toward exploration and development of new biological weapons. What the United States, the Soviet Union, and other nations do in the next few years is likely to determine whether the risks of biological warfare are dealt with destructively (by adding an ominous and unpredictable dimension to international rivalry) or constructively (through international law and diplomatic cooperation). In this final chapter, we analyze the dynamic of a potential arms race with respect to biological warfare and address the question of how this process can be contained and ultimately halted.

A fundamental element of any arms race is the ability of military establishments to assimilate and redirect new forms of science and technology into weapons applications. This process has both conceptual and institutional dimensions. That is, science and technology are absorbed by the military through the incorporation of knowledge and techniques into military frameworks as well as through their institutionalization as feeder technologies in military development programs. At the same time, assimilation also involves an ideological dimension; the process must be rationalized, particularly in the case of science or technology that originates in the civilian sector.

A variety of interests operate either to promote or restrain the present military assimilation of the biological sciences.[3] The military may exert a "pull" toward assimilation by pressing for expansion of research and development programs and justifying this expansion in terms of protecting national security, as discussed in earlier chapters of this book. In this connection, the level of government support critically shapes the response to military demand. In the case of the United States, as long as considerable funding for the Biological Defense and Chemical Warfare Programs is made available for research and development and in light of the Defense Department's justifications for expansion of these programs, it may be anticipated that these funds will be used to support exploratory activities that go beyond the requirements of a purely passive defense (protective clothing, detection devices and decontamination processes). As the Defense Department's plans for reactivating and expanding test facilities at Dugway Proving Ground suggest, exploration of the weapons potential of biogenetics can be justified in terms of anticipating and countering a perceived threat to national security. Quite beyond the public rationale one cannot entirely dismiss more sinister possibilities carried on beneath the cover of defensive research or conducted secretly, for that matter. It is not our intention to generate such suspicions, but merely to suggest that past patterns of governmental behavior do not reassure us that what is said openly tells the entire story about what is happening.

In addition to the "pull" exerted by the military itself, the scientific and corporate communities may also exert a "push" on the biological sciences toward militarization. As long as civilian support for the biological sciences remains uncertain, competition for support will be intense. This means that if moral barriers to the militarization of research are weak, then it is likely that military establishments will be actively encouraged to support research and development projects by some scientists and corporations who seek sponsorship for their work.

Fortunately, some social forces presently oppose the military assimilation of the biological sciences. In the first place, biological and chemical weaponry provokes a cultural aversion that goes beyond attitudes towards violence and warfare and is associated with a revulsion toward reliance on poison and disease as weapons of war. (This aversion is relative and varies from time to time, from place to place, and from individual to individual.) Although unstable and inconsistent, these attitudes indicate a strong societal and cultural capacity to repudiate warfare conducted with biological and chemical weapons. The international reaction against Iraq's reliance on chemical weaponry in the war against Iran is suggestive of a general consensus on these matters (as well as of the distinct limits of international willingness to develop effective sanctions for violations of the firm legal prohibition on the use of chemical weapons). Additionally, the societal support sanctioning the use of the biological sciences to *enhance* life seems to imply that inverting this goal is widely viewed with abhorrence (both inside and outside the scientific community). Even the military as a whole tends to manifest these normative attitudes regarding CW, and even more so BW, as beyond the pale of professionalism in war. Obviously, it becomes important to reinforce these attitudes by various educational undertakings. Such ethical perspectives may be influential if military justifications for development are themselves contested. Normative factors tend to be influential in official policy-forming circles when the proposed course of action is otherwise controversial.

A second barrier to the militarization of the biological sciences is provided by international law. The relative utility of international law is a variable product of all of the factors noted above, especially its perceived effectiveness, nations' images of what others are doing, public attitudes, and the vitality of cultural norms and professional constraints. In the BWC, as with most measures of arms control, there exists no sanctioning or enforcement process. In order for the treaty regime to work, it must be perceived by its actors to serve their continuing interests. This stress on perception is crucial and often overlooked. The actuality of Soviet (or United States) behavior may be less influential than what intelligence agencies, political analysts, and policy advisors on each side perceive the other side to be doing, and what this implies about capabilities and intentions. For this reason, reassurance is indispensable; the treaty regime must continue to be perceived by participants as a useful instrument of agreed controls if it is to achieve mutual restraint without possessing effective sanctions within its structure. It is thus important for diligent treaty partners to show that the treaty is being taken seriously in the internal political and economic life of their countries as well as in their external relations with other nations.

Finally, the military assimilation of the biological sciences may be checked by a variety of political forces. In its most limited form, often at a local level, societal resistance stems from a grass-roots fear of contamination from military facilities engaged in research relating to biological weaponry. This pressure, if limited to fear of immediate harm rather than moral abhorrence or respect for legal barriers, can sometimes be mollified by the production of a technical solution, by providing economic benefits to the immediate vicinity, or even through the relocation of the offending facility to some remote location. However, political resistance based on moral

revulsion or a commitment to the maintenance of high legal barriers is likely to endure even if military establishments argue persuasively on behalf of the safety or propriety of their activities.
Moreover, these public attitudes and related activities might well
produce pressures for major reductions in military spending on the
biological sciences.

The danger posed by military assimilation of the biological sciences is more a long-term threat to international security than a
matter of immediate concern. While some Pentagon officials have
claimed that exotic bioweaponry is potentially within reach of even
the world's technologically less advanced nations, that scary vision
is not borne out by most responsible evaluations of the present state
and prospects of the biological sciences (chapter 5). Developments
in biotechnology have been impressive since the emergence of genetic engineering techniques in the early 1970s; the rapid advance
into industrial production has strengthened the view that military
utility is within reach. Biogenetic techniques make it feasible to
change the characteristics of living things, produce novel toxins,
and greatly increase the efficiency of production of biological
agents. But none of these developments radically alter the characteristics of biological weapons that have made them unattractive to
military establishments in the past: their delayed action, uncertain
and indiscriminate impact, and potential to rebound on the user.
Regardless of the feasibility issue, however, the mere attention
being given to the possible military use of biotechnology is likely to
engender military interest in biological warfare.

What is of greatest concern is the *dynamic* of the present military
use of the biological sciences, with its potential for proliferation, escalation, and unanticipated breakthroughs. The United States, the
acknowledged world leader in biotechnology, is establishing a pattern of military-funded projects in biotechnology. Other Western
countries—notably the United Kingdom and West Germany—
are following the U.S. lead. And it must be assumed—although
little reliable evidence seems available—that the Soviet Union has
also initiated military programs in biotechnology. In addition, the
United States has begun to sponsor military research in the biological sciences in several other countries including Argentina, Brazil,
Britain, China, Israel, Liberia, South Korea, and West Germany.[4]
While professing concern about the potential proliferation of military applications of biotechnology, the Reagan administration fol-

lowed a course of action that actually promoted the spread of these applications to other governments.[5]

A further problem derives from the secrecy that usually envelops these biological research programs. For example, while the United States claims that its Biological Defense Research Program is entirely unclassified, the planning of this program, its rationale, and the results of some of its projects are secret. Other nations' defensive biological warfare programs appear to be enmeshed in a web of even greater secrecy. For example, the British Ministry of Defence acknowledged in 1987 that the Chemical Defence Establishment at Porton Down was sponsoring some sixty-five contracts for university research related to chemical and biological warfare, but refused to provide details about the contracts.[6] Little is known about the Soviet military sponsorship of research in the biological sciences beyond the names, addresses, and broad categories of research conducted in the Soviet Union's high- and moderate-containment facilities.[7] It needs to be stressed that what governments acknowledge in security-related activities is not necessarily what they actually do; full and honest disclosure is a rarity when it comes to weapons innovations, and the standard practice is to enshroud all activity pertaining to weapons innovation in as much secrecy as possible.

Particularly during periods of heightened geopolitical rivalry, the secrecy that characterizes much military research in the biological sciences makes it easy to accept worst-case analyses and to initiate projects that explore the weapons potential of new technologies on the grounds that hostile nations must be doing the same thing. The present U.S. guideline for biological defense research, approved by the National Security Council in 1969, accepts as permissible such forms of defensive exploration (appendix H).

As previous chapters have shown, biological defense programs in the 1980s in the United States and elsewhere have emphasized defenses against specific biological and toxin agents. Such "defensive" research is not merely ambiguous; paradoxically, it is also likely to produce results more useful for offensive applications than for defense (chapter 8). Furthermore, specific defenses of this type (as opposed to general defenses such as protective clothing) can only be perfected in tandem with certain components of an offensive capability. Not only does this tend to make a country into a latent BW country (analagous to one that has not exploded a nuclear device, yet possesses the presumed capabilities to produce nuclear weapons within a short time period), but by manifesting the existence of this "defensive" capability, a government inevitably communicates some degree of "offensive" threat. This ambiguity in "defensive" activities runs a high risk of generating suspicion and escalatory responses. And once inquiry is undertaken, it would seem naive to suppose that militarily enticing avenues of development will be entirely resisted through a discipline of self-restraint.

It must also be borne in mind that the coverage of the Biological Weapons Convention does not entirely foreclose application of the biological sciences for weapons purposes. The biological sciences play an essential collateral role in the development of chemical weapons, and the emergence of the new techniques of biotechnology is likely to enhance that role. (For example, genetic engineering and sequencing techniques make it possible to pinpoint the action of lethal chemicals far more easily than in the past—an essential step in the development of novel weapons.) Until a parallel and complementary chemical weapons convention has been successfully brought into force, this use of the biological sciences is unrestricted. It is also possible that, because of certain ambiguities in the Biological Weapons Convention, bioengineering might be used to produce artificial toxins or other biochemical substances not categorized as "toxins" without contravening the letter of the treaty.[8] The recent increase in military interest in the use of biotechnology for this purpose has drawn attention to this problem (chapters 2 and 5).

Furthermore, although most experts rate the present military utility of biological weaponry currently as low, particularly for strategic or tactical use, this perception could shift radically if persuasive scenarios demonstrating military effectiveness were developed. The military mindset has long been dominated by the search for innovative and effective capabilities to achieve battlefield victory at acceptable costs. The restraints of international law, designed to protect civilians from direct attack in wartime, were easily set aside with the advent of such militarily devastating weapons systems as submarines and bomber aircraft. The use of the atomic bomb in World War II was premised upon its military (and political) effectiveness—saving lives, inducing an early surrender, intimidating Moscow, controlling the peace process in Japan— with virtually no thought devoted to the relevance of prior inhibitions upon using toxic weaponry of mass destruction against predominantly civilian targets. The "criminal" character of this reliance on atomic bombs is apparent if one reverses identities—does anyone doubt that if Germany or Japan had used such bombs against Allied cities, and then gone on to lose the war, that such action would have been indicted as criminal behavior and punished as prime instances of war crimes? The Iraqi breakout of the chemical weapons regime in the 1980s confirms again that battlefield imperatives can overcome legal and social inhibitions. The main message here is that legal inhibitions upon biological weaponry alone cannot hope to restrain weapons development if there emerges the perception within government or policymaking circles that these weapons confer a definite advantage in relation to either strategic bargaining or actual warfare, and if they produce no serious international or domestic backlash. Secondarily, if doubts increase on these matters, regardless of actual utility and policies of others, the pressure to develop and acquire BW, and produce plans for possible use, would rise dramatically. Containing a BW arms race is a social and psychological challenge, although its difficulty can be altered greatly by perceptions and technical developments that pertain to feasibility in a range of battlefield situations.

These general reflections have a special bearing on current international relations in view of the nuclear stalemate. In East-West strategic interaction there has often been an assumption that a new class of weaponry might tip the balance of power and undermine the stability of deterrence. If the Soviet Union were to acquire a credible biological weapons capability and the United States did not, it is assumed that the resolve of the West to defend its interests would diminish; in an extreme version the United States could become vulnerable to BW blackmail or even a disarming first strike. Such a thesis has been seriously argued by some conservative defense analysts.[9] The converse, less frequently discussed at least in the open literature, is a new strategic opening by way of BW that could again make general warfare a viable option. A biological weapons capability might build a definite national advantage; it could even be regarded as a less catastrophic form of warfare than that based on nuclear weapons or even on most forms of conventional weapons. If disease vectors were disabling and of short duration, their "humanitarian" properties (as compared to other weaponry) could be used to justify clandestine development and even use. It would not even be necessary that novel forms of biological weapons be developed to tempt use for covert operations or by threatened governments with no apparent alternative means of effective defense available. Possibly not only clandestine but overt use could be justified as a basis for avoiding the physical annihilation of the earth, a line of argumentation that earlier surfaced in the course of the debate in the late 1970s on "the neutron bomb." In the absence of strong oppositional pressure, public and cultural attitudes against BW could be dismissed as "biased" or old-fashioned and a bureaucratic initiative based on reformulation of national values and interests could be relied upon.

If barriers to the development of biological weapons were to be lowered, the relative ease and low cost of production would almost certainly induce rapid proliferation of such capabilities. This concern is reinforced by a notorious instance of extensive and illegal use of chemical weapons in the 1980s; by concern about proliferation of chemical and biological weapons stimulated in part by the claims of U.S. intelligence agencies; and by recent disclosures of the ease of access of Middle Eastern countries to Western supplies of precursor chemicals and hardware required for the production of chemical weapons.[10] This evidence is instructive, if discouraging, in relation to parallel prospects of biological weapons manufacture. Also relevant here is the increasing allegation by Third World representatives that chemical and biological weapons are "the poor man's atomic bombs." These allegations were frequently made at the Paris Conference on Chemical Weaponry (January 1989) and evidently influenced the mood of the proceedings. In the background is the growing demand by some Third World representatives that *all* weapons of mass destruction be effectively repudiated, contending that objections to their availability raise largely common issues of concern. This emphasis on interrelatedness cuts against the grain of U.S. policy emphasis on nonproliferation and its continuing insistence on retaining a nuclear weapons option for itself as an essential instrument of foreign policy.[11]

At present, the major difference between the biological area and other fields of science and technology is the presence of a legal regime that inhibits possession of weapons. However, as noted earlier, the BW legal regime does not absolutely block the path to weapons development. Even if the treaty language were perfected it might still be undermined by covert undertakings or direct violations. The weakness of the sanctions imposed by other nations on Iraq for its use of chemical warfare against Iran (and internally against the

Kurds) reveals the need for much stronger international commitments to upholding the chemical and biological warfare legal regime. At best a legal regime adds weight to a wider pattern of societal, cultural, and political inhibitions; by itself, it can never generate full confidence in the national security area, given the character of the states system, the unconditional role of war within this system, and the tendency of states to introduce advantageous weapons innovations regardless of their legal status.

Present uncertainties are illustrated by the achievements and limitations of the Second Review Conference held in 1986. At one level, that conference made some notable progress in both a formal sense and in exhibiting unexpectedly strong support by important governments for the BWC. What was achieved was a commitment to restoring confidence in the treaty and an agreement to try to do so by expanding the operational meaning of the BWC by encouraging treaty partners to proceed with a series of voluntary measures (chapter 12). Whether this first limited achievement will be followed up with appropriate behavior and specific measures, thereby generating greater confidence that restraints on defensive biological warfare activities will continue to be respected in the future, remains to be seen. The measures articulated in the Final Declaration can be important in manifesting a commitment to the treaty, as well as a willingness to confirm the conviction that the national interests of treaty participants are still consistent with the goal of maintaining biological disarmament. However if the pace of expansion of military use of the biological sciences initiated in the 1980s continues, if leading military establishments continue to pursue biological research and development in secret, and if doubts about compliance remain prominent, legal barriers to the militarization of biotechnology and the biological sciences are certain to be eroded. Because of the interplay of defensive and offensive capabilities in the BW research process it is unavoidable that any kind of BW research, other than on passive measures, will over time weaken the overall atmosphere surrounding the basic treaty commitment to the unconditional and irreversible rejection of BW as a permissible weapons option.

At the present time, there are four principal arenas for action on the biological warfare issue: first, the legislative bodies of national governments, with their abilities to influence military policy and to regulate activities in civil society; second, the international system of sovereign states, with both collective and individual opportunities to work to either strengthen or dissolve the present system of international law inhibiting recourse to biological and chemical warfare; third, the scientists and corporations generating the knowledge and techniques that are in danger of becoming militarized who are linked largely through a common involvement, expressed in professional and business organizations at the national and international levels in the pursuit of knowledge, the quest for ever greater budgets and profits, and the drive toward the continuous application of technology; fourth, the citizens of each national state who, depending on the degree of democracy, possess a capacity and responsibility to act collectively to reinforce the legal regime of BW prohibition. Actions taken within any one of these arenas may affect perceptions and actions within the other arenas. For example, irresponsible military policies of national governments may produce repercussions in the international system; governmental respect for international law is likely to help constrain the military policies of national governments; collective action on the part of scientists and citizens can be influential in reinforcing cultural norms.

In considering possible action within these various arenas, we distinguish between *short-term goals*, aimed at achieving immediate changes in political behavior that will ensure continuing support for the existing CBW legal regime, and *long-term goals* aimed at developing and adopting new and more effective measures to achieve treaty compliance, international reassurance, and restriction of military activity to passive defense.

Proposals

A National Governments
All national governments are urged to take the following steps:

1. Implement in a comprehensive and effective fashion the Biological Weapons Convention in accordance with their constitutional processes as proposed in the Final Declaration of the Second Review Conference. This step is of particular importance in a market economy where, in the absence of domestic legislation, it is quite plausible that engineering or pharmaceutical companies might undertake weapons research, development, and even production activities for governmental or political clients on a confidential, for-profit basis. Several coun-

tries, including Australia, Belgium, Bulgaria, France, and the United Kingdom have already taken this step. In the United States, the Bush administration endorsed, and the Senate approved, domestic legislation in 1989 (appendix I).[12]

2. Take official action to restrict military research and development in the biological sciences. Article I of the Biological Weapons Convention allows development activities that can be justified for "prophylactic, protective or other peaceful purposes" and does not address research at all. As a step towards strengthening the Convention, national governments should place the following conditions on military-sponsored biological research and development:

   (a) Openness of all military research related to biological warfare must be maintained. Details of all military projects should be publicly and fully disclosed and results reported.

   (b) Novel plant, animal, and human pathogens and toxins should not be constructed by military institutions or under military sponsorship for any purposes. These activities cannot produce effective defenses (chapters 6 and 8); on the other hand they may profoundly destabilize the CBW legal regime.

   (c) There should be no military use of pathogens or toxins in the form of aerosols, either contained or in the open, for any purpose. Tests requiring the use of aerosols should be conducted only with simulants as now used in the development and testing of protective equipment, decontamination procedures and detection devices. Open-air testing with simulants should be publicly announced in advance, confined to unpopulated areas, and not carried out against animals or plants.

   (d) Full, informed consent from human subjects of military research should be required.

3. Sign and ratify the Chemical Weapons Convention without reservation when it is ready, thereby bringing it into force unencumbered and with least possible delay.

4. Confine strictly intelligence activities related to chemical and biological warfare to intelligence gathering, evaluation, and assessment. Intelligence agencies should not engage in any research and development activities related to CBW, much less possess weaponry for potential use.

5. Provide immunity for whistle-blowing disclosures, including arrangements for anonymity if preferred, and for the processing of allegations to ensure that irresponsible reports of violative activity do not weaken the BWC regime.

6. Avoid irresponsible allegations of violations by other nations and take all possible steps to resolve ambiguity and uncertainty with respect to the evidence regarding a suspected violation, including consultation as provided by Article V of the Biological Weapons Convention.

7. Report regularly to their legislatures and citizenry on steps taken to improve compliance with the BWC.

8. Impose trade restrictions on chemical and biological agents implicated in the production of chemical and biological weapons.

B The United States Government

How the general proposals for national governments made under (A) are implemented depends on the specific machinery of each government for oversight, regulation, and policymaking as well as on the level of military activity related to biological warfare. As a world leader in biotechnology and as one of the governments most extensively engaged in biological defense activities, the United States government has a special responsibility at the present time to review its biological warfare policy and to take steps to reinforce international commitment to biological disarmament. Just as President Nixon's unilateral renunciation of biological weaponry in 1969 reinforced international commitments to negotiate the Biological Weapons Convention, so unilateral renunciation of the exploration of potential military applications of biotechnology at this time could generate the confidence and momentum needed to ensure that this new field of science and technology will never be exploited for military purposes. Specifically, the United States Government should take the following steps:

1. Initiate a comprehensive review of the Biological Defense Research Program that includes detailed examination of the military implications of the present range of research and development projects. The implications of present projects should receive special scrutiny with the goal of eliminating those projects that are more likely to lend themselves to direct military applications. The present guideline for research conducted under the BDRP (appendix H) should be revised to restrict

the range of activities to development of *passive defense*—development of protective clothing, decontamination procedures, generic therapies, and generic detection devices. As noted in A, novel plant, animal, and human pathogens and toxins should not be constructed by military institutions or under military sponsorship for any purposes. Research aimed at threat assessment (the testing of aerosols of biological warfare agents or the exploration of the properties of genetically engineered pathogens) should be renounced as both provocative and a danger to public health.

2. Eliminate the program of medical defense against BW agents. This provocative program causes suspicion and cannot provide an effective defense. All remaining medical research aimed at prophylaxis or therapy should be transferred from military to civilian control. This would enable the use of genetic engineering and other biogenetic technologies for medical purposes to be administered by a civilian agency, such as the National Institutes of Health; such use would be subject to the full application of the Freedom of Information Act, the Federal Advisory Committees Act and the Federal Administrative Procedures Act.

3. Subject all research under the Biological Defense Research Program (as well as the Chemical Warfare Program) to the requirements of the human subjects review regulations. (Research conducted at Department of Defense facilities not funded by the Department of Health and Human Services is not covered by the 1981 regulations that protect subjects of research.)[13]

4. Extend the responsibility of human experimentation committees to include review of chemical and biological warfare research for its social and ethical impact. Scientists engaged in such work should be required to file a Secondary Impact Statement indicating foreseeable societal consequences of their work in terms of (a) the likelihood of misuse; (b) the probability of harm to the environment or public health associated with the research and with future applications; and (c) the explicit reassurance that no military relevance is foreseen or intended and that if it becomes evident in the course of research, further review will be immediately sought.

5. Require the Department of Defense to provide a full breakdown of support for research under the Biological Defense Program and the Chemical Warfare Program in its budget requests.

6. Publish the annual reports of the Department of Defense to Congress on the Chemical Warfare and Biological Defense Research Programs. These reports should also be published in the *Congressional Record*.

C The Soviet Union

The Soviet Government also bears a major responsibility for strengthening the BW treaty regime. In this case, it is the *secrecy* of Soviet activities that have been the principal cause of international concern. The Soviet Union could greatly strengthen the context of the regime by taking the following steps:

1. Provide details of its present military-sponsored biological research programs, including descriptions of the goals of projects and the means used to pursue these goals, the biological agents under study, and the locations of projects.

2. Open its biological defense facilities for visits by scientists and officials from other nations that are parties to the Biological Weapons Convention.

3. Limit its biological defense program in a manner parallel to the restrictions proposed in B for the U.S. Biological Defense Research Program.

D Organized International Community

1. *Universal Adherence to the Geneva Protocol and to the Biological Weapons Convention.* All states not currently parties to either the Geneva Protocol or to the Biological Weapons Convention should be encouraged to give their unconditional adherence as an urgent priority. (As of January 1, 1988 there were approximately 55 non-parties to the Geneva Protocol and 55 non-parties to the Biological Weapons Convention—see appendix E.) States Parties to the Geneva Protocol should be encouraged to withdraw any reservations which they have attached to their acceptance of the treaty. Many parties have reserved their right to use chemical and biological weapons in retaliation (even though with respect to biological and toxin weapons the reservation is inconsistent with the provisions of the BWC). To this point, only four nations—Australia, Barbados, Ireland, and New Zealand—have withdrawn their right of retaliation with respect to chemical as well as biological warfare. The Netherlands and

the United States have reserved a right of retaliation for chemical warfare only.[14]

2. *U.N. Investigation of Violations of the Geneva Protocol.* All nations should press for the appointment of a special U.N. committee to study the use of chemical weapons in the Iran-Iraq war and the character of responses by states and by the UN to these violations, to develop recommendations for future international responses to violations of the Geneva Protocol, and to consider whether this experience carries lessons for the reliable maintenance of the BWC regime. An expert group was formed by the U.N. General Assembly in response to Resolution 42/37C in 1987 to address technical guidelines and procedures for the investigation of allegations of use of chemical, biological and toxin weapons. This group is due to report in the fall of 1989.[15] Political dimensions of the problem—for example, the responsibility for decisions to investigate charges of noncompliance and the nature of international sanctions that might be applied against countries that use chemical or biological weapons, and against suppliers of materials and technology for chemical or biological warfare—remain to be considered.

3. *Chemical Weapon Conventions.* All delegations to the Conference on Disarmament should be encouraged to complete negotiation of the Chemical Weapons Convention as a high priority.

4. *Biological Weapons Convention* (a) All nations should be encouragreed to at the Second Review Conference. By May 1989, only twenty-seven States Parties had participated in these information exchanges. The majority of these reports were from industrial nations. No reports were made by Latin American and Middle Eastern nations, and only two by Asian and African nations.[16]

(b) *Third Review Conference on the Biological Weapons Convention*

   i. The Preparatory Committee for the Third Review Conference should encourage serious, active preparation for the Conference, including inviting contributions from scientists, lawyers, and nongovernmental organizations concerned about upholding and strengthening the BWC.

   ii. The voluntary measures agreed upon at the Second Review Conference should be extended to fully encompass all facilities where military-sponsored research relevant to the Convention is conducted, information on military development of vaccines and toxoids, data on military vaccination programs, and information on research involving animal and plant pathogens and vectors that transmit human, animal, or plant diseases. It must be emphasized, however, that the essential need with respect to biological defense activities is to *eliminate* certain types of research and development (as proposed under A.5 and B.1 and 2 above) rather than to *share* them.[17]

iii. Further confidence-building measures should be initiated, including exchanges of scientists and the opening of high-containment facilities for visits by representatives of other States Parties.

iv. Credible procedures to explain suspicious events within the treaty process should be designed.

v. Development of ways to extend the scope of Article I, including preparation of language for a more precise interpretation of its prohibition and for possible amendment of the text itself, should be planned.

5. *Development of Verification Procedures for the Biological Weapons Convention.* The institutions and procedures for verification elaborated for the Chemical Weapons Convention will provide important models for developing verification and enforcement arrangements for the Biological Weapons Convention. (If the CWC encompasses toxins, these models will provide a direct bridge between the two treaties.) Parties to the BWC should build on these provisions as a basis for strengthening the Convention; one course of action is to formulate plans at the Third Review Conference for negotiating a Protocol on Enforcement and Verification as an add-on to the BWC. This protocol could adopt, possibly without change, any requirements for monitoring laboratory research and production technology for toxins developed for the CWC.

6. *Dissemination of the Nuremberg Principles.* The role of individual responsibility that is relevant to upholding international law in the area of war and peace should be widely addressed in connection with the requirements of the Geneva Protocol and the Biological Weapons Convention. In this regard dissemination of the text of the BWC together with the Nuremberg Principles (appendix D) would provide a helpful foundation for understanding the character of legal obligations in the context of activities linked to

research and development of biological weaponry, including the duty to uphold international legal obligations even if inconsistent with official policies, governmental orders and laws at the national level (legal obligations to maintain secrecy, for example).

E Scientists and Corporations Responsible for Research and Development in the Biological Sciences and Biotechnology

1. Scientists, engineers and corporate employees should develop and circulate a code of ethics committing them not to use the biological sciences and biotechnology for research and development aimed at the development or production of chemical and biological weapons and to renounce all CBW activities except for the development of passive defenses; such a commitment should also be related to a willingness to question the imperatives of national security justifications when these conflict with international law or international morality.

2. Scientific, medical, and industrial organizations that engage in activities involving the biological sciences should disseminate such a code of ethics.

3. In addition, scientists, administrators, and corporations should be informed in effective ways that any activity that evades or breaks the commitments of the BWC is a violation of international law for which they as individuals can be held criminally accountable regardless of whether or not they were carrying out official governmental policy. War crimes trials held after World War II imposed such responsibility on scientists, engineers, and corporate officers as well as on political and military leaders, who knowingly engaged in activity that violated international law of war. Preparation and planning for illegal warfare is itself a crime in international law and arguably the inherently illegal character of biological weapons makes any act toward their development and production, let alone their use, a crime against the law of nations. It may be appropriate to circulate a Nuremberg Pledge that defines responsibilities in relation to scientific and technical activities relevant to the scope of the Biological Weapons Convention.

4. In light of proposal E.3, scientists and corporate officers and employees have a particular duty to disclose any activity that might reasonably be regarded as a violation of international law.

F Citizens

1. Individual citizens can support the BWC through the development of curricula on the social, cultural, moral, and legal dimensions of biological and chemical warfare and disarmament; by
emphasizing international and national approaches to strengthening barriers to CBW; and by speaking out on the roles of
national governments, scientists, corporations, and citizens in
achieving disarmament. These efforts should relate to a wider
questioning of the unconditional character of war and state
policy as well as to the proper limits on waging war, given the
existence of nuclear weaponry. They should also address the
shaping of scientific research by military goals and the responsibilities of scientists for military use of their knowledge. The
question whether a particular weapons system can be prohibited
reliably through legal and moral prohibition within the existing
world order remains an open, yet crucial, question.

2. Journalists have a special responsibility to achieve balanced,
accurate coverage of the issues associated with biological warfare; they should neither sensationalize these issues nor under-
state their importance. Journalists should be especially careful
in reporting allegations of noncompliance to clarify the status of
any scientific claims made in support of allegations and the
range of international responses to such charges.

3. There should be support for an ethos of disclosure pertaining to
dubious activities associated with either research on or development of biological weaponry, regardless of governmental policy,
whether such disclosure is described as whistle-blowing or upholding obligations under international law. This ethos should
be reinforced by rewarding public-minded disclosures as well as
by protecting the individual from any adverse consequences as a
result of efforts to disclose information that is embarassing or
harmful to the reputation of a government or corporation. Such
protective measures should be reliably embodied in regular legal
procedures, as well as accompanied by educative reinforcement
as to the evolving character of good citizenship.

4. Upon exhausting normal means to expose and terminate activity by governments, corporations, or individuals that appears to
violate the Biological Weapons Convention, citizens have a right,
(see Nuremberg Principles, appendix D) and possibly a duty, to

engage in nonviolent civil resistance, including initiatives that may violate domestic law.

The recent expansion of defensive biological warfare activities has been justified in the United States on the grounds that it is required in order to assure an effective defense against biological warfare agents. Even assuming that this explanation is accurate, it is based on fallacious thinking. An effective biological defense is certainly no more attainable than a nuclear one—and some would argue even less so. The general line of reasoning is the same in each case: it is impossible to anticipate accurately the choices of a determined adversary among a virtually infinite set of options. Paradoxically, striving for a perfect defense against all conceivable biological warfare agents is likely actually to *foster* the discovery of novel weapons applications, in the long run encouraging deployment, use, and proliferation of biological warfare capabilities. Elsewhere, nations engaged in biological warfare research may or may not have a rationale similar to that of the United States. The secrecy that often surrounds such programs and the fact that governments may not feel obliged publicly to justify them add elements of uncertainty that are difficult to assess and could, if only for this reason, be destabilizing for the BW legal regime. The course of action proposed in this book—disarmament achieved through opening up national biological warfare programs to national and international scrutiny and through strengthening the social, cultural, and legal barriers to biological warfare activities—provides the most constructive approach to removing these threats.

Four conditions support adoption of this course of action at the present time: first, the continuing improvement in U.S.-Soviet relations (catalyzed by Mikhail Gorbachev's acceptance of arms control and disarmament, including a dramatic shift on verification machinery); second, the strength of the cultural aversion to the use of disease and poison as weapons; third, the existence of an international community of biologists and biomedical scientists that is especially sensitive to an ethical norm of commitment governing the use of science and technology to improve rather than harm the human condition; fourth, the apparent absence of developed military-industrial-scientific lobbies for promoting biological weaponry. This opportunity to strengthen barriers to biological weaponry should be embraced immediately, especially to ensure that the new biogenetic technologies are directed solely to peaceful purposes.

Acknowledgments

This chapter is the result of a broad collaboration and exchange of ideas with many of the contributors to the book and with members of the Council for Responsible Genetics. In particular we thank the following for their proposals and detailed comments on drafts: Francis Boyle, Gordon Burck, Leonard Cole, Erhard Geissler, Paul Grams, Jonathan King, Sheldon Krimsky, Marc Lappé, Richard Novick, Charles Piller, Julian Perry Robinson, Barbara Rosenberg, Seth Shulman, Robert Sinsheimer, Nicholas Sims, and Keith Yamamoto. We remain responsible for details of the views expressed in this chapter and the specific set of recommendations developed with the generous help of our colleagues.

Notes

1. U.S. Senate, Committee on Government Affairs, *Hearings: Global Spread of Chemical and Biological Weapons: Assessing Challenges and Responses*, 9 February 1989: Testimony of William H. Webster, Director, CIA. For comprehensive reviews of claims of proliferation of chemical and biological weapons in 1985–1987, see Julian Perry Robinson, "Chemical and Biological Warfare: Developments in 1985," *SIPRI Yearbook 1986* (Oxford: Oxford University Press, 1986); "Chemical and Biological Warfare: Developments in 1986," *SIPRI Yearbook 1987* (Oxford: Oxford University Press, 1987); and S.J. Lundin, J.P. Perry Robinson, and Ralf Trapp, "Chemical and Biological Warfare: Developments in 1987," *SIPRI Yearbook 1988* (Oxford: Oxford University Press, 1988).
2. For use of "yellow rain" charges by the Reagan administration, see chapters 2 and 9; for use of charges of proliferation of chemical weapons, see U.S. House of Representatives, Committee on Appropriations, Subcommittee on Defense Appropriations, *Hearings: Fiscal Year 1987*, Testimony of General Wickham, Part 1, 114.
3. For discussion of the interplay of the factors promoting and restraining military assimilation, see Julian P. Robinson, "The Changing Status of Chemical and Biological Warfare: Recent Technical, Military and Political Developments," in *SIPRI Yearbook, 1982*.
4. U.S. Office of the Under Secretary of Defense, Office of the Director of Environmental and Life Science, "Recombinant DNA Research Projects Currently Conducted in DoD Biomedical Laboratories," 3 August 1987; United States Department of the Army, U.S. Army Medical Research and Development Command, *Draft Programmatic Environmental Impact Statement: Biological Defense Reasearch Program*, May 1988.

5. John H. Cushman, "U.S., Defending Research Efforts, Cites Increase in Biological Arms," *New York Times* (5 April 1988), 16.

6. Steven Rose, "Biotechnology at War," *New Scientist* (19 March 1987), 33–37.

7. Soviet Union, "Information Presented by USSR in Compliance with the Agreements Reached at the Second Conference for Examination of the Convention of the Prohibition of Development, Production and Stockpiling of Bacteriological (Biological) and Toxin Weapons and Their Elimination, and in Accordance with the Resolutions and Recommendations of the Special Meeting of Scientific and Technological Experts from the Participating Countries," 13 October 1987. Subsequent disclosures by the Soviet Union to the U.N. Department for Disarmament Affairs, made in accordance with the confidence-building procedures agreed upon at the Second Review Conference on the Biologcial Weapons Convention, have provided some further details of Soviet biological defense activities.

8. Erhard Geissler and Karlheinz Lohs, "The Changing Status of Toxin Weapons," in E. Geissler, ed., *Biological and Toxin Weapons Today* (Oxford: Oxford University Press, 1986), 36–56.

9. See, e.g., Joseph D. Douglass and Neil C. Livingstone, *America the Vulnerable* (Lexington, MA: Lexington Books, 1987).

10. John Fialka, "Western Industry Sells Third World the Means to Produce Poison Gas," *Wall Street Journal* (15 September 1988).

11. See *Discriminate Deterrence* (Report of the Commission on Integrated Long-Term Strategy) (Washington, D.C., U.S. Department of Defense, January 1988).

12. Although we welcome this initiative, we have some reservations about the form of the Senate legislation. Apparently as a result of concerns expressed by the Department of Defense, private industry, and some members of the American Society of Microbiology about the risks of "chilling" legitimate military and industrial activities, the legislative language approved by the Senate on November 21, 1989 specifically allows possession of biological agents, toxins, and delivery systems for prophylactic, protective, and other peaceful purposes (appendix I, note 2). To the extent that this language invites misunderstanding or suggests a gray area of activities that is not explicitly excluded by the Biological Weapons Convention but could erode its primary purpose, it requires either modification of the bill or clarification in the report accompanying the bill.

13. "Final Regulations Amending Basic HHS Policy for the Protection of Human Research Subjects: Final Rule 45 CFR 46," *Federal Register: Rules and Regulations* 46 (16) (26 January 1981), 8366–8392, and chapter 4 of this volume.

14. Nicholas Sims, *The Diplomacy of Biological Disarmament* (London: Macmillan, 1988), and chapter 12 of this volume.

15. *Chemical Weapons Convention Bulletin* 1 (Summer 1988), 6; 2 (Autumn 1988), 8; 4 (May 1988), 3.

16. Erhard Geissler, ed., *Strengthening the Biological Weapons Convention by Confidence-Building Measures*, SIPRI Chemical and Biological Warfare Studies, no. 10 (London: Oxford University Press, 1990).

17. The question of further confidence-building measures is addressed in *Strengthening the Biological Weapons Convention by Confidence-Building Measures*, ed. E. Geissler.

Appendix A

Biological, Chemical, and Toxin Warfare Agents

Gordon M. Burck

This appendix provides a brief review of chemical and biological warfare (CBW) agents, including toxins. Although this book concentrates on biological and toxin agents, chemical agents are addressed because chemical and biological weapons:

- have properties that generally distinguish them from other categories of weapons. While extremely diverse in their specific properties, chemical and biological agents are generally characterized by their biospecificity (that is, they inflict damage on living rather than on material things), their delayed effect and indiscriminate impact, and by the fact that relatively small weights of these agents may be used over large areas. The last two properties mean that many, although not all, chemical and biological agents are classified as weapons of mass destruction.

- are interrelated at the level of institutional sponsorship and management. In the United States historically there have been close ties between the institutions responsible for chemical and biological warfare (chapters 1 and 2). At present, the same Pentagon office—Deputy Assistant Secretary of Defense (Atomic Matters) (Chemical Matters)—is responsible for both areas. Several activities which have both chemical and biological warfare applications—for example research and development, protective clothing and detection equipment, and testing and evaluation—are each the responsibility of a single military institution, in large part because of the multiple functions of much defensive equipment. A direct consequence of these institutional relationships is that funding for the U.S. Chemical Warfare and Biological Defense program is treated as a single item in the U.S. budgetary process.

- are interrelated at the level of biochemistry—chemists can synthesize naturally-occurring toxins as well as lethal chemical agents; biotechnology can also be used to produce new types of chemical agents as well as toxins.

• are interrelated at the level of international law and arms control. The use of chemical and biological weapons as a group is banned by the Geneva Protocol; their acquisition, development and possession are banned by the Biological Weapons Convention (BWC) and potentially, for toxins, by the Chemical Weapons Convention (CWC) currently being negotiated.

1 Definitions

No brief set of definitions of chemical and biological weapons can be either precise or noncontroversial.

Chemical Warfare Agents

These are chemicals of any origin (natural, biological or synthetic) which are used with the primary intent to incapacitate and/or kill by means of the toxicity of the chemical. Lethality is rated by the amount of skin contact (in milligrams per kilogram of body weight) or the quantity inhaled (in milligrams per minute per cubic meter of air) that kills 50% of the subjects. Thus, a weight of chemical agent has a calculable—based on optimum dispersal—maximum number of victims. Because the agents blow away, they also have a limited time during which the lethal presence is maintained. Injury and death take place within minutes to a few hours of exposure. Table A.1 shows the chemical names and toxicity for the chemicals mentioned below.

The principal classes of lethal chemicals which have been used for warfare in the 20th century are:

• Blood or asphyxiating agents. After inhalation, some of these agents initially cause tearing and choking due to irritation but, in the manner of carbon monoxide poisoning, they also cause rapid death by blocking the capacity of the blood to carry oxygen. The principal warfare agents in this class are hydrogen cyanide (prussic acid) and cyanogen chloride. It is sometimes alleged that small compounds are being sought which may be less readily absorbed by mask filters and can therefore serve the purpose of "discipline breakers" (that is, they penetrate the filter and cause the soldier to choke and remove his mask to be killed by another agent), but none are known at present.

• Choking or lung agents. After inhalation, these cause severe inflammation of the lungs, which fill with fluid, resulting in drowning. The principal agents are chlorine, phosgene, and chloropicrin.

• Sternutators. These cause sneezing, coughing and sometimes vomiting. The principal agent has been Adamsite (DM).

• Blister agents, or vesicants. These agents attack any interior or exterior surface of the body, causing skin blisters, temporary blindness, and lung inflammation; vomiting and nausea also result. The principal agents are sulfur mustard and Lewisite (an arsenic compound).

• Nerve agents. After being absorbed through the skin or lungs, these agents block the enzyme that terminates nerve impulses, thereby disrupting bodily functions and resulting in intense sweating, bronchial congestion and constriction, dimming of vision, uncontrollable vomiting and diarrhea, convulsions, and death within minutes through respiratory failure. The only known stockpiled nerve agents are tabun, sarin, soman (GA, GB and GD in Western nomenclature) and VX, all of which are organophosphate chemicals related to pesticides such as parathion. The U.S. is developing a new "intermediate volatility agent" (IVA), but the composition has not yet been standardized.

Nonlethal chemical agents have also been stockpiled:

• Irritant agents, most notably CS tear gas, have been used in both military and police actions (see discussion below).

Two other classes of chemical agents—psychochemicals (e.g., LSD) and incapacitating chemicals (e.g., BZ or 3-quinuclidinyl benzilate)—have also been investigated, and BZ was produced by the U.S.; they have not been used in war.

Other classes of chemicals that have been used in war are *not* considered chemical warfare agents. Examples are:

• napalm and white phosphorus (not to mention smoke generators, explosives and gunpowder), whose effects are based on combustion. However the first two substances as well as smoke are included in military budgets for chemical weapons, and may be employed by soldiers such as the Soviet Chemical Troops and the U.S. Chemical Corps. Thus, such substances may confuse discussions of chemical budgets, stockpile size and location, training time, and manpower allocations.

• highly toxic fuels, such as nitrogen tetroxide, which is used to propel rockets.

• nuclear weapons, which are triggered by a chemical fuse and explosive, but kill by nuclear blast and radiation.

With respect to their coverage under international law, two classes of chemical warfare agents—herbicides and riot control agents (RCAs)—remain controversial. Herbicides and defoliants are used to kill crops and other vegetation. The largest use in war was in Vietnam by the U.S., where 2,4-D, 2,4,5-T, and arsenic chemicals were employed. It is well known, even from agricultural experience with lower rates of application, that such chemicals can cause long-term health problems. Further, the minute impurity dioxin, found in Agent Orange (as well as in the pollution from the Seveso explosion and the waste-oil spread in Times Beach, Missouri) is a super-toxic chemical that has devastating health effects, including cancer and damage to fetuses.

The second of these "grey area" classes is riot control agents (RCAs)—vomiting and tear gases. ("Tear gas," technically called a lachrymator, is actually a solid dispersed as a fine dust cloud.) According to official definition, RCAs incapacitate the victim only during exposure (unlike DM, which has a persistent effect). These irritants are the descendants of the irritants used prior to the lethal chemicals, including those used from the start of WWI and stockpiled during WWII—the most successful were arsenic and bromine compounds. Although RCAs may reach lethal concentrations in enclosed areas, the primary use is to force the victims to leave the area where the agent is released. The principal military agents have been CN and, later, CS. In Vietnam, RCAs were used to, among other things, force the evacuation of tunnels and other closed spaces (usually with the goal of forcing the victim into the line of fire). In the United States, South Korea, Israel, Yugoslavia, China, and the USSR, RCAs have been used by police forces to control the population. In several countries small numbers of victims have died due to the toxicity of the chemicals.

The status of these two classes of chemicals has not yet been settled in the negotiations on the Chemical Weapons Convention, and there is disagreement on the applicability of the Geneva Protocol.

Biological and Bacteriological Agents

This group includes organisms (bacteria, viruses, rickettsia, and fungi), or infectious material derived from them, which are intended to'enter the body and cause illness and death. Toxicity occurs in several ways that are difficult to distinguish in practice:

• infection (overwhelming life processes and the body's defenses by rapid reproduction),

• poisoning (reproducing until able to produce sufficient amounts of a nonliving but toxic substance), or

• cytotoxicity (a virus being absorbed into and killing host cells).

Biological agents include human, animal, and plant pathogens.

Unlike chemical agents, biological agents can reproduce. If they are also communicable from person to person, the ultimate number of victims is limited only by preexisting immunity, possibly by the genetic limits of susceptibility, and by public health measures. The organisms may survive indefinitely by reproduction, or simply lie in wait—for instance, anthrax spores may lie dormant in soil for decades, waiting for activation after ingestion.

An ideal biological agent would be robust in the environment, highly infectious (requiring only a few organisms for infection) and virulent after a short incubation period; *not* contagious from person to person (so that it can be targeted and confined); difficult to treat or protect with vaccines; naturally present in the region of attack (hence allowing plausible denial); suitable for mass production; and terrifying.

The most notable agents produced for the military have been anthrax, botulinum toxin A, ricin, and saxitoxin (shellfish poison). Table A.2 provides information on the biological agents that have been studied for applicability to biological warfare. Since the beginning of the various BW defense programs, the emphasis of concern has shifted from bacteria and fungi to viral agents.

Toxins

Toxins are supertoxic chemicals at the convergence of the chemical and biological agent categories in both chemistry and arms control, as mentioned above. They are nonliving substances (both proteins and non-proteinaceous) and distinguished from biological agents by their inability to reproduce. They kill primarily by direct toxicity. Some toxins may be interesting to the military due to incapacitating, rather than lethal, effects (food poisoning, for example).

Table A.1
Production of toxin agents

Reproductive technique	Variation in technique	Conceptual type of agent	Treaty coverage
Organism	in host	biological	BWC
	or		
	in test tube	chemical	BWC, CWC
Synthesis	recreating a natural toxin	chemical	BWC, CWC
	or		
	novel toxin[a]	chemical	BWC, CWC

a. Having structures similar to those of natural toxins or affecting physiological processes in a novel way.

Table A.3 provides data on natural toxins which have been studied for applicability to warfare.

Toxins may come from two sources:

• natural living sources (bacteria, protozoa, fungi, plants, coelenterata, mollusks, and amphibians), and

• synthetic sources.

Among the three categories of agents, the toxin category is experiencing the greatest growth in knowledge about their characteristics and production techniques, with two results. On the one hand, toxins may be found that are much more difficult to detect and treat, and the methods used to study them and other BW in defensive research might be applied to creating a toxin weapons production program in a short time. On the other, no effective toxin agents are known and the real threat may be illusory. But the perception of the possibilities puts toxins at the crux of the new problem of biological warfare—the breakout potential could make them the chemical weapons of choice, while their controllability could make them preferred over other biological weapons.

Table A.1 shows the various origins of toxin agents, and the applicability of the BWC and potential CWC. The new biotechnology affects each of the origins.

2 Modern History of CBW Agents

The recorded use of chemical and biological agents in warfare began in ancient times, but the sustained development of CBW agents for use in modern warfare began in World War I. Indeed, the historical development of biological weapons shows a hiatus of nearly 200 years between the British use of smallpox-infected blankets against American Indians and the Japanese campaign in Manchuria.

World War I
All of the classes of chemical agents except nerve agents were used in WWI, beginning with irritants (particularly bromoacetone), then chlorine (April 1915), and progressing to phosgene, hydrogen cyanide, and then sulfur mustard (July 1917), where each with the exception of HCN became the dominant chemical in turn. Overall agent production has been estimated at 200,000 tons.

This race was initiated by the availability of large volumes of chlorine, made available through new developments in German industrial chemistry. Once the use of chemicals commenced, innovation was spurred by the search for military advantage and also by parallel innovations in gas masks and protective clothing.

Interwar Period
Between World War I and World War II, the Geneva Protocol banning the use of chemical, biological, and toxin weapons was negotiated, signed in 1925, and entered into force in 1928. (The U.S. did not deposit its ratification until 1975.)

Visible advances in CBW weaponry were minor. Nevertheless, WWI chemical warfare establishments survived; Germany conspired with the USSR to build and operate the CW research facility at Shikhany, USSR; biological warfare (BW) programs began in the 1930s in several countries. All of the BW agents studied were naturally occurring; the programs sought ways to produce and disseminate them, and to protect against them. The WWI chemicals were used by the Italians in Ethiopia.

Unknown to the world was the secret military development by Germany in the late 1930s of supertoxic nerve agents. Tabun was discovered and patented in the course of German research on organophosphate pesticides, but it was also the first nerve agent to be produced for military purposes and weaponized.

World War II
Also largely unknown to the general public until recent years (despite a 1949 Soviet trial of 12 Japanese) was the use of chemical and biological agents by the Japanese in Manchuria from the late 1930s

until the Soviet entry into the far eastern war in 1945, both in experiments on prisoners and in military operations against cities. The biological agents included anthrax, plague, gas gangrene, encephalitis, typhus, typhoid, hemorrhagic fever, cholera, smallpox, tularemia, and glanders. The U.S. acquired the results of this "research" after the war.

Other than in China, chemical and biological warfare agents were not used in WWII (although a U.S. ship sunk at Bari released mustard, and the USSR claimed a German chemical attack in the Crimea). However, the WWI chemical agents were produced in tremendous quantities, perhaps 500,000 tons, by all of the major belligerents. The German nerve gas program progressed to production of tabun from 1942 (12,000 tons is the usual estimate), construction of a soman production plant (which never operated), and construction of a sarin pilot plant.

Biological agents were also produced by other countries in addition to Japan. For example, the U.S. biological weapons program began in 1941, and Germany conducted BW experiments in the concentration camps. The U.S. program included construction in 1943 of a plant in southern Indiana for the production of anthrax bombs for the British. This was the first Allied biological weapon, but only a prototype was actually produced and tested in Utah.

Postwar Period

Outside the military sphere, the medical, chemical and biological sciences have boomed, resulting in thousands of new industrial, agricultural and pharmaceutical chemicals, many of which are extremely toxic, as well as in production methods to make these chemicals in large quantities.

After the war the United States, United Kingdom, USSR and France proceeded to produce nerve gas weapons in varying amounts. Britain abandoned its program in the 1950s. France now claims to have no chemical weapons. U.S. production was suspended in 1969, pending evaluation of the binary munitions then in development, and resumed in 1987. Soviet production ended in 1987. Iraqi production began in the early 1980s.

The estimated U.S. and declared Soviet stockpiles are of comparable sizes, whereas the estimated French stock is under 1000 tons of chemical agents. Much of the German stockpile captured by the Allies was disposed of, often carelessly (barrels are still pulled up in the nets of North Sea fishermen), and both East and West Germany have uncovered and destroyed German stocks from both world wars; other countries continue to discover residual stocks.

Most of the postwar chemical agent production in the four major producing countries—the U.S., the United Kingdom, the USSR, and France—was probably of mustard and the German nerve agents, except for VX nerve agent (a more lethal and less volatile organophosphate chemical) produced by the U.S. in the 1960s and the USSR at some time, and possibly hydrogen cyanide produced by Iraq. Hallucinogenic chemicals such as LSD and BZ were studied, and the latter was produced by the U.S. CS became the principal harassing agent in the late 1950s. Distilled sulfur mustard (HD) supplemented the type (H) produced during the wars. Despite, or perhaps because of, such slow technical change, the U.S. and USSR accuse each other of secretly investigating "novel" chemical agents, but none of the allegations has been substantiated.

The second postwar innovation in chemical weaponry after nerve agents is the U.S. binary chemical program. While conceptual work has continued since World War II, the U.S. progressed slowly to production with the Army announcement of plans in 1973, construction starting in 1981, and final assembly of the sarin binary artillery shell on December 16, 1987. Although the packaging of the chemicals is different from previous unitary munitions, the known binary nerve agents are the same—sarin, and VX in the Bigeye bomb. The intermediate volatility agent for the multiple launch rocket system warhead is not yet publicly known, but no radical change in the composition of the chemical agent is expected. France has also declared its intent to produce binary weapons, but by 1989 the program seems close to being abandoned.

There have been many allegations of the use of chemical agents since World War II, with little substantiation other than of Iraq's use of mustard gas and possibly nerve agents against Iran in the 1980s. Other than that, the use of chemicals by Egypt in Yemen has the most solid evidence. Toxins have been implicated as assassination weapons used by the secret services of both East and West.

The largest, and acknowledged, use of the "grey area" herbicide and RCA chemicals was by the U.S. in Vietnam. Some 13.7 million pounds of CS tear gas and 18,850,000 gallons of herbicides, particularly Agent Orange (containing as much as 300 pounds of dioxin), were used. Herbicide use was stopped in 1970.

Most major powers probably conducted biological weapons programs after World War II, although only the U.S. acknowledged a stockpile of biological and toxin agents and munitions (for use against both humans and plants). Following President Nixon's renunciation of biological warfare in 1969, the United States stockpile of biological weapons and toxins was eventually destroyed.

The Biological Weapons Convention (BWC) was negotiated between 1969 and 1972 and went into force in 1975. Although it bans any acquisition, development, production, or possession of biological weapons, it allows defensive activities. Immediately after the BWC entered into force negotiations began, and have continued to the present in a variety of venues, on a Chemical Weapons Convention to complete the eradication of CBW weapons and warfare.

In the 1980s, military interest in biological and chemical weapons has revived, stimulated in part by the invention of "binary" nerve munitions and in part by advances in the biological sciences and biotechnology. A broad program of research and development involving the new techniques of biotechnology has been launched. At the same time, the number of natural agents mentioned as potential BW agents has also increased. The most lethal ones—named Marburg, Lassa, Legionnaires' disease, and Ebola viruses—were first identified in 1967, 1969 and two in 1976, respectively.

Acknowledgments

I greatly appreciate the comments of Susan Wright, Matthew Meselson, and Barbara Rosenberg on the text of this appendix, and especially the research by Stuart Ketcham on the tables.

Table A.2
Principal twentieth-century chemical warfare agents

Common name and U.S. Army symbol	Chemical name by category	Lethal dosage[a]
Incapacitants and harassing agents		
CAP (CN)	chloracetophenone	11,000
CS	2-chlorobenzalmalononitrile	25,000
Adamsite (DM)	10-chloro-5,10-dihydrophenarsazine	15,000
Choking agents		
Chlorine		19,000
Phosgene (CG)	carbonyl chloride	3,200
Chloropicrin (PS)	trichloronitromethane	20,000
Blood agents		
Hydrogen cyanide (AC)		2,000–5,000
Cyanogen chloride (CK)		11,000
Sulfur mustard (H, HD)	bis(2-chloroethyl)sulfide	1,500
Nitrogen mustard (HN-3)	tris(2-chloroethyl)amine	1,500
Lewisite (L)	2-chlorovinyldichloroarsine	1,300
Nerve agents		
Tabun (GA)	O-ethyl N,N-dimethylphosphoramidocyanidate	400
Sarin (GB)	isopropyl methylphosphonofluoridate	100
Soman (GD)	1,2,2-trimethylpropylmethylphosphonofluoridate	70
VX	O-ethyl S-diisopropylaminoethylmethylphosphonothiolate	36
Herbicide contaminant		
dioxin	2,3,7,8-tetrachlorodibenzo-*p*-dioxin	1

a. Approximate dosage (milligram-minute/meter^3) of airborne agent likely to kill about 50 percent of people exposed if unprotected. Note: the sources listed in the bibliography of this appendix give varying data for a variety of reasons; the numbers above are intended only to show the range among the chemicals.

Table A.3
Pathogenic microorganisms produced or studied as potential BW agents

Pathogen	Disease	Death rate (%) in untreated cases of natural disease	Role in U.S. biological warfare or biological defense programs
Viruses			
Chagres virus			Under study in the 1980s
Chikungunya virus	Chikungunya	0–1	Studied as potential BW agent before 1969. Under study in the 1980s
Crimean-Congo hemorrhagic fever virus			Under study in the 1980s
Dengue fever virus	Dengue fever	0–1	Under study in the 1980s
Ebola virus	Ebola fever	65–80	Under study in the 1980s
Equine encephalitis viruses			Under study in the 1980s
Eastern encephalitis virus	Eastern equine encephalitis	50	Studied as potential BW agent before 1969
Venezuelan equine encephalitis virus	Venezuelan equine encephalitis	0–2	Studied as potential BW agent before 1969 Standardized as BW agent before 1969 Produced and stockpiled in 1954–1957
Western equine encephalitis virus	Western equine encephalitis	0–3	Studied as potential BW agent before 1969
Hantaan virus	Korean hemorrhagic fever		Under study in the 1980s
Japanese encephalitis virus	Japanese encephalitis		Under study in the 1980s
Junin virus	Argentine hemorrhagic fever	5–15	Under study in the 1980s

Table A.3 (*continued*)

Pathogen	Disease	Death rate (%) in untreated cases of natural disease	Role in U.S. biological warfare or biological defense programs
Kyasanur Forest Virus	Kyasanur Forest disease		Under study in the 1980s
Langat virus			Under study in the 1980s
Lassa fever virus	Lassa fever	1–50	Under study in the 1980s
Lymphocytic choriomeningitis virus	Lymphocytic fever		Under study in the 1980s
Marburg virus	Marburg fever	35	Under study in the 1980s
Mayaro virus	Mayaro		Under study in the 1980s
O'nyong-nyong virus	O'nyong-nyong		Under study in the 1980s
Rift Valley fever virus	Rift Valley fever	0–1	Studied as potential BW agent before 1969 Under study in the 1980s
Ross River virus	Ross River		Under study in the 1980s
Sandfly fever virus	Sandfly fever		Under study in the 1980s
Sindbis virus	Sindbis		Under study in the 1980s
Tick-borne encephalitis virus (Russian Spring-Summer encephalitis virus)	Tick-borne encephalitis		Under study in the 1980s
Variola virus	Smallpox	10–30	
West Nile virus			Under study in the 1980s
Yellow fever virus (Aedes aegypti, carrier)	Yellow fever	30–50	Standardized as weapon in 1943–1969; plant designed for producing carrier in 1959; under study in the 1980s

Bacteria

Actinobacillus mallei	Glanders	90–100	Studied during World War II
Bacillus anthracis	Anthrax	95–100	Studied intensively during World War II; stockpiled during and after World War II until 1969; under study in 1980s
Legionella pneumophila	Legionnaires' disease		Under study in the 1980s
Brucella species	Brucellosis	2–5	Standardized as biological weapon in 1950s; produced and stockpiled in 1954–1967.
Chlamydia psittaci	Influenza psittacosis	10–100	Studied as potential BW agent before 1969
Clostridium tetani	Tetanus	90–100	
Clostridium perfringens	Gas gangrene	high	
Francisella tularensis	Tularemia	0–60	Standardized as biological weapon in 1950s; produced and stockpiled in 1954–1967; under study in the 1980s
Salmonella typhosa	Typhoid	4–20	
Shigella	Dysentery	2–20	
Vibrio comma	Cholera	10–80	
Yersinia pestis (*Pasteurella pestis*)	Plague	30–100	Studied as potential BW agent before 1969; under study in the 1980s

Rickettsiae

Coxiella burnetii	Q-fever	1–4	Standardized as BW agent before 1969; produced and stockpiled in 1954–1967; under study in the 1980s

Table A.4
Toxins produced or studied as potential BW agents

Toxin	Source	Lethal dosage $(LD_{50})^a$	Role in U.S. biological program
Batrachotoxin	Colombian frog	100	Under study in the 1980s
Botulin	*Clostridium botulinum*	0.6	Standardized and produced as a toxin weapon in 1954–1967; under study in the 1980s
Cobrotoxin	Chinese cobra	50	Produced as a toxin weapon in the 1950s and 1960s; under study in the 1980s
Conotoxin	Marine Cone snail		Under study in the 1980s
Crotoxin	South American rattle snake		Under study in the 1980s
Ricin	castor beans	100	Under study in the 1980s
Saxitoxin	shellfish	200	Standardized and produced as a toxin weapon in 1950s and 1960s; under study in the 1980s
Staphylococcus aureus Type A Type B		1,300 6,000	Standardized and produced as a toxin weapon in 1954–1967; under study in the 1980s
Taitoxin	Taipin snake		Under study in the 1980s
Tetanus toxin	*Clostridium tetani*	2.5	Under study in the 1980s
Trichothecene mycotoxins	*Fusarium* species	1–15,000,000	Under study in the 1980s
Sarin (for comparison)		200,000–1,500,000	

a. nanogram/kg (parenteral dose) estimated to have 50 percent chance of killing subject

References

The following sources each contain sections, of varying levels of detail and technicality, describing past and present chemical, biological, and toxin weapons:

W.C. Anderson III and J.M. King, *Vaccine and Antitoxin Availability for Defense Against Biological Warfare Threat Agents*, September 1983 (U.S. Army Health Care Studies Division Report No. 83-002).

Robin Clarke, *The Silent Weapons* (New York: D. McKay Co., 1968).

John Cookson and Judith Nottingham, *A Survey of Chemical and Biological Warfare* (London & New York: Monthly Review Press, 1969).

Department of Defense, *IBC-Approved Recombinant DNA Research Projects*, February 10, 1984.

Erhard Geissler, ed., *Biological and Toxin Weapons Today* (New York: Oxford University Press, 1986).

Julian Perry Robinson, "Environmental effects of chemical and biological warfare," in Royal Swedish Ministry of Agriculture Environmental Advisory Council, *War and Environment* (Stockholm: Liber Förlag, 1981), 73–117.

Jeanne McDermott, *The Killing Winds* (New York: Arbor House, 1987).

Naval Biosciences Laboratory, School of Public Health, University of California, Berkeley, *Annual Report*, 1982–1983.

Charles Piller and Keith R. Yamamoto, *Gene Wars* (New York: Morrow, 1988).

Stockholm International Peace Research Institute, *The Problem of Chemical and Biological Warfare*, Vol. I: *The Rise of CB Weapons*, and Vol. II: *CB Weapons Today* (Stockholm: Almqvist and Wiksell, 1971 and 1973, respectively).

Stockholm International Peace Research Institute, "The Effects of Developments in the Biological and Chemical Sciences on CW Disarmament Negotiations" (Stockholm: SIPRI, 1974).

United Nations, *Chemical and Bacteriological (Biological) Weapons and the Effects of their Possible Use* (U.N. Document A/75/75) July 1, 1969.

United States Army, Field Manual 3-9, "Military Chemicals and Chemical Compounds" (Washington; D.C.: Department of the Army, October 1975).

U.S. Army Medical Research Institute of Infectious Diseases, *Biological Defense, Functional Area Assessment: Overview*, January 4, 1985.

Work Unit Summaries for Research supported by the U.S. Army Medical Research and Development Command, 1980–1987.

World Health Organization, *Health Aspects of Chemical and Biological Weapons*, report of a WHO group of consultants (Geneva: WHO, 1970).

Appendix B

Text of the 1925 Geneva Protocol

Protocol for the Prohibition of the Use in War of Asphyxiating, Posionous or Other Gases, and of Bacteriological Methods of Warfare

Signed at Geneva on 17 June 1925
Entered into force on 8 February 1928
Depositary: French government

The Undersigned plenipotentiaries, in the name of the respective Governments:

Whereas the use in war of asphyxiating, poisonous or other gases, and of all analogous liquids materials or devices, has been justly condemned by the general opinion of the civilised world; and

Whereas the prohibition of such use has been declared in Treaties to which the majority of Powers of the world are Parties; and

To the end that this prohibition shall be universally accepted as part of International Law, binding alike the conscience and the practice of nations;

Declare:

That the High Contracting Parties, so far as they are not already Parties to Treaties prohibiting such use, accept this prohibition, agree to extend this prohibition to the use of bacteriological methods of warfare and agree to be bound as between themselves according to the terms of this declaration.

The High Contracting Parties will exert every effort to induce other States to accede to the present Protocol. Such accession will

Source: *League of Nations Treaty Series*, Vol. 94 (1929).

be notified to the Government of the French Republic, and by the latter to all signatory and acceding Powers, and will take effect on the date of the notification by the Government of the French Republic.

The present Protocol, of which the French and English texts are both authentic, shall be ratified as soon as possible. It shall bear today's date.

The ratifications of the present Protocol shall be addressed to the Government of the French Republic, which will at once notify the deposit of such ratification to each of the signatory and acceding Powers.

The instruments of ratification of and accession of the present Protocol will remain deposited in the archives of the Government of the French Republic.

The present Protocol will come into force for each signatory Power as from the date of deposit of its ratification, and, from that moment, each Power will be bound as regards other Powers which have already deposited their ratifications.

Appendix C

Text of the 1972 Biological Weapons Convention

Convention on the Prohibition of the Development, Production and Stockpiling of Bacteriological (Biological) and Toxin Weapons and on Their Destruction

Signed at London, Moscow and Washington on 10 April 1972
Entered into force on 26 March 1975
Depositaries: UK, US and Soviet governments

The States Parties to this Convention,

Determined to act with a view to achieving effective progress towards general and complete disarmament, including the prohibition and elimination of all types of weapons of mass destruction, and convinced that the prohibition of the development, production and stockpiling of chemical and bacteriological (biological) weapons and their elimination, through effective measures, will facilitate the achievement of general and complete disarmament under strict and effective international control,

Recognizing the important significance of the Protocol for the Prohibition of the Use in War of Asphyxiating, Poisonous or Other Gases, and of Bacteriological Methods of Warfare, signed at Geneva on June 17, 1925, and conscious also of the contribution which the said Protocol has already made, and continues to make, to mitigating the horrors of war,

Reaffirming their adherence to the principles and objectives of that Protocol and calling upon all States to comply strictly with them,

Source: *Treaties and Other International Acts, Series 8062* (US Department of State, Washington, D.C., 1975).

Recalling that the General Assembly of the United Nations has repeatedly condemned all actions contrary to the principles and objectives of the Geneva Protocol of June 17, 1925,

Desiring to contribute to the strengthening of confidence between peoples and the general improvement of the international atmosphere,

Desiring also to contribute to the realization of the purposes and principles of the Charter of the United Nations,

Convinced of the importance and urgency of eliminating from the arsenals of States, through effective measures, such dangerous weapons of mass destruction as those using chemical or bacteriological (biological) agents,

Recognizing that an agreement on the prohibition of bacteriological (biological) and toxin weapons represents a first possible step towards the achievement of agreement on effective measures also for the prohibition of the development, production and stockpiling of chemical weapons, and determined to continue negotiations to that end,

Determined, for the sake of all mankind, to exclude completely the possibility of bacteriological (biological) agents and toxins being used as weapons,

Convinced that such use would be repugnant to the conscience of mankind and that no effort should be spared to minimize this risk,

Have agreed as follows:

Article I

Each State Party to this Convention undertake never in any circumstances to develop, produce, stockpile or otherwise acquire or retain:

1. Microbial or other biological agents, or toxins whatever their origin or method of production, of types and in quantities that have no justification for prophylactic, protective or other peaceful purposes;

2. Weapons, equipment or means of delivery designed to use such agents or toxins for hostile purposes or in armed conflict.

Article II

Each State Party to this Convention undertakes to destroy, or to divert to peaceful purposes, as soon as possible but not later than nine months after the entry into force of the Convention, all agents, toxins, weapons, equipment and means of delivery specified in article I of the Convention, which are in its possession or under its jurisdiction or control. In implementing the provisions of this article all necessary safety precautions shall be observed to protect populations and the environment.

Article III

Each State Party to this Convention undertakes not to transfer to any recipient whatsoever, directly or indirectly, and not in any way to assist, encourage, or induce any State, group of States or international organizations to manufacture or otherwise acquire any of the agents, toxins, weapons, equipment or means of delivery specified in article I of the Convention.

Article IV

Each State Party to this Convention shall, in accordance with its constitutional processes, take any necessary measures to prohibit and prevent the development, production, stockpiling, acquisition or retention of the agents, toxins, weapons, equipment and means of delivery specified in article I of the Convention, within the territory of such State, under its jurisdiction or under its control anywhere.

Article V

The States Parties to this Convention undertake to consult one another and to cooperate in solving any problems which may arise in relation to the objective of, or in the application of the provisions of, the Convention. Consultation and cooperation pursuant to this article may also be undertaken through appropriate international procedures within the framework of the United Nations and in accordance with its Charter.

Article VI

1. Any State Party to this Convention which finds that any other State Party is acting in breach of obligations deriving from the provisions of the Convention may lodge a complaint with the Security

Council of the United Nations. Such a complaint should include all possible evidence confirming its validity, as well as a request for its consideration by the Security Council.

2. Each State Party to this Convention undertakes to cooperate in carrying out any investigation which the Security Council may initiate, in accordance with the provisions of the Charter of the United Nations, on the basis of the complaint received by the Council. The Security Council shall inform the States Parties to the Convention of the results of the investigation.

Article VII

Each State Party to this Convention undertakes to provide or support assistance, in accordance with the United Nations Charter, to any Party to the Convention which so requests, if the Security Council decides that such Party has been exposed to danger as a result of violation of the Convention.

Article VIII

Nothing in this Convention shall be interpreted as in any way limiting or detracting from the obligations assumed by any State under the Protocol for the Prohibition of the Use in War of Asphyxiating, Poisonous or Other Gases, and of Bacteriological Methods of Warfare, signed at Geneva on June 17, 1925.

Article IX

Each State Party to this Convention affirms the recognized objective of effective prohibition of chemical weapons and, to this end, undertakes to continue negotiations in good faith with a view to reaching early agreement on effective measures for the prohibition of their development, production and stockpiling and for their destruction, and on appropriate measures concerning equipment and means of delivery specifically designed for the production or use of chemical agents for weapons purposes.

Article X

1. The States Parties to this Convention undertake to facilitate, and have the right to participate in, the fullest possible exchange of

equipment, materials and scientific and technological information for the use of bacteriological (biological) agents and toxins for peaceful purposes. Parties to the Convention in a position to do so shall also cooperate in contributing individually or together with other States or international organizations to the further development and application of scientific discoveries in the field of bacteriology (biology) for prevention of disease, or for other peaceful purposes.

2. This Convention shall be implemented in a manner designed to avoid hampering the economic or technological development of States Parties to the Convention or international cooperation in the field of peaceful bacteriological (biological) activities, including the international exchange of bacteriological (biological) agents and toxins and equipment for the processing, use or production of bacteriological (biological) agents and toxins for peaceful purposes in accordance with the provisions of the Convention.

Article XI

Any State Party may propose amendments to this Convention. Amendments shall enter into force for each State Party accepting the amendments upon their acceptance by a majority of the States Parties to the Convention and thereafter for each remaining State Party on the date of acceptance by it.

Article XII

Five years after the entry into force of this Convention, or earlier if it is requested by a majority of Parties to the Convention by submitting a proposal to this effect to the Depositary Governments, a conference of States Parties to the Convention shall be held at Geneva, Switzerland, to review the operation of the Convention, with a view to assuring that the purposes of the preamble and the provisions of the Convention, including the provisions concerning negotiations on chemical weapons, are being realized. Such review shall take into account any new scientific and technological developments relevant to the Convention.

Article XIII

1. This Convention shall be of unlimited duration.

2. Each State Party to this Convention shall in exercising its national sovereignty have the right to withdraw from the Convention if it decides that extraordinary events, related to the subject matter of the Convention, have jeopardized the supreme interests of its country. It shall give notice of such withdrawal to all other States Parties to the Convention and to the United Nations Security Council three months in advance. Such notice shall include a statement of the extraordinary events it regards as having jeopardized its supreme interests.

Article XIV

1. This Convention shall be open to all States for signature. Any State which does not sign the Convention before its entry into force in accordance with paragraph (3) of this Article may accede to it at any time.

2. This Convention shall be subject to ratification by signatory States. Instruments of ratification and instruments of accession shall be deposited with the Governments of the United States of America, the United Kingdom of Great Britain and Northern Ireland and the Union of Soviet Socialist Republics, which are hereby designated the Depositary Governments.

3. This Convention shall enter into force after the deposit of instruments of ratification by twenty-two Governments, including the Governments designated as Depositaries of the Convention.

4. For States whose instruments of ratification or accession are deposited subsequent to the entry into force of this Convention, it shall enter into force on the date of the deposit of their instruments of ratification or accession.

5. The Depositary Governments shall promptly inform all signatory and acceding States of the date of each signature, the date of deposit of each instrument of ratification or of accession and the date of the entry into force of this Convention, and of the receipt of other notices.

6. This Convention shall be registered by the Depositary Governments pursuant to Article 102 of the Charter of the United Nations.

Article XV

This Convention, the English, Russian, French, Spanish and Chinese texts of which are equally authentic, shall be deposited in the archives of the Depositary Governments. Duly certified copies of the Convention shall be transmitted by the Depositary Governments to the Governments of the signatory and acceding States.

Appendix D

Text of the Nuremberg Principles

Principle I

Any person who commits an act which constitutes a crime under international law is responsible therefor and liable to punishment.

Principle II

The fact that internal law does not impose a penalty for an act which constitutes a crime under international law does not relieve the person who committed the act from responsibility under international law.

Principle III

The fact that a person who committed an act which constitutes a crime under international law acted as Head of State or responsible government official does not relieve him from responsibility under international law.

Principle IV

The fact that a person acted pursuant to order of his Government or of a superior does not relieve him from responsibility under international law, provided a moral choice was in fact possible to him.

Source: Report of the International Law Commission Covering Its Second Session (5 June–29 July 1950), U.N. Doc. A/CN.4/34 (2 August 1950), 31–41.

Principle VI

The crimes hereinafter set out are punishable as crimes under international law:

    a. Crimes against peace:

        (i) Planning, preparation, initiation or waging of war of aggression or a war in violation of international treaties, agreements or assurances;

        (ii) Participation in a common plan or conspiracy of the accomplishment of any of the acts mentioned under (i).

    b. War crimes:

Violations of the laws or customs of war which include, but are not limited to, murder, ill-treatment or deportation to slave-labour or for any other purpose of civilian population of or in occupied territory, murder or ill-treatment of prisoners of war or persons on the seas, killing of hostages, plunder of public or private property, wanton destruction of cities, towns, or villages, or devastation not justified by military necessity.

    c. Crimes against humanity:

Murder, extermination, enslavement, deportation and other inhuman acts done against any civilian population, or persecutions on political, racial or religious grounds, when such acts are done or such persecutions are carried out in execution of or in connexion with any crime against peace or any war crime.

Principle VII

Complicity in the commision of a crime against peace, a war crime, or a crime against humanity as set forth in Principle VI is a crime under international law.

Appendix E

States Parties to the 1925 Geneva Protocol and the 1972 Biological Weapons Convention

Country	GP	BWC
Afghanistan	1986	1975
Albania		
Algeria		
Antigua and Barbados	S[a]	
Argentina	1969	1979
Australia	1930	1977
Austria	1928	1973
Bahamas		1986
Bahrain	S[a]	
Bangladesh	S[a]	1985
Barbados	1976	1973
Belgium	1928	1979
Belize		1986
Benin	1986	1975
Bhutan	1978	1978
Bolivia	1985	1975
Botswana		S
Brazil	1970	1973
Brunei Darusalaam		
Bulgaria	1934	1972
Burkina Faso (formerly Upper Volta)	1971	
Burma		S
Burundi		S
Byelorussia	1970	1975
Cameroon	A	
Canada	1930	1972

Country	GP	BWC
Cape Verde		1977
Central African Republic	1970	S
Chad		
Chile	1935	1980
China	1929	1984
Colombia		1983
Congo		1978
Cook Islands		
Costa Rica		1973
Cuba	1966	1976
Cyprus	1966	1973
Czechoslovakia	1938	1973
Denmark	1930	1973
Dominica		
Dominican Republic	1970	1973
Ecuador	1970	1975
Egypt	1928	S
El Salvador	S	S
Equitorial Guinea		
Ethiopia	1935	1975
Fiji	1973	1973
Finland	1929	1974
France	1926	1984
Gabon		S
Gambia	1966	S
German Democratic Republic	1929	1972
FR Germany	1929	1983
Ghana	1967	1975
Greece	1931	1975
Grenada	S[a]	1986
Guatemala	1983	1973
Guinea		
Guinea-Bissau	S[a]	1976
Guyana		S
Haiti	A	S
Holy See (Vatican City)	1966	
Honduras		1979
Hungary	1952	1972
Iceland	1967	1973

Country	GP	BWC
India	1930	1974
Indonesia	1971	S
Iran	1929	1973
Iraq	1931	S
Ireland	1930	1972
Israel	1969	
Italy	1928	1975
Ivory Coast	1970	S
Jamaica	1970	1975
Japan	1970	1982
Jordan	1977	1975
Kampuchea	1983	1983
Kenya	1970	1976
Kiribati		
Korea, Democratic People's Republic	S[a]	1987
Korea, Republic of (South)	S[a]	1987
Kuwait	1971	1972
Lao People's Democratic Republic	S[a]	1973
Lebanon	1969	1975
Lesotho	1972	1977
Liberia	1927	S
Libya	1971	1982
Liechtenstein		
Luxembourg	1936	1976
Madagascar	1967	S
Malawi	1970	S
Malaysia	1970	S
Maldives	1966	
Mali		S
Malta	1970	1975
Mauritania		
Mauritius	1970	1972
Mexico	1932	1974
Monaco	1967	
Mongolia	1968	1972
Morocco	1970	S
Nauru		
Nepal	1969	S
Netherlands	1930	1981

Country	GP	BWC
New Zealand	1930	1972
Nicaragua	S	1975
Niger	1967	1972
Nigeria	1968	1973
Niue		
Norway	1932	1973
Pakistan	1960	1974
Panama	1970	1974
Papua New Guinea	1981	1980
Paraguay	1933	1976
Peru	1985	1985
Philippines	1973	1973
Poland	1929	1973
Portugal	1930	1975
Qatar	1976	1975
Romania	1929	1979
Rwanda	1964	1975
Saint Lucia	S[a]	1986
Saint Vincent and the Grenadines		
Samoa, Western		
San Marino		1975
Sao Tome and Principe		1979
Saudi Arabia	1971	1972
Senegal	1977	1975
Seychelles		1979
Sierra Leone	1967	1976
Singapore		1975
Solomon Islands		1981
Somalia		S
South Africa	1930	1975
Spain	1929	1979
Sri Lanka	1954	1986
Sudan	1980	
Suriname		
Swaziland		
Sweden	1930	1976
Switzerland	1932	1976
Syria	1968	S
Taiwan[b]		1973

Country	GP	BWC
Tanzania	1963	S
Thailand	1931	1975
Togo	1971	1976
Tonga	1971	1976
Trinidad and Tobago	1970	
Tunisia	1967	1973
Turkey	1929	1974
Tuvalu		
Uganda	1965	
UK	1930	1975
Ukraine		1975
United Arab Emirates		S
Uruguay	1977	1981
USA	1975	1975
USSR	1928	1975
Venezuela	1928	1978
Viet Nam	1980	1980
Yemen Arab Republic	1971	S
Yemen, People's Democratic Republic	1986	1979
Yugoslavia	1929	1973
Zaire	A	1977
Zambia		

Sources: *SIPRI Yearbook* 1988; *Chemical Weapons Convention Bulletin* 3 (February 1989).

Note: This table gives the year of ratification, accession or succession (except where indicated otherwise). As of December 31, 1987, 110 states were parties to the Geneva Protocol and 110 states were parties to the Biological Weapons Convention.

GP = Geneva Protocol (1925)

BWC = Biological Weapons Convention (1972)

S = signed treaty

S^a = Signed treaty at the Paris Convention on Chemical Weapons, January 7–11, 1989.

A = announced intention to sign at the Paris Conference on Chemical Weapons, January 7–11, 1989.

b. The Geneva Protocol, signed in 1929 in the name of China, is taken to be valid for Taiwan. However, Taiwan has not confirmed its accession to the Geneva Protocol.

Appendix F

Final Declaration of the First Review Conference of the Parties to the Biological Weapons Convention

The States Parties to the Convention on the Prohibition of the Development, Production and Stockpiling of Bacteriological (Biological) and Toxin Weapons and on their destruction, having met in Geneva 3-21 March 1980 under the provisions of Article XII to review the operation of the Convention with a view to assuring that the purposes of the preamble and the provisions of the Convention are being realized:

Reaffirming their determination to act with a view to achieving effective progress towards general and complete disarmament including the prohibition and elimination of all types of weapons of mass destruction and convinced that the prohibition of the development, production and stockpiling of chemical and bacteriological (biological) weapons and their elimination, through effective measures, will facilitate the achievement of general and complete disarmament under strict and effective international control,

Recognizing the continuing importance of the Convention and its objectives and the common interest of mankind in the elimination of bacteriological (biological) and toxin weapons,

Affirming their belief that universal adherence to the Convention would enhance international peace and security, would not hamper economic or technological development, and further, would facilitate the wider exchange of information for the use for peaceful purposes,

Reaffirming their adherence to the principle and objectives of the Geneva Protocol of 17 June 1925 and calling upon all States to comply strictly with them,

Source: U.N. Doc. BWC/CONF.I/10.

Recalling that the General Assembly of the United Nations has repeatedly condemned all actions contrary to the said principles and objectives,

Recognizing the importance of achieving international agreement on effective measures for the prohibition of the development, production and stockpiling of chemical weapons and for their destruction as a matter of high priority.

Noting the relevant provisions of the Final Document of the Tenth Special Session of the General Assembly devoted to Disarmament,

Appealing to all States to refrain from any action which might place the Convention or any of its provisions in jeopardy,

Declare as follows:

The States Parties to the Convention reaffirm their strong determination for the sake of all mankind, to exclude completely the possibility of bacteriological (biological) agents and toxins being used as weapons. They reaffirm their strong support for the Convention, their continued dedication to its principles and objectives and their commitment to implement effectively its provisions.

Article I

The Conference notes the importance of Article I as the Article which defines the scope of the Convention and reaffirms its support for the provisions of this Article.

The Conference believes that Article I has proved sufficiently comprehensive to have covered recent scientific and technological developments relevant to the Convention.

Article II

The Conference notes the importance of Article II and emphasizes that States which become Parties to the Convention, in implementing the provisions of this Article, shall observe all necessary safety precautions to protect populations and the environment.

The Conference welcomes the declarations of several States Parties to the effect either that they do not posses and have never possessed agents, toxins, weapons, equipment or means of delivery specified in Article I of the Convention, or that having possessed

them they have destroyed them or diverted them to peaceful purposes. The Conference believes that such voluntary declarations
contribute to increased confidence in the Convention and believes
that States not having made such voluntary declarations should
do so.

Article III

The Conference notes the importance of the provisions of Article
III which proscribes the transfer of agents, toxins, weapons, equipment or means of delivery specified in Article I of the Convention to
any recipient whatsoever and the furnishing of assistance, encouragement or inducement to any State, group of States or international organizations to manufacture or otherwise acquire them.

Article IV

The Conference notes the provisions of Article IV, which requires
each State Party to take any necessary measures to prohibit and
prevent the development, production, stockpiling, acquisition or
retention of the agents, toxins, weapons, equipment and means of
delivery specified in Article I of the Convention, within its territory,
under its jurisdiction or under its control anywhere, and calls upon
all States Parties which have not yet taken any necessary measures
in accordance with their constitutional processes to do so immediately.

The Conference invites States Parties which have found it necessary to enact specific legislation or take other regulatory measures
relevant to this Article to make available the appropriate texts to
the United Nations Centre for Disarmament, for the purposes of
consultation.

Article V

The Conference notes the importance of Article V which contains
the undertaking of States Parties to consult one another and to
co-operate in solving any problems which may arise in relation
to the objective of, or in the application of the provisions of, the
Convention.

The Conference considers that the flexibility of the provisions
concerning consultations and co-operation on any problems which

may arise in relation to the objective, or in the application of the provisions of, the Convention, enables interested States Parties to use various international procedures which would make it possible to ensure effectively and adequately the implementation of the Convention provisions taking into account the concern expressed by the Conference participants to this effect.

These procedures include, *inter alia*, the right of any State Party subsequently to request that a consultative meeting open to all States Parties be convened at expert level.

The Conference, noting the concerns and differing views expressed on the adequacy of Article V, believes that this question should be further considered at an appropriate time.

Article VI

The Conference also notes the importance of Article VI, which in addition to the procedures contained in Article V, provides for any State Party, which finds that any other State Party is acting in breach of its obligations under the Convention, to lodge a complaint with the United Nations Security Council, and under which each State Party undertakes to co-operate in carrying out any investigation which the Security Council may initiate.

The Conference further notes that no State Party has invoked these provisions.

Article VII

The Conference notes with satisfaction that it has not proved necessary to invoke the provisions of Article VII.

Article VIII

The Conference reaffims that nothing contained in the Convention shall be interperted as in any way limiting or detracting from the obligations assumed by any State under the Protocol for the prohibition of the use in war of asphyxiating, poisonous or other gases and of bacteriological methods of warfare, signed at Geneva on 17 June 1925. The Conference calls on those States Parties to the Convention which are Parties to the Protocol to comply strictly with its provisions and those States not yet Parties to the said Protocol to ratify or accede to it at the earliest possible date.

Article IX

The Conference notes the importance of the provisions of Article IX and of the preambular paragraphs concerning the commitment of States Parties to continue negotiations in good faith with a view to reaching early agreement on effective measures for the prohibition of the development, production and stockpiling of chemical weapons and for their destruction. The Conference deeply regrets that such agreement has not yet become a reality despite the fact that eight years have already elapsed since the Convention was opened for signature.

The Conference urges the Committee on Disarmament to undertake negotiations on an agreement on the complete and effective prohibition of the development, production and stockpiling of all chemical weapons and on their destruction, as a matter of high priority, taking into account all existing proposals and future initiatives. To this end, the Conference welcomes the establishment, by the Committee on Disarmament, of an *ad hoc* working group on chemical weapons and urges all the members of the Committee to contribute towards the fulfilment of its mandate.

The Conference takes note of the bilateral USA-USSR report (CD/48) presented to the Committee on Disarmament on the progress of their negotiations undertaken with a view to presenting a joint initiative to that Committee and notes their stated intention to continue intensive negotiations to this end.

The Conference reaffirms the obligation assumed by States Parties to the Convention to continue negotiations in good faith towards the recognized objective of an early agreement on complete, effective and adequately verifiable measures for the prohibition of the development, production and stockpiling of chemical weapons and for their destruction.

Article X

The Conference notes that since the entry into force of the Convention, increasing importance has been attached by the International community to the principle that the disarmament process should help promote economic and social development, particularly in the developing countries. Accordingly, the Conference calls upon States Parties, especially developed countries, to increase, individually, or together with other States or international organizations, their scientific and technological co-operation, particularly with developing countries, in the peaceful uses of bacteriological (biological) agents and toxins. Such co-operation should include, *inter alia,* the transfer and exchange of information, training of persoonel and transfer of materials and equipment on a more systematic and long-term basis.

Furthermore, the Conference notes with satisfaction that the implementation of the Convention has not hampered the economic or tehnological development of States parties.

The Conference requests the United Nations Secretariat to include in the background materials prepared for the second Review Conference of the Parties to the Convention on the Prohibition of the Development, Production and Stockpiling of Bacteriological (Biological) and Toxin Weapons and on Their Destruction, information on the implementation of Article X by States Parties.

Article XI

The Conference notes the importance of the provisions of Article XI and that during the first five years of the operation of the Convention these provisions have not been invoked.

Article XII

The Conference welcomes the spirit of co-operation in which this Review Conference was conducted, and believes that such conferences constitute an effective method of reviewing the operation of the Convention with a view to ensuring that its purposes and provisions are being realized, in particular with respect to any new scientific and technological developments relevant to the Convention.

The Conference decides that a second Review Conference shall be held in Geneva at the request of a majority of States Parties not earlier than 1985 and, in any case, not later than 1990.

Any information provided by States Parties on scientific and technological developments relevant to the Convention, and on its implementation, shall be made available periodically to States Parties, in particular through the United Nations Centre for Disarmament.

Article XIII

The Conference notes the provisions of Article III and expresses its satisfaction that no State Party to the Convention has exercised its right to withdraw from the Convention.

Article XIV

The Conference notes with satisfaction that 81 States have ratified the Convention, 6 States have acceded to the Convention and a further 37 States have signed but have yet to ratify the Convention. The Conference calls upon all signatory States which have not ratified the Convention to do so without delay and upon those States which have not signed the Convention to join the States Parties thereto in their efforts to eliminate the risk of biological warfare.

Article XV

The Conference notes the provisions of Article XV.

Appendix G

Final Declaration of the Second Review Conference of the Parties to the Biological Weapons Convention, September 1986

Preamble

The States Parties to the Convention on the Prohibition of the Development, Production and Stockpiling of Bacteriological (Biological) and Toxin Weapons and on their Destruction, having met in Geneva 8-26 September 1986 in accordance with a decision by the First Review Conference 1980 and at the request of a majority of States Parties to the Convention, to review the operation of the Convention with a view to assuring that the purposes of the preamble and the provisions of the Convention are being realized:

Reaffirming their determination to act with a view to achieving effective progress towards general and complete disarmament including the prohibition and elimination of all types of weapons of mass destruction and convinced that the prohibition of the development, production and stockpiling of chemical and bacteriological (biological) weapons and their elimination, through effective measures, will facilitate the achievement of general and complete disarmament under strict and effective international control,

Recognizing the continuing importance of the Convention and its objectives and the common interest of mankind in the elmination of bacteriological (biological) and toxin weapons,

Affirming their belief that universal adherence to the Convention would enhance international peace and security, would not hamper economic or technological development, and further, would facilitate the wider exchange of information for the use of bacteriological (biological) agents for peaceful purposes,

Confirming the common interest in strengthening the authority and the effectiveness of the Convention, to promote confidence and co-operation among States Parties,

Source: U.N. Doc. BWC/CONF.II/13.

Affirming the importance of strengthening international co-operation in the field of biotechnology, genetic engineering, micro-biology and other related areas,

Reaffirming their adherence to the principle and objectives of the Geneva Protocol of 17 June 1925 and calling upon all States to comply strictly with them,

Recalling that the General Assembly of the United Nations has repeatedly condemned all actions contrary to the said principles and objectives.

Recognizing the importance of achieving as a matter of high priority an international convention on the complete and effective prohibition of the development, production and stockpiling of chemical weapons and on their destruction,

Noting the relevant provisions of the Final Document of the tenth Special Session of the General Assembly devoted to Disarmament,

Appealing to all States to refrain from any action which might place the Convention or any of its provisions in jeopardy,

Declare their strong determination for the sake of all mankind, to exclude completely the possibility of microbial, or other biological agents, or toxins being used·as weapons and reaffirm their strong support for the Convention, their continued dedication to its principles and objectives and their legal obligation under international law to implement and strictly comply with its provisions.

Article I

The Conference notes the importance of Article I as the Article which defines the scope of the Convention and reaffirms its support for the provisions of this Article.

The Conference concludes that the scope of Article I covers scientific and technological developments relevant to the Convention.

The Conference notes statements by some States Parties that compliance with Articles I, II and III was in their view subject to grave doubt in some cases and that efforts to resolve these concerns had not been successful. The Conference notes the statements by other States Parties that such a doubt was unfounded and, in their view, not in accordance with the Convention. The Conference agrees that the application of States Parties of a positive approach in questions of compliance in accordance with the provisions of the Convention was in the interest of all States Parties and that this would serve to promote confidence among States Parties.

The Conference, conscious of apprehensions arising from relevant scientific and technological developments, *inter alia*, in the fields of microbiology, geneic engineering and biotechnology, and the possibilities of their use for purposes inconsistent with the objectives and the provisions of the Convention, reaffirms that the undertaking given by the States Parties in Article I applies to all such developments.

The Conference reaffirms that the Convention unequivocally appies to all natural or artifically created microbial or other biological agents or toxins whatever their origin or method of production. Consequently, toxins (both proteinaceous and non-proteinaceous) of a microbial, animal or vegetable nature and their synthetically produced analogues are covered.

Article II

The Conference notes the importance of Article II and welcomes the statements made by States which have become Parties to the Convention since the First Review Conference that they do not possess agents, toxins, weapons, equipment or means of delivery referred to in Article I of the Convention. The Conference believes that such statements enhance confidence in the Convention.

The Conference stresses that States which become Parties to the Convention in implementing the provisions of this Article, shall observe all necessary safety precautions to protect populations and the environment.

Article III

The Conference notes the importance of Article III and welcomes the statements which States that have acceded to the Convention have made to the effect that they have not transferred agents, toxins, weapons, equipment or means of delivery, specified in Article I of the Convention, to any recipient whatsoever and have not furnished assistance, encouragement or inducement to any State, group of States or international organizations to manufacture or otherwise acquire them. The Conference affirms that Article III is sufficiently comprehensive so as to cover any recipient whatsoever at international, national or sub-national levels.

The Conference notes that the provisions of this article should not be used to impose restrictions and/or limitations on the transfer for purposes consistent with the objectives and the provisions of the Convention of scientific knowledge, technology, equipment and materials to States Parties.

Article IV

The Conference notes the importance of Article IV, under which each State Party shall, in accordance with its constitutional processes, take any necessary measures to prohibit or prevent any acts or actions which would contravene the Convention.

The Conference calls upon all States Parties which have not yet taken any necessary measures in accordance with their constitutional processes, as required by the Article, to do so immediately.

The Conference notes that States Parties, as requested by the First Review Conference, have provided the United Nations Department for Disarmament Affairs with information on and the texts of specific legislation enacted or other regulatory measures taken by them, relevant to this Article. The Conference invites States Parties to continue to provide such information and texts to the United Nations Department for Disarmament Affairs, for purposes of consultation.

The Conference notes the importance of:

• legislative, administrative and other measures designed effectively to guarantee compliance with the provisions of the Convention within the territory, under the jurisdiction or control of a State Party;

• legislative regarding the physical protection of laboratories and facilities to prevent unauthorized access to and removal of pathogenic or toxic material; and

• inclusion in textbooks, and in medical, scientific and military educational programmes of information dealing with the prohibition of bacteriological (biological) and toxin weapons and the provisions of the Geneva Protocol

and believes that such measures which States might undertake in accordance with their constitvtional process would strengthen the effectiveness of the Convention.

Article V

The Conference notes the importance of Article V and reaffirms the obligation assumed by States Parties to consult and co-operate with one another in solving any problems which may arise in relation to the objective of, or in the application of the provisions of, the Convention.

The Conference reaffirms that consultation and co-operation pursuant to this Article may also be undertaken through appropriate international procedures within the framework of the United Nations and in accordance with its Charter.

The Conference confirms the conclusion in the Final Declaration of the First Review Conference that these procedures include, *inter alia*, the right of any State Party to request that a consultative meeting open to all States Parties be convened at expert level.

The Conference stresses the need for all States to deal seriously with compliance issues and emphasizes that the failure to do so undermines the Convention and the arms control process in general.

The Conference appeals to States Parties to make all possible efforts to solve any problems which may rise in relation to the objective of or in the application of the provisions of the Convention with a view towards encouraging strict observance of the provisions subscribed to. The Conference further requests that information on such efforts be provided to the Third Review Conference.

The Conference, taking into account views expressed concerning the need to strengthen the implementation of the provisions of Article V, has agreed:

• that a consultative meeting shall be promptly convened when requested by a State Party,

• that a consultative meeting may consider any problems which may arise in the relation to the objective of, or in the application of the provisions of the Convention, suggest ways and means for further clarifying, *inter alia*, with assistance of technical experts, any matter considered ambiguous or unresolved, as well as initiate appropriate international procedures within the framework of the United Nations and in accordance with its Charter,

• that the consultative meeting, or any State Party, may request specialized assistance in solving any problems which may arise in relation to the objective of, or in the application of, the provisions of the Convention, through, *inter alia*, appropriate international procedures within the framework of the United Nations and in accordance with its Charter,

• The Conference considers that States Parties shall co-operate with the consultative meeting in its considerations of any problems which may arise in the relation to the objectives of, or in the application of, the provisions of the Convention, and in clarifying ambiguous and unresolved matters, as well as co-operate in appropriate international procedures within the framework of the United Nations and in accordance with its Charter.

The Conference, mindful of the provisions of Article V and Article X and determined to strengthen the authority of the Convention and to enhance confidence in the implementation of its provisions, agrees that the States Parties are to implement, on the basis of mutual co-operation, the following measures, in order to prevent or reduce the occurence of ambiguities, doubts and suspicions, and in order to improve international co-operation in the field of peaceful bacteriological (biological) activities.

1. Exchange of data, including name, location, scope and general description of activities, on research centres and laboratories that meet very high national or international safety standards established for handling, for permitted purposes, biological materials that pose a high individual and community risk, or specialize in permitted biological activities directy related to the Convention.

2. Exchange of information on all outbreaks of infectious diseases and similar occurences caused by toxins, that seem to deviate from the normal pattern as regards type, development, place, or time of occurrence. If posible, the information provided would include, as soon as it is available, data on the type of disease, approximate area affected, and number of cases.

3. Encouragement of publication of results of biological research directly related to the Convention, in scientific journals generally available to States Parties, as well as promotion of use for permitted purposes of knowledge gained in this research.

4. Active promotion of contacts between scientists engaged in biological research directly related to the Convention, including exchanges for joint research on a mutually agreed basis.

The Conference decides to hold an *Ad Hoc* meeting of scientific and technical experts from States Parties, to finalize the modalities for the exchange of information and data by working out, *inter alia*, appropriate forms to be used by States Parties for the exchange of information agreed to in this Final Declaration, thus enabling the States Parties to follow a standardized procedure. The group shall meet in Geneva for the period of 31 March-15 April 1987 and shall communicate the results of the work to the States Parties immediately thereafter.

Pending the results of this meeting the Conference urges States Parties to promptly apply these measures and report the data agreed upon to the United Nations Department for Disarmament Affairs.

The Conference requests the United Nations Department for Disarmament Affairs to make available the information received to all States Parties.

Article VI

The Conference also notes the importance of Article VI, which in addition to the procedures contained in Article V, provides for any State Party, which finds that any other State Party is acting in breach of its obligations under the Convention, to lodge a complaint with the United Nations Security Council, and under which each State Party undertakes to co-operate in carrying out any investigation which the Security Council may initiate.

The Conference notes the need to further improve and strengthen this and other procedures to enhance greater confidence in the Convention. The Conference considers that the Security Council may, if it deems it necessary, request the advice of the World Health Organization in carrying out any investigation of complaints lodged with the Council.

Article VII

The Conference notes that these provisions have not been invoked.

Article VIII

The Conference reaffirms the importance of Article VIII and stresses the importance of the Protocol for the prohibition of the use in war of asphyxiating, poisonous or other gases and of bacteriological methods of warfare.

The Conference reaffirms that nothing contained in the Convention shall be interpreted as in any way limiting or detracting from the obligations assumed by any State under the Protocol for the prohibition of the use in war of asphyxiating, poisonous or other gases and of bacteriological methods of warfare, signed at Geneva on 17 June 1925. Noting the report of the Security Council (S/17911), the Conference appeals to all States Parties to the Geneva Protocol of 1925 to fulfil their obligations assumed under that Protocol and urges all States not yet Parties to the said Protocol to adhere to it at the earliest possible date.

Article IX

The Conference reaffirms the obligation assumed by States Parties to continue negotiations in good faith towards an early agreement on effective measures for the prohibition of the development, production and stockpiling of chemical weapons and for their destruction.

All States parties participating in the Conference reiterate their strong commitment to this important goal.

The Conference notes with satisfaction the substantial progress made in the negotiations on a convention on the prohibition of chemical weapons in the Conference on Disarmament during the period under review. The Conference also takes note of the bilateral talks between the Union of Soviet Socialist Republics and the United States of America on all aspects of the prohibition of chemical weapons.

The Conference nevertheless deeply regrets that an agreement on a convention on chemical weapons has not yet been reached,

The Conference urges the Conference on Disarmament to exert all possible efforts to conclude an agreement on a total ban of chemical weapons with effective verification provisions by the earliest possible date.

Article X

The Conference emphasizes the increasing importance of the provisions of Article X, especially in the light of recent scientific and technological developments in the field of bio-technology, bacteriological (biological) agents and toxins with peaceful applications, which have vastly increased the potential for co-operation between

States to help promote economic and social development, and scientific and technological progress, particularly in the developing countries, in conformity with their interests, needs and priorities.

The Conference, while acknowledging what has already been done towards this end, notes with concern the increasing gap between the developed and the developing countries in the field of biotechnology, genetic engineering, microbiology and other related areas. The Conference accordingly urges States Parties to provide wider access to and share their scientific and technological knowledge in this field, on an equal and non-discriminatory basis, in particular with the developing countries, for the benefit of all mankind.

The Conference urges that States Parties take specific measures within their competence for the promotion of the fullest possible international co-operation in this field through their active intervention. Such measures could include *inter alia*:

• transfer and exchange of information concerning research programmes in bio-sciences;

• wider transfer and exchange of information, materials and equipment among States on a systematic and long-term basis;

• active promotion of contacts between scientists and technical personnel on a reciprocal basis, in relevant fields;

• increased technical co-operation including training opportunities to developing countries in the use of bio-sciences and genetic engineering for peaceful purposes;

• facilitating the conclusion of bilateral, regional and multiregional agreements providing on a mutually advantageous, equal and non-discriminatory basis, for their participation in the development and application of biotechnology;

• encouraging the co-ordination of national and regional programmes and working out in an appropriate manner the ways and means of co-operation in this field.

The Conference calls for greater co-operation in international public health and disease control.

The Conference urges that co-operation under Article X should be actively pursued both within the bilateral and the multilateral framework and further urges the use of existing institutional means within the United Nations system and the full utilization of the possibilities provided by the specialized agencies and other international organizations.

The Conference, noting that co-operation would be best initiated by improved institutionalized direction and co-ordination, recommends that measures to ensure co-operation on such a basis be pursued within the existing means of the United Nations system. Accordingly, the Conference requests the Secretary-General of the United Nations to propose for inclusion on the agenda of a relevant United Nations body, a discussion and examination of the means for improving institutional mechanisms in order to facilitate the fullest possible exchange of equipment, materials and scientific and technological information for the use of bacteriological (biological) agents and toxins for peaceful purposes. The Conference recommends that invitations to participate in this discussion and examination should be extended to all States Parties, whether or not they are members of the United Nations, and concerned specialized agenices.

The Conference requests the States Parties and the United Nations Secretariat to include in the document materials prepared for the above-mentioned discussion of States Parties, information and suggestions on the implementation of Article X, taking into account the preceding paragraphs. Furthermore, it urges the specialized agencies, *inter alia*, FAO, WHO, UNESCO, WIPO and UNIDO, to participate in this discussion and fully co-operate with the Secretary-General of the United Nations and requests the Secretary-General to send all relevant information of this Conference to these agencies.

The Conference, referring to paragraph 35 of the Final Document of the First Special Session of the General Assembly, devoted to Disarmament, stresses the importance of the obligations under Article X promoting economic and social development of developing countries, particularly in the light of the United Nations Conference on the Relationship between Disarmament and Development, for the States participating therein, scheduled for 1987.

The Conference, to ensure compliance with Article X, also requests States Parties and the United Nations Secretariat to provide information relevant to the implementation of the Article for examination by the next conference of States Parties.

The Conference upholds that the above-mentioned measures would positively strengthen the Convention.

Article XI

The Conference notes the importance of Article II and that since the entry into force of the Convention the provisions of the Article have not been invoked.

Article XII

The Conference decides that a Third Review Conference shall be held in Geneva at the request of a majority of States Parties not later than 1991.

The Conference, noting the differing views with regard to verification, decides that the Third Review Conference shall consider, *inter alia*:

• the impact of scientific and technological developments relevant to the Convention,

• the relevance for effective implementation of the Convention of the results achieved in the negotiations on prohibition of chemical weapons,

• the effectiveness of the provisions in Article V for consultation and co-operation and of the co-operative measures agreed in this Final Declaration, and

• in the light of these considerations and of the provisions of Article XI, whether or not further actions are called for to create further co-operative measures in the context of Article V, or legally binding improvements to the Convention, or a combination of both.

Article XIII

The Conference notes the provisions of Article XIII and expresses its satisfaction that no State Party to the Convention has exercised its right to withdraw from the Convention.

Article XIV

The Conference notes with satisfaction that a significant number of States have ratified or acceded to the Convention since the First Review Conference and that there are now more than 100 States Parties to the Convention, including all the permanent Members of the Security Council of the United Nations.

The Conference calls upon States which have not yet ratified or acceded to the Convention to do so without delay and upon those States which have not signed the Convention to join the States Parties thereto thus contributing to the achievement of universal adherence to the Convention.

The Conference makes an urgent appeal to all States Parties to the Convention on the Prohibition of the Development, Production and Stockpiling of Bacteriological (Biological) and Toxin Weapons and on their Destruction, which did not participate in its work, to give their effective co-operation and take part more actively in the common endeavour of all the Contracting Parties to strengthen the objectives and purposes of the Convention. In this connection, the Convention urges all States Parties that were absent to take part in the future work envisaged in this Final Declaration.

Article XV

The Conference notes the provisions of Article XV.

Appendix H

Text of National Security Decision Memorandum 35, November 25, 1969

National Security Decision Memorandum 35

To: The Vice President
       The Secretary of State
       The Secretary of Defense
       The Director, Central Intelligence Agency
       The Director, Arms Control and Disarmament Agency
       The Director, Office of Emergency Preparedness
       The Director, Office of Science and Technology

Subject: United States Policy in Chemical Warfare Program and Bacteriological/Biological Research Program

Following consideration by the National Security Council, the President has decided that:

1. The term Chemical and Biological Warfare (CBW) will no longer be used. The reference henceforth should be to the two categories separately—The Chemical Warfare Program and The Biological Research Program.

2. With respect to Chemical Warfare:

   a. The objective of the U.S. program will be to deter the use of chemical weapons by other nations and to provide a retaliatory capability if deterrence fails.

   b. The renunciation of the first use of lethal chemical weapons is reaffirmed.

   c. This renunciation is hereby applied to incapacitating chemical weapons as well.

Note: This version of NSDM 35 was released following a classification review on March 16, 1989. The withheld portions are classified for national security reasons under provisions of Executive Order 12356.

d. This renunciation does not apply to the use of riot control agents or herbicides. A special NSDM on authorization for their use will be issued.

e. The Administration will submit the Geneva Protocol of 1925, "Protocol for the Prohibition of the use in War of Asphyxiating Poisonous or Other Gases, and of Bacteriological/Biological Methods of Warfare," to the Senate for its advice and consent to ratification. An appropriate interpretive statement will be prepared by the Department of State in coordination with the Department of Defense to the effect that the United States does not consider that the Protocol prohibits the use of chemical herbicides or riot control agents, widely used domestically, in war. The statement will be unilateral in form and will not be a formal reservation.

f. [Classified]

g. The Secretary of Defense, in cooperation with the Director of the Office of Science and Technology, shall continue to develop and improve controls and safety measures in all Chemical Warfare programs.

h. [Classified]

i. The Under Secretaries Committee shall conduct an annual review of United States Chemical Warfare programs and public information policy, and will make recommendations to the President.

3. With respect to Bacteriological/Biological programs:

a. The United States will renounce the use of lethal methods of bacteriological/biological warfare.

b. The United States will similarly renounce the use of all other methods of bacteriological/biological warfare (for example, incapacitating agents).

c. The United States bacteriological/biological programs will be confined to research and development for defensive purposes (immunization, safety measures, et cetera). This does not preclude research into those of offensive aspects of bacteriological/biological agents necessary to determine what defensive measures are required.

d. The Secretary of Defense will submit recommendations about the disposal of existing stocks of bacteriological/biological weapons.

e. The United States shall associate itself with the principles and objectives of the Draft Convention Prohibiting the Use of Biological Methods of Warfare presented by the United Kingdom at the Eighteen-Nation Disarmament Conference in Geneva, on 26 August 1969. Recommendation as to association with specific provisions of the Draft Convention should be prepared by the Secretary of State and the Director of the Arms Control and Disarmament Agency, in coordination with other interested agencies, for the President's consideration.

f. The Secretary of Defense, in conjunction with the Director of the Office of Science and Technology, shall continue to develop controls and safety measures in all bacteriological/ biological programs.

g. [Classified]

h. The Under Secretaries Committee shall conduct an annual review of United States Bacteriological/Biological Research Programs and public information policy, and will make recommendations to the President.

                                        Henry A. Kissinger

cc: Chairman, Joint Chiefs of Staff

Appendix I

Text of S. 993

A BILL To implement the Convention of the Prohibition of the Development, Production, and Stockpiling of Bacteriological (Biological) and Toxin Weapons and Their Destruction, by prohibiting certain conduct relating to biological weapons, and for other purposes

Be it enacted by the Senate and House of Representatives of the United States of America in Congress assembled,

Section 1. Short Title.
This Act may be cited as the "Biological Weapons Anti-Terrorism Act of 1989".

Section 2. Purpose and Intent.
    (a) PURPOSE.—The purpose of this Act is to—

        (1) implement the Biological Weapons Convention, an international agreement unanimously ratified by the United States Senate in 1974 and signed by more than 100 other nations, including the Soviet Union; and

        (2) protect the United States against the threat of biological terrorism.

    (b) INTENT OF ACT.—Nothing in this Act is intended to restrain or restrict peaceful scientific research or development.

Section 3. Title 18 Amendments.
    (a) IN GENERAL.—Title 18, United States Code, is amended by inserting after chapter 9 the following:

Note: Text is that of the bill approved unanimously by the United States Senate on November 21, 1989.

"*Chapter 10—Biological Weapons*

"Sec.
"175. Prohibitions with respect to biological weapons.
"176. Seizure, forfeiture, and destruction.
"177. Injunctions.
"178. Definitions.

"*§ 175. Prohibitions with respect to biological weapons*

"(a) IN GENERAL.—Whoever knowingly develops, produces, stockpiles, transfers, acquires, retains, or possesses any biological agent, toxin, or delivery system for use as a weapon, or knowingly assists a foreign state or any organization to do so, shall be fined under this title or imprisoned for life or any term of years, or both. There is extraterritorial Federal jurisdiction over an offense under this section committed by or against a national of the United States.

"(b) DEFINITION.—For purposes of this section, the term 'for use as a weapon' does not include the development, production, transfer, acquisition, retention, or possession of any biological agent, toxin, or delivery system for prophylactic, protective, or other peaceful purposes.

"*§ 176. Seizure, forefeiture, and destruction*

"(a) IN GENERAL.—(1) Except as provided in paragraph (2), the Attorney General may request the issuance, in the same manner as provided for a search warrant, of a warrant authorizing the seizure of any biological agent, toxin, or delivery system that—

"(A) exists by reason of conduct prohibited under section 175 of this title; or

"(B) is of a type or in a quantity that under the circumstances has no apparent justification for prophylactic, protective, or other peaceful purposes.

"(2) In exigent circumstances, seizure and destruction of any biological agent, toxin, or delivery system described in subparagraphs (A) and (B) of paragraph (1) may be made upon probable cause without the necessity for a warrant.

"(b) PROCEDURE.—Property seized pursuant to subsection (a) shall be forfeited to the United States after notice to potential claimants and an opportunity for a hearing. At such hearing, the government shall bear the burden of persuasion by a preponderance of the evidence. Except as inconsistent herewith, the same procedures and provisions of law relating to a forefeiture under the customs laws shall extend to a seizure or forfeiture under this section. The Attorney General may provide for the destruction or other appropriate disposition of any biological agent, toxin, or delivery system seized and forfeited pursuant to this section.

"(c) AFFIRMATIVE DEFENSE.—It is an affirmative defense against a forfeiture under subsection (a)(1)(B) of this section that—

"(1) such biological agent, toxin, or delivery system is for a prophylactic, protective, or other peaceful purpose; and

"(2) such biological agent, toxin, or delivery system, is of a type and quantity reasonable for that purpose.

"§ 177. Injunctions

"(a) IN GENERAL.—The United States may obtain in a civil action an injunction against—

"(1) the conduct prohibited under section 175 of this title;

"(2) the preparation, solicitation, attempt, or conspiracy to engage in conduct prohibited under section 175 of this title; or

"(3) the development, production, stockpiling, transferring, acquisition, retention, or possession, or the attempted development, production, stockpiling, transferring, acquisition, retention, or prossession of any biological agent, toxin, or delivery system of a type or in a quantity that under the circumstances has no apparent justification for prophylactic, protective, or other peaceful purposes.

"(b) AFFIRMATIVE DEFENSE.—It is an affirmative defense against an injunction under subsection (a)(3) of this section that—

"(1) the conduct sought to be enjoined is for a prophylactic, protective, or other peaceful purpose; and

"(2) such biological agent, toxin, or delivery system is of a type and quantity reasonable for that purpose.

"§ 178. Definitions

"As used in this chapter—

"(1) the term 'biological agent' means any microorganism, virus, or infectious substance, capable of causing—

"(A) death, disease, or other biological malfunction in a human, an animal, a plant, or another living organism;

"(B) deterioration of food, water, equipment, supplies, or material of any kind; or

"(C) deleterious alteration of the environment;

"(2) the term 'toxin' means, whatever its origin or method of production—

"(A) any poisonous substance produced by a living organism; or

"(B) any poisonous isomer, homolog, or derivative of such a substance;

"(3) the term 'delivery system' means—

"(A) any apparatus, equipment, device, or means of delivery specifically designed to delivery or disseminate a biological agent, toxin, or vector; or

"(B) any vector; and

"(4) the term 'vector' means a living organism capable of carrying a biological agent or toxin to a host."

(b) WIRE INTERCEPTION.—Section 2516(c) of title 18, United States Code, is amended by adding "section 175 (relating to biological weapons)," after "section 33 (relating to destruction of motor vehicles or motor vehicle facilities),".

(c) CLERICAL AMENDMENT.—The table of chapters for part I of title 18, United States Code, is amended by inserting after the item relating to chapter 9 the following new item:

"10. Biological Weapons .... *175.".*

Appendix J

Text of H.R. 806

101st Congress, 1st Session, H.R. 806

To require the Secretary of Defense to disclose all biological agents used in, or the subject of, research, development, testing, or evaluation which is conducted under the Biological Defense Research Program.

In the House of Representatives

February 2, 1989
Mr. OWENS of introduced the following bill; which was referred to the Committee on Armed Services

A Bill

To require the Secretary of Defense to disclose all biological agents used in, or the subject of, research, development, testing, or evaluation which is conducted under the Biological Defense Research Program.

Be it enacted by the Senate and House of Representatives of the United States of America in Congress assembled,

Section 1. Short Title.
This Act may be cited as the "Biological Defense Safety Act of 1989".

Sec. 2. Identification of Biological Agents.
(a) IDENTIFICATION REQUIRED.—Not later than 60 days after the end of a fiscal year, the Secretary of Defense shall publish in the Federal Register a report identifying—

(1) each biological agent used in, or the subject of, research conducted under the Biological Defense Research Program during such fiscal year;

(2) the unique and complete biological properties of such agent;

(3) the location at which research under the Biological Defense Research Program involving such agent is conducted; and

(4) the biosafety level utilized in conducting such research.

(b) TYPES OF RESEARCH PROJECTS AFFECTED.—Subsection (a) shall apply to research conducted under the Biological Defense Research Program whether such research is performed—

(1) by contract with, or by grant to, educational or research institutions, private businesses, or other agenices of the United States;

(2) through one or more of the military departments; or

(3) by using employees and consultants of the Department of Defense.

Sec. 3. Definitions.
For purposes of this Act:

(1) The term "biosafety level" means the applicable biosafety level described in the publication entitled *Biosafety in Microbiological and Biomedical Laboratories* (CDC-NIH, 1984).

(2) The term "research" includes research, development, testing, and evaluation.

Appendix K

The Pledge against the Military Use of Biological Research

We, the undersigned biologists and chemists, oppose the use of our research for military purposes. Rapid advances in biotechnology have catalyzed a growing interest by the military in many countries in chemical and biological weapons and in the possible development of new and novel chemical and biological warfare agents. We are concerned that this may lead to another arms race. We believe that biomedical research should support rather than threaten life. Therefore, we pledge not to engage knowingly in research and teaching that will further the development of chemical and biological warfare agents.

Circulated by the Council for Responsible Genetics and the Coalition of Universities in the Public Interest.

Appendix L

Recombinant DNA Projects Funded by U.S. Military Agencies

Recombinant DNA Projects Pursued under the U.S. Biological Defense Research Program and the Chemical Warfare Defense Program, June 30, 1988

U.S. Army

1. J. M. Middlebrook, J. Schmidt, L. S. Trusal (USAMRIID)
   Basic Studies of Conventional Toxins of Biological Origin and Development of Medical Defensive Countermeasures
2. J. M. Dalrymple, S. H. Leppla, C. S. Schmaljohn (USAMRIID)
   Basic Studies on Conventional Agents of Biological Origin and Development of Medical Defensive Countermeasures
3. P. B. Jahrling, R. H. Kenyon, M. H. Crumrine (USAMRIID)
   Exploratory Vaccine Development Studies on Conventional Agents of Potential BW Threat
4. L. S. Baron, D. J. Kopecko, J. A. Wohlhieter (WRAIR)
   Microbial Genetics and Taxonomy
5. D. S. Burke, C. Hoke (WRAIR)
   Viral Infections of Man
6. K. W. Hedlund, T. R. Jerrells, C. Hickman, R. M. Rice (WRAIR)
   Rickettsial Diseases of Military Personnel
7. E. C. Tramont, J. Sadoff, A. Cross (WRAIR)
   Bacterial Diseases of Military Importance
8. T. L. Hale, S. B. Formal, J. Newland (WRAIR)
   Pathogenesis of Enteric Disease
9. W. T. Hockmeyer, W. R. Ballou (WRAIR)
   Immunological Mechanisms in Microbial Infections
10. W. T. Hockmeyer, J. S. Williams (WRAIR)
    Immunity in Protozoan Diseases

11. W. T. Hockmeyer, K, Esser, B. T. Hall (WRAIR)
    Identification of *Trypanosoma rhodesiense* Protective Antigens
12. K. W. Hedlund, E. V. Oaks, C. K. Stover (WRAIR)
    Rickettsiae-Host Interactions in Pathogenesis of Disease
13. W. T. Hockmeyer, J. L. Weber, P. R. Jackson (WRAIR)
    Exploratory Vaccine Development Against Malaria
14. J. C. Sadoff, B. M. Kaufman (WRAIR)
    Immunochemistry of Nerve Agents
15. W. T. Hockmeyer, W. R. Ballou (WRAIR)
    Vaccine Development/Malaria
16. S. B. Formal (WRAIR)
    Vaccine Development/Shigella
17. E. C. Boedeker, J. Andrews, R. H. Reid (WRAIR)
    Development of Vaccines for Enterotoxigenic *Escherichia coli*
18. E. A. Henchal, B. L. Innis, A. Nisalak (WRAIR)
    Rapid Diagnosis of Flavivirus Infections Using Nucleic Acid
    Hybridization
19. W. T. Hockmeyer, P. R. Jackson (WRAIR)
    Rapid Diagnosis of Leishmaniasis by DNA-DNA Hybridization
20. J. A. Wohlhieter, D. J. Kopecko, F. A. Rubin (WRAIR)
    Rapid Diagnostic Procedures
21. D. S. Burke, C. Hoke, R. Feighny (WRAIR)
    Flavivirus Nucleic Acid Probes
22. K. Stover, E. Oaks (WRAIR)
    Cloning of *Rickettsia tsutsugamushi* Antigens
23. R. J. Neill, P. Gemski (WRAIR)
    Protein Secretion in Gram Negative Bacteria
24. F. H. Top, C. A. Nacy, M. S. Meltzer (WRAIR)
    Immunomodulators for Defense Against Biological Warfare
    Agents
25. J. R. Putnak, P. C. Charles, D. S. Burke (WRAIR)
    Cloning and Expression of Dengue Virus Nonstructural Proteins
26. R. M. Rice, C. K. Stover, K. W. Hedlund (WRAIR)
    Development of Diagnostic Nucleic Acid Probes for Scrub
    Typhus
27. D. Kopecko, J. Buysse (WRAIR)
    Cloning Shigella Pili Genes

28. D. S. Burke, R. R. Redfield (WRAIR)
    Nonsystems Development for Vaccines Versus Retrovirus Infections
29. W. T. Hockmeyer, K. M. Esser, B. T. Hall (WRAIR)
    Molecular Immunology
30. M. S. Meltzer, C. A. Nacy, R. G. Wolff (WRAIR)
    Immunomodulation of Latency in HIV Infections
31. P. Gemski, J. Olenick, R. Neill (WRAIR)
    Molecular and Cell Biology of Bacterial Toxins
32. K. W. Hedlund, R. M. Rice, C. K. Stover (WRAIR)
    Scrub Typhus Antigens Isolation and Characterization
33. H. Schneider (WRAIR)
    Immunochemistry of Gonoccal Lipooligosaccharides
34. W. A. Reid, Jr., M. Grogl (WRAIR)
    Molecular Biology of Drug Resistance
35. J. W LeDuc, F. Knauert, J. W. Ezzell (USAMRIID)
    Exploratory Development Studies on Conventional Agents of Potential BW Threat

U.S. Navy

1. Y. Charoenvit, R. Beaudoin, A. Szarfman (NMRI)
   Exploratory Vaccine Development Against Malaria
2. R. Wistar, Jr., D. Burr, G. Dasch (NMRI)
   Technology Development on Rapid Diagnosis of Infectious Diseases of Military Importance
3. R. Beaudoin, R. Hedstrom, R. Campbell (NMRI)
   Cloning of Plasmodium DNA and Characterization of the Recombinants for Vaccine Production
4. R. Beaudoin, Y. Charoenvit, F. Rollwagen, W. Weiss (NMRI)
   Basic Studies on Infectious Disease of Military Importance: Animal Model for Studies of Malaria Vaccines
5. G. Dasch (NMRI)
   Cloning DNA in *Escherichia coli* From Species of Aeromonas
6. G. Dasch (NMRI)
   Cloning DNA in *Escherichia coli* From Species of Rickettsiales
7. P. Guerry, R. Campbell (NMRI)
   DNA Probes for the Rapid Diagnosis of Malaria
8. P. Guerry (NMRI)
   Cloning of Surface Antigens of Campylobacter for Vaccine Production

9. S. Hoffman, R. Beaudoin, W. Weiss (NMRI)
   Basic Studies on Infectious Diseases of Military Importance:
   Vaccine Development, Malaria Sporozoite

U.S. Air Force
1. J. Spain (AFESC)
   Factors Influencing Biodegradation Kinetics and Pathways
2. J. Spain (AFESC)
   Biodegradation of Hazardous Chemicals
3. J. Spain (AFESC)
   Biodegradation of Mixed Chlorinated Solvents

Uniformed Services University of the Health Sciences, Bethesda, MD
1. S. Serrate, R. Friedman, C. Dieffenbach
   Production of Acid-Labile-Alpha Interferon by AIDS Patients
2. A. Holmes
   The Cloning and Expression of DNA Sequences Coding for
   DNA Polymerase
3. R. Holmes
   Toxinogenesis and Virulence in *Vibrio cholerae*
4. A. O'Brien
   Genetic Control of Natural Resistance to Murine Typhoid
5. A. Maurelli
   Isolation of Shigella Virulence Gene Products by lacz Protein
   Fusions
6. R. Friedman
   Genetic Recombination and Other Interactions of AAV and
   Human Cellular DNA
7. K. Minton
   Characterization of a New UV-Induced DNA Photo Product

Acronyms for Research Centers Cited
AFESC   Air Force Engineering Services Center, Tyndall Air
           Force Base, Florida

NMRI   Naval Medical Research Institute, Bethesda,
           Maryland

USAMRIID   United States Army Medical Research Institute of

Infectious Diseases, Fort Detrick, Frederick, Maryland

WRAIR   Walter Reed Army Institute of Research, Washington, D.C.

University/Industry Recombinant DNA Projects Funded by DOD Biomedical Organizations, June 30, 1988

1. R. E. Johnston, N. L. Davis—North Carolina State University, Raleigh, NC
   Molecular Strategy for the Construction of a Genetically Engineered Vaccine for Venezuelan Equine Encephalitis Virus.
2. S. C. Merritt—University of North Carolina, Chapel Hill, NC
   Molecular Characterization of Mefloquine Resistance in *Plasmodium falciparum*
3. C. A. Rosen—Dana-Farber Cancer Institute, Boston, MA
   Molecular Biology of STLV-III and HTLV-IV
4. H. Soreq—Hebrew University, Jerusalem, Israel
   Molecular Biological Studies on the Biogenesis of Human Cholinesterases *in vivo* and as Directed By Cloned Cholinesterase DNA Sequences
5. D. P. Bolognesi, B. F. Haynes, T. J. Matthews—Duke University Medical Center, Durham, NC
   Biological Significance of the Immune Response to HTLV-III/LAV
6. I. S. Y. Chen, D. Ho, J. Rosenblatt—University of California, Los Angeles
   Virological and Molecular Studies of AIDS-Related CNS Disorders
7. D. L. Robertson—Brigham Young University, Provo, UT
   Use of Recombinant DNA Techniques for the Production of a More Effective Anthrax Vaccine
8. M. S. Collett—Molecular Genetics, Inc., Minnetonka, MN
   Rift Valley Fever Virus: Molecular Biologic Studies of the M Segment RNA for Application in Disease Prevention
9. E. Paoletti—Health Research, Inc., Albany, NY
   Genetically-Engineered Poxviruses and the Construction of Live Recombinant Vaccines

10. J. W. Patrick, P. Mason, K. Evans—Salk Institute for Biological Studies, La Jolla, CA
    Primary Structure of Nicotinic Acetylcholine Receptor

11. J. V. Ravetch—Sloan Kettering Institute, New York, NY
    Organization and Expression of Plasmodial Genes Required for Erythrocyte Invasion

12. J. J. Iandola—Kansas State University, Manhattan, KS
    Cloning Sequencing and Structural Manipulation of the Enterotoxin D&E Genes from *Staphylococcus aureus*

13. O. Lockridge, B. Ladu—University of Michigan, Ann Arbor, MI
    Isolation of Genomic Clone for Human Cholinesterase

14. M. A. Cochran, G. Smith, B. Ericson—Microgene Sys, Inc., West Haven, CT
    Baculovirus Recombinants that Express Hepatitis B Virus Surface Antigen: Demonstration of a General Method for Production of Subunit Vaccines

15. J. Lindstrom, J. Ralston—Salk Institute for Biological Studies, La Jolla, CA
    Use of Monoclonal Antibodies to Study the Structure of the Function of Nicotinic Acetylcholine Receptors on Electric Organ and Muscle to Determine the Structure of Nicotinic Acetycholine Receptors on Neurons

16. I. I. Kaiser, J. D. Johnson—University of Wyoming, Laramie, WY
    Crotoxin: Structural Studies, Mechanism of Action, and Cloning of its Gene

17. M. I. Fournier—University of Massachusetts, Amherst, MA
    Structure and Expression of Genes for Flavivirus Immunogens

18. M. J. Buchmeier—Scripps Clinic & Research Foundation, La Jolla, CA
    Synthetic Vaccines for the Control of Arenavirus Infection

19. M. Manak—Biotech Research Laboratories, Inc., Rockville, MD
    Molecular Mechanisms of Cytopathogenicity of Primate Lymphotropic Retroviruses: Relevance to Treatment and Vaccine for AIDS

20. M. Lubet—Biotech Research Laboratories, Inc., Rockville, MD
    Development and Evaluation of Adeno-HTLV-III Hybrid

Virus and Non-Cytopathic HTLV-III Mutant for Vaccine Use

21. P, R, Oeltgen, R. D. Myers, J. Coupal—University of Kentucky, Lexington, KY
Characterization of an Opioid-Like Hibernation Induction Trigger

22. C. M. Rice, J. I. Cohn—Washington University, St Louis, MO
Expression of Yellow Fever Antigens and Infectious Virus From Cloned CDNA

23. P. Taylor—University of California, San Diego
The Primary Sequence of Acetylcholinesterase and Selective Antibodies for the Detection of Organophosphate Toxicity

24. P. A. Nuttall, D. H. L. Bishop, G. M. Steele—Natural Environment Research Council, Swindon, UK
Diagnosis and Prevention of Infection by Nairoviruses

25. H. Wigzell—Karolinska Institute, Stockholm, Sweden
Potential Benefits and Hazards of Humoral Reactions Against HTLV-III

26. G. A. Cole—University of Maryland, Baltimore, MD
T Cell Responses to Arenavirus Infection

27. F. McCutchan—Bionetics Research, Inc., Rockville, MD
Molecular Biological Approaches to Disease Prevention and Diagnosis

28. D. W. Trent—Centers for Disease Control, Fort Collins, CO
Development of a Genetically-Engineered Venezuelan Equine Encephalitis Virus Vaccine

29. G. Horwith—Wyeth Laboratories, Philadelphia, PA
Cooperative Study of Adenovirus Vectored Vaccines

30. M. J. Blaser, M. Vasil, W. Wang—Veterans Administration Medical Center, Denver, CO
Studies of the Outer Membrane Proteins of *Campylobacter jejuni* for Vaccine Development

31. B. K. Sim—Johns Hopkins University, Baltimore, MD
Isolating and Characterizing Genes of Liver Stage Antigens with Vaccine Potential

32. L. L. Muldrow—Spelman College, Atlanta, GA
Genetic Engineering of *Clostridium difficile* Toxin A Vaccine

33. S. Falkow—Stanford University, Stanford, CA
Molecular Basis of Pathogenicity in Enteric Bacteria

34. V. Finnerty—Emory University, Atlanta, GA
    Development of a DNA-Based Method for Distinguishing the
    Malaria Vectors *Anopheles gambiae* from *Anopheles arabiensis*
35. C. Thorne—University of Massachusetts, Amherst, MA
    Genetic and Physiological Studies of *Bacillus anthracis* Related
    to Development of an Improved Vaccine
36. J. Ivy—Hawaii Biotechnology Group, Aiea, Hawaii Development of Dengue Vaccine Phase I
37. D. H. L. Bishop—Natural Environmental Research Council,
    Oxford, UK
    Diagnosis and Prevention of Infection by Phlebotomus Fever
    Group Viruses
38. L. Ratner—Washington University, St Louis, MO
    Development of a Sensitive DNA Assay for the AIDS Virus,
    HTLV-III/LAV
39. L. Ratner—Washington University, St Louis, Mo
    Mechanism of Cytotoxicity of the AIDS Virus, HTLV-III/
    LAV
40. M. W. Eklund—U.S. Department of Commerce
    The Role of Plasmids and Bacteriophages in Toxigenicity of
    Clostridium botulinum and Characterization of Converting Bacteriophages
41. E. Ehrenfeld—University of Utah, Salt Lake City, UT
    Studies on the Pathogenesis of Hepatitis and Feasibility Studies on a Hepatitis A Vaccine
42. S. Lemon—University of North Carolina at Chapel Hill
    New Approaches to Attenuated Hepatitis A Vaccine Development: Cloning and Sequencing of Cell Culture Adapted Viral
    CDNA
43. R. K. Padmanabhan—University of Kansas, Lawrence, KS
    Cloning and Expression of Genes for Dengue Virus Type 2
    Encoded Antigens for Rapid Diagnosis and Vaccine Development
44. S. Sawicki—Medical College of Ohio, Toledo, OH
    Detection of Arboviruses using Specific RNA Probes
45. J. A. Berzofsky—National Cancer Institute
    Prediction and Testing of Antigenic Sites of the AIDS Virus
    HTLV-III Recognized by T Lymphocytes for the Development of Possible Synthetic Vaccines

Note: This list does not include any recombinant DNA projects which may be
conducted under the auspices of the Chemical Warfare Offensive Program.

Appendix M

Obligations for Research, Developments, Evaluation, and Testing for the U.S. Chemical Warfare and Biological Defense Programs, FY1974–FY1987

Fiscal Year[a]	Chemical warfare	Ordnance[b]	Biological defense	Total
Current dollars				
1974	28.2	6.9	14.4	49.5
1975	24.2	4.8	11.5	40.5
1976	30.2	6.5	14.2	51.0
1977	28.6	5.9	15.9	50.5
1978	34.9	16.5	7.6	59.0
1979	42.3	10.4	16.5	69.2
1980	47.6	5.1	16.0	68.7
1981	101.0	7.5	15.1	123.7
1982	167.8	9.9	21.6	199.2
1983	163.4	9.0	30.8	211.1
1984	258.8	6.3	62.5	327.5
1985	286.0	18.3	68.5	372.8
1986	257.6	n.a.	90.6	348.2[c]
1987	271.4	n.a.	62.5	333.9[c]
Constant 1982 dollars				
1974	54.1	13.2	27.6	94.9
1975	42.1	8.3	20.0	70.4
1976	48.6	10.5	22.9	82.0
1977	42.7	8.8	23.7	75.2
1978	48.7	23.0	10.6	82.3
1979	54.3	13.4	21.2	88.8
1980	56.5	6.0	18.9	81.1
1981	108.4	8.0	16.2	132.7
1982	167.8	9.9	21.6	199.2
1983	156.8	8.6	37.2	202.5

Fiscal Year[a]	Chemical warfare	Ordnance[b]	Biological defense	Total
1984	239.0	5.8	57.7	302.5
1985	255.4	16.3	61.2	332.9
1986	233.6	n.a.	78.6	302.2[c]
1987	228.8	n.a.	62.5	281.5[c]

Sources: Department of Defense, Annual Reports on the Chemical Warfare and Biological Research Program Obligations, published in the *Congressional Record* from 1973 to 1979.

a. From 1974 until 1977, fiscal years ran from July 1 until June 30 the following year. In 1976, the fiscal year was redefined to run from October 1 until September 30 the following year. The Department of Defense report issued in 1977 covered the period July 1, 1975 to September 30, 1976. The amounts given in this table have been prorated for 12 months.

b. The term "ordnance" covers tear gases and herbicides—agents that are not considered by the United States to be "chemical agents" under the Geneva Protocol. In 1986, the Department of Defense stopped reporting amounts spent on research and development for this category in its annual reports.

c. Does not include "ordnance" agents.

Appendix N

The Reagan Administration's Biological Warfare Policy

1. Walter J. Stoessel et al., Report of the Chemical Warfare Review (Washington, D.C.: U.S. Government Printing Office, 1985), chapter 18, Biological Weapons.

The Commission's charter does not formally extend to the realm of biological weapons. Yet the nature of modern biochemistry, where daily press reports on "genetic engineering" and "designer drugs" are common, has blurred the line between the chemical and the biological. Toxins already occupy a middle ground. From the military point of view, the employment and characteristics of chemical and biological weapons have similarities that would make it artificial to look only at chemicals and pretend that the biological threat does not exist, and would be to ignore what may turn out to be the most serious aspect of the problem.

In 1969 the United States abandoned its research into biological weapons. Unfortunately, there is evidence that the Soviet Union has done just the opposite, and since the 1970's has been pursuing an active program of research into biological agents for military use. The exact scope and nature of the Soviet effort is unclear. The deaths caused by anthrax spread from a Soviet weapons laboratory in Sverdlovsk in 1979 are an example that this country cannot ignore.

The threat such Soviet activity poses is grave. The rapid advances of genetic technology—in which the United States for now is fortunately the leader—offer the predictable likelihood of new agents being developed for which no vaccines or counteragents are known or available. Moreover, unlike chemical research, even ordinary modern biological research often has direct and obvious military applications as well as perfectly legitimate peaceful ones.

Chemical weapons, because of the volume of agent required to cover a large area, are unlikely to be employed as strategic weapons directed against homeland populations. The largest targets militarily attractive for them would be port facilities or other concentrations and bottleneck areas.

Biological weapons, on the other hand, could be designed to spread disease and kill indiscriminately in wider fashion, and thus are adaptable for targets far from one's own population. They could infect enormous areas. At the same time, the very lack of precise control of biological weapons makes their battlefield use less likely, as does the fact that, unlike most chemical weapons and toxins, biological agents usually have a period of delay before they take effect.

Perhaps most seriously, the Soviets also are believed to be pursuing development of both lethal and incapacitating toxins, that could produce, for example, sudden panic or sleepiness in defending forces. Toxins are of particular concern because they can be developed to be hundreds of times more lethal than agents in existing munitions, or to be less susceptible to countermeasures. Once developed, their manufacture is relatively simple, making proliferation a problem. Toxins often can be countered, however, if studied in advance and rapidly detected.

The Commission was warned eloquently by distinguished biological scientists that advances in biology are leading toward a danger of tampering with life itself, with consequent horrors difficult to visualize. The Commission was impressed with these warnings, and particularly with the evidence that the Soviet Union has not heeded them, and that the Soviets are conducting active research on how biological science advances might be turned to military ends. Representatives of others governments also expressed to the Commission their concern about Soviet biological warfare activity.

The only sensible response, we believe, is again for the United States not to ignore the problem, but rather to conduct comprehensive defensive research on biological agents and toxins under conditions of extreme care. The need is to be able to assess the likely threat, to develop detection measures and defenses, and to create sufficient uncertainty in the minds of Soviet leaders as well as those of other governments that they would hesitate to trust in such a method of warfare.

At this time, the Department of Defense does not have an adequate grasp of the biological-warfare threat and has not been giving it sufficient attention. Both intelligence and research in this area, though improved after a virtual halt during the 1970s, are strikingly deficient. The Department should be devoting much more resources and talent to addressing the chemical and biological threats of the future as well as those of the present. A moderate but intensive course of research, which does not include actual development of biological weapons, appears the only prudent one to follow.

2. Douglas J. Feith, Deputy Assistant Secretary of Defense for Negotiations Policy, Testimony before the Subcommittee on Oversight and Evaluation of the U.S. House of Representatives Permanent Select Committee on Intelligence, 8 August 1986.

I appreciate the opportunity to address this Subcommittee on the military problem of biological and toxin weapons. Biological agents (i.e., live organisms) and toxins (i.e., toxic chemicals produced by live organisms) are similar in essential respects and I shall refer to them collectively as "BW."

The stunning advances over the last five to ten years in the field of biotechnology—the advances that have brought into common parlance such terms as genetics engineering, recombinant DNA techniques, monoclonal antibodies, and Nutrasweet—mean more than new foods, pharmaceuticals, and fertilizers. They mean new and better biological weapons for any country willing to violate what the U.S. Government still insists is an international norm against the possession of such weapons. New technology has exploded the standard ideas about BW that prevailed ten or more years ago.

The Old Conventional Wisdom
Those old ideas can easily be summarized: BW was thought to be a small problem solved. It was thought small because BW was judged militarily insignificant or, at most, of highly restricted utility. Agents best suited for military use—those, for example, like snail or shellfish toxins, which disseminate well in effective concentrations and work quickly and somewhat controllably—could not be produced affordably in large quantities. Those that could efficiently be produced worked in general less quickly and spread infectious disease, with large attending risk to the attacker as well as the target. BW was deemed a strategic weapon and, from a milit-

ary point of view, far inferior to other—that is, nuclear—strategic weapons.

Lessening further BW's value was the difficulty of safely storing filled munitions or bulk agent. The dangers of BW storage were made graphic in 1979 when a leak or explosion at a Soviet BW facility in Sverdlovsk caused the release of large quantities of anthrax spores, resulting in many deaths. (The official Soviet explanation has been that the victims died from eating contaminated meat. This, however, does not jibe with the evidence. For example, the military took charge of the clean-up operations, which were the kind required for decontaminating surfaces coated by an infectious aerosol; moreover, the symptoms of many victims indicated pulmonary anthrax, which results from inhaling, not eating.)

The BW problem was thought solved because over a hundred states, including the major powers, have subscribed to the Biological and Toxin Weapons Convention of 1972 ("BWC"), which makes it illegal to "develop, produce, stockpile or otherwise acquire or retain" or transfer biological or toxin agents or weapons. This prohibition, it should be noted, does not extend to very small quantities of agent, possession of which is necessary for "prophylactic, protective, or other peaceful purposes." It was obvious that a ban on tiny quantities could not be policed effectively and, in any event, substantial stockpiles of agent were believed to be a prerequisite for an offensive BW capability.

The BWC came into being three years after the Nixon Administration unilaterally destroyed all U.S. BW stocks, renounced future acquisition of BW, and terminated the U.S BW program, sparing only the facilities for BW defense. This unilateral U.S. action reflected the judgment that BW lacked military usefulness. Under the circumstances, it was not considered necessary that the treaty afford the parties any means of ascertaining each other's compliance. Accordingly, the BWC included no verification provisions. The U.S. Government reasoned that it had already renounced BW unilaterally, so there could be no harm in signing an unverifiable ban.

Bioengineered BW

The BW picture has been radically altered by recent scientific developments. It is now possible to synthesize BW agents tailored to military specifications. The technology that makes possible so-called "designer drugs" also makes possible designer BW. States unconstrained by their treaty obligations can now produce BW agents of varying effects—different types of fast-acting incapacitants as well as lethal substances. Agents can be developed for various climatic conditions. They can be mixed to complicate identification and their chemical structure can easily be altered to circumvent immunogens or antigens that the other side is suspected to possess.

The BW field favors offense over defense. It is a technologically simple matter to produce new agents but a problem to develop antidotes. New agents can be produced in hours; antidotes may take years. To gauge the magnitude of the antidote problem, consider the many years and millions of dollars that have thus far been invested, as yet without success, in developing a means of countering a single biological agent outside the BW field—the AIDS virus. Such an investment far surpasses the resources available for BW defense work.

New technology can yield BW agents against which a state could immunize its own forces. A state could therefore employ BW without having to require all its own troops in the area to don cumbersome protective clothing. This would enhance BW's military advantage over chemical weapons, such as nerve agent, against which no reliable prophylaxis is available.

It has been hoped that the risk of exposure would help deter BW use, for such exposure might trigger special, undesirable consequences, which, depending on circumstances, could range from the international community's condemnation and possibly sanctions to nuclear retaliation. New technology, however, makes it easier to develop BW agents that would defy identification after use. Their effects can be symptoms of endemic diseases. If it cannot clearly be demonstrated that BW has been used—if, for example, the effects of the attack are attributable to natural causes—the risks of BW use diminish. And this concern is not just hypothetical.

Evidence of many types and from a variety of sources has established that the Soviets and their clients have, in Southeast Asia and Afghanistan, used mycotoxin weapons banned by the BWC. That mycotoxins occasionally occur in nature in certain colder areas has, however, clouded the picture and made it easy for states to refuse to come to the unpleasant conclusion that BW has been used and something should be done about it. One must suppose that the Soviets have drawn appropriate lessons from the heated controversy in the West about the natural occurrence theory of Yellow

Rain. They can hardly have failed to observe that, at least in part because of that controversy, the costs of BW use have proven altogether manageable, indeed virtually nonexistent.

Easy, Fast, and Clean

Bio-engineered substances are now produced around the world in large quantities by various commercial ventures. The production equipment, though newly invented, is not very "high tech." The equipment can be housed in a standard industrial or manufacturing facility that offers no distinctive sign of the kind of production activity occurring within.

An example: Recent discoveries in mammalian cell culture make possible the growth of mammalian cells on the surface of minute beads, rather than on the inner surface of glass roller bottles. The beads provide the ideal environment for the growth of viruses. One small bottle partially filled with beads can now yield quantities of product that previously would have required much larger production facilities. This single technical advance has effectively erased the distinction between a biological agent production plant and an ordinary-looking small scientific laboratory.

The new type of biological production equipment works fast. Substances sutiable for BW use can be synthesized within hours— a day or two at most. Seed stock of BW agent—that is, test tube quantities—can be fermented into large production quantities in three or four weeks. After a production run, the equipment, operating more or less as self-cleaning ovens do, destroys within an hour or two whatever residue there is, thereby preventing contamination of the next production run and, incidentally, making it impossible for anyone to prove that a given substance has been produced.

The Soviet BW Program

The Soviet Union evidently appreciates the military opportunities created by the biotechnological revolution of recent years. Though U.S. policy remains what it was in 1969 after President Nixon's unilateral renunciation of BW (and there is no thought within the Administration to change the policy), the Soviet Union has built a large organization devoted to the development and production of offensive BW. At the very time when Soviet officials were negotiating and signing the BWC, a high-ranking Soviet defector has reported, the Politburo decided to intensify the Soviet BW program.

The Soviets retain stockpiles of BW agent produced in pre-recombinant-DNA days. At known biological warfare facilities in the Soviet Union, they maintain highly-secured weapons storage facilities under military control. They have, as alluded to above, transferred BW to their clients in Southeast Asia. They have themselves used toxins against their enemies in the Afghanistan war. And they are developing new means of biological warfare based on current bio-engineering technologies. In other words, the Soviet Union has not only violated the BWC, but every major prohibition in it.

The scale and seriousness of the Soviet BW program are formidable. There are at least seven biological warfare centers in the USSR under military control, all with unusually rigorous security. One such facility constitutes a veritable city with a large number of residents who work and live there full time, isolated from the rest of society. There residents must possess extraordinary security clearances, a requirement that excludes individuals or ethnic groups considered disloyal. The level of effort committed to research on various natural poisons—such as snake venoms—is far in excess of what could be justified to deal with such substances for purely medical or public health purposes.

Versatile BW
All of this, of course, has implications for both the military and the arms control aspects of the BW problem. The prevailing judgment of years ago that BW is not a militarily significant weapon is now quite unsustainable. BW can be designed to be effective across the spectrum of combat, including special operations and engagements at the tactical level. No field equipment has yet been developed that can detect BW agents, let alone identify them. There are no antidotes now available against many possible agents. And it is not certain that our troops' protective gear would be effective against all such agents.

The Limits of Arms Control
As for the arms control implications, these divide into two categories. The first can be labeled "crime and non-punishment," the second "technology overtakes the treaty."

The systematic violations of the BWC by the Soviet Union and its clients undermine the treaty and the anti-BW norm it symbolizes. At least equally grave, however, is the international community's unwillingness to take a collective interest in the evidence of those violations. A treaty may survive breaches by some parties. But can it long survive general indifference as to whether it is violated?

What is unwholesome, I wish to emphasize, is not the failure of many BWC parties to endorse the U.S. Government's conclusions about Soviet violations, but their refusal even to inquire into them or urge formal investigation. Some states explain their inaction by asserting that the U.S. Government's case is not conclusive. Reasoning like Lewis Carroll's Queen of Hearts, they contend in effect that treaty parties have no responsibility to investigate charges of violations until the allegations are proved.

Many states, after dismissing violation controversies as mere politics between the "superpowers," feel justified in exhorting the U.S. Government to conclude new arms control agreements with the Soviet Union. They claim standing on the grounds that they, as members of the international community, are affected by the quality of relations between the powers. They do not in general take this stand cynically, wryly acknowledging its irony. On the contrary, they earnestly assert their responsibility for promoting new arms control treaties and equally earnestly assert, once a treaty has been signed, the propriety of their not heeding Soviet violations. Their earnestness notwithstanding, however, they have dimmed severely the prospects for arms control agreements ever contributing to international security.

The major arms control implication of the new biotechnology is that the BWC must be recognized as critically deficient and unfixable. A state contemptuous of international law and unconstrained by anti-BW public or parliamentary opinion could now maintain an offensive BW capability without violating any of the specific prohibitions of the BWC. (Maintaining such a capability would necessarily violate the BWC's general prohibition; the treaty's purpose, after all, is to ban BW. But if a state refrains from stockpiling large quantities of agent, it would as a practical matter be impossible to prove any such violation.)

Given the ability to produce militarily significant quantities of BW from seed stock within a month or so, it is not necessary to stockpile agent. Such a state need only maintain in a freezer a few hundred test tubes full of seed stock and a production facility which, in the normal course of things, makes agricultural or medical products. In the unlikely event the freezer were discovered, a closed society would have little difficulty characterizing it as part of a research effort for BW defense. In fact, because seed stock can be synthesized in a matter of days, one could get by even without the freezer.

As for the rest of the infrastructure required for a BW capability—such as munitions-filling equipment, aerosolization and dissemination testing, and training—it could be maintained openly. It is essentially identical to the infrastructure entailed in a chemical weapons capability.

While it in no way excuses or belittles the importance of the Soviet Union's BWC violations, the fact is that their compliance with the treaty's specific prohibitions would not obviate concern about their BW capabilities. Because new technology makes possible a massive and rapid break-out, the treaty constitutes an insignificant impediment at best. Its principal failing, therefore, is no longer the absence of verification provisions or lack of effective complaint mechanisms, the commonly acknowledged shortcomings, but its inability to accomplish its purpose—to ensure that even states respecting its specific terms pose no BW threat.

A Problem with No Apparent Solution
What therefore is to be done and not done? First of all, the Administration is not interested in altering the longstanding U.S. policy against possession of BW or development of an offensive BW capability.

Secondly, the United States will remain a party to the BWC and will remain in full compliance with it. Though the treaty has been overtaken by technology as well as systematically violated, the Administration continues to support the idea behind it— prohibiting BW.

Third, aware that the BWC serves as a false advertisement to the world that the BW problem has been solved, the Administration will make an effort—especially at the second BWC Review Conference, which will convene in Geneva in September 1986—to highlight the nature of the problem and the critical defects of the BWC. The danger of not publicizing these matters is that friends and allies will continue to neglect BW defense work aimed at developing detection and medical capabilites and protective gear.

It is not a pleasant task to deliver so dismal a report to the Congress. The material's distressing nature probably accounts in large part for why it is so little treated in the public debate on national security issues. It is axiomatic that the only successful politics in a democracy is the politics of hope. But can one responsibly inflate hope for an escape from the military problems posed by the Soviet BW program? There can be no Deus ex Arms Control in this arena. In answer to those who crave a constructive suggestion under even the least promising circumstances, one can recommend only: Defense.

Contributors

Barton J. Bernstein is Professor of History and Mellon Professor of Interdisciplinary Studies at Stanford University, where he directs the International Relations Program and the International Policy Studies Program. He has written extensively on the nuclear arms race, including *Politics and Policies of the Truman Administration* and *The Atomic Bomb: The Critical Issues*.

Gordon Burck, a chemist by training, also holds a Master's degree in International Affairs from Columbia University. He is Staff Associate for Chemical and Biological Warfare for the Federation of American Scientists. He previously served as a consultant on chemical weapons issues at the Center for Defense Information.

Leonard A. Cole, a political scientist, teaches in the Program in Science, Technology, and Society at Rutgers University. His most recent books are *Politics and the Restraint of Science* (1983) and *Clouds of Secrecy: The Army's Germ Warfare Tests Over Populated Areas* (1988).

Richard Falk is Albert G. Milbank Professor of International Law and Practice at Princeton University. His most recent books are *Revolutionaries and Functionaries: The Dual Face of Terrorism* (1988) and *Revitalizing International Law* (1989).

Jeanne Guillemin is Professor of Sociology at Boston College and specializes in social anthropology and medical sociology. Her most recent books are *Anthropological Realities. Readings in the Science of Culture* (1983) and, with Lynda L. Holmstrom, *Mixed Blessings. Intensive Care for Newborns* (1986).

John Isaacs is Legislative Director of the Council for a Livable World. He writes regularly for *The Bulletin of the Atomic Scientists*, *Nuclear Times*, and *Arms Control Today* on Congress and national security policy, elections, the defense budget, strategic nuclear arms negotiatios, and major weapons programs.

Stuart Ketcham is a molecular biologist in the Department of Biology at the University of Michigan, specializing in the mitotic cell cycle in yeast. He received his doctorate in biochemistry from Cornell University in 1985.

Jonathan King is Professor of Molecular Biology and Director of the Biomedical Electron Microscopy Laboratory at MIT. His scientific research is in the area of protein folding and the genetic control of virus assembly.

Marc Lappé is Professor of Health Policy and Ethics at the University of Illinois College of Medicine. He is the author of *The Broken Code: The Exploitation of DNA* (1985) and *Germs That Will Not Die: The Medical Consequences of the Misuse of Antibiotics* (1983).

Matthew Meselson is Thomas Dudley Cabot Professor of the Natural Sciences and professor of Biochemistry and Molecular Biology at Harvard University. He is a member of the United States National Academy of Sciences and the Royal Society (London), and the recipient of many awards for his research in biochemistry and molecular biology. With Julian Perry Robinson, he edits *Chemical Weapons Convention Bulletin*.

Richard Novick is the Director of the Public Health Research Institute of New York. A molecular biologist specializing in the molecular genetics of *Staphylococcus aureus*, and its plasmids and toxins, he is a founding editor of the journal *Plasmid*.

Charles Piller is an investigative reporter focusing on science, biological warfare, and labor and international relations. he is co-author, with Keith Yamamoto, of *Gene Wars: Military Control Over the New Genetic Technologies.* He has served as an adviser on military research to several congressional committees and as a consultant on biological warfare issues to CBS News and ABC World News Tonight.

Julian Perry Robinson, a chemist and lawyer, is a Senior Fellow of the Science Policy Research Unit of the University of Sussex, England. He has written extensively on the subject of chemical and biological warfare and serves as a consultant to a wide range of national and international organizations on this subject, including the World Health Organization, other agencies of the United Nations, and the International Committee of the Red Cross. With Matthew Meselson, he edits *Chemical Weapons Convention Bulletin*.

Barbara Hatch Rosenberg, a molecular biologist at Memorial-Sloan Kettering Cancer Center, is also a professor in the Division of Natural Sciences of the State University of New York, Purchase. She has served as a consultant to several congressional committees on legislation relevant to the 1972 Biological Weapons Convention.

Seth Shulman is the Boston correspondent for *Nature*. He also writes about science, technology, and the environment for *The Atlantic, Smithsonian, Technology Review*, and other journals and is currently writing a book on the environmental consequences of the military infrastructure.

Nicholas A. Sims is Lecturer in International Relations at the London School of Economics and Political Science, specializing in international organization and biological and chemical disarmament diplomacy. His books include *International Organization for Chemical Disarmament* (1987) and *The Diplomacy of Biological Disarmament* (1988).

Robert L. Sinsheimer, a molecular biologist and Chancellor Emeritus of the University of California, Santa Cruz, is Professor of Biology at the University of California, Santa Barbara. He is a member of the National Academy of Sciences and a former editor of its *Proceedings*. He has written widely on the ethical and social implications of advances in modern biology.

Harlee Strauss, a molecular biologist, is the founder and president of H. Strauss/Associates, a consulting firm in toxicology and risk assessment of chemicals and microorganisms in the environment. She teaches toxicology at Tufts University and Boston University and is currently editing *Risk Assessment in Genetic Engineering: Environmental Release of Organisms*.

Susan Wright, a historian of science specializing in the history of contemporary science policy, directs the Science and Society Program at the Residential College of the University of Michigan. She is currently completing *Molecular Politics: The Development of Policy for Recombinant DNA Technology in Britain and the United States*.

Keith R. Yamamoto, a molecular biologist, is Professor and Vice Chairman in the Department of Biochemistry and Biophysics at the University of California, San Francisco. He is also Chairman of the Molecular Biology Study Section of the National Institutes of Health and coauthor, with Charles Piller, of *Gene Wars: Military Control Over the New Genetic Technologies*. His research addresses the mechanisms of gene expression.

Index

Secretary-General, investigation of
  compliance questions by, 309–310
Security, National Security Council
  guideline for, 335
Security clearance, for military labs, 155
Seeley, Thomas, 204, 207, 224
Senate Human Resource Committee
  Hearings, 176
Sims, Nicholas A., 302
Simulants, 36, 50
  Army rejects, 146, 151
  tests on effectiveness of, 175–176
SIPRI. *See* Stockholm International
  Peace Research Institute
Smidovich, Nikita, 323–324
Sovereign state, interpretation of, 249–
  250
Soviet Union
  agrees to verification measures, 349
  on BW disarmament, 41
  possible BW superiority of, 30, 31
  and purported rise of lethal chemicals,
    44, 45, 46
  responsibilities of, 344
Soviet *Military Encyclopedia* reference to
  BW, 210
Soviet Military Power, DOD report, 202
Soviet threat, as rationale for U.S.
  biotechnology program, 135
Special Operations Division (SOD), 36
Sternutators, 354
Stevenson, Earl P., 31
Stewart, Walter W., 11
Stimson, Henry L., 10–11, 15, 19
Stockholm Conference on Confidence
  and Security Building Measures
  (CSBMs) and Disarmament, 273
Stockholm Document, 273
Stockholm factor, 273
Stockholm International Peace Re-
  search Institute, 56–57, 315, 319
Stockpiles, destruction of, 252, 253
Stoessel, Walter J., Jr., 203, 423–425
Storella, Mark, 44
Strategic scenario, 105
Streptococcus fecalis, 115–116
Structure of Scientific Revolutions (Kuhn),
  171
Subsequent practice, 310
Sverdlovsk, 246
  accident at, 199–202
  anthrax epidemic at, 55
  and vaccine use, 83

Sweden
  on confidence-building measures, 305
  leads reformists, 268, 269
Swyter, Han, 40
Szilard, Leo, 187

Tactical scenario, 105
Tear gas, 34
Technical Secretariat, joint BWC/
  CWC, 320–321
Technology and science, 172–173. *See
  also* Biotechnology; Genetic engineering
Terrorists
  present lack of interest in weapons of
    mass destruction, 263
  use of biological weapons by, 105–
    107, 117
  and use of CBW, 56
Test and Evaluation Command (U.S.),
  33, 42, 134
Thant, U, 38
Top, Col. Franklin H., 161–162
Toxin(s), 34–35, 356–357
  artificial, 336
  definition of, 308
  as weapons, 308–309
Toxin genes
  cloning of for vaccine development,
    182
  introduction of, 115–116
Toxoids
  declaration of, 314
  as useless, 180
Treaty compliance, verification of, 54.
  See also Compliance; Verification
Treaty of Tlatelolco, 306
Tricothecenes, 203, 205, 206–207, 208–
  209, 226, 231
Truman, Harry S., 16, 18, 20
Tu quoque, 242

"Umbrella murder," 92
United Kingdom, 301
  disarmament efforts of, 38
United Nations (UN)
  Department for Disarmament Affairs,
    277
  General Assembly Resolution 41(I)
    (1946), 28
  General Assembly Resolution 2603A
    (1969), 37, 249, 250